THE DECADE
THAT
TRANSFORMED
THE POP MUSIC SCENE

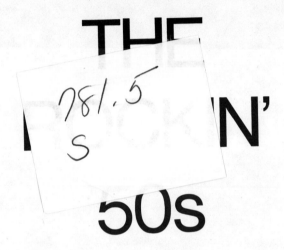

THE ROCKIN' 50s

ARNOLD SHAW

HAWTHORN BOOKS, INC.
Publishers / New York

To the memory of my parents,
Sarah and David,
and my sisters,
Alice and Rose

Library of Congress Catalog Card Number: 73-332

ISBN: 0-8015-6432-8, Hardbound edition
       0-8015-6434-4, Paperbound edition

First Printing: February 1974
Second Printing: April 1974
Third Printing: October 1974

CONTENTS

Acknowledgments   xi

Introduction   xv

1 SUMMER OF 1955   1

Col. Tom Parker · Elvis Presley · Bill Randle · Sam Phillips · "I Forgot
to Remember to Forget" · Steve Sholes

I

DEATH OF AN ERA
TIN PAN ALLEY
1950–1953

2 IT'S LATER THAN YOU THINK   13

Pop Music at Midcentury · Song Forms and Shibboleths of the Tin Pan
Alley Era

3 MUZAK AND MISTER IN-BETWEEN   19

Perry Como · Sinatra · Nat "King" Cole · Billy Eckstine · Johnny Mathis

4 THE BEARD   27

Mitch Miller · Guy Mitchell · Hank Williams · "Come On-A My House"

5 THE EXCITERS   32

The Weavers · Teresa Brewer · The Ames Brothers · The Four Aces · Mario Lanza · Tony Bennett · Les Paul and Mary Ford · Joni James · Sunny Gale · Georgia Gibbs · The Bunny Hop · Julius La Rosa · Patti Page · Eartha Kitt · Jo Stafford · Harry Belafonte

6 THE BEATS AND THE BELTERS   45

Sinatra · FRANKIE LAINE INTERVIEW · Eddie Fisher · JOHNNIE RAY INTERVIEW

7 THE PERSONALITY DEEJAYS   61

Dick Haynes · Martin Block · Al Jarvis · Eddie Hubbard · Kurt Webster · Al Collins · Bob Horn · Bill Randle · Howie Richmond · Gene Rayburn

8 "YOUR HIT PARADE"   67

II

UPHEAVAL IN POP
1954–1955

9 "SH-BOOM"   73

The Chords · The Crew Cuts · JERRY WEXLER INTERVIEW

10 BLUES WITH A BEAT   80

Louis Jordan · AHMET ERTEGUN INTERVIEW · R & B Grows

11 THE BACK OF THE CHARTS   89

The Orioles · Joe Liggins and his Honeydrippers · Percy Mayfield · Roy Milton and his Solid Senders · Little Esther and Johnny Otis · Fats Domino · Ivory Joe Hunter · Ruth Brown · Memphis Slim ·

Lowell Fulson · BMI · The Clovers and A. Nugetre · Billy Ward and the Dominoes · Earl Bostic · Jackie Brenston · Johnny Ace · Chuck Willis · Howlin' Wolf · Lloyd Price · B. B. KING INTERVIEW · Clyde McPhatter · The Drifters · The Five Royales · Big Mama Thornton · Leiber and Stoller

12 ROCK 'N' ROLL'S SUPERPROMOTER   104

Alan Freed · Paul Sherman

13 CONFRONTATION   112

Rebel Without a Cause · "Shake, Rattle and Roll" · Joe Turner · White Balladeers · ASCAP · Muddy Waters · Hank Ballard and the Midnighters · The Penguins · The Charms · Roy Hamilton · "Let Me Go Lover"

14 BLACK ORIGINALS AND WHITE COVERS   122

The Blackboard Jungle · The Mambo · Georgia Gibbs · LaVern Baker · Randy Wood · Pat Boone · Ray Charles · Little Willie John · Little Walter · The El Dorados · The Four Fellows · BO DIDDLEY INTERVIEW · Leiber and Stoller · The Cheers · The Robins

15 "ROCK AROUND THE CLOCK"   136

BILL HALEY INTERVIEW · The Platters · Chuck Berry

III

THE ROCK 'N' ROLL YEARS
1956–1960

16 THE GOD OF R 'N' R ARRIVES   149

Elvis Presley

Contents

17 KNOCKING THE ROCK 154

Alan Freed · The Celler Committee · ASCAP vs BMI · Nat "King" Cole

18 TEEN-AGE ERUPTION 161

Little Richard · Fats Domino · James Brown · Ivory Joe Hunter · Carl Perkins · Johnny Cash · George Hamilton IV · Gene Vincent · The Cadillacs · The Coasters · Frankie Lymon and the Teenagers · "Flying Saucer" · James Dean · Calypso · Record Hops

19 THE AMERICAN BANDSTAND 175

"Young Love" · Dick Clark · "Lip-Syncing"

20 THE AUDACIOUS AMATEURS— AND THE COUNTRY ROCKERS 182

Fabian · Sal Mineo · The Tune Weavers · The Bobbettes · The Rays · Charlie Gracie · Bobby Helms · Tommy Sands · Buddy Knox · Jimmy Bowen · Tex-Mex Sound · Buddy Holly · The Everly Brothers · JERRY LEE LEWIS INTERVIEW · Bill Justis · Link Wray · Duane Eddy

21 WE'RE SO YOUNG—AND THEY'RE SO OLD 194

PAUL ANKA INTERVIEW · Ricky Nelson · Jimmie Rodgers · Eddie Cochran · Johnny Mathis · Sam Cooke · DELLA REESE INTERVIEW · Mickey and Sylvia · Larry Williams · The Stroll · Chuck Willis · The Coasters · Thurston Harris · Huey Smith and the Clowns · The Del Vikings · Little Richard

22 GET PRESLEY! 211

Skiffle · Ray Anthony

23 GOING STEADY 216

"Lollipop" · Danny and the Juniors · The Silhouettes · Billy and Lillie · Frankie Avalon · Connie Francis · Four Preps · The Champs · Laurie London · Sheb Wooley · Jack Scott · Ed Townsend · Bobby Freeman

24 HULA HOOPS, CHIPMUNKS,
AND THE KINGSTON TRIO   232

Perez Prado · Bobby Darin · George "Hound Dog" Lorenz · "*Volare*"
· Peggy Lee · The Elegants · The Poni-Tails · Little Anthony and the
Imperials · Jimmy Clanton · Hula Hoop Craze · The Olympics ·
Bobby Day · Jerry Wallace · Dion and the Belmonts · Earl Grant
· Tommy Edwards · The Kingston Trio · Conway Twitty · The Big Bopper
· Cozy Cole · Bob Braun · "The Chipmunk Song" · Phil Spector ·
The Playmates · "The Little Drummer Boy"

25 WHAT A DIFFERENCE A DECADE MAKES   252

Johnny Horton · Jimmy Driftwood · Marty Robbins · Bobby Darin ·
The Browns · Ritchie Valens · Neil Sedaka · Bobby Rydell · Freddy
Cannon · Brenda Lee · The Fleetwoods · The Crests · Santo and
Johnny · Lloyd Price · Dinah Washington · Sarah Vaughan · Jackie
Wilson · Brook Benton · Nina Simone · Ray Charles · The Isley
Brothers

26 PAYOLA   268

Discography   282

Selected Bibliography   289

Index   291

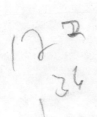

ACKNOWLEDGMENTS

Although I was active in the music scene of the 1950s and had firsthand contact with much of what I have described, I welcomed the recollections of other participants and observers in rounding out the picture. I am grateful to the following, not only for interviews included in these pages, but for incidental insights that emerged in taping sessions: Paul Anka, Ray Charles of "Your Hit Parade," Bo Diddley, Ahmet Ertegun of Atlantic Records, Bill Haley, B. B. King, Frankie Laine, Jerry Lee Lewis, Johnnie Ray, Della Reese, and Jerry Wexler of Atlantic Records.

Others who supplied information, photographs, and/or contacts include Eddy Arnold, Tony Bennett, Johnny Mathis, Johnny Tillotson, Jerry Vale, my good friend (conductor-composer) Henri René, Tom Dowd of Atlantic Records, Henry Glover of King Records, Bobby Shad of Time Records, manager Lee Magid, James K. Makrianes, Jr., of Young & Rubicam, William G. Clotworthy of Batten, Barton, Durstine, Osborn, C. A. Jackson, Jr., of the American Tobacco Co., Herbert N. Gottlieb and Richard Frohlich of ASCAP, Russ Sanjek, Burt Korall, and Dick Kirk of BMI, Kenn Scott of MCA Records, Bob Altschuler of Columbia Records, Herb Hellman of RCA Records, Sol Handwerger of MGM Records, my daughter Elizabeth Hilda Adams, my niece Joni Friedman Walden, publicist Richard Gersh, producer Richard Nader of the "1950s Rock 'n' Roll Revival," and Doug Allen, editor of *Cavalier,* in whose pages a cameo view of the '50s and the interviews with Paul Anka and Frankie Laine appeared originally.

Among my Las Vegas neighbors, I acknowledge the help of radio–TV commentator Joe Delaney, Art Engler of Associated Booking Corp., Muriel and Maury Stevens of radio and TV, June Paramore of the *Las Vegas Review-Journal,* Ralph Pearl of the *Las Vegas Sun,* Forrest Duke of the *Review-Journal,* Bill Willard of *Variety*, publicist Jimmy Snyder, and, especially, publicist Jim Seagrave.

The columns of *Variety* and *Cash Box* were important sources. But a special word must be said for *Billboard* whose amiable publisher, Hal Cook, allowed me (during the many research trips I made to Hollywood) to use its offices, bound volumes, Xerox machine, and on one accidental occasion, its doctor.

Other persons to whom I am indebted are mentioned in the book. And here is a list of songs to which I refer in the text, with their copyright notices:

"Ac-cent-tchu-ate the Positive (Mister In-Between)." W by Johnny Mercer. M by Harold Arlen. Copyright 1944 by Edwin H. Morris & Co., Inc. 26

"Come On-a My House." W & M by Ross Bagdasarian and William Saroyan. Copyright 1950 by Duchess Music Corp. 30

"Music! Music! Music! (Put Another Nickel In)." W & M by Stephen Weiss and Bernie Baum. Copyright 1950 by Cromwell Music, Inc. 34

"Too Young." W by Sylvia Dee. M by Sid Lippman. Copyright 1951 by Jefferson Music Co., Inc. 36

"Mockin' Bird Hill (Tra-la La Twittle Dee Dee Dee)." W & M by Vaughn Horton. Copyright 1949 by Southern Music Publishing Co., Inc. 37

"High Noon" a.k.a. "Do Not Forsake Me." W by Ned Washington. M by Dimitri Tiomkin. Copyright 1952 by Leo Feist, Inc. 38

"Matilda, Matilda." W & M by Harry Thomas. Copyright 1953 by Duchess Music Corp. 43

"Please Send Me Someone to Love." W & M by Percy Mayfield. Copyright 1951 by Venice Music, Inc./Hill & Range Songs, Inc. 90

"Fool, Fool, Fool." W & M by Ahmet Ertegun. Copyright 1951 by Progressive Music Publishing Co., Inc. 92

"Honey Love." W & M by Clyde McPhatter and J. Gerald. Copyright 1954 by Progressive Music Publishing Co., Inc. 102

"Work with Me Annie." W & M by Henry "Hank" Ballard. Copyright 1954 by Lois Publishing Co. 117

"Annie Had a Baby." W & M by Henry Glover and Lois Mann. Copyright 1954 by Jay & C Music Corp. 117

"Shake, Rattle and Roll." W & M by Charles Calhoun. Copyright 1954 by Progressive Music Publishing Co., Inc. 137

INTRODUCTION

In the current '50s revival, *bland* and *halcyon* are two of the most
frequent epithets one encounters in nostalgic flashbacks. Remembrance of things past *tends* toward soft-focus views of a given time.
But how can one apply these adjectives to days filled with the
rumblings of the Cold War, fears about the race in space, and the
hysteria of the McCarthy witch-hunts. "Bland" when people were
building bomb shelters and schoolchildren were being drilled in
what to do in an atomic attack?

Similarly, historians of rock are given to such words as *fun,
joy,* and *innocence* in recalling the songs. The songs were simpler
than they became in the '60s and were made for dancing. But the
new generation was seeking to define itself through them—and it
was an embattled generation, for the Establishment fought the
new music with bans, arrests, lawsuits, not to mention actual
physical destruction of recordings on and off the air.

Like Dover Beach, the '50s were "swept with confused alarms
of struggle and flight." At their beginning, the Tin Pan Alley
era of lush balladry was in the doldrums. Seeking dance music,
the children of World War II found it in the big beat of rhythm
and blues. And then R 'n' R came rolling in with Bill Haley,
Elvis, Alan Freed, and a flock of young singers. *Teen-age* became a war cry as an older generation of singers, songwriters, and
publishers fought the new wave. And then, as the decade ended,
the payola investigations shook up television and rocked the entire world of entertainment.

The '50s were a time of flux, of sound and fury. The sound was
made by young people creating their own culture; and the fury,
that of the older generation resisting, hating, and opposing something they could not and did not want to understand. Mutual

trust between those under and over thirty splintered until the generation gap of the '6os became a dismal reality.

Although I grew up with the pop of the older generation, the '50s were my era. As a publisher, record producer-and-promoter, I early learned to like and work with the new sounds—as a list of hits I picked amply reveals. I remember the days of ducktail haircuts and swinging ponytails, skintight pedal pushers and pegged pants, coonskin caps and sack dresses, frisbies and hula hoops, sock hops and sputniks, *Peyton Place,* sexy Marilyn and T-shirted Marlon as raunchy, rockin', and rewarding years.

1

SUMMER OF 1955

In the spring of 1955, I took over the creative reins of one of New York's oldest music publishing companies.

"Edward B. Marks Music Corporation is proud," an advertisement in *Billboard*'s May 7 issue read, "to welcome Arnold Shaw as its General Professional Manager." The lower half of the ad advised that the "Malagueña" girl Caterina Valente was "Blowing Up a Record Storm" with Ernesto Lecuona's Latin ballad "The Breeze and I." A storm was brewing in pop music. No one seemed to know exactly in which direction the wind was a-blowin'.

Confusing to people outside music business, my title (Gen. Prof. Mgr., as it was abbreviated) meant in its simplest and most terrifying terms: finder and maker of hits—a round-the-clock syndrome, ulcer-making and hair-graying, that involved auditioning songs, making demos, getting recordings, and plugging-promoting-publicizing them until they made the charts or were shelved as "dogs," "flops," or "bombs."

Except for two or three New York publishers who had staked out Nashville and signed accessible recording-writers, most Gotham firms then had little or no contact with the Tennessee music scene. A maverick in more ways than one—I was six credits from a Ph.D. in American literature when I quit academia—I had been paying periodic visits to the home of the "Grand Ole Opry" for five years. Now, in the waning weeks of the summer, I decided to head south again.

As I got into a taxi on the Fiftieth Street, eastbound side of the RCA Building, Nat "King" Cole's silk-and-satin baritone came oozing out of the radio speaker. Each syllable printed out of Cole's Steeplechase mouth like the illuminated letters on Times

Square's running news sign, or the General Motors bulb-bright
ad above Columbus Circle. Subconsciously, I thought: the color
is right. But the sound and this type of pretty, pseudopoetic
ballad are passé. As if in answer to my thoughts, Sinatra winged
in with "Learnin' the Blues," a finger-snapping rhythm ballad,
belted with bluesy-bent notes. The Voice had just reasserted his
priority on the vocal scene with "Young at Heart," and the blues
were no longer part of a career flying phoenixlike into a new, expansive phase. No, his choice of song was motivated by the change
in taste sensed by Perry Como, Georgia Gibbs, and others who
were copying—"covering" in music-biz euphemistic lingo—driving
rhythm-and-blues recordings by black artists.

On the way to La Guardia, I had the taxi stop on Fifty-ninth
Street between Third and Second Avenues. The block was a Little
Italy, and I bought several pounds of pepperoni packed in dry
ice. The long, spicy, Italian frankfurters were a favorite food of
portly Tom Parker, former manager of the Tennessee Plowboy,
Eddy Arnold, and I happened to savor Mrs. Tom Parker's
cooking.

Not that I had an invitation to visit with the Parkers. It was
just that Nashville food was then the worst. Operating in a dry
state, the restaurants could not make it without liquor revenue
and the food suffered. You could, of course, drink in public eating
places. But you had to go to a Package Store, buy a bottle, carry
it in in a brown paper bag, and have the waitress bring set-ups.

And so I bought the pepperoni, hoping that once Colonel Tom
Parker knew I was in town—at the old Andrew Jackson Hotel—
he would invite me to stay at his home. The gamble paid off in
unexpected ways. You could almost say that the rock revolution
was started by pepperoni.

Nashville music folk, I had found, were convivial and out-
going in a way that pop people seldom were. I cannot recall a visit
to Music City, as it is now known, without an invitation to have
dinner or lunch at Eddy Arnold's home. Not long after I settled
at the Andrew Jackson, the room phone would ring and Arnold's
booming, Tennessee-accented voice would sound out, "Mr. Shaw,
this is Ed-*dy* Ar-nold." Later in the day, he would drive up to the
hotel in an air-conditioned Cadillac—Nashville even then had
the highest per capita number of Caddies—and take me out to his
rambling farm on the outskirts of town. And he knew for a cer-
tainty that I was carrying songs and demos to audition for a possible recording by him.

I knew Eddy much better than I knew Jim Denny, program
director of WSM, talent coordinator of the "Grand Ole Opry,"

and later a most successful publisher artists manager. But one day as I was hurrying along a Nashville street, late for an appointment, I ran into Denny. When he learned where I was headed, he held up a small ring of car keys, pointed to a garage about two blocks away, and offered me his Cadillac. I was surprised, startled in fact. When he explained the distance I had to traverse, I gladly accepted, thanked him, and not without a sense of disbelief, started on a trot to the garage—then turned quickly around and trotted back after Denny.

"I've got a series of appointments," I explained, out of breath, "and I don't know how soon I can return your car."

He shrugged. "Whenever you are finished, bring 'er in. Tonight. Tomorrow morning. We've got other cars in the office. An' remember this is not New York. Slow down."

During the plane ride to Nashville, I tried to sort out my intuitions about the music-record scene. As E. B. Marks' new hit finder, I had succeeded one of the industry's highest-paid Gen. Prof. Mgrs. A giant during the '30s and '40s—he was a legendary liar and a man whose nervousness manifested itself in the twisting of handkerchiefs—Harry Link had laid an egg during the '50s. I was uneasy as the occupant of his former office because of both his success and failure, also because for the first time I was up at bat alone. From 1950 to 1955 I had served in a similar capacity with two other large firms; but the working owners liked you best when you had egg on your face.

As I looked ahead into the fall of '55, I was certain that the future of the business was not in Hollywood, not on Broadway, and certainly not in good old Tin Pan Alley. Everybody felt that something was happening when a nice Jewish girl like Georgia Gibbs got hits by copying (and cloroxing) records by black-and-gritty LaVern Baker. Old-line publishers who had dominated the hit parade for years couldn't understand it. They both feared and hated it without really knowing what it was and without suspecting what a tidal wave was soon to inundate the pop mainstream.

They felt uneasy when they read in *Billboard* (July 23, 1955): "Negro Artists Rise as Solid Pop Sellers." Their edginess was reflected in a slogan that kept appearing under the trade paper's all-important Honor Roll of Hits: "KEEP THE POPS ALIVE IN '55." They tried to believe that these were not storm warnings, only a temporary situation. Some months later, *Billboard* would eliminate their wishful thinking: "Pop Crapehangers Hex But R & B in '56 Boom—Death Certificate Premature; R & B Ain't Even Been Sick."

My first move at Marks had been to contact R & B record labels with small publishing adjuncts: companies that owned copyrights but lacked the staffs and/or capital to promote them. Within weeks, I acquired from Herman Lubinsky at Savoy Records the rights to "Pitter Patter," a black ballad recorded by gravel-voiced Nappy Brown. (Nappy had just come off "Don't Be Angry" whose cover by the Crew Cuts yielded a hit disk for the Canadian lads of "Sh-Boom" fame). By the time I was on the way to Nashville, "Piddilly Patter Patter," as I retitled the tune, had been covered on Mercury by Patti Page. Not long after, I purchased from another small R & B label (Glory Records) a tune called "Soldier Boy," as recorded by the Four Fellows.

Neither tune made it real big, though "Soldier Boy" scored as one of 1955's Top R & B Records and was recorded by a large number of artists, including at a later date Elvis Presley. But both songs served notice to music business that the seventy-year-old firm of Marks, moribund for almost a decade, was alive and well and moving aggressively back onto the pop scene.

My trip to Nashville had a similar purpose. Though '55 was a year of white major covers of small black records, Nashville had been a strong source of pop hits in the early '50s. Apart from "Tennessee Waltz" and "Chattanoogie Shoe Shine Boy," Patti Page and Bing Crosby covers respectively of Cowboy Copas and Red Foley originals, there had been Tony Bennett, Rosemary Clooney, and Jo Stafford covers of Hank Williams originals. I was interested in finding material in the other area not readily accessible to old-line publishing companies and I wanted to hire a field representative in the Tennessee capital.

I was at the Andrew Jackson only one day before the Colonel's hoarse voice with the rising inflections—as if he were making a point or expected applause—was on the phone. Late that day, he came by the hotel and drove me to his home in Madison, about twenty-five miles from Nashville. While Marie Parker busied herself preparing dinner, the Colonel took me down to his basement. After a while, he opened a desk drawer and pulled out a four-page, legal-size, printed document.

"That's the contract promoters have to sign if they want to book one of my artists," he said, a sly look in his washed-out blue eyes.

I glanced through the document. It was drawn in typically heavy legal jargon. As I flipped to the back page, the kicker came: "I prepared that contract myself," said the Colonel.

My amusement must have shown in my face. You see, the

Colonel had, on several occasions, boasted that he was a public-school dropout.

"I'm not snowin' you," said the Colonel, employing one of his favorite expressions. "I prepared that contract myself, every single clause of it. See, here's where you city slickers can learn a little somethin' from us country boys." Having indulged himself in another favorite gambit, the Colonel paused, pacing his act like one of his artists.

"I started in the carny business when I was very young," he continued. "County fairs, livestock shows, rodeos, circuses, tobacco promotions, Saturday-night dances, carnivals—cleaning, doing odd jobs, selling programs. Finally, I got to where I sold an act to a promoter and I had to sign a contract. Took me all night to read that piece of paper. But I read every word, signed it—and got taken to the cleaners, as you city folk say.

"Raised a ruckus but couldn't do a thing. It was all legal. So I went home, found the clause that did me in, cut it out, and pasted it on a piece of paper. The next time I got a contract, I went lookin' for this son-of-a-bitchin' clause. It wasn't there. But I got taken by another clause. So I pasted that one on a piece of paper. After several years, I had all these stinkers that I was watchin' out fer."

Now, the Colonel paused, gave me one of his sly, squinty-eyed looks, flicked some ash from a cigar, and waited. "One day," he said slowly, "I put all those smart-assed clauses together—and that's the contract you're holdin' in yer big-city hands."

It was a gem, as more than one lawyer at the big booking agencies told me. And the Colonel was himself a gem of a not-too-rare species. In the early years when he was presenting his own shows for Purina products in southern towns, he always scheduled a lengthy intermission. Apart from providing an opportunity to hawk souvenir programs, buttons, and other items—all of which he himself sold in prodigious quantities—it permitted another money-making gambit. The Colonel sent a kid through the tent or auditorium to pick up every program left temporarily on a chair or seat. These were resold at the next show, picked up again, and sold again.

The Colonel used a more involved scheme on other occasions, particularly in poor, rural areas when he had to keep his admission price low to get an audience. He would pitch his tent in a field where a farmer had a herd of cows. By the time the show went on, the area around the exit would be rather well inundated with cow dung. To get to an access road, the audience had to trudge through this deep layer of mush. But no, the good Colonel came to the rescue of the ladies in their Sunday fineries. He provided donkeys to help them across the sea of cow shit. Only the short donkey ride cost more than an admission to the show.

As I anticipated, I had a delectable dinner that evening. The following morning, Marie Parker made like a good Jewish mother, and I could not leave the breakfast table without absorbing a meal that was like a seven-course dinner. Afterwards, the Colonel took me out to a shack in back of his house which served as an office and where his assistant, Tom Diskin, functioned.

Quite casually, he put a 45 disk on the record player. I listened to another side by the same singer, wondering what the Colonel had in mind. When he put on a third side, I glanced at the singer's name. It was unknown to me. The voice sounded white southern, but the style was black. The background by a small string combo was a cross between white country and western and black rhythm and blues. I couldn't decide whether the singer was black or white, though I didn't think the Colonel would be managing a black artist.

At about that time, he handed me several glossy 8½ by 10s. The singer was a tough-looking white youngster. His lips were curled in a wise-guy sneer, later eliciting the epithet "surly." An action shot showed him with his knees bent in a branch-clipper cross.

"In Georgia and Florida," the Colonel said, "the girls are tearing off his clothes."

I could see the animal sex appeal flowing from the youngster. And though I could not always understand the lyrics, as he worried and spit them out, he had a chesty, throaty, rasping sound that was quite sensual.

"He's unknown north of the Mason and Dixon line," the Colonel added, eyeing me as if fitting a suit. You're a big man up north. Let me see you get his records played in the Big City."

"What's your interest, Colonel?" I asked. The Colonel, who had managed Eddy Arnold very successfully for almost ten years, was then heading Hank Snow Jamboree Attractions. The Parker-Arnold partnership had broken up, partly as I understood it, because the Colonel wanted to handle other talent and despite his willingness to share the take with Eddy.

"This kid is now managed by Bob Neal of Memphis," the Colonel replied. "But I'll have him when Neal's contract finishes in less than a year."

And so I left Madison, carrying with me two copies each of

three Sun recordings. The then-unknown singer, as you have perhaps surmised, was Elvis Aaron Presley.

Back in New York, I played the disks for several people in my office. The over forty's reacted as antagonistically as they did to most "unmusical" R & B disks. I got the feeling in watching some of the under twenty girls that despite their noncommital comments, Presley was getting to them. The movements of their eyes and slight movements of their bodies told me that they were reacting to something visceral and vibrant in the grooves. Glancing at his pictures, my secretary remarked: "His eyes look like soft-boiled eggs."

I frankly did not know what to make of the records. They puzzled me but they had a quality, despite their crudeness, that intrigued me. I decided to try them on a disk jockey whom I greatly respected. Bill Randle was a well-known Cleveland platter spinner (on station WERE) who came into New York once a week to do a Saturday-morning show over CBS. In 1955 he was one of a select group of personality deejays who had demonstrated a rare and consistent ability to "break" records i.e., to attract and create an audience for a new disk. Randle had a suave, scholarly appearance and was, in fact, taking courses toward a Ph.D. degree. Publishers, artists, and record men were so anxious to get recordings on his turntable that they slipped him advance copies of disks before the actual release date. This was a no-no. But the practice continued until all the other disk jockeys in Cleveland ganged up and issued an ultimatum that they would boycott any record on which Randle was given the jump.

When I approached him about the Presley recordings, he evinced the instantaneous excitement of a uranium seeker who hears the clicking of a Geiger counter. Randle had big owl eyes that looked even larger because of the shell-rimmed glasses he wore. They opened wide as I repeated what I had learned from the Colonel. The fact that Presley was then unknown in the North and Midwest added the extra touch so prized in the world of entertainment—the prestige of discovery. Nevertheless, Randle decided that Presley was too primitive for his metropolitan CBS show.

Just three days later, my phone rang and an excited Randle was on the line from Cleveland. "I don't know what those Presley records have," he shouted. "But I put them on yesterday and, Arnold, the switchboard lit up like Glitter Gulch in Las Vegas. I still can't make out half the words of 'Mystery Train' and 'I

Forgot to Remember to Forget.' But the kids seem to get them.
He hits them like a bolt of electricity. If you can, if I were you,
I'd pick up every one of those songs. My phone hasn't stopped
ringing and I haven't been able to stop playing those sides. Take
my word . . . he's gonna bust wide open into the biggest thing
that ever hit music business. Gotta cut. All my phones are ringing
again. Bye."

I had not said one word and he was off the phone before I
could. Remember, this was the early fall of '55. Randle had a
great track record for picking winners. But he was also known to
be a hype artist by nature. He never just liked something. He
loved it. And when he loved, everybody knew it. As I sat mulling
the situation, my secretary buzzed: "Dee Kilpatrick of Mercury
Records in Nashville is on the line."

"Is it true that Presley's Sun contract is up for grabs?" he
asked. The Randle hype was already producing action. Before I
could reply, Kilpatrick added: "You know, Arnold, we've been
watching this kid for a while. He's dynamite in personals. But
his records haven't meant a thing. Randle thinks he's ready for
the big time. Can you help us? I hear you have the inside track
with Sun."

During the succeeding week, virtually every record executive
in the business phoned me. When they called Randle to hype a
disk of their own, he obviously hit them with: "Hey, have you
heard this new Presley kid?" Since Randle knew of Presley
through me, they immediately came after me. And then they
were on the phone with Sam Phillips of Memphis, the man who
recorded Presley and owned Sun Records.

Except for the South where Presley's records were getting airplay on C & W (country and western) stations, Randle was then
the only urban disk jockey programing Elvis—and I mean, four
and five times an hour. Considering the stir inside the record
business, the charts of the day hardly revealed the upheaval that
was in the making. The top three songs then were: "Yellow Rose
of Texas," an old-style sentimental-patriotic march with records
by Mitch Miller and Johnny Desmond; "Love Is a Many-Splendored Thing," the Oscar ballad of the year; and "Autumn
Leaves" in a rippling, piano version by Roger Williams.

Despite the absence of Presley from all of the national charts,
the kid was (in show-biz parlance) *hot* and the record business
buzzed with offers and counteroffers, deals, and superdeals. At
one point, I heard that Sam Phillips was asking $15,000 for Elvis's
contract and that Mitch Miller of Columbia dismissed the figure
as ridiculous.

In the midst of the maneuvering, I picked up the phone early one morning to hear Colonel Parker's husky voice at the other end. He was in New York staying at the Hotel Warwick, and could he come over and see me? We were four and one-half blocks from each other—and that was the time that it took for him to be at my desk in Rockefeller Center.

When he had talked to me at his home in Madison, he was a minister without portfolio. Presley was then, as he was at the moment, under the exclusive personal management of Bob Neal of Memphis, Tennessee. Parker was merely helping to arrange some of Presley's personal appearances. But now as he stood at my desk in the RCA Building, he unfurled a telegram that was literally more than a foot long. Addressed to him, it was signed by Presley's mother and father—Elvis was then not yet twenty-one—and it stated in repetitious legal jargon that Col. Thomas A. Parker was fully empowered by them, Gladys and Vernon Presley, to negotiate a recording contract for their son, Elvis Aaron.

As a matter of fact, Parker was not technically Presley's manager even when RCA Victor, the record company that bought his Sun contract, announced the release of his first Victor disk on December 3, 1955. "The most talked about new personality in the last 10 years of recorded music," was the caption on a full-page *Billboard* ad. The titles of the first release: "I Forgot to Remember to Forget" b/w (backed with) "Mystery Train" (20/47-6357). These were not new recordings but sides that Victor had bought from Sun. The credits at the bottom of the ad read: "Bob Neal, manager/ under direction of Hank Snow Jamboree Attractions/ Col. Tom Parker, general manager/ Box 417, Madison Tennessee."

There is a mistaken impression that the deal between Victor and Sun was made in Nashville at WSM's annual disk-jockey convention, held late in September of '55. The deal was first announced there and Presley made an appearance at the convention. But negotiations were conducted and terms set in New York. Just about the time that the Colonel was ensconced at the Warwick, Sam Phillips also was in the city. By then his asking price had risen to $40,000, the generally reported closing figure. It was paid jointly by RCA Victor and the brothers Jean and Julian Aberbach, owners of Hill & Range and other C & W publishing companies. RCA ostensibly put up $25,000 for Presley's recording contract while the Aberbachs paid $15,000 for publishing rights and the purchase of Hi Lo Music, a Sam Phillips company that owned the songs recorded on Sun by Presley. The only song that

Hill & Range did not acquire 100 percent was "I Forgot to Remember to Forget."

You see, I had phoned Sam Phillips immediately after my long-distance conversation with the excited Mr. Randle. Phillips's executive assistant, Marion Keisker, served as intermediary and indicated a willingness to sell 50 percent of one of the songs. When Phillips was in New York negotiating with RCA and the Aberbachs, he came to my office. It was a Saturday morning. We were closed, as were many of the restaurants in the RCA Building. We had difficulty finding a quiet spot for breakfast.

I must confess that Phillips was a more considerate man than the Colonel. He could easily have reneged on a very tentative promise made over a long-distance phone by Marion Keisker. But he did not, and Edward B. Marks Music, the company I was running, acquired 50 percent of "I Forgot to Remember to Forget," Presley's first release on Victor. As for the dear Colonel, I cannot remember receiving an acknowledgment of any kind, let alone a thank-you in writing or orally, for the contribution that Bill Randle (and I) had made to the successful conclusion of a game he had been playing for some time.

What I did not learn until sometime later was that the Colonel had been trying to peddle Elvis's Sun contract to RCA for almost a year before he brought the disks to my attention. (He was also working on Gladys and Vernon Presley to ditch Bob Neal.) His contact at RCA was Steve Sholes, a topnotch record producer who spent all of his working life at Victor and who was then in charge of its C & W department. The Colonel had worked with Sholes, as he had with the Aberbachs, during his years with Eddy Arnold. Both Arnold and Hank Snow recorded for RCA and owned publishing companies with the Aberbach *freres.*

Presley's first Sun disk ("That's All Right Mama" b/w "Blue Moon of Kentucky") was released in August 1954. By the time I stayed at the Colonel's home in Madison, there were five Presley platters on the market. Some of them had made C & W regional charts and, through Sam Phillips, he had appeared on the "Grand Ole Opry" over WSM and was a regular on "Louisiana Hayride," originating over KWKH out of Shreveport, Louisiana. But he had not created more than a regional stir, and Sholes kept telling the Colonel that he had no basis on which to approach the financial powers at RCA. Randle (and I) created the stir.

Of greater concern and consequence to me than the absence of any overt manifestation of gratitude by the Colonel was friction that he apparently created between me and Sholes. Steve and I had a friendly working relationship that began in 1949 when he recorded, with Elton Britt and Rosalie Allen, a song on which I had collaborated, "Acres of Diamonds." Through the years, we occasionally lunched together and his door had always been open to me. Suddenly, at the time of the Presley negotiations, I felt a cold wind blowing from his direction. I never knew what the Colonel told Sholes that caused this alienation, and by the time the breach was healed several years later (fortunately before Steve's sudden death), there seemed no point in asking.

My last personal contact with the Colonel came early in 1956. It was a cold, rainy day in New York. Presley was making his first appearance on national television, on of all conceivable programs, the "Tommy Dorsey Show." The rehearsal was being held in the Nola Studios on Broadway between Fifty-first and Fifty-second Street, over the new Lindy's, now a Steak & Brew restaurant. I came without an invitation. Tommy was munching an apple— he was later to choke to death on one—as the band, seated in tiers at one end of the rehearsal studio, went over the numbers. The truculent trombonist was in a lively mood, but could not resist needling, as was his wont, trumpeter Charlie Shavers. Presley sat in a corner quietly and unobtrusively. After a while, the Colonel motioned to me and I went over to shake hands with his charge. When Dorsey gave the band a "take five" the Colonel, accompanied by an agent from the William Morris office, brought Presley over to meet the famous bandleader. The formalities were brief, and Elvis exhibited a kind of deference and courtesy that patently puzzled Dorsey. As I recall it, Presley did not rehearse since he had brought his own small combo to accompany him.

Considering that the Pelvis's appearance that Saturday night (January 28, 1956) elicited angry phone calls, violent telegrams, and vituperative letters from many parents—and there were network-agency conferences about canceling his two other Dorsey appearances—his demeanor at the rehearsal made a strange contrast to the knee-jerking, face-leering, hip-bumping, pelvis-twisting figure that viewers saw on the tube.

If I were to pick any one moment when Broadway's big music companies, also the established artists of the day, sensed the handwriting on the wall, Elvis's first appearance on the Dorsey TV show would be it. *Billboard*'s slogan "KEEP THE POPS ALIVE IN '55" looked, indeed, like wishful thinking. The "Pops" should have read "Pop."

By then, *Billboard's* Honor Roll of Hits had a really ominous cast. Sure, there were old-style ballads like "Memories Are Made of This," "Love and Marriage," and "All at Once You Love Her" by established singers like Dean Martin, Frank Sinatra, and Perry

Como. But more than one-third of the list consisted of items like
"The Great Pretender" and "Only You" by the Platters, Bill
Haley's "See You Later, Alligator," "Tutti Frutti" by Little
Richard (also Pat Boone), and "I Hear You Knockin' " by Smiley
Lewis (also Gale Storm). There were also—and in the Top Ten—
"Rock and Roll Waltz," "Teen-Age Prayer," and "Dungaree
Doll," a song on which I collaborated. At this moment in time,
it was hard to brush aside the possibility that pop music was
making a sharp turn and that new songwriters and artists, most
of them young and gifted and black, were about to take over the
music scene.

I

DEATH OF AN ERA

Tin Pan Alley 1950-1953

2

IT'S LATER
THAN YOU THINK

In March 1950 Sen. Joseph McCarthy made a five and one-half hour speech, charging that the State Department harbored 81 Reds. He previously had cited figures of 205 and 57. The following month, "It Isn't Fair" made the *Hit Parade*.

"We're not at war," said President Harry Truman of the Korean conflict. "We're just engaged in a police action." At about the same time, record buyers began purchasing large quantities of a song titled "I Said My Pajamas (And Put on My Prayers)."

Not long before he fired Gen. Douglas MacArthur as field commander of the Korean operation, Harry Truman flew to Wake Island for a conference. MacArthur might have greeted the president with a then-popular ditty, "If I Knew You Were Comin', I'd've Baked a Cake." And Harry might have responded with a current torch ballad, "The End of a Love Affair."

In the schools, junior was being drilled on how to survive an atomic attack. "Fall instantly face down, elbow out, forehead on arms, eyes shut . . ." One of 1950's biggest songs was "There's No Tomorrow."

But in actuality, pop music at midcentury had no relevance to the day's events or problems—in fact, it avoided them. A story is in order. In 1951 when I was the song picker at Duchess Music Corporation, our West Coast representative telegraphed that he was forwarding a hot song he had just acquired. As I recall, he paid a $500 advance for "It Is No Secret." Since romantic ballads commanded the highest advances except in unusual situations, we assumed that the lyric would take the form of "It Is No Secret" that I love you, or that I miss you, or that I need you, or that I want you (the most intense form).

When the lead sheet arrived, we were surprised to find that the sequential words after the title were "what God can do . . ." My staff as well as song pluggers on associated staffs—Duchess was part of a combine including Pickwick Music and Leeds Music, the parent company—all wrote the song off.

I thought that Stuart Hamblen's religioso (as this type of religious ballad was typed in the trade) had emotional appeal, inspirational impact, and a memorable country melody. Since it was my function to get new songs recorded, I pitched for country artists at the labels I contacted. To my great satisfaction, I was able to interest some record producers in cutting "Secret" pop. In fact, in a short time I secured about fifteen different recordings, with some companies covering the song three ways—country, pop, and rhythm and blues. "It Is No Secret" never made the charts and logged only limited performances. (Compare the recent acceptance of "Bridge over Troubled Water.") But it was a solid seller on records and sheet music, and went on to become a well-loved standard.

I recount this experience by way of suggesting the dead-end generalizations that held pop music in a vise in the Tin Pan Alley era. Most publishers would not even audition three categories of song: patriotic, current events, and religious. The Alley lived on three other types: ballads, i.e., romantic songs; rhythm tunes, considered lightweight, like "I'm Looking over a Four-Leaf Clover" or "Cruising Down the River," and novelty songs like "I Taut I Taw a Puddy Cat" or "Papa Loves Mambo"—these were either overnight smashes or bombs.

Ballads, the mainstay of the business, took one of several simplistic directions: a declaration of undying love ("I'm Yours"); an appeal for love ("My Heart Cries for You"); or a troubled query ("Undecided"). As in the movies, happy endings were perferred. Unrequited love—torch songs—and triangles were accepted with uneasiness although they were a staple of country ballads. (By contrast, consider recent hits like "Gentle on My Mind" and "Honey.")

Direct references to physical contact or sex were taboo. But lyric writers had a drawerful of Victorian euphemisms that conveyed the idea. Words like "need," "love," "desire," "want," were all soft sells for bedding down, and so understood by listeners as well as singers. No one had any doubts about what was meant when a femme chirper sang, "If I give my heart to you . . ." As Randy Newman, a contemporary songwriter has said: "A lot of tunes in the guise of romanticism have mainly fucking behind them."

A portmanteau word like "charms" covered everything in the epidermis department, rhyming in ninety-nine out of one hundred songs with "arms," as "sorrow" inevitably brought on "tomorrow." It was up to the singer to infuse cliché lyrics with subtleties of feeling, emotion, and sex. And the power of Sinatra, who took lessons from Billie Holiday, lay in his ability to convey a degree of warmth, physical contact, and intimacy that brought female listeners to the verge of orgasm.

Even into the '50s, monosyllables were the lyric writer's staple, except in show songs. Larry Hart of the great musical-theatre team of Rodgers and Hart, once wrote an outstanding ballad whose underlying purpose was to poke fun at the kindergarten vocabulary of Tin Pan Alley. It went "I took one look at you/ That's all I meant to do/And then my heart stood still . . ." With just a few departures, the hit ballad from *A Connecticut Yankee* made its point in monosyllables. This severe limitation taxed the lyric writer's ingenuity, with the result that plays on words were frequent. One of the most-prized gimmicks was to switch the meaning of the title in its final repetition: for example, in "Even Now," a chartmaker for Eddie Fisher in '53, the first word of the title changes from an abverb (*just* now) to an adjective (emotionally equal) in the final strain.

If one wanted to be unkind and doubtless unjust, one might dismiss lyric writing during the Tin Pan Alley era as an exercise in word play. It was that in large part—outside the musical theatre —since lyricists sought not to express themselves or their own feelings so much as viable sentiments of the average sheet-music and record buyer. The publishers in the Brill Building at 1619 Broadway and in its adjuncts at 1650 and 1674 Broadway were not concerned with creativity but commercialism—a rather elusive concept for which Gen. Prof. Mgrs. and their intuitions commanded sizable salaries and expense accounts. There was no interest in expanding the craft, enlarging its coverage, or extending its vision, though songwriters occasionally did these things. The round-the-clock search was for a hit, a syndrome that has since overwhelmed every type of business and all the media.

One aspect of "commercialism," akin to a shibboleth of advertising, was repetition. Publishers were enthralled by a title like "You, You, You," a hit for the Ames Brothers in '53 or "It's Over, It's Over," a Sinatra perennial, where the repetition becomes almost hypnotic. Unfortunately, sheet-music and record buyers tended to confirm the practical validity of this esthetic canon. When a title was not "on the nose" (at the beginning), they frequently went into stores asking for a song by its first or other memorable line. That's how a '53 ballad "I Get So Lonely" came to be known as "Oh, Baby Mine." And "The Three Bells" was also known as "The Jimmy Brown Song."

The song form that dominated the Tin Pan Alley era was itself an exercise in repetition. Except for show tunes, pop music consisted preponderantly, overwhelmingly, almost exclusively, of thirty-two measure songs in which an eight-bar phrase (a) was repeated (a), then followed by a "bridge" or "release" (b), and repeated once again at the end (a).

Adult-oriented, pop was only occasionally adult-minded. Its focus was the urban courting generation. The expense-account crowd and the Serutan set supported the Broadway musical theatre and helped account for the popularity of show tunes like Cole Porter's "So in Love" from *Kiss Me Kate* and Rodgers and Hammerstein's "Some Enchanted Evening" from *South Pacific*, two of the big ballads of 1949. Mainstream pop emphasized sentiment and sentimentality, heartbreak and the homely virtues, romance and dreams, sometimes humor. It eschewed realism, gut truth, down-to-earth situations, and the joys and problems of the flesh. It addressed itself to the heart, not the stomach, nerves, or genitalia, and seldom the mind. It was music for people who put the lights out when they made love—like the films that panned to the sky or showed waves breaking on the beach when the stars made it to bed.

As we celebrated New Year's eve in 1949, "Mule Train" was racing across the music charts at the head of ballads like "I Can Dream, Can't I," revived by the Andrews Sisters, "A Dreamer's Holiday" by Perry Como, "Don't Cry, Joe" by Frank Sinatra, also Gordon Jenkins, his orchestra and chorus, and the folksy "Dear Hearts and Gentle People" by Bing Crosby.

In hot pursuit of Frankie Laine, who had the best-selling disk of the clippity-cloppity pacemaker, were seventeen other artists. Gordon McRae, Vaughn Monroe, and Crosby were each trying to grab a slice of the urban, mainstream market. Burl Ives was after the folk crowd. The Syncopators on National Records sought the race or rhythm-and-blues buyer. Tennessee Ernie, Cowboy Copas and Grandpa Jones, among others, competed for hillbilly or country-and-western sales. Like America, pop music was divided along regional and color lines. The generation split was yet to come.

Two of the day's best sellers suggested a crossover from country into mainstream. Western-gaited, "That Lucky Old Sun" had the sound of Beasley Smith of Nashville, Tennessee, and Haven Gillespie of Covington, Kentucky. Recorded originally by country writer-singer Floyd Tillman, "Slippin' Around," a downsouth euphemism for screwing around, was a pop hit for Margaret Whiting and Jimmy Wakeley.

But these occurrences were like shooting stars, ephemeral or so it seemed, and as they expired in a burst of sales, a sign of the things that would not change. Despite the cold war, atom-bomb hysteria, mounting Korean casualties, the fear of Communism, Whittaker Chambers's hollowed-out pumpkin and Alger Hiss's Woodstock typewriter, and McCarthyism—CBS and Campbell Soup required non-Commie oaths—there was "Arthur, the-man-with-the-natural-look Godfrey" . . . Jack Benny feuding with sharp-tongued Fred Allen . . . Boston Blackie, friend to those who have no friends . . . "Kukla, Fran and Ollie" . . . "Life Can Be Beautiful" . . . "The Lone Ranger," "Hi-ho, Silver! Awaaaayyy" to the *William Tell* Overture . . . seventy-nine-year-old Grandma Moses and her cheerful paintings of farm life in upper New York State . . . the "Joe Penner Show," "Wanna Buy a Duck?" . . . Rita Hayworth and Ingrid Bergman giving birth to "premature" babies . . . the Hollywood Ten going to jail . . . the "Eddie Cantor Show" with Parkyakarkus and the Mad Russian . . . Ethel Merman, who was Madame Du Barry, Panama Hattie, Annie Oakley, and now was Perle Mesta in *Call Me Madam* . . . the "Romance of Helen Trent," romance at thirty-five and beyond. . . .

And in pop music, there were the big baritones crooning big, romantic ballads to the accompaniment of big, fiddle-faddle orchestras—Hugo Winterhalter, Percy Faith, Henri René, and so on, some of whom like David Rose and Leroy Anderson ("Blue Tango") played lush, mood music for relaxing, cocktails, and vacationing in faraway places. There were also the Mickey-Mouse, swing-and-sway bands of Sammy Kaye, Guy Lombardo, Lawrence

Welk, Blue Barron, and Art Mooney playing the Businessman's Bounce for middle-aged, middle-class dancers.

In 1950 live entertainment returned to Broadway's Palace Theatre—once the Taj Mahal of vaudeville—with a bang-up bill headed by Belle Baker, the Barbra Streisand of the 1920s, Ukulele Ike, and the old-hat comic duo, Joe Smith and Charles Dale, formerly of the Avon Comedy Four. The entertainment Establishment was ecstatic at the possible return of the "good old days." All through the early '50s, it kept trying and trying to bring back the Big Bands . . .

3

MUZAK AND
MISTER IN-BETWEEN

From small-town barber to best-selling baritone—Perry Como's voice had the soothing quality of a hot towel or a gentle massage of the scalp. In the year that World War II ended, he marched onto the record scene with an adaptation of Chopin's Polonaise in A Flat. "Till the End of Time" contained an echo of the war in the stately, martial rhythms of the polonaise. But its appeal was doubtless in the expression of a world's yearning for permanence. To the men and women who survived the travail of the war, his low-keyed style became the sonic projection of the peaceful life, clean fun, controlled ebullience, and tranquil rather than passionate love.

Extolling the virtues of the childhood sweetheart he married, Perry said: "She's almost like a daughter to me. I have always had such a deep protective feeling for Roselle that it's as though I were her father. That's what love means to me." Coming onto the pop scene as the Big Baritones superseded the Big Bands, Perry was at the other end of the emotional spectrum from Frankie Boy. Perry was cool, relaxed, whereas the Voice was intense and frenetic; detached where Sinatra was involved; friendly and protective while the Voice was fleshy and possessive. In the early '50s, Como was the Eisenhower of the baritones, a gentle father figure.

Arriving several years after Sinatra had prompted the Paramount panics and swooning syndrome, he enjoyed great acceptance into the early '50s when the Voice had temporarily toppled from his pedestal. Como scored at first with melodramatic and impassioned ballads like "Prisoner of Love"—"upon my knees to her I'm creeping"—the song that brought fame to short-lived Russ

Columbo in the early '30s; Rodgers and Hammerstein's "If I
Loved You"; and Irving Berlin's "They Say It's Wonderful." His
low-pitched approach hardly seems appropriate to these high-
powered love ballads. But it may well be that postwar world
welcomed a retreat from the unbuttoned emotionalism of the war
years. Como mused rather than emoted, evincing a bland kind of
sincerity. And he also spent every spare moment swinging at little
white balls on a golf course.

Hybrids were really his forte—a pseudo–folk song like "Seattle,"
a pseudo–country tune like "Here Comes My Baby" or "My One
and Only Heart." Apparently neither he nor his audience could
take their songs straight and looked for sweeteners and mixes.
Como was most adept in handling novelty songs and humorous
ditties, a talent he manifested early when he sang "Dig You Later,
A-Hubba-Hubba-Hubba" in a film, *Doll Face*. Through the years,
he made best sellers of such cutie pies as "Hot Diggity (Dog
Diggity! Boom! What You Do to Me)," "Papa Loves Mambo,"
and "Delaware," an inventive play on the names of states. "What
did Delaware? . . . She wore a brand New Jersey . . ." In these,
as on his television show, he displayed a genuine flair for low-
keyed comedy.

The theme of his large-as-life weekly television program,
"Dream Along with Me . . . I'm on My Way to a Star," reminded
one of Sinatra's '42 radio theme, "Put Your Dreams Away for
Another Day." But itsy-poo lines like "We can wink at the moon
as we hold each other tight" sounded as if they came from an
1898 ballad, "When you were sweet sixteen, and I met you on the
village green," a Como favorite. Unquestionably, it was the TV
program's popularity that helped sustain his own through the '50s.
Mr. C., as he came to be known, registered a hit record, "Catch
A Falling Star," as late as 1958.

His record sessions in a period when vocalists tried to cut four
tunes in three hours—overtime rates after that—were models of
decorum. An aura of high soberness and contained power caused
A & R (artist and repertoire) producers to address him in hushed
tones. They never made suggestions or corrections over the studio
speaker, as they did with lesser artists. No, they came out of the
glass-fronted engineering booth, marched into the large studio
used for Como sessions, and whispered to him. Mr. C. smiled
occasionally but generally fixed them with the expressionless stare
of a father listening to a possibly misguided son. Sinatra was
treated with the same deference. But he always had a live audience
of friends, the girl of the hour, and hangers-on in the studio, and
he handled his sessions as if he were putting on a show, kidding

with the musicians, producers, and engineers when he was in a good mood.

Not unlike Sinatra, Como never went anywhere without an entourage. Headed by his brother-in-law, swarthy Dee Belline, and balding, bright-eyed Mickey Glass, who managed Mr. C.'s publishing interests, its personnel was quite constant and all male. It consisted mostly of song pluggers and small publishers, many of whom were Perry's golfing companions. These were the people with whom he felt at ease. Some said it was basically because he was a shy man. Others pointed to his background—his pa was a poor millhand in Canonsburg, Pennsylvania, where Perry, one of thirteen children, started barbering early enough to have his own shop at the age of sixteen. Friends claimed that he was always uncomfortable among strangers, particularly VIPs. Monte Proser said that when Como played the New York City Copa, he seldom left his dressing room between shows.

For a long while, his favorite restaurant (after telecasts and rehearsals) was a music-biz hangout, Al & Dick's Steak House on West Fifty-fourth Street. One evening when rehearsals ran long, Mr. C. and entourage arrived to find his customary table—large and round in a corner—occupied. Always self-contained, he manifested his irritation only in the set of his mouth. Turning on his heels, he led his entourage out of the restaurant. It was the last time that Al & Dick's saw him. Thereafter, his dining post, despite its distance from the CBS studio in the West Fifties, was Danny's Hideaway on East Forty-fifth Street. And before long, music business' influentials were dining regularly on Danny Stradella's Italian and by no means inexpensive cuisine.

More than Danny's dishes were flavored with garlic, oregano, and Parmesan cheese. Consider, if you will, the names of the leading male balladeers of the 1950s. Besides Sinatra and Como, both *paisanos,* there were Vic Damone, Al Martino, Tony Bennett (Benedetto), Jerry Vale, Eddie Fisher, Frankie Laine (Lo Vecchio), Alan Dale, Don Cornel, Billy Eckstine, Johnnie Ray, Guy Mitchell, Nat Cole, Johnny Desmond, and Dean Martin—not to mention Mario Lanza. Considering the preponderance of *paisanos,* is it any wonder that mainstream pop, until the advent of rock 'n' roll, was a *pasta* of Neapolitan, *bel canto,* pseudooperatic singing? The accompaniment, a gentle undercurrent of swirling strings, woolen woodwinds, and light rhythm, led an adverse critic to type the style as "the out-of-tempo, rustle-of-spring sound."

As America moved into midcentury, the swooning was over for Frank Sinatra, somebody tried to assassinate President Truman, and Harry advised a critic who assaulted his daughter Margaret's singing with the epithet "flat": "Someday I hope to meet you. When that happens, you'll need a new nose, a lot of beefsteak for your eyes and, perhaps, a supporter below."

Sinatra's personal life was in a domestic spin as he tried to free himself from his first wife (and legalize his relationship with Ava Gardner) but could not free himself of destructive guilt feelings about deserting his children. The travail was in his voice as it was in his erratic and intemperate behavior—brawls with newsmen, arguments with Ava, conflict with his advisors. To add to his trauma, in 1950 he lost two close friends—George Evans, his longtime publicist, prematurely dead of a heart attack, and Manie Sachs, his longtime A & R man and mentor, who left Columbia for RCA Victor.

Recordwise, Sinatra spent the early '50s trying to adjust to a new Columbia regime and experimenting with different arrangers. Nothing halted the downdraft in his career. By the time his contract expired in '52, he owed Columbia $110,000 in unearned advances and both he and the record company were anxious to call it "splitsville," in Sinatra lingo.

Blonde, balding Axel Stordahl, architect of his Columbia sound and the smashes of 1940s, arranged and conducted his first date at Capitol. Soon thereafter, he deserted what looked like a sinking ship and accepted a position with a new, rising vocal star, Eddie Fisher. In April 1953 Sinatra turned to Nelson Riddle as his arranger-conductor.

By December of that year, they had "Young at Heart" in the grooves. It was the turning point of his record career, as *From Here to Eternity,* released that year, was the start of a new, fabulously successful, film career.

"Young at Heart" was a finger snapper. It had the sound of the Big Bands enhanced by a large fiddle section. It was swing with strings, the brass imparting drive as the strings contributed lyricism. "Young at Heart" said something to the veterans of World War II but it caught the ears of their kids with its fresh, kick-ballad style.

"Man, I'm buoyant," Sinatra said, after he won the Academy Award as Best Supporting Actor of 1953. But just before he recorded "Young at Heart," he and Ava separated. The costly marriage had not lasted quite two years. For some years after '54, the Phoenix of the Films, as he was called, flew about carrying a burning torch. Always the autobiographical singer on an emotional level—and unique in this respect among pop vocalists—he kept recording songs that hinted at his lingering feelings for Ava.

"Why Should I Cry over You?" he asked in December '53. "Last Night When We Were Young," he mused in March '54. "Just One of Those Things," he observed the following month, and tried to "Get Happy" and "Wrap Your Troubles in Dreams." In May, he was lamenting "The Gal That Got Away" and in August confessed, "When I Stop Loving You."

By February of '55, he was asking, "Why Can't We Be Friends?" and giving assurances, "I'll Be Around." The same month, he announced "I Get Along Without You Very Well" but at the same time, recorded the tortured "In the Wee Small Hours of the Morning" and "When Your Lover Has Gone." The following month, he admitted, "I'll Never Be the Same" and asked, "How Could You Do a Thing Like That to Me?" That I have not manufactured a story out of titles becomes evident when one considers Frank's conduct. Once, in this period, he ripped a photograph of Ava to shreds, then made his cronies assist him in piecing it together. A delivery boy whose entrance helped uncover a missing scrap received a wrist watch in gratitude. His singing had such immediacy and depth of feeling because his choice of songs allowed him to externalize his own innermost feelings.

Sinatra remained high in the vocal firmament all through the rest of the '50s, scoring chart songs and mammoth album sellers— "Love and Marriage" from a TV show in '55; "All the Way," the Academy Award song of '57; and "High Hopes," the Oscar winner of '59. Not even the rock avalanche bothered him. The kids admired his truculence and felt a kinship, when he challenged authority, bucked the Establishment, and behaved like a bastard.

By the end of the '50s when most artists of his generation were kaput, he still felt potent enough to leave Capitol Records and found his own diskery. On Reprise Records, as late as the mid-'60s, he came up with three of the biggest singles of his entire career: "Strangers in the Night," "That's Life," a hard-rock blues, and "Something Stupid," a duet with daughter Nancy—all No. 1's and all Gold Records. By then, he was just Nancy's pop to the kids.

However, it was during the rock 'n' roll days of the '50s that he developed the singular style, which I have described in my biography of Sinatra as "a swinging ballad genre (that) combines pop lyricism with jazz inflections, deep feeling with a driving beat . . . the self-pitying tenderness of the lonely with the improvisational toughness of the flip." It is a style that appealed to young, old, and those in-between. While others have imitated it, for him the style was the man.

Apart from his Bogartlike image, his appeal to the rock 'n' roll

generation inheres in two factors. As a lover, he was vulnerable
as well as aggressive, tender as well as tough, and as ready to say
"Please love me" as "Frig you." The other factor, Sinatra has
himself described: "It's because I get an audience involved, personally involved in a song. . . . Having lived a life of violent
emotional contradictions, I have an over-acute capacity for sadness
as well as elation. . . . Whatever else has been said about me
personally is unimportant. When I sing, I believe . . ."

When New York's Fifty-second Street was still swinging in the
'40s, the King Cole Trio played Kelly's Stable, arriving from the
West in an old secondhand car. Gifted Oscar Moore on guitar
and Wesley Price on bass ably abetted Nat Cole's imaginative
excursions at the keyboard.

One afternoon, co-owner Ralph Watkins received a phone call
from his sister, who was the Stable's bookkeeper. She couldn't do
her work because Nat was "singin' this one number over and over
until I'm goin' nuts." Watkins said, "Nat doesn't sing," and
hopped into a cab and sped over to the club. Making a quiet
entrance, he parked himself in a corner of the darkened club and
listened—in surprise. He said nothing to Nat until a few nights
later when Billie Holiday, the starring vocalist on the bill, called
in sick. Then he tackled Cole about taking the vocal spot for the
evening. Cole balked, exhibiting an uneasiness that surprised
Watkins. But that evening, he sang. It was the first time that
King Cole, jazz pianist, appeared as Nat Cole, singer.

It took several years before the billing of the King Cole Trio
changed to Nat "King" Cole. The partial explanation is startling.
No one who has ever heard Cole in person or on wax has failed
to marvel at the flawless clarity of his diction. (They prized good
diction in pre-rock singing.) Yet Cole was afraid to sing in public
because he had a speech problem and did so only after he had
been helped by a speech therapist.

Although the King Cole Trio had a hit in "Straighten Up and
Fly Right" in 1944, Nat Cole did not attain his vocal maturity
until 1947 with "Nature Boy." The offbeat ballad, with a sinuous,
East-Indian-type melody, was written by a Los Angeles amateur,
who might well claim that he was the country's first hippie. Sport-
ing long hair and a Christlike beard, Eden Ahbez walked Hollywood's boulevards in sandals and a white cassock that anticipated
today's Hare Krishna devotees. The unusual character of the
song, with its nature-boy message of "loving and being loved in
return," set a pattern for Cole's future records.

Through the mid-'50s, he popularized such melodically rich

and lyrically poetic ballads as "Mona Lisa," the Oscar song of 1950, "Too Young," "Somewhere Along the Way," "Answer Me, My Love," "A Blossom Fell," and a revival of "Ballerina" with its Pagliacci theme. Inside the business, publishers knew that Cole could not be interested in the average Tin Pan Alley ballad, regardless of how commercial it might be.

Neither as involved a singer as Sinatra nor as detached as Como, Coles vocals were triumphs of sheer style. His sound, muted strings or a soft tenor sax, was unique and unmistakable. In the pre-rock days before black became beautiful, he was one of two male vocalists who penetrated the mainstream. Billy Eckstine, the other, is remembered for "I Apologize" and "My Destiny." Though the reaction to Mr. B., as Eckstine became known, was more intense—he subbed for Sinatra at the Copa when the Swooner lost his voice—Eckstine's tenure in the rarified atmosphere of the Top Ten was much shorter lived than Cole's, possibly because of an exaggerated, sometimes almost laughable vibrato.

The entertainment world, including music business, has always prided itself on its freedom from prejudice. Yet in an overall list of 197 recordings, designated by *Billboard* as "All-Time Juke Box Favorites," how many were by blacks? Only sixteen. And many of these artists, including Cole, performed in an imitative white style. In the pre-rock '50s, white-mainstream disk jockeys would not spin platters that sounded too black. As a result, when Ray Charles was struggling to get started in the early '50s, he imitated Cole. Fortunately for him and for pop, acceptance came when, as in Aretha Franklin's career, he tapped his gospel roots.

Young and black, Johnny Mathis had his first hit after the rise of rock 'n' roll. But he is a direct descendant of the big, white balladeers of pre-rock, intense but uninvolved, an adagio singer without a beat, and the master of a soaring lyrical style.

Mathis holds the record for an album that remained on *Billboard*'s best-seller charts for over 400 consecutive weeks. Sixteen weeks short of eight years, they lapped from the late '50s into the '60s. "When Columbia's research department," he told me, "tried to discover the reason for the longevity, they found that it was aiding lovers of all ages to find and relive their most tender and romantic moments." The album is *Johnny's Greatest Hits*.

In an analytical vein, Johnny added: "Since other media cannot be controlled to give a continuous flow of relaxing songs at the exact time that people choose to cuddle up on their sofas or bearskin rugs, phonograph records become a catalyst to generate sensuous vibrations that induce the closest form of love-making. Call it sex. But not if you mean that my records gyrate the listener into a frenzied aphrodisial state of mind. No, I select songs that are void of protest, hate, violence, grief, and all negative aspects—and choose arrangements that will make people love one another by portraying everything that is beautiful and optimistic."

And there you have the pre-rock '50s in a cassette. Singers strove to relax their listeners and create an atmosphere of warmth and affection. They tried to conjure up a dream world in which everybody lived happily after. No four-letter thoughts. No four-letter words. Don't sing out—croon, hum, reflect, daydream. Wish on a star, wink at the moon, laze in the sun. Don't make waves. As Johnny Mercer wrote, and Bing Crosby and the Andrews Sisters sang: "Ac-cent-tchu-ate the positive, ee-lim-i-nate the negative." But forget Mercer's further admonishment—DO stick with Mister In-Between. Pre-rock pop was a background hum of sound before the trade papers concocted the term *Easy Listening* and before Muzak speakers were pouring out a never-ending stream of lobby-to-elevator-to-bank-to-restaurant-to-airport-to-washroom swirl of music.

"The Eisenhower years? The clothes told much of the story," Stephanie Harrington wrote recently in *Cavalier*. "The men embalmed in their three-button gray flannels; the college boys in their tweed jackets, button-down shirts, crew neck sweaters and rep ties (and, of course, fraternity blazers); and the coeds in their cashmere sweaters, Bermuda shorts or kilt-style skirts, knee socks and camel's-hair coats. And the women. The poor trussed-up women! With their mid-calf-length skirts and pulled-in waistlines; their short, fitted peplum jackets; and their dumpy coats, with big clumsy dolman sleeves. . . . It was a tight little time and the very garments . . . seemed designed to shield them from hostile forces outside, from the Communists waiting to get them or the anti-Communists waiting to prove they were Communists."

4

THE BEARD

Snapping bullwhips . . . honking wild geese . . . barking dogs
. . . braying French horns . . . bearded Mitch Miller brought
sound gimmickry and excitement into the pop record scene of
the early '50s, then ruled by an all-powerful junto of the Six.

The Six were the A & R chieftains at the major record companies. Not a junta at all, they were so frequently overthrown
that the Six were seldom the same six. But at one moment in the
early '50s, there were balding, moon-faced, cigar-chomping Milt
Gabler at Decca (successor to tall, suave Dave Kapp to Morty
Palitz to Jimmy Hilliard), crew-cut Charlie Grean at RCA Victor,
hulking Joe Carlton at Mercury, dour-faced Harry Meyerson at
MGM, amiable Andy Wiswell at Capitol. This was the New
York Phalanx. There was another cabal in Hollywood. The Six
were not really the men so much as the nationwide record companies with distributors, sales managers, advertising budgets, PR
and promo staffs, regional offices, etc., and what they poured out
of their pressing plants combined to make up the mainstream
of pop.

From February 1950 when he took over the reins at Columbia
until the advent of rock 'n' roll, Mitchell Miller was the most consistent producer of hits, also the most colorful personality. His
beard and moustache were then a novelty. In a world where
executives were razor clean and their trousers bore knife-sharp
creases, they instantly established his unique identity. A graduate
of the Eastman School of Music, he was an oboist of distinction.
He was also a self-advertised supercocksman, which may explain
why his records were earthy but not sexy.

When well-loved Manie Sachs left Columbia for RCA Victor,

Goddard Lieberson, also an Eastman School alumnus and then executive head of Columbia, brought Mitch from Mercury Records where he had already made a name for himself. The Chicago-based company was just beginning to advertise Frankie Laine's disk of "Cry of the Wild Goose," produced by Miller. "Mule Train," on which Miller had snapped a mule-driver's bullwhip, had just slipped from the coveted No. 1 slot on *Billboard's* Honor Roll of Hits. Another Laine hit, "That Lucky Old Sun," was recognized as No. 2 of the Top Tunes of '49.

Despite Miller's move to Columbia, Mercury featured him in an ad for a new disk, "The Flying Dutchman" by young Richard Hayes. Dressed as the legendary sailor in a hurricane hat, Miller's face appeared along with Hayes's. Only it was four times larger than Hayes's. As Columbia was the most successful of the major diskeries in the early '50s, so Miller was the most publicized and self-advertised producer.

Columbia Records was then situated at 799 Seventh Avenue on the corner of Fifty-second Street, a long block west of its present location in the copper-toned skyscraper on Sixth Avenue. Miller arrived each morning with the elevator operator who opened the building. Publishers accustomed to reaching their own offices in the forenoon found that 8:00 A.M. was the best hour to audition songs for him. The Beard also seldom took lunch out, as most A & R men preferred to do—at Al & Dick's, defunct Toots Shor, Oak Room of the Plaza, defunct Dinty Moore's, or defunct Lindy's across from the defunct Capitol Theatre. Mitch kept a small refrigerator in his office and nibbled on cheese and health foods, smoking long, thick cigars through the day. He never wore a jacket. Collar open, tie loose, wrinkled shirt crawling out of creased trousers, he was energy in motion.

When he turned a song down, all you got was a negative swivel of the head. If you caught his eye, the lids fluttered sympathetically. When he liked a song, he became voluble on how it could be improved. His comments were generally sensitive. Since it spelled the difference between getting a record or not, his suggestions prevailed regardless.

Unlike most A & R men of the early '50s who dealt exclusively with publishers and their Gen. Prof. Mgrs., Mitch opened his door to songwriters. Terry Gilkyson, the folk buff who wrote "Cry of the Wild Goose," was a frequent visitor, as were Bill Engvick, who authored the lyrics to "Song from Moulin Rouge," Alec Wilder as arranger and songwriter, and Bob Merrill ("My Truly, Truly Fair").

Soon after Miller settled at Columbia, Frankie Laine followed him from Mercury. In the Miller group, one found Doris Day, organ-voiced Jo Stafford, colorless Mindy Carson, and belter Rosemary Clooney; among the men, Tony Bennett, Guy Mitchell, weeper Johnnie Ray, the Four Lads ("Moments to Remember"), silver-voiced Vic Damone, and later Johnny Mathis.

Working with his orchestra and chorus—really hand-picked studio musicians, Miller himself accounted for best sellers, like "Yellow Rose of Texas," one of the Most Played Records of 1955, and "The River Kwai March." As in his own recordings, he went for the happy, jouncy, vim-and-vigor sound, anticipating the virility and lustiness of the Kingston Trio. Toward the end of his tenure at Columbia when he became the Grandpa Moses of the Sing-A-Long syndrome, he racked up the largest volume of album sales aggregated (until then) by any record artist on any label.

As the tidal wave of R 'n' R began peaking around 1958, he became the only outspoken antagonist among major record-company execs. Yet in his work as a producer, he both foreshadowed and anticipated aspects of rock 'n' roll.

Threading through his choice of songs was a multicolored skein of folk-oriented material. "The Roving Kind," a hit for Guy Mitchell, was based on the English folk song "The Pirate Ship," a.k.a. "The Rakish Kind." From the South African repertoire of Josef Marais, Miller picked material for Jo Stafford, Doris Day, and Frankie Laine. An adaptation by Oscar Brand of an ancient bawdy song, known in World War II as "A Gob Is a Slob," became in '52 the best seller "A Guy Is a Guy" for Doris Day.

Miller prodded Bob Merrill into writing songs that sounded as if they had folk origins. Tailormade for Guy Mitchell, who flopped in several record debuts under other names (including his own), were such hits as "Belle, Belle," "Sparrow in the Tree Top," "Pittsburgh, Pennsylvania," and "Feet Up (Pat Him on the Po-Po)." It was on these disks that Miller made use of the French horn with the hollow, whooping sound that was so new in the world of pop.

All of these songs were published by Joy Music under whose managerial aegis Guy Mitchell and Mindy Carson, the wife of Eddie Joy, came to Columbia. Miller accorded the company—also lanky Howard Richmond's firms—the rare privilege of visiting its quarters to audition material instead of having Georgie Joy or son Eddie bring it to his office.

Despite his own sophisticated musical background—even in this period, Miller made appearances as solo oboist with symphony orchestras—he manifested a superb sensitivity to popular taste,

including hillbilly material. Nashville people sometimes refer
to songs originating in its environs as "white blues" while *Rolling
Stone* uses the underground epithet "shit-kickin'."

Be that as it may, as early as 1951, Miller took a Hank Williams
ballad, "Cold, Cold Heart," recorded by its writer on MGM,
covered it with Tony Bennett and produced a resounding hit for
the man with the chesty baritone. The following year, Miller did
the same for Rosemary Clooney with another Hank Williams
ballad, "Half As Much," and for Jo Stafford with the Williams
Cajun swinger "Jambalaya (On the Bayou)." The pour of
C & W material into the mainstream involved other major diskeries than Columbia. (More about this later.) It helped prepare
the market for rockabilly, the earliest form of R 'n' R.

In the summer of '51, Columbia's custom-pressing department
received a West Coast master for reproduction. The singer was
Kay Armen and the song was a novelty written by author William
Saroyan and his cousin Ross Bagdasarian, later famous as the
creator of the Chipmunks. The two Armenians—Kay was also
Armenian—had written the song during an auto trip ten years
earlier, and Saroyan had interpolated it in an off-Broadway play
Son, produced in 1950. No one went out of the theatre whistling
it, or recalling its comical lines.

How Mitch Miller learned of the tune is not known. Generally,
A & R and customs departments have no contact with each other.
But once he heard it, Miller wasted not a moment. He rushed a
new vocalist, just out of Tony Pastor's band, into a studio. By
the following day, New York City deejays had copies, and vinylites
were being rushed by airmail to key disk jockeys around the
country. In a matter of weeks, "Come On-A My House . . .
I'll geeve-a you candy . . ." was No. 1 on the Honor Roll of Hits,
and Rosemary Clooney was launched on a career as a star vocalist.
(Clooney was of a new breed of dynamic singers, and her vocal,
abetted by a jangling harpsichord, had tremendous drive.)

Kay Armen's original recording was left at the starting gate.
Her supporters claimed that Columbia delayed delivery on her
pressings to give the Clooney disk a head start. "Come On-A My
House" was published by a company that I was running at the
time, Duchess Music. Because it was felt that Kay was really
responsible for launching the song, Lou Levy, the owner of
Duchess, arranged for Armen to receive a share of the song's
earnings.

As far as I know, Mitch made only one foray into rock 'n' roll,
and that was through a songwriter-singer whom I published and
managed. Beverly Ross, daughter of a Jewish chicken farmer of

New Jersey, was cowriter of "Dim, Dim the Lights," recorded by Bill Haley and the Comets. She was also cowriter of "Lollipop," a rock ballad that I published, recorded with her, and that was a smash for the Chordettes.

When Beverly brought me two autobiographical songs, I approached Mitch about recording her. He bought the idea. "Stop Laughing at Me" and "Headlights" were cut with a typical rhythm-and-blues combo and a heavy afterbeat. Mitch was so excited that he brought Beverly (and me) before an enlarged meeting of the sales, promotion, advertising, and executive staffs when he unveiled the sides. I believe that the Columbia crowd was impressed by the sides and pleased that Mitch was tackling the teen-age market.

Beverly had a strident quality a' la Shirley Bassey and she sang with heart. "Headlights" described the longing of a lonely girl on a farm, watching the headlights of cars on the darkened walls of her room, and imagining the wonderful times that other girls were having with attentive boyfriends. "Stop Laughing at Me" was the poignant, angry outcry of an unattractive girl.

Despite the power of the sides, Beverly's appearance then worked against her. Built like Mama Cass, she had coarse features and dressed garishly, anticipating the hippies of the '60s. Columbia was enthusiastic enough to finance a disk-jockey promo trip. Inexperienced, Beverly was undoubtedly on the defensive and her tough manner irritated many of the platter spinners. Her disk impressed the producer of the "Ed Sullivan Show." But when Beverly showed in person, her appearance was canceled. *Life* magazine sent a camera crew to her father's chicken farm where they shot scores of pictures of her in the locale out of which the songs came.

After five exciting weeks, it all came to naught. The record did not "get off the ground," as they said in the business. I would hesitate to say that this experience soured Mitch completely on R 'n' R, though he was not a man to take even minor failures lightly. Yet it is a fact that he never again signed a rock singer and he did become the record Establishment's prime antirock spokesman.

Arguing that the deejays were mishandling their responsibilities by neglecting audiences that prized "variety, musicianship and a bit more sophistication in their music," he warned that the sale of single records would be downgraded by LP purchases "to satisfy a grown-up musical appetite." The Beard was prophetic, but in a way that he did not anticipate. Album sales did pyramid. But so did singles. And teen-agers bought albums in greater quantities, perhaps, than adults.

5

THE EXCITERS

After Bacharach and David became hot in pop, show composer Vernon Duke asked me to arrange a meeting with lyricist Hal David. The three of us spent part of an afternoon together, during which Duke, who was a fast, bright, nervous talker, regaled David with anecdotes, analyzed music trends, discussed different lyricists with whom he had worked (an impressive list), and pitched for their collaborating. It was quite a performance and Hal, who is not chit-chat verbal, was overwhelmed by Duke's display of enthusiasm.

Afterward, Duke exclaimed: "I had him mesmerized, didn't I?"

It was a concept one encountered constantly in music business. In a large sense, it ran the business during the Tin Pan Alley era. Songs and records, even songwriters and singers, were so ephemeral, how could you sell them except through a show of enthusiasm and excitement. Publishers used it to acquire songs for small advances. Gen. Prof. Mgrs. like myself employed it to persuade producers and artists to record a new song. A & R men used it to hype disk jockeys into programing their new releases. The game was to detect when it was manufactured rather than genuine.

As for the public, it was always eager for a new exciting singer or sound, though its loyalties seemed longer lived in pre-rock days. And so here are some of the *exciters* of the early '50s. There is no such word. But there were those artists who created excitement and aroused enthusiasm.

1950

"So Long, It's Been Good to Know You . . ." The voices were vigorous, across the plains, lusty. Three guys and a girl. They called themselves the Weavers. They sang Woody Guthrie's dust-bowl ballad with the barbaric yawp and vitality of latterday Walt Whitmans. "Tzena . . . tzena . . . tzena" had the robust rhythm and hand-clapping joy of an Israeli hora. They first made it in 1950 with Huddie Ledbetter's lumberjack balled, "I-i-rene, good-ni-i-ight, Irene good-night . . ." Leadbelly died the year before and now his ballad of heartbreak was the biggest song of the year.

The shimmery sound of the zither was new, heard as the ominous theme of a Carol Reed thriller, *The Third Man*. Played by Austrian composer Anton Karas, it was also known as the "Harry Lime Theme" after the key figure of the suspense film. Guy Lombardo, exponent extraordinaire of the "businessman's bounce," had the hit recording. Art Mooney tried to capitalize on the sound by recording (and publishing) a Tin Pan Alley–written "Zither Serenade." But the nabobs at Selznick Studios and Loew's got together—and MGM Records pulled back the Mooney recording.

From Hollywood also came "My Foolish Heart" with a schmaltzy Victor Young melody. Introduced in the film of the same name by that tear-swept, heartbreak gal Susan Hayward, it became a best seller on disks by Gordon Jenkins and His Orchestra and Billy Eckstine. In the Oscar race, "My Foolish Heart" lost out to "Mona Lisa," introduced in a so-so Alan Ladd film *Captain Carey, U.S.A.* but hyped by an imaginative lyric, Nat Cole's superlative rendition, and one of Nelson Riddle's earliest hit arrangements. Arrangers did not receive label credit in those days—only bandleader/conductors—and it was assumed that Les Baxter was responsible until Riddle committed the no-no of talking.

The year's most important importation was "La Vie En Rose," introduced here by Edith Piaf, who wrote the original French lyric. Known as Kid Sparrow in her native country and widely publicized as a former prostitute, Piaf scored a sensation at Manhattan's chi-chi club, the Versailles—but Tony Martin had the best-selling record.

The freak song of the year was a ten-year-old ballad by Rodgers and Hart. Introduced originally in *Pal Joey*, "Bewitched . . . bothered . . . and bewildered." made no impact, possibly because the show was then comparatively short lived (270 performances). In 1950, a piano version sans lyrics on an unknown label (Tower) by an unknown pianist (Bill Snyder) brought a revival that sent the torcher high on the charts and gave Doris Day a big platter.

And then there was "The Thing," a freak novelty by Charlie

Grean, RCA Victor's A & R chieftain. Phil Harris spoke the words in his gravelly, southern, chuckling baritone. There were two loud thumps at the critical moment when he looked in the mysterious box. Everybody wondered but nobody ever learned what "The Thing" was—just thump-thump.

Among newcomers, you could see her jouncing around and snapping her fingers just by listening to her up-tempo, ricky-tick recording of "Music, Music, Music . . . put another nickel in . . . in the nickelodeon . . ." Her voice was hard, young and shrill, and her name was Teresa Brewer, and she was at the beginning of a long-lived career.

Their voices were resonant and musical, but they were young and newcomers. The Amory Brothers of Boston, recording as the Ames Brothers, covered a song on an offbeat label (Bullet) and made a mainstream chart song of "Rag Mop," originally cut by one of its writers, westerner Johnny Lee Wills and his Boys. "R-a . . . R-a-g-g . . . M-o-p-p . . ." was good two-beat Dixieland. But its sock afterbeat carried a suggestion of rhythms that were soon to become the dance music of a new generation. For the time being, "Sentimental Me," the other side, received the main play.

There were other signs of possible impending change. A country song, "Chattanoogie Shoe Shine Boy," written by two Nashville radio men, went to No. 1 on the pop Honor Roll of Hits. Red Foley recorded it first but his Decca colleague, Bing Crosby, made the cloth-snapping version that moved it into the mainstream.

In the fall of '50, Crosby gave a hint of the passage of time by recording two songs with his oldest son. The record label credited "Play a Simple Melody" and "Sam's Song" to Gary Crosby and Friend. But everyone knew that the friend was papa.

"Sam's Song" was published by what was known in the business as a "one-lung" operation. The reference was to a firm functioning out of a bedroom and a briefcase. The personnel of Sam Weiss, Inc., was Sam Weiss, a contact man (song plugger) who had worked with major publishers for years. In the late '40s, dwindling sheet-music sales and an increasing concern with record spins rather than live performances, not to mention payola for small sustaining plugs, led to the paring of song-plugging staffs.

By 1950 quite a number of former contact men were trying to operate as independent publishers. Songs were not hard to come by. Printing a copy was inexpensive. The problem was to get a recording. Suddenly, in '50, A & R men at the major diskeries opened their doors to anybody with acceptable material. Weiss was able to sell the Crosbys and Decca on the soft-shoe-styled rhythm tune as well as Lou Busch at Capitol, who recorded "Sam's Song" under his piano-playing pseudonym, Joe "Fingers" Carr. The incipient open-door policy augured a loosening of the grip of major publishers on the business.

In '50, too, Birdland, a jazz cellar named after genius improviser, Charlie "Bird" Parker, opened on Broadway on the site of the defunct Clique Club. It signaled the end of Fifty-second Street, mecca of jazz fans the world over, as Swing Street. More important, it provided a major showcase for bop, the postwar jazz style that incubated in Harlem and came downtown via Swing Street. Birdland's success confirmed that jazz fans were ready for the complex harmonies and polyrhythms of bop. Everybody was a soloist, includings the drummer man who once was a metronome. Between beatless old-time ballads and the new concert jazz, the gap was opening for music to which an adolescent youngster could dance.

Where would it come from? In New Orleans a singer-pianist named Antoine "Fats" Domino was just getting started; in fact, had just cut his first disk for Imperial Records of Los Angeles. He called the "a" side "Fat Man" because that's what he was. It made the R & B charts. No one paid too much attention.

And in Akron, Ohio, a disk jockey named Alan Freed was enjoined by a local court from broadcasting for a year within a seventy-five-mile radius. Seems that Freed had walked out of Station WAKR to accept a position at WADC across the street. The management of WAKR was up in arms. Freed had been making $43.00 a week at Station WKST in New Castle, Pennsylvania, when he joined WAKR at $60.50 a week in 1945. In requesting an injunction, it noted that his earning in '49 had risen to $10,000.00.

Having reached a dead end in Akron, Freed headed for Cleveland where he began, as he had at New Castle, by spinning classical records. Within a year, he was in command of "The Moon Dog Show," sponsored on Station WJW by a Cleveland record shop with a growing business in R & B disks. One wonders what would have happened to R 'n' R had he been allowed to go on spinning records in Akron . . .

Meanwhile, Gene Autry started "Rudolph, the Red-Nosed Reindeer" on a sleigh ride that turned the Xmas ditty into the biggest money-making song of the past three decades and possibly of all time. For a while, "White Christmas" was the claimant to this mark. But in the past few years, partly because of black objections, "Rudolph" has surpassed the Berlin ballad in the number of different recordings, gross sales, and annual performances.

Since 1950 songwriter Johnny Marks has been able to live more than comfortably on the income of the one song.

1951

The airwaves were dancing the "Tennessee Waltz" as the year began. Clara Anne Fowler of Tulsa, Oklahoma, better known as Patti Page, had scored a number of hits before she did a duet with herself, a comparatively new gimmick on records, and made the waltz so popular that it later became the state song. Her saccharine, country-ballad style contrasted sharply with the growing trend toward tough singers like the perky blonde out of Maysville, Kentucky, Rosemary Clooney, who was offering to "geeve-a you figs and dates and ev-e-ry-ting if you 'Come On-A My House.' "

Out of Chester, Pennsylvania, came the Four Aces, a new male group that sounded as if they were harmonizing on motorcycles and wearing black denim trousers. ("It's No) Sin," their first disk was produced in Chester for Victoria Records, a local label. But it made so much noise that the master and the group were quickly snapped up by Decca. Before year-end, they were riding a new hit, "Tell Me Why," with lyrics by lead singer Al Alberts, in which they pleaded—no, asked—no, requested—no;—hell, they demanded to know why they kept falling in love. Soon they were so popular that Hollywood producers paid top coin to have them sing the title tune of *Three Coins in a Fountain*, Oscar song of '54, and "Love Is a Many-Splendored Thing," Oscar song of '55. When Al Alberts left the group, they folded and he failed to make it on his own. And then there were the Four Lads with a sound like theirs.

If "Tennessee Waltz" was not the biggest song of '51, then "Too Young" could claim the honor. It remained in the coveted No. 1 spot on the Saturday night "Hit Parade" for more weeks than any song in its entire history. Strange, indeed, when you consider that at least five years before the rash of teen-age ballads deploring the lack of parental understanding, it sounded a major theme of the generation gap—"They tried to tell us we're too young . . . too young to really fall in love . . ."

He sounded like Caruso come to life, with the throbbing, dramatic tenor, the rangy operatic thrust, and the long notes held until you lost your breath. A former piano mover, he took the screen name of Mario Lanza and generated such excitement that moviegoers viewing *The Toast of New Orleans* and *The Great Caruso* applauded wildly in movie houses—and some shouted "bravo" and "encore." "Be My Love," an Academy Award nominee from *Toast* and "The Loveliest Night of the Year" from *Caruso,* launched Alfred Arnold Cocozza on a roller-coaster regimen of overeating and dieting that brought him to a premature death.

"I tried everything from being a race singer to doing Mario Lanza," said Anthony Dominick Benedetto, better know as Tony Bennett. "Then we decided to get some strings and I would just sing sincerely and honestly." The ballad Tony sang at Percy Faith's suggestion was a ten-year-old music-hall melody by Arthur Hammerstein, brother of old-time impresario Oscar and aging uncle of Oscar II, librettist-lyricist of *South Pacific.* "Because of You," in a version that was an echo of Lanza, became a Gold Record. It was not long before Bennett and his appealing lisp had literally gone from "Rags to Riches," a hit in '53.

Nineteen fifty-one brought a fresh, new sound into the record field. There seemed to be gobs of guitars and many voices. But there was really only one guitar played by Lester Polfus of Waukesha, Wisconsin, and there was just one voice emanating from the throat of Colleen Summers, a former member of Gene Autry's hillbilly troupe. A synthetic process known as "overdubbing" was the secret.

Neither Lester nor Colleen could read music. Polfus learned songs as a youngster by watching and numbering the keys on a pianola. Nor did he have any schooling in electronics or engineering. Somehow he mastered the trick of delaying sound one-tenth of a second (to produce an echo), delaying it by half (to stop reverberation) and, most important, eliminating the surface scratch in multiple overdubbing. He always worked at home, an apartment over a butcher shop in Jackson Heights, Long Island, an abandoned inn in New Jersey, an isolated country house in Stroudsburg, Pennsylvania—places where no neighbors were around at 4 A.M.

It was an ear-arresting recording of an old show tune with involved chord changes that brought him recognition. "How High the Moon" sold over a million copies in a matter of weeks, sounding as if it was played by a guitar orchestra and sung by a large vocal group. But it was just Les Paul and Mary Ford, as they called themselves. In '51, too, they had "Mockin' Bird Hill . . . Tra-la la twittle dee dee dee . . ." And the following year, "Meet Mr. Callaghan," an instrumental I found in London— it was played as an "overture" for a suspense play—and airmailed to Les in Oakland, New Jersey.

1952

The surprise song of the year was "High Noon," theme of a great Hollywood western starring Gary Cooper and Grace Kelly. Frankie Laine had the hit record. On the screen, it was sung by western star Tex Ritter. And it sounded like an authentic American folk tune, even unto the lyric, "Do not forsake me, oh, my darlin'." But the memorable melody was composed by Dimitri Tiomkin, one of the gifted Europeans (Bakaleinikoff, Amfitheatrof, Rosza, Steiner, etc.) who had been composing and conducting background film scores for years. When he made his acceptance speech at the Academy Awards, Tiomkin followed tradition in thanking those who made his Oscar possible, except that he proceeded to reel off the names of a long list of European composers of the past.

A surprise of a different order—freak would be more accurate—was the song "Oh, Happy Day." It was the work of an eighteen-year-old Cleveland lad, Don Howard, who recorded it in his own garage and managed to have it released by a small, local label, Triple A. Rumor had it that Cleveland disk jockeys programed the record because it was so bad as to be ludicrously entertaining. Some thought it was a put-on—it had a melancholy melody despite its title. Apparently it made enough noise so that enterprising Dave Miller of Essex Records in Philadelphia bought and released it. Then, despite music pros, to whom the record was a laugh, the unexpected happened. "Oh, Happy Day" became a runaway hit. No one realized it then, but the day of the indie (independent) record companies was at hand. Also, this was an early instance of the lucky amateur. And like most amateurs of the rock 'n' roll era, Don Howard never had another song that mattered, even though he was signed as a recording artist by Coral Records.

Two new thrushes saw songs they launched become hits for other singers, Joni James with "You Belong to Me" and Sunny Gale with "Wheel of Fortune." "You Belong to Me" was the work of a southern housewife, Chilton Price, and two Nashville performers, Pee Wee King and Redd Stewart, a trio also responsible for another hit of '52, "Slow Poke." For Joni James, the declarative ballad marked her record debut. Quick covers by Jo Stafford on Columbia and Patti Page on Mercury took the play away from her. But before year-end, Joni had a hit for herself in the cry and plea of "Why Don't You Believe Me?"

Sunny Gale, who somehow never attained her majority as a record artist, made her debut on Derby Records, a small, New

York City indie, with "Wheel of Fortune." Again the majors
rushed in with quick covers, Capitol with brassy Kay Starr and
Mercury with belting Georgia Gibbs. At her record session,
Georgia spent almost three hours cutting the "Wheel" ballad,
and in the waning moments, did a spirited song I had brought
her, in two quick takes, an American adaptation of the Argentine
tango "El Choclo," titled "Kiss of Fire."

Of course, the wheel of record fortunes spun to a stop on the
"wrong" number. "Kiss of Fire," slated for the "b" side, swept
through the disk scene like a blaze out of control and shot up to
No. 1 on the Honor Roll of Hits. "Wheel of Fortune" did nothing
for Georgia. But it launched country-shouter Kay Starr, who
stole most of the sales away from Sunny Gale. Kay's vocal
benefitted from a touch of realism—the whirring of a roulette
wheel in the background.

Another disk to which sound gimmickry made a contribution
was Ella Mae Morse's "Blacksmith Blues." The effect of a
blacksmith's hammer clinking on an anvil was used to enhance
the rhythm.

The sensational figure of the year was the newcomer who became known as Mr. Emotion or the Sobber Baron. Johnnie Ray
literally wept his way to the top of the year's best-selling records
with two *cry* songs, back to back.

Three other important newcomers were not nearly as emotional or exhibitionistic but all delivered with a wallop: Don
Cornel on "I'm Yours," Al Martino, another *paisano*, on "Here in
My Heart," and young Eddie Fisher, who had been a synagogue
singer and a fruit vendor, on "Anytime," "Lady of Spain," and
three or four other fast sellers.

The increasing toughness of the music scene was evident even
in some of the big song titles of the year: "Be Anything But Be
Mine)," a hit for Eddy Howard; "Be My Life's Companion," a
Mills Brothers best seller; "Botch-A-Me" by Rosemary Clooney.
Lovers were not asking for love; they were demanding it.

And yet the airwaves were not devoid of sentiment and cutie
pies. "The Glow Worm," dating back to the first decade of the
century, became a million seller for the Mills Brothers as Johnny
Mercer electrified the critter and employed clever volts-and-watts
metaphors in a new lyric. Of German origin, too, was Vera Lynn's
nostalgic ballad "Auf Wiederseh'n, Sweetheart."

For those who had an ear for lilting instrumental music, there
was "Blue Tango" by Leroy Anderson, an arranger for the
Boston Symphony's Pop Concerts, whose succeeding orchestral
novelties included "The Typewriter" and "The Syncopated

Clock." (Is there a New Yorker who does not recall the metro-nomelike melody, sounded on xylophone, that heralded CBS's "Late, Late Show"?)

Percy Faith, whose magic with strings magnetized England's Mantovani, made the Top Ten with "Delicado," a Latin-inflected instrumental that featured the harpsichord. (It was a spur-of-the-moment decision when he found the instrument in the recording studio—and Mitch Miller and he had to pick a lock to open it.)

A dance called the "bunny hop" got its start in '52 with a Ray Anthony record. You formed a line, boys alternating with girls, both hands on shoulders, waist or hips of the girl or boy in front. You kicked twice to the left, twice to the right, hopped forward on both feet, hopped back, then forward, hop, hop, hop—and started all over with the kicks. The band speeded up the tempo as the dance progressed so that after a while, the line went to pieces.

1953

"Why Don't You Believe Me?" by Joni James was the No. 1 song, and moppet Jimmy Boyd's "I Saw Mommy Kissing Santa Claus" was just behind it when the country awoke on New Year's day, 1953. But Hank Williams, known as Luke the Drifter and the Hillbilly Shakespeare, was dead. A heart attack, apparently brought on by a combination of drugs and alcohol, killed him as he was traveling in a car to Canton, Ohio, for a New Year's eve engagement. He was just twenty-nine.

"I could draw more people in Montgomery, Alabama, dead," he once told a fellow artist, who was griping about Hank's hometown audiences, "than you can alive." And he did at his funeral. Twenty-five thousand tried to attend rites in the Municipal Auditorium—only three thousand could—in what was described as "the greatest emotional orgy in the city's history since the inauguration of Jefferson Davis."

MGM Records was just about to release a new disk of his. "Kaw-Liga," the tale of a wooden Indian with an "Ode on a Grecian Urn" theme, became the No. 1 best seller on C & W charts and "Your Cheatin'" Heart" No. 2 Three other songs written and recorded by Williams finished posthumously among the Top Twenty: "Jambalaya," "Take These Chains from My Heart," and the ironic "I'll Never Get Out of This World Alive." In pop Joni James had a chart song with "Your Cheatin' Heart," later the title of a Hank Williams biopic.

"Sincerity," Williams once said, "makes our kind of music successful. A hillbilly sings more sincere than most entertainers because he was raised rougher. You got to have smelt a lot of mule manure before you can sing like a hillbilly."

The repressive atmosphere in the country found expression in show biz in two January events. Playwright-wit George S. Kaufman was summarily dismissed as emcee of the CBS program "This Is Show Business." "Let's make this one program," he had said, "on which no one sings 'Silent Night.' " He was objecting, he later explained, to the overcommercialization of Christmas carols. But listeners flooded CBS with cries of "antireligious!"

In Boston Station WHDH banned a disk of "I Went to Your Wedding" by Spike Jones and his famous Musical Depreciation combo. Station management claimed that the record was risqué and cited the line: "You walked down the aisle and fell on your smile."

The big story in record business was the launching of a new label (Cadence) and a new singer (Julius La Rosa). More excitement, one recalls, than when Al Martino hit with "Here is My Heart" on BBS, a small, indie label, and Capitol signed him. The record was plugged on the Arthur Godfrey morning show where La Rosa was a featured singer and Cadence founder Archie Bleyer was the bandleader-arranger. The takeoff of "Anywhere I Wander," from the film *Hans Christian Anderson* was taken as a token of Godfrey's amazing power of a supersalesman.

The excitement created a public for La Rosa without giving him a hit. His big seller was a later release, *"Eh Cumpari."* And in '53 Dean Martin, trying to make it on his own as a crooner-comic, had his first disk click in "That's Amore," another Italian-spiced ballad.

But before the year was over, Godfrey and La Rosa split in a sensational parting witnessed by the country's TV viewers. Godfrey brusquely fired the young singer while they were on the air on an October Tuesday, accusing La Rosa of lacking humility. Comics and a rash of satiric songs helped establish '53 as the "humility year." Eddy Arnold and Colonel Parker also split up after an eight-year association, opening the door to the good Colonel's pursuit of a then-unknown rockabilly singer. Al Alberts, lead voice of the best-selling Four Aces, initiated a breakaway from the quartet. Recording his first solo single, Alberts started himself and the group on the road to oblivion.

The year included a number of curiosities, among them Patti Page's "Doggie in the Window." That it could have become the No. 3 best seller of '53 is a testimonial to Patti's hold on the public—and to dogs. The barking for the song was done by the contractor and arranger on the date. Homer and Jethro had their own fun with a humorous parody, in "That Hound Dog in the Window." Patti demonstrated her power also on a different type of song, "Changing Partners," when she outsold competitors like Bing Crosby, Helen Forrest, Pee Wee King, Dinah Shore, and Kay Starr.

Sound gimmicks were still noisemakers—the roar of the sea and the squeaking of sea gulls on "Ebb Tide" by Frank Chacksfield, who scored a best seller also with Charlie Chaplin's theme for *Limelight* a.k.a. "Terry's Theme." The harmonica, rarely heard on pop records, seemed to have just the right, romantic sound for Richard Hayman on a lovely ballad, "Ruby."

The theme of Jack Webb's "Dragnet" series—Boom! de-da Boom!—was recorded in a marathon Capitol session that ran close to five hours—after four tunes in three hours, musician rates rose to time and a half and double time. Ray Anthony's record aroused so much comment that Stan Freberg rushed to record a parody, "St. George and the Dragonet."

Jack Webb's ex-wife surprised everybody by delivering a hit on her first vocal outing. Julie London's deadpan style was just right for the imaginative torch ballad "Cry Me a River," written by Arthur Hamilton, cowriter of "How High the Moon." The broken marriage, contrasting with her own visual appeal, contributed overtones that enhanced the disk's impact.

Ballads, some of them quite corny, seemed to be "in." "You . . . you . . . you" they harmonized in simplistic monosyllables to a German beer-stein melody—and the Ames Brothers barreled with their rich, baritone-bass voices into the Top Ten. Eddie Fisher outsold Sinatra on the English torcher, "I'm Walking Behind You," despite an imaginative touch on the Voice's platter—a high soprano in the background to suggest the title concept—"walking behind . . ."

The most intriguing vocal sounds of the year emanated from the throat of a new RCA Victor artist, who prospered with "Santa Baby" and *"C'est Si Bon,"* previously a hit for Johnny Desmond. Eartha Kitt, guided by Henri René, had an erotic, catlike quality vocally as well as visually, also an attractive, exotic accent. The appeal to "Santa Baby" for Cadillacs and furs had an irreligious suggestiveness that offended some parents. Eartha was really more an in-person cat's meow than a record seller.

Sex reared its attractive head on several sides by Jo Stafford. Her sustained nasalism had an astringent coolness that took the edge off patently suggestive songs like "Make Love to Me" and "Teach Me Tonight."

Walking through the headquarters of RCA Victor on East Twenty-fourth Street in Manhattan. I heard a strange voice and rhythms that drew me into a studio. A handsome, light-skinned Negro was singing a calypso tune in pidgin English. I purchased the publishing rights to "Matilda, Matilda"—"she took me money and go Ven-e-zue-la . . ." It anticipated the calypso trend and Harry Belafonte's emergence as a major record artist by three years.

The two biggest songs of the year tapped two contradictory veins of music. The score for the film *Moulin Rouge* came from the pen of one of France's longhairs, Georges Auric. From it, Percy Faith extracted and constituted the melody that became known as "Song from Moulin Rouge"—in its lyric version, "Where Is Your Heart?" it vied for '53's top honors with a sentimental, Tex-Mex type of waltz, "Vaya Con Dios," recorded with multiple, overdubbed voices and guitars by Les Paul and Mary Ford.

But on the basis of performance, as logged by the Peatman sheet, "I Believe" came first. Wailing Frankie Laine, wallowing in tears, had the biggest disk of many versions. The *religioso* asserted that even the smallest prayer was heard "by someone in the great somewhere." *I believe, the lyric read, when I hear a new-born baby cry*—but in what? The vagueness was characteristic of the times.

Despite the seemingly traditional character of the record scene— Perry Como had a giant disk on Rodgers and Hammerstein's ballad "No Other Love" from *Me and Juliet*—there were growing signs of impending change.

Out of Texas came a seventeen-year-old songwriter-performer who created tremendous excitement among teen-agers on a tour with Bob Hope. Darrell Glenn's record of a country weeper, "Crying in the Chapel," meant little, except that it led to a Rex Allen cover on Decca, a disk by the Orioles, a hot R & B group, on Jubilee, and a June Valli platter on RCA Victor. Allen made Top Twenty on C & W charts. The Orioles hit Top Five on R & B charts. And June Valli carried the song into the pop Top Thirty. It was an early instance of the influence of regional and mainstream currents.

"The King of Tin Pan Alley," *Variety*'s Abel Green wrote in a year-end wrap-up, "is the deejay and the record is the sceptre with which he can knight any artist, song or publisher. Of course, what's 'in the groove' is what counts."

Perhaps even more indicative was a second Perry Como record that made the Top Ten. "Don't Let the Stars Get in Your Eyes" was an offbeat country song, odd structured and odd metered. Co-writer Slim Willet launched it on Four Star, a West Coast label.

Skeets McDonald on Capitol outdistanced Willet on C & W charts and Como had a surprise smash in pop.

Nineteen fifty-three saw the rise of two new indie publishers. Out of Chicago, Brandom Music was able to put three songs on the Honor Roll of Hits: "Why Don't You Believe Me?" with Joni James, "Have You Heard?" also with Joni, and "Pretend," a hit for Nat Cole and, instrumentally, for Ralph Marterie.

It was somewhat longer lived than Village Music Company, a Brill Building firm launched by Sidney Prosen. Writer of one of the year's big ballads, "Till I Waltz Again with You," Prosen opened house in a big way, with contact men in Chicago, the South, and Hollywood. Despite the earnings of the Teresa Brewer disk, Prosen could not follow up, and the firm went bankrupt.

Significant as these developments were, they reflected rather than affected the future. It was what has happening outside of pop and the major diskeries and publishers—in the R & B field— that was of the greatest consequence. To the youngsters then growing up and slated to emerge as future stars, the sounds of Tin Pan Alley and Tin Pan Valley were dull, lifeless, uninteresting. These young people were turning their radio dials and searching for fresh sounds on offbeat black stations.

One of them, who lived in a Memphis public housing development, heard "That's All Right, Mama," a rhythm-and-blues ballad by Arthur "Big Boy" Crudup. And he was excited by Big Mama Thornton's disk of "Hound Dog," the No. 1 best seller in black ghettos across the country. Perhaps he heard "Crazy Man Crazy" by an unknown country singer named Bill Haley on Essex. It was two years before the latter's "Rock Around the Clock" girdled the globe and three years before the youngster himself shook up the national record scene.

6

THE BEATS
AND THE BELTERS

In 1952 Frank Sinatra played the New York Paramount where he had created panics in the mid-'40s and where the swooning hysteria started, genuine or provoked by publicist George Evans. The *New York World-Telegram* greeted Sinatra's return in a compact and cruel headline: *"Gone on Frankie in '42: Gone in '52."* The article was in the form of an open letter: "I saw you last night," wrote a femme feature writer, "but I didn't get 'that old feeling' . . . I sat in the balcony. And I felt kind of lonely. . . . The usher said there were 750 seats—and 749 were unfilled. . . . Later I stood outside the stage entrance. Three girls were saying 'Frankie' soft and swoonlight. I said, 'How do you like Frankie?' They said, 'Frankie Laine, he's wonderful' . . . I heard a girl sighing, 'I'm mad about him' so I asked her who. 'Johnnie Ray!' she cried. All of sudden, Mr. Sinatra, I felt sort of old . . ."

Some attributed Sinatra's fall from stardom to bad publicity and public disapproval of his love life. Others claimed a deterioration of vocal quality. Sinatra blamed Mitch Miller, especially since the Beard was producing hits with another Frankie. Playing the Copa in New York City, Sinatra donned a coonskin cap, snapped a bullwhip, and honked derisively like a wild goose.

Truth is that, regardless of the Swooner's personal problems and their impact on his career, a new, postwar generation of youngsters did not react to soft, tender, reflective, moolike singing. Bedroom idol during the war to girls without men, he was no longer communicating to the former bobbysoxers, now young marrieds and bedeviled by the tensions of a postwar economy.

45

And he certainly was not talking to their kids who were seeking excitement and a viable dance beat.

The stage was set for the emergence of a style whose dynamics, metrics, and physical expressiveness had been suggested by Frankie Laine in the late '40s on his recording of "That's My Desire." His treatment was demonstrative, dynamic, demanding. He did not sigh. He shouted. He did not crawl. He stamped his feet. Originally, "Desire" was a wistful Tin Pan Alley ballad introduced in '31 by crooner Lanny Ross. Laine's "Desire" had flesh and passion in it. As I wrote in a 1953 *Variety* article, "Sex-Vex-Wrecks Supersedes June-Spoon-Moon."

"Belting," as the style came to be known, was in drive, tension, and decibels at the other end of the sound spectrum from crooning. It almost seemed that, as the McCarthy witch-hunts of 1950–54 created a Silent Generation, young artists raised their voices in psychological inversion—and young listeners welcomed the loud, declamatory outcries as a vent for their frustrations.

FRANKIE LAINE INTERVIEW

"I'm not a crooner. I'm a singer who shouts," said Frankie Laine, back in the days when he had "That's My Desire" (1947), "Mule Train" (1949), "Cry of the Wild Goose" (1949), "Swamp Girl (1949), "Jezebel" (1951), "High Noon" (1952), and "I Believe" (1953).

"My first consciousness of blues and jazz," he told me recently, as we sat on the lush, green lawn of his Shelter Island waterfront apartment in San Diego, "was accidental." His speaking voice is much like his singing voice, vigorous, well phrased, and emotive. "When we moved to 351 Schiller Street in Chicago . . . it was to a house that Mom and Dad bought. They kept some of the furniture, including an old wind-up phonograph. Most of the records were classical—Caruso, Gigli, Galli-Curci—along with some pop Italian records like Carlo Bucci, who was a favorite of mom's. Among these I found a strange record. I often wonder how it got there. It was a Bessie Smith recording of a song called 'Bleeding Heart Blues.' This was the record that grabbed me. I was then ten to twelve years old. The only music I knew at the time was church music that I sang in the altar-boy choir and whatever stuff we heard in the movies.

"One day I skipped school to see a movie. It was *The Singing Fool* with Al Jolson. He absolutely laid me out. And we stayed for two performances. I was so impressed, without knowing what was happening to me, that when I got home, I told my younger brothers that I had learned a new song. As I was doing it down on one knee the way Jolson did it, mom appeared. She quickly surmised that I had skipped school and I was in Dutch.

"After Jolson, the artist who worked her magic on me was Mildred Bailey—the Rockin' Chair Lady, as she was known, after the Hoagy Carmichael song that became her theme. The Bailey impact came via the Merry Garden Ballroom at Belmont & Sheffield on Chicago's north side. . . .

"One night, when I was about fifteen, I attended a party for the sister of my closest friend. She was older and so were most of the kids at the shindig. . . . After some guy named Tony Benson played the tipple—a bastard instrument somewhere between a guitar and a ukulele—I did an Italian pop song called 'Mia Bella Rosa.' When I finished, there was a deathly silence, probably because they were so surprised. But in that silence, you could hear some of the girls crying. I had to repeat the song. And with that, I became part of the crowd—I was in. They wanted me for parties. But they also got me into a dance instruction class at the Merry Garden Ballroom, where I not only learned to dance but became a half-assed teacher. This meant that I got a pass to Ballroom events. It was important because even though I was working as an office boy at International Harvester—going to high school in the daytime—I had an allowance of only a dollar a week. This was for lunches and carfare. Once in a while I'd sneak a free ride on the El. With a Ballroom pass, all I needed was carfare.

"The regular orchestra at the Merry Garden was Joe Kayser's It had Dave Rose on piano, Gene Krupa on drums, Muggsy Spanier on trumpet, Frankie Trumbauer on C-melody sax, and Frank Silvano handling the vocals. Occasionally the crowd would get me up to sing a number. Charley Agnew's Orchestra succeeded Kayser's. During his sojourn, the Ballroom began bringing in featured bands on big holidays. It was on one of these occasions that Paul Whiteman came in and I heard Mildred Bailey sing 'Rockin' Chair.' Her record of it had knocked me on my ass. But once I heard her in person, it became *my song* and she became *my* singer.

"During much of this time, Louis Armstrong was playing at the Sunset Cabaret. I never went there and never heard him in person. But I heard his recordings and every once in a while I caught him on the radio.

"My fifth influence was like an explosion of dynamite. It happened on Lincoln's birthday in twenty-eight or nine. The Ballroom brought in a guy named Cab Calloway to front what I now know as a pick-up band. We didn't know about such things in

those days. We thought it was his band. He absolutely gassed me—
the way he *moved* as well as the way he sang. His style is an in-
credible thing even today. It shook me up and propelled me in
the direction I was going without my knowing where I was going.
I'll never forget the way he sang 'Ploddin' Along.' This was long
before he had 'Minnie the Moocher.'

"After I started traveling, I began listening to jazz. In New
York I heard Billie Holiday and she really got to me. After Billie,
it was Nat Cole. In Cleveland I worked with a white pianist who
played two-beat Dixie. Now, I never cared for Dixieland style. But
on quiet nights, we used to try to stump each other with songs.
When I didn't know one, he'd tell me my key and we'd make up
a copy. That's how I learned 'West End Blues.' 'River St. Marie,'
'Blue Turning Gray,' 'Black and Blue,' and 'Shine,' which I later
recorded.

"By 1943 I was in Hollywood. I had come in from a warplant
in Cleveland and was working in Southgate. I worked the five
P.M. to five A.M. shift. Then I'd grab a few hours of sleep and by
noon, I'd hit the street, Vine Street, that is. That's how I met
Carl Fischer and we began writing together. He already had
'Who Wouldn't Love You?' to his credit. It took us six months
before we wrote 'We'll Be Together Again,' and another two years
before it was on wax. Carl later became my accompanist. . . .

"The story reached its climax at Billy Berg's club in Hollywood
where at about the same time the first bop quintet met such
hostility that Charlie "Bird" Parker suffered a mental breakdown.
Slim Gaillard of Slim and Slam, and author of the famous "Flat
Foot Floogie (With the Floy-floy)," was then a big drawing card
at the club. On occasion he would call on Frankie to sing.

"One evening when I sang 'Rockin' Chair,' Hoagy Carmichael
happened to be in the club. The next I knew I was booked at
Billy Berg's. I worked there for about sixteen weeks with a group
called Milton de Lugg and the Swing Wing. . . . After he left,
I sang with Edgar Hayes. And now a strange web of coincidences
enmeshed me.

"Hayes was the black pianist whose band recording had made
a hit of 'Star Dust,' Hoagy's imperishable standard. You listen to
the second chorus on the record, and it's pure rock 'n' roll, including the triplets. One night I arrived early. Hayes was at the
clubs and we sat down to dinner together. While we were
feasting on some spaghetti, I asked Edgar if he knew a song called
'That's My Desire.' Now, if he had been a young man, he would
not have known that ballad, first introduced in 1931. . . .

"We were the intermission act and nobody paid any attention

to us. Edgar played three, I sang three, and he played three. The audience waited for Slim, who was the star. But this particular night, I did what I had never done before: I spoke about the song before I did it, and I presented it as a *brand new song that we wanted to try out.* After I sang it, Mrs. Billy Berg came rushing up to the bandstand and asked me to encore it. Soon I was doing the tune six or seven times a night.

"I started singing it sometime in May, 1946. I never told anybody that I had originally heard a singer named June Hart do it in Cleveland. She could have been another Mildred Bailey had she been able to straighten herself out. I kept singing it as if it were a new song. . . . Finally, in September, 1946, I cut 'That's My Desire' for Mercury Records. Disc jockey Al Jarvis, who originated the 'Make Believe Ballroom,' jumped on the record. Ed Hurst of WPEN in Philadelphia picked up on it. And by February, 1947, we were off to the races.

"But it happened in a very strange way. In those days, *Billboard* carried Harlem charts as well as pop. The Harlem charts—Harlem Detroit, Harlem Chicago, Harlem Los Angeles—reflected the taste of black buyers. Well, 'Desire' was number one on all these charts before it ever appeared on a pop chart.

"Everybody thought I was colored. They didn't use the word 'black' in those days. My manager, Sam Lutz, kept getting into arguments with disc jockeys who argued that 'no white man sang like that. . . .' "

"From Billy Berg's, I went to the Morocco on Vine Street, where I worked with Red Nichols. In fact, it was Red who gave me my first four band-arranged songs: 'Georgia on My Mind,' 'Black and Blue,' 'Sunny Side of the Street,' and 'I'm in the Mood for Love.' ('Georgia' became one of my first big records after 'Desire.') Now things began to go haywire. Carl Fischer, with whom I had written some songs, was then playing with Pee Wee Hunt. In fact, he was responsible for Pee Wee's hit record 'Twelfth Street Rag' on Capitol—he played the piano part. On my urging, Fischer left Pee Wee and joined me at the Morocco in June, 1947. . . .

"In September, 1947, I went into the Million Dollar Theatre in downtown Los Angeles. The week before that at the Morocco I was getting $750. At the end of the first week at the theatre, my percentage of the box office brought $11,700. When Carl and I saw the check, we were so overwhelmed we both started to cry."

In the summer of 1950 Frankie (Sinatra, not Laine) returned from abroad—buffeted by the winds of Hurricane Ava—to find record buyers avidly reading about "That Lucky Old Laine," a new singing star who had sold more than eight million discs in three years. In the widely read article, the writer noted that Frankie (Laine, not Sinatra) "had none of the fragile, wistful qualities of Sinatra, Damone, or Mel Torme." Laine was described as the crooner "with steel tonsils," who flailed the air with his arms, stamped out the beat with his feet, and who did not bend notes but crippled them.

The Wild Goose was flying long before the pelvic god of rock donned Blue Suede Shoes and came hip-swiveling into Heartbreak Hotel, there to offer his white, Memphis, country-styled version of black R & B.

The Philip Roth of Pop

When he broke into the big time, Laine was a man in his mid-thirties with thinning hair. Edwin Jack Fisher, son of a Philadelphia produce vendor, was just twenty-two when the record market broke open for him with "Bring Back the Thrill" and "Thinking of You," revival of a '27 ballad. Fisher's disk of "Thinking" opened cold with a long, sustained monosyllable "Why-y-y-y-y-y is it I spend the day?" Blues singers call the device "worryin'" while longhairs refer to the stretching of a syllable over several notes as *melisma*. Fisher was not worryin' a syllable but simply *extending* its duration suspensefully over one long note. It became an earmark of his style. "An-ny-ti-i-i-i-i-ime . . ." Also, "You've got to have hear-ar-ar-ar-ar-art . . ." And "I'm walking be-hi-i-i-i-ind you . . ."

"He's strong as a bulldog," said Joe Carlton, who produced his records at RCA Victor. "He can do seventeen or eighteen takes when other singers begin to tire after four or five."

Hugo Winterhalter, who arranged and conducted all of his early dates, said: "Eddie doesn't have to depend on tricks or fancy phrasing. His success comes from the basic sound of his voice. It's a voice that can stand much more background than most voices. He never seems to be overcrowded on a recording." Recall "Lady of Spain" and the way he soared over a huge complement of howling brass and a mass of racing fiddles.

Like many of the belters, Eddie bit and spat out his words. Not surprisingly, he favored dental sounds—titles like "Trust in Me," "Tell Me Why," "Downhearted," and "Dungaree Doll," the last song written by Ben Raleigh and Sherman Edwards, lyricist-composer of *1776*, to a title and ideas that I developed.

There he was at the opening of the decade with his boyish good looks, the thick thatch of unruly black hair, the high forehead symmetrically framed by curving insets and the ingratiating, little-boy smile with the squinty eyes, and deep, long dimples along the jawline. Most of all, it was the young, vigorous, full-throated baritone that caught the ears of the younger generation.

Fisher began singing professionally when he was just twelve over Station WFIL in Philadelphia. Not a good student, he dropped out of school in the eleventh grade. Later, he had diffi-culty remembering lines, despite extended rehearsals, and Charlie Ventura, with whose band he sang, complained that he had "trouble with time and meter."

The big break in Fisher's career came at a borscht-circuit hotel in the New York Catskills, later the scene of his scandalous wooing of Elizabeth Taylor when he was still married to Debbie Reynolds. When comic Eddie Cantor heard him sing at Gross-inger's, he took him on a cross-country tour that netted him an RCA Victor record contract.

While Grossinger's and Cantor were accidents, the setting and auspices were right. Eddie Fisher was to pop music what Philip Roth and Bernard Malamud were to the American novel. He was the Jewish boy who made good in a field dominated by *goyim*. "He appeals to women," a music publisher suggested, "as though he were there own son," an appeal confirmed by the smashing success in '53 of "Oh, My Pa-Pa," with its sentimental, Yiddish melody.

Fisher was attractive also to the youngsters of the day. Two years he spent in the Army after attracting attention helped rather than hurt him. As soloist with the U.S. Army Band, he made hundreds of personal appearances throughout Korea, Japan, Europe, and the U.S.A. He was also able to make records that became his first giant sellers: "Anytime" (over a million), "Turn Back the Hands of Time," "I'm Yours," and "Wish You Were Here," the last credited with saving the Broadway show of the same name.

When he came out of the Army in April 1953, he went into the New York Paramount, along with the first 3-D film (remember *House of Wax* that had to be viewed through colored, plastic spectacles?). The kids were waiting for him, as they had once waited for Frankie Boy. Bringing their lunch boxes, they squealed hysterically so that he could not hear himself sing. By the follow-ing year, he had "Coke Time," a twice-a-week NBC-TV show aimed at the high school crowd. It went out over seven hundred television stations in the biggest, nationwide hookup of the day.

Asked to explain his appeal, veteran songsmith Irving Berlin said: "Something in his voice is the closest thing I have heard to

what Al Jolson had in his." The dynamic emoter who sang originally in blackface and received his training in minstrel shows, was,
in fact, Eddie's favorite singer. After he got out of the Army,
Fisher's accompanist was Harry Akst, who had worked with Jolson.

Eddie Fisher was a bridge from the era of the intimate crooners
into rock 'n' roll. While his belting style helped prepare the way
for the turnaround of 1956, his own record star sank below the
horizon just about that time. "Cindy, Oh, Cindy," a song I promoted that year, was his last big record.

The Anatomy of Self-Pity

Johnnie Ray, out of Oregon, had been singing professionally,
if unprofitably, for half a dozen years and had made several blues
records for Okeh before he burst as an original on a startled
world. No one seemed prepared for the extreme kind of emotive
singing Ray represented even though black gospel singers had
pursued the style for decades.

So violent was his impact that *The New York Times'* classical-
music critic felt impelled to investigate and paid a visit to Manhattan's Copa. "Ray sings like a man in an agony of suffering," he
wrote. "Drenched in tears . . . he tears a passion to tatters and
then stamps on the shreds. . . . His hair falls over his face. He
clutches at the microphone and behaves as if he were about to
tear it apart. His arms shoot out in wild gesticulations and his
outstretched fingers are clenched and unclenched . . ."

Critic Howard Taubman had some fleeting doubts about the
authenticity of Ray's "unassuageable grief": "It is to be noted,"
he wrote, "that, possessed or not possessed, tortured or not tortured by spasms of movement, he never forgets to bring his lips
to the microphone when the time comes to sing a phrase. The
most convulsive writhings occur in the pauses between notes."

The extreme of feeling came across even to those who just heard
Ray's records with the convulsive stuttering and the tense, almost
painful stretching of syllables—devices long used, by the way, by
black gospel preachers. "E-e-e-eef yo-o-o-oar s-s-s-sw-sw-sw-sweet
h-h-h-h-ar-ar-rr-rr-art s-s-s-sennzzz a ll-ll-llett-ta-a-a-a u-u-uuffff goo-
oo-oo-b-b-b-by-y-y-y . . ."

Released late in 1951, "Cry" stood at No. 1 on the hit parade
by February '52. The "b" side, "The Little White Cloud That
Cried," written by Ray himself, surprised everbody by making the
Top Thirty on its own. When "Cry" ranked No. 5 in the annual

Peatman performance survey for '52, "Little White Cloud" was No. 29. In this survey, Eddie Fisher captured the No. 1 and No. 2 slots with "Anytime" and "Wish You Were Here." But Johnnie Ray's two-sided hit mounted a phenomental sales of over four million disks, a mark never reached by Eddie on any of his hits.

It was an impossible mark for Johnnie himself to duplicate. Nevertheless, he later racked up a number of Gold Records, among them, a '52 revival of Harry Richman's hit of 1930 ("Walkin' My Baby Back Home") and four years later, "Just Walking in the Rain."

In trying to determine the character of Ray's audience and appeal, *The New York Times* critic concluded: "This young man's style speaks for young people beset by fears and doubts in a difficult time. His pain may be their pain. His wailing and writhing may reflect their secret impulses. His performance is the anatomy of self-pity."

While he was still a youngster, Johnnie Ray began to go deaf, a condition that proved emotionally destructive. "I couldn't communicate," he recalls, "with other children of my age. I withdrew, was alone a lot. I used to fantasize a lot about being a star." Self-pity was surely the poignant emotion that gave "The Little White Cloud that Cried" its manifest appeal.

An artist that generates as much excitement as Ray did generally descends from the heights almost as fast as he rises. Johnnie followed the pattern, "assisted" by scandal that alienated as it attracted. Rumors that he was a homosexual and drug addict, which would not have hurt him in the '70s, did great harm in the repressive atmosphere of the early '50s.

JOHNNIE RAY INTERVIEW

"Billie Holiday influenced me a great deal," Johnnie Ray told me, "her style. I've always enjoyed originals. There was no one you could compare her to.

"In those early days, I was most influenced by spiritual music. A lot of it, you could just put dirty lyrics to and tag rhythm and blues. But basically they're spiritual songs. And when I wrote, I was under the influence. . . .

"You take the Flame Show Bar in Detroit. It was a continuous show, right through the night. And I was the only white guy; as far as the show was concerned, it was a black and tan club. . . .

"When my first record hit, a lot of people thought that I was black—and a lot of people thought that I was a woman. And GAC

[General Amusement Corporation] didn't know I existed. When I called Bill Weems at GAC, he didn't even know I was on their list. Then in four weeks my price went from $150 to $6,000. . . .

What do you do when you live on a farm in Oregon? Except that I had this calling: I was gonna be in show business, come hell or high water. I didn't want to be a singer, I wanted to be an actor—which is basically what I am anyway, as it turns out.

"I was a second-generation Billie Holiday fan. Billie had just recorded 'Lover Man' and 'That Old Devil Called Love,' [late in 1944]. My sister had it lying around the house. I happened to run across it, and played it. It was like *being possessed* by something. . . . "Then I discovered all the things she had done in the 1930s, with her own orchestra and all that. Became a Billie Holiday collector so that now I have virtually everything she ever recorded. . . .

"I lived to see the day when she came into the Flame Show Bar and saw me in person. When I realized that she was there, I thought . . . I just can't go on. Not with Billie Holiday out front. There isn't any way to get me on. [Laughing.] She musta heard something. Because she latched right onto me. She asked me over to her table, where I promptly got an invitation to come back to her hotel after the last show to have a drink. And that began a friendship. . . .

"The songs I was singing then? Wailing the Blues: 'Pretty-Eyed Baby'; 'I Almost Lost My Mind'; a lot of Ivory Joe Hunter stuff and things like it that I had written myself. Two of the biggest things in the act I wrote myself 'Whiskey and Gin' and 'Tell the Lady I Said Goodbye,' which were the first recordings I ever made. These basically were inspired by my association with the black community. I was the only white kid around and the first white singer to leave the microphone.

"There were no black people in Oregon. I had to get into show business to find out what nigger and kike and all those words were. In Oregon I never heard them. . . .

"I recorded 'Whiskey and Gin' and 'Tell the Lady I Said Goodbye' for Okeh. Oddly enough I was signed on Okeh for rhythm and blues. . . . After the first two sides came out, Mitch Miller snatched me from Danny Kessler's arms—and what followed was 'The Little White Cloud That Cried' and 'Cry.' That, strangely enough, was still on Okeh. After that, they put me on the parent label and the old contract was renegotiated. . . .

" 'Walkin' My Baby Back Home' was a song that I heard in my youth. Me and Buddy Cole were recording on the coast. And just off the top of my head, I said, 'Let's do "Walkin' My Baby Back

Home." ' And we just winged it. Next I knew, they handed me a Gold Record.

"Lots of hits came out that way—just winging it with him. We ad-libbed 'Somebody Stole My Gal.' Also 'All of Me,' which sold a lot of records. Songs I remembered kicking around the house when we were kids.

"My basic background in music came from both gospel and country and western. There was a lot of western music around Oregon. Still is as a matter of fact. When I was a kid, I was taken to square dances. Dad used to fiddle at them. We were well aware of the Roy Acuff things and far-out people you wouldn't expect us to hear, like the Maddox Brothers and Rose, Homer and Jethro. . . . I sang in church a bit. Don't know whether you'd call it gospel. It depended on the spirit in which you sang it. After all you can take 'Bringin' in the Sheaves,' which is a hymn, and make a gospel song out of it. Basically, it was a combination, a wedding of the two kinds of influences—that plus a burning ambition to be in the business, which is strange in itself given my environment. But it was something like a calling. I had to become what I had to become. And it never occurred to me that, given the chance, I wouldn't succeed.

"So that's why when it happened to me, everybody was surprised except me. A lot of people laugh when I tell that story. How confident can you get?

"I went from Oregon to Detroit through a gal named Jan Mitchell. She and her partner had a comedy act. . . . They talked their agent in Cleveland into booking me for two weeks in Ashtabula, Ohio, at $150 a week. . . . I figured with $300 less commission, I could always get bus fare back home if nothing happened. I sent about $50 to my father and hopped a Greyhound to Cleveland. My friends had in the meantime gone to Detroit on a gig.

"At Ashtabula, I was fired after the second week and I starved the rest of that year. But I managed to grab a job playing background music in Akron, Ohio. Picked up a couple of jobs here and there in Cleveland until Jan, to whom I was almost engaged then, called me and said, 'Come on up to Detroit, lot of clubs here, and you can audition.'

"The day I got there, we took a streetcar out to a place in Canfield, Woodward really, and I auditioned for a man named Al Green, who is now dead, and some other guys. They liked me and signed me for about $125 a week. That was the start and I stayed. I quit the Flame once and went over to the Clover Club but I came back and got a salary raise. Without knowing it, I had developed a following—important enough for them to want me to come back. . . .

"One night, Robin Seymour, a local disk jockey, happened to catch me. He got hold of Danny Kessler, who offered me a contract with Okeh, which I refused. I had made some demos and sent them out to Dave Cavanaugh at Capitol, cocky as hell. I wouldn't give Kessler an okay because the best artists seemed to be on Capitol. When Cavanaugh sent my demos back, I said okay to Okeh.

"We recorded 'Whiskey and Gin' and 'Till I Say Goodbye' in Detroit. By this time, GAC had become interested and signed me sight unseen. First place they booked me into was the Capitol Lounge in Chicago. About $300 a week. Without my knowing it, in towns like Boston, Philadelphia, Buffalo, Pittsburgh, which were record-breaking towns at the time, both my sides had gone up to the top of the charts. And so Columbia suggested that I go down to Cleveland for some record promotion.

"It was just an overnight train ride from Chicago. I wasn't prepared. When I got off the train, I thought there was a celebrity arriving. Tons of people were there to see me. This happened because Bill Randle, with the power that he then had, had driven my record right up to the top—and the rest of the towns had followed his lead. No question, it was Randle who was most responsible for the exposure of the early Johnnie Ray.

"Mitch got word of all this. And he came up with the idea of my doing 'Cry.' When I came into New York, he played it for me. It had already been recorded by some girl on an obscure label. And it was a straight, pretty, sugar-dripped little ballad. We got to the record session with 'Cry' and two old songs selected by Mitch—'Broken-Hearted' and 'Please Mr. Sun,' which turned out to be million sellers, too. The session was done with the Four Lads, Jimmy Carroll, and Sam Butera on sax. I wasn't told what to do. The style of 'Cry' is just something that came to me. It was the way I felt it.

"We even had some time left over. And that's how 'The Little White Cloud That Cried' happened to be recorded. I think that they thought: We'll do the kid a favor since we have some extra time and do one of his songs. Stick it on the back of 'Cry.'

"The interesting thing is that when I heard the playbacks, I knew what we had. I just knew it. I didn't guess that the record was going to circumnavigate the globe like it did. But I sensed the excitement, without realizing that there had never been anything quite like me around. . . . I don't believe that it's a matter of being at the right place at the right time. . . .

" 'Walkin' in the Rain' was very strange because Mitch came up with it. I was going off to England on one of my merry little tours. The original recording was by convicts at the Tennessee State Penitentiary. Mitch came up with the whistler and the banjo. . . . But I didn't think that the song had anything. . . . I just couldn't take it seriously. Horsin' around. Two takes like at five minutes to seven. Sometimes you get lucky, like on 'With These Hands,' which I did in one take. I wanted to sing a couple of notes differently. . . . But Mitch said the record has it; don't touch it. . . .

"On 'Walkin'' he came out of the booth and got his beard right up to the microphone like he was eating cooze. 'Get in there,' he said, 'this could do it for you.' So I did a couple of takes, and went off to England. Forget about it. Didn't spend a nickel on promotion. . . . Came back and that damn thing was No. 1 on the hit parade.

"*Cash Box* wanted to do a cover story. They had to come down to the Chase Hotel in St. Louis. Did a picture of me outside, in a raincoat with an umbrella, between shows. . . .

" 'Walkin' in the Rain' was my last Gold Record—1956. It was my sixth. Once you're past the hit records, audiences are unpredictable. There'll always be somebody they're screaming about. Ten years before me, it was Sinatra. Six years after me, it was Presley. Now it's Bobby Sherman and David Cassidy. I went through the teen-age idol thing . . . and not only here, but everywhere around the world. . . . Now, audience response varies from night to night and place to place. . . .

"Talking about Las Vegas, some years ago when *Confidential*, that so-called exposé magazine, was being printed, they ran a sensational story about me. A few facts and a lotta fabricated stuff. Moe Dalitz made one phone call and you couldn't find a copy of the rag in Vegas or anywhere in Nevada.

"When I was a record sensation, the Mob once tried to buy my contract. They offered my manager $50,000. We said a polite no. I was sure I'd get mutilated. But they never bothered me. I was a big drawing card at the Sands then. The girls loved me. Maybe Jack Entratter and Moe Dalitz also said a polite no."

Bounding onto the stage of the Desert Inn lounge in '72, Ray was slender, tall, handsome, and knock kneed. There was the metallic rasp in his voice, like a saw being sharpened, and the sharp, jerky motions of his legs and arms, the clenching of his hands, and the grimaces of pain. Fooling around with something hidden in his dress shirt, he explained that he could adjust his hearing aid that way. "Big deal about my being partly deaf," he

commented. Then he did a medley of walking songs, chewing on
some syllables and hissing others. For "The Little White Cloud
That Cried" he set the mood by sitting on the steps leading offstage and talking about an unhappy seventeen-year-old who was
living in Rosebud, Oregon. He walked off to resounding applause after his ninth song, a furious, up-tempo gospel number.
When he returned, he turned his back on the audience, struck a
dramatic pose, threw his right hand out as if he were shooting
craps and went into "Cr-r-r-r-rhyeh . . ." He was back in the
'50s and the audience, sipping the watered drinks, sighed audibly
and reveled in the nostalgia.

The Cool Generation and the Beats

Before they said "Crazy, Man, Crazy," as Bill Haley did in a
'53 recording, they were saying "Cool, man, cool!"

Cool jazz developed in the same years as belting in pop. Tenorman Lester Young and trumpeter Miles Davis led a counterrevolu-
tion to the bop revolution promulgated by altoist Charlie "Bird"
Parker, trumpeter Dizzy Gillespie, and others. Their introversion
and detachment was the other side of the coin of alienation.

In '53 at a smart nitespot in Los Angeles, the leader of a small
combo interrupted his group's playing of "How High the Moon"
and angrily dressed down the audience for talking while his men
performed. When he was taken to task by the management, Gerry
Mulligan explained: "Most of the Haig's customers are here to
listen. When anyone talks it not only annoys those who are trying
to listen but disturbs the continuity of our collective musical
thinking."

Everything was in reverse. Instead of the get-happy spirit
customary in a nitespot, there was studied quiet. Instead of sweating, gyrating performers, a group of placid, "thinking" musicians.
Instead of aggressive showmanship, something approximating re-
pose. "Moldy fig" became the term of opprobrium hurled at
Dixieland/swing fans and the cats who played it. They were not
hip.

"Hot jazz, Dixieland and swing, was (and is) happy music," I
wrote in an *Esquire* article in May 1954. "It had bounce, spirit,
movement, kaleidoscopic colors. . . . It was (and is) a music of
action, excitement, confusion, but, above all, of release. In violent
contrast, cool jazz is introspective. It is a state of numbness. The
musician—Lennie Tristano at the piano, Stan Getz on tenor, or

Cal Tjader at the vibraphone—is a study in still life. At the peak of 'coolness,' he betrays no emotion whatsoever. This is the musical mind seeking order out of chaos and fearful of discovering only a void."

In '54 I called the musicians and their followers the "Cool Generation." Later, during the Eisenhower era, Jack Kerouac called it the "Beat Generation." *Beat* had nothing to do with rhythm—it meant spent or beatific. We were both concerned with the same motivations—the withering sense of being alone arising from alienation from family and established values, the lack of roots in the past and the fear of the future, and the resulting tendency to play with oneself and live-live-live in the present. The beats were "on the road," trying to escape from the square world around them. They made no effort to change things. They were contemplators, and when what they contemplated became unbearable, they sought to narcotize themselves.

The belters in pop were surely not aware of the psychological basis of their style. But through it, they gave unconscious expression to the tensions and frustrations of the growing generation.

Howl!

Eddie Fisher and Johnnie Ray represented the two strains of belting that dominated pop in the early '50s. There were the *shouters* like Eddie, Don Cornel, Guy Mitchell, Al Hibbler, Roy Hamilton, the Four Aces, the Four Lads, Tony Bennett, the Ames Brothers—also hard-voiced females like Rosemary Clooney, Georgia Gibbs, Teresa Brewer, Kay Starr, the McGuire Sisters. And there were the *emoters* and exhibitionists like Johnnie Ray and Jackie Wilson, vocal descendants of Billy Daniels and Little Richard.

Frankie Laine embodied both strains—the screamer on records like "Mule Train" and the impassioned emoter on disks like "Swamp Girl" and "Jezebel"—"If ever there was a devil in disguise . . . it was you! Jezebel! Jezzz-eheheh-ehbellllll!" When he brought black drive into pop, after trying to make it with the intimate, crooning style of Crosby or Sinatra, Laine anticipated the rockabilly pioneers by a good six years.

Screamers or emoters (the two overlap), the belters used their voices like shafts. It had thrust, muscle, animation. It was an explosion of pain or pleasure. They were men and women in motion—not Como musing or Sinatra caressing a mike but dynamic figures whose high-decibel vocals found expression in clenched hands, gritting teeth, flailing arms, and stamping feet. And they climaxed their performances with a *Roxy ending*, one in which the final notes had so much volume, duration, and wallop that they rattled windows, even those of giant movie palaces like the now defunct Paramount Theatre and the Roxy.

Belting was a spiritual descendant of gospel shouting. Transitional to R 'n' R, it was influenced, directly or indirectly, by the urban type of blues know as R & B.

7

THE PERSONALITY
DEEJAYS

In Los Angeles in the 1950s, as you bumper-to-bumpered to work on the freeways, you avoided blowing your cool by listening to "Haynes at the Reins," a Texas Yahoo whose main, imaginary collaborator was Gum Drop Gus, a Mortimer Snerd–type cornball. Dick Haynes was the waker-upper of the Big Five at KLAC, then the area's top station. Other disk jockeys were Alex Cooper, Bob McLaughlin, Gene Norman, and Peter Potter. The powerhouse figure was Al Jarvis, who was not exclusively contracted to the "Station of the Stars," as KLAC called itself at 570 on the dial.

Martin Block, a regular on New York City's WNEW, is sometimes spotlighted as the nation's first disk jockey. In February 1935, as he awaited bulletins on the trial of Bruno Hauptmann, the house painter who was ultimately found guilty of kidnapping and killing the Lindbergh baby, he began playing phonograph records. At the time, there was not a single disk in the station's library, and Block got the platters by purchasing them at nearby Liberty Music Shop on Madison Avenue and Fiftieth Street. Playing disks by Clyde McCoy, the "Sugar Blues" trumpeter, he pretended that the music was coming live from a ballroom. Station management was not too receptive to a program made up of phonograph records until Block got his own sponsor.

The idea was not his, as he later admitted. Having worked on stations in Southern California, he was familiar with "The World's Largest Make-Believe Ballroom," a program presented by Al Jarvis over KFWB in L.A. at least three years earlier. So, credit for being the nation's first deejay should go to Jarvis, who also played a critical role in launching swing.

Benny Goodman's 1937 stand at the Palomar Ballroom in L.A.

is generally recognized as the take-off of Big Band swing. Because the band had not been doing well in its cross-country tour, Goodman sent an advance man to spark the Hollywood scene. Charlie Emge, editor of *Tempo* and later a *Down Beat* staffer, turned to Jarvis whose spins of Goodman disks brought an overflow crowd to the Palomar. The crowd's roaring approval, heard over a coast-to-coast remote, helped animate a wave that led to the crowning of B.G. as the king of swing.

When Jarvis left KFWB to go with KLAC, it was with a seven-year contract guaranteeing him $1,700,000, or roughly $245,000 a year. As KLAC was the first all deejay station with identifiable platter spinners, so in the '50s Jarvis became one of the most successful personality disk jockeys. The station he left made a deal with Martin Block in which he spun disks live over L.A.'s KFWB, did a recorded show for WNEW in New York City, and was syndicated on thirty other stations. In 1948 this setup promised Block a gross of $2 million.

Apart from Jarvis, the development of personality deejays gained impetus in the late '40s when disk jockeys in three different parts of the country broke records single handed. In Chicago Eddie Hubbard, spinning disks on Station WIND, stuck his needle in the grooves of a 1913 ballad, "Peg O' My Heart" and handed a novelty instrumental group, the Harmonicats, the biggest and most unexpected hit of their careers.

An even more impressive demonstration of disk-jockey power occurred the same year (1947) when a Charlotte, North Carolina platter spinner took an old 78 rpm disk made in 1931 and spun it into a national hit. Decca Records was amazed when orders suddenly began pouring in for Ted Weems's out-of-print platter of "Heartaches" and so dubious about a revival that it had popular Guy Lombardo cut a new treatment. There was no stopping the avalanche that Kurt Webster, "The Midnight Mayor of Station WBT," had started. Ted Weems's recording finished as the No. 3 disk of the year.

Weems was so delighted with his renewed popularity that he played a date at the Charlotte Armory in June 1947 and turned the proceeds over to Webster. And Leeds Music, the publisher of "Heartaches," with whom I was then associated as publicity and ad director, gave the North Carolina jockey a free-expense trip and week's vacation in New York. As Webster's guide, I found it interesting to see my home city through the eyes of a young Southerner. What eventually became trying was his night-after-night fondness for Lindy's food, especially a rich, cloying dessert known as strawberry cheesecake.

Nineteen forty-eight brought an even more curious affirmation of the selling impact of a colorful knight of the new round table. Emcee of a program called "Jazzbo Jamboree" out of Salt Lake City, Al Collins (later known as Jazzbo Collins) one day received a new disk from MGM Records. It featured an ex-Paul Whiteman, hunchbacked banjo player, Mike Pingatore, performing a ricky-tick tune of 1927, "I'm Looking over a Four Leaf Clover," to the accompaniment of Art Mooney's squeaky-mouse band. Collins's short-fused temper exploded because such a disk was sent to an established jazz deejay. His anger lasted for three and a half hours during which he played the record over and over, and vented his spleen by giving the song a different title each time. It was a tour de force that shook up listeners in Salt Lake City and started a chain reaction that made Mooney's recording the No. 4 best seller of the year.

By the early '50s, there was hardly a city that did not boast one or more flamboyant, weird, or offbeat platter spinner. Station management was interested in their ratings and ability to attract sponsors. Music business was concerned with their power in breaking hits. Though New York had its share of personalities, among them Ted Brown and the Redhead at WMGM, Bob and Ray at WNEW, Klavan and Finch also at WNEW, it had no standing as a breakout town. Honors went to nearby Jersey City with Paul Brenner at WAAT; to Boston with Bob Clayton at WHDH; Philadelphia with Joe Grady of WPEN; Washington, D.C., with Eddie Gallagher at WTOP; Cincinnati with Bill Dawes at WCKY; Chicago with Howard Miller and Eddie Hubbard at WIND; St. Louis with Gil Newsome at KWK; and Detroit with Ed McKenzie, "Jack the Bellboy," at WJBK.

At the beginning of the '50s, one of the country's most potent record sellers was Bob Horn at Station WFIL in Philadelphia. Tom Donahue, a competitor, described him as "the closest thing to a Roman Emperor I've ever known." Alleged involvement with one of his teen-age femme fans brought his downfall, and the payola investigations of '59 led to an indictment for income tax evasion. But Caesar encountered his Mark Anthony as early as 1952 when a young man named Dick Clark joined his daily "Bandstand" show.

In '52 the deejay regarded as "the single most important and powerful record spinner in the country", according to *Down Beat*, broadcast daily from Station WERE in Cleveland. Bill Randle looked like a young college professor and was as literate. "A seemingly casual plug on his show," *Down Beat* wrote, "carries the weight of a blockbuster." The jazz publication made the admission, lamenting Randle's defection as a proponent of jazz. (From '42 on, for six years, Randle had conducted "Strictly Jive" over Station WJLB in Detroit, across the street from WJBK where "Jack the Bellboy" was the hitmaker.)

By the time he settled in Cleveland in '49, Randle defined his policy very simply: "I don't care what it is. I want to make hits." And a hitmaker he became. One of his first finds was a young singer out of Oregon named Johnnie Ray, who was playing a local club. Another was a Brooklyn-born paisano with whom Randle would tour the Cleveland high schools and whose records he plugged constantly on his four-hour afternoon program. "I would not be where I am," Tony Bennett has said, "without the help of Bill Randle."

One of his earliest demonstrations of power came, not with a pop artist, but with a rhythm-and-blues man, Louis Jordan. After an initial play of "Saturday Night Fish Fry" by Jordan and his Tympany Five, Randle responded to listener calls—he took them while he was on the air—by playing the disk every fifteen minutes. Then he cued the Decca distributor in the area, a technique that in turn brought him advance information on records breaking in other areas. Competitors claimed that he got many tips from his mother, who lived in Detroit and monitored motor town's Ed McKenzie for her son.

It was not long before record salesmen found themselves constantly assailed by the query: "Is Randle laying on it?" And they found it difficult to stock stores with new disks unless they could assure dealers that the Cleveland Monster was, indeed, on it. In an effort to assure a concentrated play by Randle, many artists, publishers, and A & R men slipped him advance copies of forthcoming disks.

Through the '50s, Randle had as much as 80 percent of the afternoon listening audience. The varied record hits that came off his turntable reached from a revival of the 1926 film ballad "Charmaine" by Mantovani to the Crew Cuts and Elvis Presley.

Vinylites Instead of "Pro" Copies

"A hit is a hit only 50 percent on its merit," publisher Howie Richmond said early in 1951. "The other 50 percent is the treatment the deejays give it. When I get the best record I can of a new song, I air-mail copies to three hundred deejays who are personal friends of mine."

It was a technique that was not entirely new. But no publisher before Richmond employed it so assiduously. And no one demonstrated its efficacy so dramatically as young Richmond. A former publicist who went into the publishing business in 1950 and functioned as a one-man operation out of a walkup office over a Fifty-second Street chop house, Howie racked up six smash hits in one year. It was an unheard of achievement in an industry where even the large, major publishing companies consider themselves fortunate to score one or two best sellers a year. In '50–'51 Richmond's proliferating companies accounted for "Hop Scotch Polka," "Music! Music! Music!" "Goodnight Irene," "Molasses Molasses," "Tzena Tzena Tzena," and "The Thing."

The hit that brought him into the business was, in fact, called to his attention by three disk jockeys, Eddie Gallagher of WTOP in Washington, D.C., and Gene Rayburn and Dee Finch of WNEW in New York. "Scotch Hot," as it was then known, was available on a London recording by Billy Whitlock, an aging music-hall performer then working as a night watchman. Rewritten as "Hop Scotch Polka," on Richmond's initiative, by Carl Sigman and Gene Rayburn, it became a best seller on a new Guy Lombardo recording, the foundation of an international publishing combine (TRO), and a confirmation of growing deejay power.

It was only after "The Thing" became a runaway smash—his sixth in a row—that Richmond revealed his *modus operandi*. After dropping out of the University of Pennsylvania, he had gone to work for a Broadway publicist. Since he worked for free, the publicist decided to try an experiment: in addition to publicizing his artist clients, he would promote their records. Thus, Richmond came to know the new titans of the turntable, a friendship that grew as he went into publicity business on his own and promoted the recordings of Sinatra, Dinah Shore, and others. By the time he embarked on publishing, after a four-year stint in the Army, at least three hundred deejays knew him on a first-name basis.

All of them had his office and home numbers, and carte blanche to phone collect any hour of the day or night. At least half of his own working day was spent telephoning these "friends." On Saturdays and Sundays, he reportedly spent a full sixteen hours on long-distance calls to platter spinners all over the country. In the eyes of publishing competitors, who had plugging and promo staffs, this mode of operation was forced upon him—since as a one-man operation, it was the only way he could get exposure of his new songs.

Whether it was necessity or choice, the fact is that about the time that Howard Sam Richmond came into the music-publishing business, disk jockeys became the fulcrum of song promotion. Where song pluggers had once carried professional copies neatly folded in their back pants pockets and romanced live performers, in the 1950s they were trotting around with vinylite disks in attaché cases and wooing the country's platter spinners.

The power of the personality deejay peaked with the rise of rock 'n' roll. But by then he faced the competition of a mechanized type of programing known as Top Forty. Presumably, it was started as early as 1953 when Todd Storz, later head of a potent chain, bought WTIX in New Orleans and saw a way of keeping personnel costs down with a format of "Top Forty at 1450." Not long after, the owner of another chain, Gordon McLendon, followed suit with a playlist from which jockeys on Station KLIF of Dallas had to program.

Some say that the personality deejays priced themselves out of the radio scene. Others claim that station managers were anxious to eliminate them and thereby enhance their earnings and position (as program directors). The history of radio after the rise of R 'n' R is a story of the losing battle of the personality deejay against Top Forty. But the '50s were his era and his turntable spelled the difference between "smash" and "bomb."

8

"YOUR HIT PARADE"

" 'Your Hit Parade,' America's Taste in Popular Music," made its debut on coast-to-coast radio on Saturday night, April 20, 1935, in the period when the moon came over the mountain for Kate Smith and the blues of the night met the gold of the day for Bing Crosby.

It opened cold with an announcer saying: "With men who know tobacco best, it's Luckies two to one." And a tobacco auctioneer sounded the singsong mumbo-jumbo of calling prices and ended with a melodic "Sold to A-mer . . . i-can!" Then the clicking of a telegrapher's key in a rhythm immediately duplicated by an announcer saying: "L-S . . . M-F-T. L-S . . . M-F-T." Another voice: "You said it! Lucky Strike means fine tobacco! So round, so firm, so fully packed . . . so free and easy on the draw!" Once again, the auctioneer calling unidentifiable numbers in his singsong, climaxed by "Sold to A-mer . . . i-can!" Ascending harp glissando as the band swung into the first sixteen bars of "This Is My Lucky Day" in a brassy, lilting up-tempo. Finally. André Baruch, smooth as the cigarette itself, announced: "Lucky Strike presents 'Your Hit Parade' starring Kay Thompson, Charles Carlyle, Gogo De Lys, and Johnny Hauser."

By World War II when Sinatra was starred on the "Parade" and "Saturday night was the loneliest night in the week" for girls without boys, "Your Hit Parade" was as important as the release of a new Rolling Stones album today.

The Ten Top Tunes of the Week! Their titles and order were a closely guarded secret, intriguing the mighty as well as the mass. So secret that once when Sinatra paid a visit to the White House, FDR asked what song would be No. 1 that coming Saturday night.

Surprise was unquestionably a plus factor in the long-lived popularity of the "Parade."

As for music business, every publisher and song plugger maneuvered to get advance info. Some cultivated ad men at Batten, Barton, Durstine, Osborn (BBDO—no "and"), the agency that produced the show. Others tried to develop a pipeline through musicians in the orchestra or employees of the NBC, secretaries, mimeo operators, stagehands, guards. The most anyone could or would tell you is whether a given tune was on. Of course, the personnel of the show got to know the position of songs as rehearsals progressed. But apparently there was such cohesiveness that leaks were minor.

"It was the most familylike operation with which I've ever been involved," Ray Charles told me. Ray was the "Parade's" choral director/vocal arranger from 1949 into 1958, and worked with other TV programs including the Perry Como show. "There would be a luncheon meeting at BBDO each Monday. Mark Warnow, the conductor (later Raymond Scott), Bill Nichols (chief writer), Tony Sharmalee (choreographer), Paul Barnes (set designer), Sal Anthony (costumer), Clark Jones (director), and the coproducers, Ted Fetter and Dan Lounsberry of the agency. We had a list of the fifteen top songs from the preceding week with some preliminary dramatizations prepared by the writers.

"About midway through lunch, a phone call would come in from American Tobacco giving us the ten (later seven) songs in the week's survey. The producers would assign the songs to the different cast members, and working with the chief writer and director, check over the visualization. Then they would phone the sponsor for approval.

"Oh, yes, nothing, but nothing, was done without American Tobacco's okay. The Lucky Strike Extras were planned in advance from a list previously presented by the tobacco people. 'Fine and Dandy' was one of their favorites, probably because the famous George Washington Hill, A.T.'s prexy, liked it.

"By Monday evening, I was at work on the vocal arrangements while other arrangers labored through the night on the orchestral scores. Tuesday, the dancers began rehearsing. On Wednesday, the costumes and sets were ready. Thursday, we started vocal rehearsals with the four principals and the chorus. Late Thursday, we had an initial run through. Then at about four o'clock we watched a kine of the previous week's show. It was party time . . . a ball. We applauded, laughed at the funny bits, kidded about the boo-boos.

"Since the show was done live, there were mistakes. Dancers

missed cues. Sets would be out of kilter. And Snooky Lanson was always forgetting lyrics. Once he wrote the words on the floor and they were erased by the touch-up crew just before showtime. Did he ad-lib! Another time—and what a time—on a Christmas telecast, he had a lapse of memory on 'O, Holy Night.'

"Friday morning, the musicians showed for an orchestral rehearsal. And that afternoon, we blocked movements and positions in the studio for the camera crew. Saturday, we had a full run through, then a dress rehearsal, and at 7:30 P.M., it was showtime. We'd all go out to dinner and return at 10:30 for a repeat telecast to the West Coast."

Apart from its value as musical entertainment, "Your Hit Parade" had the appeal of any so-called "inside" survey. It never disclosed its yardstick or statistics for selecting the Top Tunes. On the air, reference was made to the sale of sheet music—there was such a thing in those days—juke-box plays, record sales, and performances on radio and TV. Publishers felt that performances were the key, and their staffs were marshaled to bunch air plugs in "drive weeks." From the '30s into the '50s, music business was, in fact, geared around "No. 1 Plugs"—songs selected for a concentrated push on radio, later TV, with no holds barred: payola, hypola, giftola, layola, get the plug.

In the summer of 1950, serving as a replacement for "Robert Montgomery Presents," "Your Hit Parade" became one of the first, long-lived radio shows to tackle television. By then TV had become a major cultural force and more Americans were, for the first time, watching TV than listening to the radio. But television and developments of the decade were the beginning of the end for the "Parade" and the sensibility it represented.

The visual factor proved a trial right from the start. Repeat appearances of the same song in the survey posed back-breaking problems to scripters to dream up new settings every week—and sometimes, the settings were less than congruous with the songs. Ingenuity was taxed even in handling the numerals indicating the position of each song in the survey—the "6" appeared one week on a tree trunk, next in a chapter heading, again on a playing card, later when a teapot was lifted, etc.

As the tenor of pop music changed after the mid-'50s, the contrast between teen-age songs and the performers was destructive. Vamp-eyed Gisele McKenzie tried to brazen it but her coyness did not work. Bucktoothed Dorothy Collins—then married to Raymond Scott—seemed puzzled and uneasy, despite her youthfulness and lisp. And Snooky Lanson? A rock critic wrote: "The creepiest of the four, Snooky Lanson, stood up in front of the cardboard sets they used, and sang out, 'You ain't nothin' but a hound dog,' with a shit-eating Lucky Strike grin on his face."

During '57–'58 the "Parade" dropped the vocal complement of Lanson, Collins, McKenzie, and Russell Arms. It substituted a group of youngsters, headed by Tommy Leonetti and Jill Corey. But even though they were younger, they were not at ease with rock 'n' roll material. And instead of retaining a conductor who understood teen-age music, an arranger-conductor of Broadway musicals was hired. During the final season, Johnny Desmond appeared to no avail and Dorothy Collins returned with her long-sleeved, white blouse and black string tie to be framed in the circle on the Lucky Strike package and lisp the "so round, so firm" commercial.

In March 1958 the "Parade" added a musiquiz feature to its presentation of the week's Top Tunes. Two-hundred thousand dollars in prizes were awarded to those who guessed the title of a mystery tune and gave the best reasons in twenty-five words or less for preferring Luckies. It was an attempt to meet the competition of musical quiz shows like "Dough-Re-Mi" on NBC-TV and a musical jackpot on Ted Steele's WOR-TV show.

A trade-paper editor contended that the "Parade" was not facing its format problem squarely: "Either junk the idea of 'top hits,' " Ren Grevatt write in *Billboard*, "and program only non-rock-and-roll hit material for adult, late-evening viewers, or revert to an out-and-out pop hit format and fill the studio with teen-age fans who can do the stroll . . ."

When the "Hit Parade" returned in the fall of '58, it still tried to straddle the issue. Switching from NBC-TV after almost a decade, it was presented on CBS-TV, choreographed by Peter Gennaro and staged by Norman Jewison—both of whom went on to notable careers in TV, films, and the theatre. In an effort to appeal to young and old, the program was divided into four departments: the Top Three Tunes of the week and three other hits from the Top Twelve *plus* numbers from albums and a medley from the All-Time Hit Parade.

Appearing as regulars, Dorothy Collins and dapper Johnny Desmond were joined by guests: The Accents, a vocal quintet, performed "Bird Dog," the No. 3 song of that week. After Desmond delivered *"Volare,"* No. 2, and Collins the No. 1 hit, "It's All in the Game," the other nine songs of the Top Twelve were named in rhymed couplets, chanted by the singing chorus.

It was a brave and inventive attempt to span the '50s, one end of the swaying structure rooted in the crumbling world of the past and the other, anchored in the present. The "Parade" was trapped in a hopeless contradiction: it needed an adult audience to sell its product (tobacco) but the music scene was teen-age.

The end came in the spring of 1959. On April 24 Dorothy Collins sang, as Eileen Wilson once had, "So long for a while. . . . So long to Your Hit Parade. . . . And the tunes you picked to be played . . ." The entire cast joined in and followed with "Be happy, Go Lucky," swaying as a group from side to side. But the "so long," despite statements that the staff would be kept intact for a fall '59 return, was not "just for a while," but for good. "Your Hit Parade" had really outlived its time.

In the twenty-four years of its existence—it passed almost on the day of its birth—it had become the embodiment, symbol, and summation of the Tin Pan Alley era in pop. Critics of the new style of song that helped destroy it, like to call the "Hit Parade" tradition "good music." The current trade paper term is "Easy Listening." It was a tradition of sentimental-romantic ballads and cutie-pie novelty tunes, structured in a thirty-two-bar form, regardless of whether they came from films, shows, or the Alley. "Entertainment" is, perhaps, an informed way of characterizing the singing style, as opposed to "emotion" or "expressiveness." Whether it was vaudeville, radio, or television, the *live* performance was the prime form of exposure and promotion, not the record, cassette, or tape. Singers were accompanied on piano, not the guitar, and by bands or orchestras, not electric combos. And the harmonies, melodies, and sensibility stemmed from Tchaikovsky, Ravel, Neapolitan song, mittel-European operetta, not blues, folk, or country.

When I asked Ray Charles how rock and roll affected the "Parade," he responded with one word: "Fatally." And added: "Of course, it was not just rock 'n' roll but several other things that happened at the same time. Until rock and roll, the *song* was the thing. Suddenly, it was the *performance*. Viewers didn't want to hear Dorothy Collins singing 'Rock Around the Clock.' They wanted Bill Haley and the Comets. They didn't want anybody except Fats Domino doing 'Blueberry Hill.' Our audience was middle generation and they didn't like the music that was coming in. And the kids whose music it was didn't like the people who were performing it. Suddenly, the star performers looked older than they were and the girls in the chorus didn't look like girls. Everything was against the show's success at that point— mostly time . . ."

The "Hit Parade" emerged with the rise of the Big Bands. Its popularity peaked in the days of the Big Baritones and waned as the Big Belters took over. Its troubles intensified when Top Forty programing provided an hourly hit parade for listeners. The element of surprise was gone—and why wait for Saturday night? A victim of the rock revolution, "Your Hit Parade" died with the passing of Tin Pan Alley as the central locus of pop music.

II

UPHEAVAL IN POP

1954-1955

9

"SH-BOOM"

In the spring of 1954 when I was vice-president and Gen. Prof. Mgr. of Hill & Range Songs, I met on a Saturday morning with Morty Craft, an arranger and independent record producer. Craft had just cut a disk that was making noise in rhythm-and-blues markets. I had requested the meeting in the hope of purchasing all or part of the copyright.

In the course of our conversation, he adverted to a strange phenomenon he had just encountered in Los Angeles. He did not tell me outright but asked whether I could guess the No. 1 record seller. As I named disks that were then on the charts—"Wanted" (Perry Como), "Make Love to Me" (Jo Stafford), "Little Things Mean A Lot" (Kitty Kallen)—he kept shaking his head in the negative. Finally, with a sly glint in his eyes, emphasized by the heavy lenses he wore, he said: "Ever hear of a song called 'Sh-

Boom?' And a group called the Chords? *That's* what's No. 1 in Los Angeles!"

After he left my office at 1650 Broadway, I went to a health club frequented by music men, The Gotham on Fifty-fourth Street, just west of what was then the famous Ziegfeld Theatre. While I was getting a massage, I kept thinking of Craft's claim that "Sh-Boom" was No. 1, not on an R & B but a pop list. Although I had a lunch date, I could not resist hurrying back to my office. Phoning a friend in Hollywood, I asked him to go over to Glenn Wallich's record store on Sunset and Vine and call me collect with a list of their best-selling records. When the call came in late that night, Craft's "tall tale" was confirmed. The Chords' disk of "Sh-Boom" was outselling Como, Kitty Kallen, etc.

I spent a restless Sunday. But by 10:00 A.M. on Monday, I had ascertained that the Chords' recording was on a Cat label, a subsidiary of Atlantic Records, and that the copyright was owned by Progressive Music, also an Atlantic subsidiary. By noon, I was with Jerry Wexler and Miriam Abramson—my impression is that Atlantic was then on the two top floors of a run-down building on West Fifty-sixth Street, between Broadway and Eighth Avenue. They were surprised that I wanted to buy the copyright and wanted to know what attracted me to "Sh-Boom." Naturally I did not tell them and they gave no indication of whether a deal would interest them. But I suspected that Wexler and his associates were not uninterested in cash and the promotion that we could put behind a song. You see, Hill & Range was known as a powerhouse publishing house while Progressive Music, like most record subsidiaries of that day, was just a holding company.

Of course, no one could have surmised, as we sat talking, how big the song would become—or how fast. But I had a hunch. And my hunch crystallized into a firm determination to purchase the copyright after I listened to the Chords recording, which they gave me. It had a curious sound and appeal, one that baffled even the Atlantic execs. After it became a hit, Ahmet Ertegun, Atlantic president, admitted that when the record was played at a sales-release meeting, everyone felt that "it had something, but what?"

What I heard was an appealing dance vitality and a beguiling horniness in the lead singer. The disk opened with two unaccompanied "Life could be a dream . . . life could be a dream," hoarse and strident, and bounced into a bright, unabating shuffle. Explosive "Sh-Booms" punctuated both the vocal and R & B tenor-sax solo (whose opening phrase sounded perilously close to "Mean to Me"). The phrase "Hello, hello again" came out of nowhere sev-

eral times to keep the rhythm going, as did other nonsense syllables. The bass voice solo, traditional on R & B records, had a
nostalgic feeling of longing. Lyrically, the song was a compound of
cliché phrases like "tell me I'm the only one you love" and "let me
spend my whole life with you." But it kept repeating the inviting
promise of "Life could be a dream." I found it irresistible.

The following morning, Jerry Wexler called. They would sell
50 percent of the copyright for a $6,000 advance. I felt that they
were asking a lot but I did not waver in my determination to
make a deal.

Now, I faced the problem of getting the owners of Hill & Range,
Jean and Julian Aberbach, to go along. Unfortunately, that Tuesday, Jean Aberbach, who made the decisions, was leaving for
California. I gave him a copy of the Chords disk the moment he
arrived at the office and tried to get him to listen before telling
him what was involved. When he pleaded the press of last-minute
business, I hit him with the $6,000 figure. His eyes opened wide,
not so much at the size of the sum as my obvious willingness to
venture it on what was then a completely unknown quantity. He
was impressed—as most entrepreneurs are by big figures—but asked
me to wait for an answer until later.

The day passed without his getting back to me. Then it was
five o'clock—and there was Jean trotting out of the office, followed
by the entourage of songwriters who usually came to see him off.
I intercepted him as he reached the door, but could get no answer
on "Sh-Boom"—and then he was gone. I raced back to my office
and grabbed a copy of the Chords disk. I reached the street just
as he and his entourage were filling two taxis. Not without difficulty, I managed to muscle my way into his cab. Jean was afraid
to fly and traveled from coast to coast in one of the day's luxury
trains, the Twentieth Century Ltd. Riding downtown to Grand
Central Station, I tried to impress him with the importance
of "Sh-Boom." But he had a captive audience of songwriters
before whom he had to display his wit. As we walked the red
carpet that the New York Central rolled out next to the Twentieth
Century Ltd.—with Jean's entourage trotting along—I handed him
a copy of the Chords disk and urged him to phone me at the
earliest.

The following day, I had lunch with Hugo and Luigi, who
were then A & R chiefs at Mercury Records. Because I wanted to
pitch a number of songs at them, I picked Camillo's, an out-of-
the-way spot on Fifty-fourth Street, east of Park Avenue. Toward
the end of the leisurely meal, the headwaiter came trotting to our

table to say that there was a long-distance call for me. I asked him to get the name and number of the caller. When he placed a slip near my plate with Jean Aberbach's name on it and the number of a Chicago operator, I regretted that I had not taken the call. In a matter of minutes, the headwaiter was back: "The gentleman is on the phone again. He says he *must* talk with you at once!"

Reluctantly excusing myself, I went to the house phone. Jean had a high-pitched voice. But he was so excited that he almost sounded like a penny whistle.

"Can you still get 'Sh-Boom'?" he shrieked. I told him I thought so.

"And is it $6,000 for 50 percent of the copyright? Is that the best you can do?" I told him it was.

"Do you still want to do it?" he asked. I asked him what he thought of the record.

"It's on your head," he replied. "But you can go ahead if you want to."

A day or two later, I handed the attorney for Atlantic Records, Warren Troub, a $6,000 check, and the Hill & Range attorney, Ben Starr, received copies of a contract signed by the Atlantic executives. Progressive Music and St. Louis Music, a Hill & Range subsidiary, were now equal partners on "Sh-Boom."

Had the Atlantic people waited little more than a week, they would have had no reason to part with half of the income, as they did. What Jean Aberbach never told me, but I learned later was the following. The Twentieth Century Ltd., departing Grand Central at six o'clock P.M. arrives in Chicago the following morning. But the train leaving for the coast from another rail station does not depart until four or five hours later. Now, no music man would spend those hours in Chicago without visiting a record company—and Mercury, the most important of the Midwest companies, was at 35 E. Wacker Drive.

When Jean walked into that office, he found A & R men and even the secretaries "flipping their lids" over a new record that was being rushed out as a Special Release. You have probably guessed. It was a recording of "Sh-Boom," a cover of the Chords R & B disk by a white, pop group from Canada, the Crew Cuts. Jean was nearly apoplectic on the long-distance phone because we had been handed—if we owned all or part of the copyright—the very thing we needed if the black ballad was then to make it in the pop market. But he had left me with the barb that the $6,000 advance was "on my head."

The Crew Cuts record "saved" my head, as you must know. Released in the week that the Chords disk hit the pop charts, it zoomed into the Top Ten one week later. By the end of July '54, it was on "Your Hit Parade" where it remained for twelve weeks, climbing only to the No. 3 slot. But in *Billboard*'s Honor Roll it monopolized the No. 1 spot during August and September, finishing as one of 1954's Top Five songs.

I feel gratified that rock historians like Carl Belz and others have singled out "Sh-Boom" as the first rock 'n' roll hit. I hasten to assure the reader that the designation is accurate even though there are two other possible contenders. Several months earlier than "Sh-Boom," an R & B song called "Gee," recorded by the Crows on Rama Records, made the pop charts. But it never made the Top Ten nor did it stir the excitement generated by the Chords recording. Almost a year earlier, a weeper recorded by the Orioles on Jubilee went pop. But "Crying in the Chapel" was a country song, recorded by Darrell Glenn (brother of writer Artie Glenn) on Valley Records.

"Sh-Boom" was unique in several respects. For one thing, it was a studio-written song, as the number of collaborators suggests. The performers were the writers. For another, it has the distinction of being not only the first nationwide smash in the new genre but the first rock 'n' roll song to draw a major attack. As we shall see, after the rise of rock 'n' roll, the older generation waged a prolonged, rear-guard action against it. In the case of "Sh-Boom," the major antagonist was parodist Stan Freberg, who did not come out sounding comical. The possible explanation emerged during an appearance on Peter Potter's CBS-TV show "Juke Box Jury." After Potter played his record of "Sh-Boom," Freberg said, "I hope this puts an end to rhythm and blues." In short, he was too full of animosity to be funny and his parody turned into epithet.

Freberg's television comments drew a barrage of criticism from industry spokesmen who felt that he had done a disservice particularly to Capitol Records, his label, in view of its expanding program of R & B recording. Freberg was among those who played some part in persuading the rising generation that it had something different and, perhaps, even dangerous. It was a pleasant summer for the young as they sunned themselves on sandy beaches and listened to their transistors pouring out the danceable strains of "Life could be a dream . . . Sh-Boom, Sh-Boom . . ."

In its style, the manner of its rise, and the animus it aroused, "Sh-Boom" was the culmination of postwar developments in pop music and society, specifically the situation of black people and black music in the American scene.

JERRY WEXLER INTERVIEW

"I came to Atlantic Records in June 1953," said Jerry Wexler, with whom I negotiated the deal on "Sh-Boom." "Herb Abramson, who founded the company with Ahmet Ertegun, was going into the Army. . . . Ahmet was constantly in the studio and he and Miriam Abramson wanted somebody who would come to the office every day. They had been wanting me to leave the Big Three (Robbins, Feist, and Miller Music Corps.) for about a year. . . . But they had been offering just a weekly salary. When they said, 'Come in and we'll sell you a piece of the company,' that interested me. But my friend, publisher Howie Richmond, said: 'Don't do it. You'll never make it. R & B ain't going nowhere.'

"I didn't listen to Howie. . . . Ahmet began breaking me into the studio. He knew I was on a pass just as he was at the beginning. He had just signed Clyde McPhatter, who was my first assignment. Having just left the Dominoes, Clyde got together a new group. We rehearsed them for several months. Then we did a session. 'Money Honey' was one of the songs. The whole session was no good. We threw it out and Clyde got a new group together and we started all over again. When we did all the tunes again, they came out. There was a lot of discussion about giving him a commercial name. . . . But Ahmet said, 'No, let's stick with his name.'

"I knew Ahmet and Herb from the days when we were all jazz record collectors. In fact, that's how they got into the recording business, as you indicate in your book *The World of Soul*. All of their early dates were jazz sessions until they found out that they had to pay for the grits and started making some funk.

"I was onto R & B and blues very much. On *Billboard*, before I went to the Big Three, I was the R & B expert. I wound up giving Atlantic terrific reviews. I guess I had a prevision of things to come! No, speaking seriously, I loved their records. And, of course, being a record reviewer, I kept thinking I could make better records—until I got into the studio and found out what it was all about.

"During the first year, I cut Ruth Brown, the Clovers, Joe Turner, and the Drifters with Clyde. In those years, a top R & B record could go to four hundred thousand. Sales were localized in ghetto markets. There was no white sale, and no white radio play. The great thing was that we had a terrific releasing pattern. We put out four records every three weeks. One release would include Ruth Brown, the Drifters, Chuck Willis, and Ray Charles.

Then, we'd put out Ivory Joe Hunter, the Clovers, LaVern Baker, and Chuck. Every one would rack up a sale of one hundred thousand. We never cared about a white market. We didn't look for it. . . .

"At some point, we became aware that southern whites were buying our records, white kids in high school and college. This happened long before the kids in the North began to dig R & B. A kid like Presley was picking up on R & B long before the other kids around him—listening to and singing Joe Turner songs.

"The southern market opened with kids at the University of Virginia and young people all through the Carolinas on the sea-coast. In May or June we always came out with what was known as a 'beach record.' It would be a hit in the pavilions—the bathing places—all through the Carolinas. We never missed.

"We know today that people like Elvis Presley, and more recently Delaney and Bonnie, were brought up in a southern family culture. It was neither black nor white. It was southern proletarian, southern agrarian, and these people—truck drivers, farm hands—worked together. Their churches were very much alike. A white Baptist church had the same screaming and carrying on as a black Baptist church—the euphoria, speaking in tongues, the falling down, rigidity, tambourines, responses, and the minister blues-talking. People can hate each other's guts even though they come from a common culture—and that's the way it was in the South. That's why I believe that the true exponents of white soul music, with some rare exceptions like Eric Clapton and Joe Cocker, come from below the Potomac.

"I don't think that Sam Phillips of Sun Records in Memphis was looking for white sales or sensed that he might get them when he cut Arthur Crudup and those other guys, and sold the masters to Chess and RCA. . . . He was cutting something he heard in these guys. It was not a teleological approach. It was ecological. He felt that they were getting at something that was not being cut in Nashville. What the Presley kid and Johnny Cash and Roy Orbison were doing, was non-Nashville country. And to this day I love country music that does not have a commercial stamp, that is not manicured. Just like I can't stand Broadway records or Hollywood records. Phillips heard something that was raw but it was new. It was a part of southern culture where black and white culture overlapped and joined."

10

BLUES WITH
A BEAT

Early in '55 I tried to interest an R & B record producer in a singing group I had discovered. When I phoned to set up an audition, his first question was: "Do they dance?"

"I'm calling about a singing group with an unusual sound," I said.

"If they can't dance," he said, "their sound won't interest me."

"Look," I said, not without irritation, "I'm calling about voices and you're talking about feet."

"I sure am," he said, "Unless a singer's feet dance, he can't sing—for my market anyway. Next time your group rehearses, watch their feet and call me back if they can dance."

The R & B producer was getting at something that eluded Stan Freberg and that some adults still do not understand. R & B is vocal music, as is R 'n' R, but it's vocal music to *dance to*—and the rhythm of the words is more important than meaning, if a choice has to be made. (Ideally, meaning should not be sacrificed.) The continuing friction between generations over rock is, among other things, a conflict of two traditions of song.

In a lecture I have given at a number of universities, I hold up several photographs. One depicts Sinatra singing as he sits relaxed on a high stool, and another, as he stands at a music stand, hands in pockets. In a third photo, we see Tom Jones, legs astride, knees bent, arms raised as if he were running, or warding off a blow. Sinatra represents, as did Como and Cole, the internalized crooning or concert tradition of song in which loveliness of sound and clarity of diction are the desiderata. There is almost no movement of body, limited hand motions, and a reliance on facial expressions. Interpretation and communication are the end, although a singer like Sinatra achieves involvement as well.

Tom Jones works in a contrasting, externalized tradition in which excitement and vitality count. He is less concerned with intelligibility than with rhythmic pulse and drive. The singer is music in motion.

Obviously, not all white singers have been static performers. Back in the days of vaudeville, Al Jolson and Eddie Cantor were movers. But it is, perhaps, no accident that both worked in black-face and were schooled in the minstrel-show tradition. The belters of the early '50s were also white. And they, too, derived their muscular style from black singers, most immediately from rhythm and blues.

In its issue of April 24, 1954, *Billboard* headlined a change that was beginning to sweep through pop: "TEEN-AGERS DEMAND/ MUSIC WITH A BEAT/ SPUR RHYTHM-AND-BLUES." "The teen-age tide," it wrote, "has swept down the old barriers, which kept music restricted to a segment of the population. . . . The present generation satisfies its hunger for 'music with a beat' in the Earl Bostic, Buddy Johnson, Tiny Bradshaw bands, or uses the rhythmically pronounced recordings of The Clovers, Ruth Brown, and others as its dance music." California juke-box operators report that wherever teen-agers congregate, "popular records take a secondary position to R & B."

There was reason to believe that teen-age boredom with pop manifested itself earlier, possibly as early '48–'49. About two years after *Billboard* began publishing a Race chart (1946), crying blues-man Roy Brown wrote and recorded "Good Rockin' Tonight," a song that became a hit for Wynonie "Blues" Harris on King Records. Both Presley and Buddy Holly later recorded the tune, suggesting that they knew it in their formative years—also that southern, white youngsters were able to vault the social prejudices of their elders before their northern and eastern compeers.

The big daddy of the dynamic tradition was Louis Jordan, who embraced many styles of black music, and influenced white rocka-billies like Bill Haley and black influentials like B. B. King and Chuck Berry. Originally a bluesman of Brinkley, Arkansas (near Memphis, Tennessee) and later a jazz saxist-vocalist with the bands of Chick Webb and Earl Hines, Jordan sold over a million copies of breakable 78s in a period when the black market was small. As they bought the Ink Spots and Mills Brothers, so white listeners helped make Gold Records in 1945 of "Choo, Choo, Ch'Boogie" and "Caldonia (What Makes Your Poor Head So Hard)." Jordan's talents as a blues comic and lyricist, enhanced by his clear diction, gave him strong, white appeal. So did his good-humored, jive portrayals of Negro life in songs like "Ain't Nobody Here But Us Chickens," "Reet, Petite and Gone," and "Saturday Night Fish Fry," all of which inescapably fed white feelings of superiority.

But "Fish Fry" was No. 1 on R & B charts in 1949–50, indicating that black people also "bought" Jordan and his Tympani Five. And well they should have since he was no Uncle Tom but simply dealt with the ghetto world he knew. "Saturday Night Fish Fry" carried local color and realism to the edge of protest. Though he was simply having a good time, police raided the fish fry, beat him up, and trundled him off to a "rotten jail." Jordan was more amused than bitter. And this Tympani Five, jumping to a great boogie beat, filled you with the joy and pleasure of a "Saturday Night Fish Fry" in a triumph of entertainment.

The year 1950 marked the high point of Jordan's record career as well as his Decca association. In the following year, he sold only moderately well on "Teardrops from My Eyes," a No. 1 R & B hit for Ruth Brown. By '54 he had moved to a West Coast independent label. "Mr. Jordan's in Town!" Aladdin shouted in large, full-page ads. But "Dad Gum Ya Hide, Boy" b/w "Whiskey, Do Your Stuff" failed to attract record buyers. The country was then just months away from the Supreme Court's ruling against segregated schools. Jordan's feeling for local color apparently was out of joint with the times. But this was not to gainsay his pioneer role as the father of rhythm and blues.

Bluesman Aaron "T-Bone" Walker, a pioneer in the use of the electric guitar and its exploitation as an erotic prop (à la Jimi Hendrix), felt that Jordan played "good blues and sang them like they were originally sung, too." And Chuck Berry paid him the supreme compliment: "If I had one artist to listen to through eternity, it would be Nat Cole. And if I had to work through Eternity, it would be Louis Jordan. I identify myself with him more than with any other artist . . ."

Jordan was on a major record label (Decca)—and Bill Haley went to Decca after making his mark on a small Philly label. But the R & B tradition that reshaped the character of pop developed through and was nurtured by numerous small independents. A few of these like Apollo Records in Harlem and Savoy in Newark started in the early years of World War II when a shortage (and rationing) of shellac prompted the majors to slough off fringe recording. But the rise of indie labels came with the end of the war: in 1945, National in New York, King in Cincinnati, Aladdin, Modern, and Specialty in Los Angeles; in 1947, Chess in Chicago and Imperial in L.A.; in 1948, Atlantic and Jubilee in New York;

and in 1949, Peacock in Houston. Between '52 and '55, when the majors trooped once again into the field, a dozen indies of some significance sprang up, with the most important, Sun Records, emerging in Memphis in 1953.

AHMET ERTEGUN INTERVIEW

Founder of Atlantic Records with Herb Abramson, Ahmet Ertegun remains today at the helm of the company and is an executive of Warner Communications, the present owners of Atlantic. Of the beginnings of the company for which Warner Brothers–Seven Arts paid $15 million, Ertegun had the following to say:

"We came to Washington, D.C., from Turkey via several European countries when my father was appointed Ambassador to the United States. After our family returned, my brother and I remained here. Nesuhi taught courses at UCLA in folk and jazz, and I went to Georgetown University in Washington, studying for my Ph.D. But I used to hang around a record shop at Seventh and T streets, about a block away from the Howard Theatre, the well-known Negro vaudeville house.

"I dug Dusty Fletcher and Pigmeat Markham, two great black was one of Dusty's famous skits. Herb Abramson, my partner when we started Atlantic, was recording director of National Records. He recorded Dusty doing *Richard*. (Weren't you working with the firm that published it, Arnold, and didn't you do an article for *The New York Times* on *Richard*?) I think it was in '47, the year we incorporated Atlantic. There were *Richard* records by Jack McVea on Black & White, Count Basie, and Louis Jordan.

"The Quality Music Shop, on Seventh and T, was owned by Max Silverman. He, I, and Lionel Hampton used to go out together after he closed the store. At the beginning of the war, there were many after-hour joints. Hampton was always talking about our starting a record company. I was interested but only in a company that made jazz and blues records, pure jazz. But I didn't know how to go about it. Hanging around Silverman's shop, I did learn what people were buying.

"I was then doing studies in the beginnings of jazz. And I became involved in the 'moldy fig' syndrome, digging for music that was played way back. I went down to New Orleans to see Monk Hazel, who had played cornet and drums with Emmett Hardy (Hardy was supposed to be Bix Beiderbecke's teacher). Went searching for Edison rolls that Hardy was said to have made so I would know how he sounded. Monk Hazel would say: 'he played something like this, and he'd beat the drums with his feet and one hand, and \.ith the other, finger the horn. He really could wail!'

"I wanted to know what Freddie Keppard sounded like and Buddy Bolden. And then we helped bring Bunk Johnson, who played with Bolden, out of retirement. At the same time, my brother reconstituted Kid Ory's band. He had a label in California called Jazzman, later changed to Crescent Records. He put together bands that had been out of action for twenty years and made some historic records. All our activity was to find these retired jazzmen and put them back in action. We did the research and we dug the music.

"But hanging around Max Silverman's store, I realized that most people were not interested in this early jazz. They were interested in modern, pseudojazz, sweet jazz, like Don Byas, Erroll Garner—good artists but with a pop feel. Like Helen Humes and her 'Be-baba-leba,' a jump blues she recorded on Aladdin, and those early disks by Apollo and Rainbow records.

"A whole new thing was developing in my consciousness. Like R & B was Big Maceo, Washboard Sam, and Leroy Carr. They were my favorite blues singers. This new thing was something else—a very young, hip approach to blues played by the pioneers, but more sophisticated and swinging. And I began to dig them as out-of-sight performers.

"I said 'Hey,' like when I heard Louis Jordan's novelties. They were like Fats Waller and they had a lot of musical value, too. They were groovy tunes and what the people were buying. People loved them and Nat "King" Cole whose singing had an R & B sensitivity. When I heard Charles Brown doing 'Drifting Blues,' I knew I was home again. Charles Brown and Amos Milburn impressed me as great R & B artists but also as great blues singers.

"And I thought, this is something I've got to go into because this is current music that people dig. Just as the music we were researching was great music in its time for people of that time.

"So we incorporated Atlantic Records in October 1947 with our first releases in '48. Our offices were a two-room suite in the old Jefferson Hotel on Broadway and Fifty-sixth Street, now the site of the Mony Building. We couldn't get good singers at first but we did get some good bands. We cut Joe Morris's band. Morris was a trumpet player who had been with Lionel Hampton. When he left, he took Johnny Griffin with him. Johnny was Hampton's tenor sax star, an all-time great jazz saxophonist. Morris had Matthew Gee on trombone, Philly Joe Jones on drums, Percy Heath on bass, Elmo Hope on piano, later replaced by Ray Charles—yeah, *the* Ray Charles. It was a real all-star band.

"Tiny Grimes was another great band we recorded. And both of these bands made our first hit records. Tiny made it with 'Blue Harlem,' which he previously had recorded for Blue Note. He re-recorded it for us, and he made a lot of standards. Like 'Old Black Magic,' only he did it with a stomping beat. Tiny had a quartet that made an awful lot of music. He played guitar in the tradition of Charley Christian, a little bit of blues and a lot of swing.

"We also did many jazz dates—all-stars out of Kenton's band, some progressive jazz with Boyd Raeburn, Erroll Garner, and others.

"The first hit I cut was Stick McGhee doing 'Drinking Wine, Spo-Dee-O-Dee.' It made me realize what a market there was in the blues. We sold three to four hundred thousand. And I said 'Man!'

"And so we went more into blues. We were lucky enough to sign Ruth Brown, a great, young singer who came from Virginia. Willis Conover of the Voice of America tipped me off. And so did Max Silverman, who phoned me about this cute, little chick appearing at the Crystal Caverns, an after-hours joint.

"I had been trying to get this other girl, Little Miss Cornshucks. But she would not sign up with us. We were an unknown record company. She also had difficult managers and I don't think that she ever got to make any records. She was a precursor of Dinah Washington. She and Dinah and all these girls used to sing songs like 'So Long,' 'In the Rain' and 'Evil Gal Blues.'

"Dinah was fantastic. But she was with Keynote—and not within our reach. And Little Miss Cornshucks was flipped out. She would come onstage without shoes to show that she was real down home, real country, like from the mud. She wore a patched-up dress and a big straw hat and carried a basket. She'd sing 'I'm an evil gal. . . . Don't you bother with me. . . .' And these little joints, like in southeast Washington, were real rough places and the people would tear off the roof.

"When I went to hear Ruth Brown, she was singing 'A—You're Adorable.' After doing a couple of Doris Day–type songs, she turned around and sang 'So Long.' It knocked me out. She had a sound that was unbelievable. We hit with her on her first record and she kept hitting after that.

"She became a symbol for other R & B singers. Other singers like Little Esther patterned themselves after her. Then we had the great LaVern Baker, an outstanding singer from Chicago via

Detroit. Joe Turner, who was an old favorite of mine from his Kansas City days with Bennie Moten and Count Basie, did well for us. And then Ray Charles came out of Joe Morris's band. He was under contract to a small label in California and we bought out the contract.

"That's how Atlantic got started, except that the going was not easy in the beginning. You see, radio and TV were really made for white people. They were like the rest of things in our segregated world. And it took time for us to break through.

"During the depression, when everything stopped selling, including records, R & B records were the only things that did sell. They called them race records then. Black people didn't have theatres to go to. The radio didn't interest them, if they had one. There were no big beautiful dance halls for them. Once in a while, an artist would come through and play a tobacco barn. All they could do if they worked all week and had some money left over after buying groceries, was buy a jug, a few records, and go home and have a ball. That's why the R & B business, small as it was, remained steady.

"Underlying this was the fact that some white people were buying R & B records even then. But I'd always say to disk jockeys: Just put them on your turntable; you'll see whether they like Ruth Brown or Dinah Washington. It was a picnic for the big majors: they'd copy our records, except that they'd use a white artist. And the white stations would play them while we couldn't get our records on. 'Sorry,' they'd say, 'It's too rough for us.' Or: 'Sorry, we don't program that kind of music.'

"And I'd say: But you're playing that song in your Top Twenty. It's a copy of our record. There'd be one excuse or another. But that was the way things were.

"The change came gradually. It started, oddly enough, in the South where white stations began to play R & B. Many white southerners liked R & B. As he was growing up, Elvis Presley was singing Clyde McPhatter's hits like 'Money Honey.' He didn't hear them in a publisher's office. He heard them on the radio. He wasn't the only one. Many of the people in Memphis dug R & B, and pop stations started playing it. Programers found their ratings going up because they were not only getting new listeners (black people) but more white listeners who happened to like the music. Time has been a great leveler since now all types of music can get on Top Forty stations . . ."

Basically, the growth of R & B, an urban, electrified, ensemble form of the blues, was prompted by the migration of southern blacks into the cities of the North, East, and West where wartime needs opened hitherto closed job opportunities. Along with the farm hands and laborers came black musicians and singers—Joe Turner from Kansas City, B. B. King from Mississippi via Memphis, T-Bone Walker from Texas, Muddy Waters and Howlin' Wolf from the delta country of Mississippi, etc.

Bars, honky-tonks, and clubs in the black ghettos of the big cities provided showcases for their talents. But gas rationing and other shortages, coupled with wartime affluence, created an expanding market for home entertainment. Chess Records, like Peacock Records, started as an extension, almost as a promotion medium, for entertainers appearing in clubs owned by the Chess Brothers in Chicago and Don Robey in Houston. Even black bluesmen who remained in their hometowns—Fats Domino in New Orleans and Little Richard in Macon—recorded for the new, burgeoning R & B labels, Domino for Imperial and Little Richard for Peacock and Specialty.

By the time that Muddy Waters began recording for the Chess Brothers in 1946, the black Big Bands had collapsed—along with their better-rewarded imitators like Benny Goodman and Glenn Miller—priced out of existence by postwar economics and economies. The availability of electrified instruments, with their increased volume, made the small combo a natural substitute.

Just as Sinatra and Como emerged from the Big Bands, so did Dinah Washington, Bullmoose Jackson, Joe Turner, and the rest. Vocalists and vocal groups were "in" just as in pop. Accompanied by dance combos instead of guitar and "harp," the blues turned into rhythm and blues, though the records were first known by such segregated epithets as "Sepia," "Race," and "Harlem." It was sensual, good-time music for dancing and revelry.

Even the ballads of frustrated and embittered love bounced with a resounding backbeat. It is strange that this most patent departure from pop has not been given more attention by historians. For fifty years of popular song, piano, bass, and drums played *OOM-pa, OOM-pa,* stressing the first and third beats of a measure. R & B was *oom-PA, oom-PA,* reviving the afterbeat stress of New Orleans and Dixieland jazz heard today on rock records. Rhythmically, R & B also brought back boogie and shuffle—the rolling eight-note figuration in the bass and the wailing blue notes in the melody—a sound absent from white pop since the 1930s.

In form, R & B underwent a curious transformation from the blues. Instead of maintaining the twelve-bar form and the simple three-chord progression (I,IV,V), it adopted gospel or pop structures of eight and sixteen bars. Progressions varied greatly but a *patterned bass* held the recording together. It was a carry-over of the *riff* in swing, save that the repetition of a group of notes assumed the form of a bass rhythm figure.

Two instruments became crucial in the sound of R & B. The electric guitar was comparatively new. But the hoarse, husky tenor sax was again a carry-over from swing. In-person, the tenor man heated up the joint. With his eyes shut and the veins bulging in his forehead, he grimaced and bobbed up and down like a rooster, the sweat beading his face in an unabating pour. Big Jay McNeely was among the best-known of a group of honkers and screechers that included Eddie "Lockjaw" Davis, Illinois Jacquet, and Willis "Gatortail" Jackson, who threw themselves on their backs and, kicking their feet in the air or bouncing erotically, burped one low note or screeched one high note over and over.

Can you imagine the reaction of white youngsters who came on this scene in clubs on Central Avenue in Los Angeles, the southside honky-tonks of Chicago, the ghetto bars of Memphis's Beale Street, or at Harlem's Apollo Theatre? Bop had no dance beat, pop was tame and static—and here was this raucous, driving, pulsating music! No wonder that in 1952 when disk jockey Alan Freed staged a now-famous shindig with all-black talent at the Cleveland Arena, a large percentage of the audience consisted of white teen-agers.

11

THE BACK
OF THE CHARTS

One day late in 1947, Frank Schiffman was standing outside
Harlem's Apollo Theatre, which he owned and operated, when
a dilapidated old Ford coughed its way to the lobby doors and
deposited six young blacks and a white girl. They had somehow
made it from Baltimore in the '34 wreck. The girl was Deborah
Chessler, a songwriter who managed the group, and who had
changed their name from the Vibranaires to the Orioles after the
Baltimore oriole.

As Schiffman's son Jack recalls: "Partly out of compassion (How
were they going to get back to Baltimore?) and partly out of his
showman's instinct, Dad gave them a hearing. He liked them and
hired them."

The following year, the Orioles had a modest hit on Jubilee
Records with Deborah Chessler's ballad, "It's Too Soon to Know,"
recorded also by Dinah Washington on Mercury—and revived in
1958 by Pat Boone. In '49, the Orioles were on the charts with
"Tell Me So."

The charts they made were—like Negroes in southern buses—
in the back of the trade papers. A small sector of the population
bought these records. A limited sector of music business paid attention to them. But this was the area in which a storm was
brewing that was to shake the rafters of pop. The Orioles became
more widely known in '54 when they covered a country record
of "Crying in the Chapel" and were in turn covered by the
majors. But some of the big black artists of the early '50s never
crossed into white markets.

In 1950 Joe Liggins and his Honeydrippers told the bluesy tale
of "Pink Champagne" . . . that stole his love from him. The

piano boogied into the vocal, with three saxes echoing and
answering in the call-and-response pattern of traditional blues.
The rhythm was a steady four à la the bands of the swing era. And
the unforgettable refrain "Cham-pagne! Cham-pagne! (pause)
Mellow, mellow wine. . . ."

Handsome Percy Mayfield, announcing that he didn't beg for
sympathy "just because I'm in misery" pleaded tenderly in a slow-
walking four, "Please Send Me Someone to Love." His ballad was
a remarkable combination of implicit protest and personal romanticism—a man asking for understanding among men and love
for himself. He was cool when he warned, "Hate will put the
world in a flame (what a shame)." And his vocal, close to Nat
Cole's but with more grit, was polished, the diction clear as a
flute and the feeling churchy, sung against his own upper-register,
rippling piano. (Songwriter-performer Curtis Mayfield of the
Impressions and the supersmash "Superfly" is his son.)

And then there was "The Hucklebuck"—you pushed your
partner out, hunched your back, wiggled like a snake, waddled
like a duck, and that's the way you did the Hucklebuck. Everyone
tried to compete with Roy Milton and his Solid Senders—Paul
Williams on Savoy, Lucky Millinder on RCA Victor, and Jimmy
Liggins and his Drops of Joy with a takeoff titled "Shuffleshuck."
With Milton's saxes wailing, the piano hammering bluesy triplets,
and the electric guitar booging, the Hucklebuck moved from
black clubs to white dancers.

Nineteen fifty was the year that a teen-ager named Little Esther
made her debut with Johnny Otis and achieved three No. 1's in
succession: "Cupid's Boogie," "Double Crossing Blues," and "Mis-
trustin' Blues." There were other records after that, then silence.
After a time, Little Esther returned as Esther Phillips. But it was
not until 1973 that she scored a Grammy nomination with her
album *From a Whisper to a Scream* and won hyperbolic plaudits
like Leonard Feather's: "Esther Phillips is the greatest, most
powerful individual feminine voice to come down the pike since
Billie Holiday."

Perhaps the most notable career that had its beginnings in '50
was that of a New Orleans pianist-singer whose first disk had
autobiographical overtones. It was called "Fat Man." Writing his
own songs and playing a toe-tapping, boogie piano, Antoine
"Fats" Domino was one of the first R & B artists to cross over in
'55. But from '50 on, he was seldom without an R & B chartmaker, and in '53 was represented by "Goin' to the River," "Please
Don't Leave Me," and "Something's Wrong." By the time he

made the transition to rock 'n' roll, he modified an early style that recalled country-blues singer Blind Lemon Jefferson in its high-pitched nasality. But he retained the Cajun accent and an almost childlike sound.

Ivory Joe Hunter was another black performer-writer who made his mark on wax in the '50s, actually from 1948 on. Although the big Texan with the owl eyes and Cheshire-cat smile racked up three chartmakers in '49, it was in 1950 that he created the big songs of his career, "I Need You So" and "I Almost Lost My Mind." Both figured in the crossover pattern of early rock 'n' roll. Later he wrote and recorded "Since I Met You Baby," a Gold Record in 1956. Both in his vocal and writing style, Ivory Joe mixed pop, blues, and spirituals in a smooth blend. Despite a successful recording career that embraced releases on King, MGM, and finally Atlantic, his creativity as a songwriter really outstripped his impact and longevity as a vocalist.

Debuting in '49 with "So Long," sloe-eyed Ruth Brown began cutting across color lines early in the growth of Atlantic Records. "Teardrops from My Eyes" made it to the top of R & B charts in '50, as did"Five-Ten-Fifteen Hours" in '52 and "(Mama) He Treats Your Daughter Mean" with its tempered screech in '53. Miss Brown made only limited use of black mannerisms, so that the tailored accompaniment and her own rhythmic drive offered white listeners easy access to black music. They came and were conquered even though the pop charts gave no evidence.

In "Five-Ten-Fifteen Hours" love assumed a very physical shape as Ruth Brown asked for just so many hours to prove her feelings. It was No. 1 for the Virginia miss with a print-out diction and a pre-Rosemary Clooney, black sound. An appealing seductiveness that Sinatra later achieved at the end of "Strangers in the Night" with a series of nonsense syllables, Ruth Brown added with a mildly-husky, gently-panting "hoo-yeah . . . hoo-yeah . . ." as the record ended.

Nineteen fifty saw the birth of one of the great standards of R & B. "Every Day I Have the Blues" was written by Peter Chatman of Memphis, Tennessee, who recorded as Memphis Slim and whose long list of vocal/piano disks remained blues oriented. But it was first cut by Lowell Fulson, a crying bluesman of Oklahoma. In '52 it was a hit for big Joe Williams on Checker and in '55 for Count Basie on Clef. By then it had been recorded by B. B. King who has used it as his theme up to the present.

In 1950 Broadcast Music, Inc., (BMI) the performing-rights organization launched by broadcasters to compete with ASCAP, celebrated its tenth anniversary. Initially locked out of pop, it spent those early years developing catalog in two areas neglected by ASCAP with its Broadway–Hollywood–Tin Pan Alley orientation. BMI may quite properly take credit for giving *blues* and *country* songwriters an outlet and larger rewards for their creativity, and for opening the mainstream to these two regional currents. As it contributed to the development of publishing (and recording) enterprise outside the New York–Chicago–Hollywood axis, it helped erode the foundations of Tin Pan Alley as the capital of pop.

The Clovers and A. Nugetre

Nineteen fifty-one brought onto the music scene one of R & B's giant groups and the first of Atlantic Records' three chartmaking vocal groups. "Ooh-DIDDly-Do Dah-Do Dey-ey . . . Ooh-DIDDly-Do Dah-Do-Dey-ey . . ." the Clovers sang on their first hit, "Don't You Know I Love You." The lead cat was cool but he said expansive things like "You're my jail, you're my prayer, you're my all in all . . ." The words and music were by A. Nugetre—Ertegun spelled backwards—who produced the disk with Herb Abramson. The recording was crude but it had an insistent, modified boogie beat to which even a lame kid could dance.

On "Fool, Fool, Fool," another Nugetre song cut in July of '51, the Clovers had grown so tall it was easy to see why they became the most influential of the early '50s groups. John (Buddy) Bailey now sang lead with impact and intensity, and the others supported him with harmonious conviction. The voices had an appealing instrumental quality as the bass, deep and horny, opened with a "do-do-do . . . Do-Do" and the others answered with a "da . . . ah-di-dey-do" in a rhythmic, twelve-bar blues. The lyric possessed a gentle earthiness: "The first time you walked down the street, I said there goes my meat . . ."

By early '52 the Clovers were on Rudolph Toombs' funky tale of "One Mint Julep" and white combos were rushing out covers —Buddy Morrow on RCA and Louis Prima on Columbia. But the Clovers' influence was much wider, turning black groups away from the polished, pop-oriented approach of the Ink Spots and Mills Brothers toward gutsy, gospel-styled R & B. They were able to maintain their priority through the '50s with a succession of best sellers, moved onto pop charts in '55 with "Love, Love, Love," and scored as late as '59 with Leiber and Stoller's blues-humored "Love Potion Number Nine."

The Dominoes, Earl Bostic, and Jackie Brenston

Another breakout group of '51 is remembered both for its best sellers as well as the important soloists that came out of it. Billy Ward and the Dominoes was responsible for one of the most controversial hits of the year in the erotic "Sixty Minute Man," coauthored by Ward. Federal Records, a King subsidiary, claimed a sale of over two million disks. With Clyde McPhatter singing lead, and arrangements and songs by Ward, the group was on the charts steadily during '51 and '52, producing among other hits, the party-spirited, hand-clapping, shuffle-gaited "Have Mercy Baby." Although Jackie Wilson succeeded McPhatter when he left to form the Drifters, something went out of the Dominoes and their popularity waned.

After-hours dancing in a dimly lit bar was the mood created by Earl Bostic and his searing, vibrant tenor sax on "Flamingo," "Smoke Gets in Your Eyes," and other pop standards. Swinging to a danceable four and the romantic overtones of a vibraharp, he was more bluesy and funky than jazzy. He improvised attractively without straying too far from the melody and without sacrificing mood to technique.

"Rocket 88" was a best-selling instrumental of another genre. A fast boogie, it featured the ballsy baritone sax of Jackie Brenston, a singing sideman who had been recording with Ike Turner's Kings of Rhythm. Brenston's Chess disk not only went to No. 1 on R & B charts but was covered that year (1951) by Bill Haley on Essex, who imitated Jackie's light-shout style.

Haley's cover was a signpost into the future, though no one paid any more mind to it than to the strange phenomenon of seeing Johnnie Ray's disk of "Cry" climb to No. 1 on R & B charts.

Two Unlucky Stars

John Marshall Alexander, better known as Johnny Ace, entered the lists in '52 along with Chuck Willis. Soulful singers, both were dead before the end of the decade and both had their biggest hits posthumously.

Ace played the piano in B. B. King's Beale Streeters, a Memphis band. When Don Robey of Houston added Duke Records to his Peacock label, Johnny Ace was part of the roster he acquired. That same year (1952), "My Song" made black listeners aware of a new talent. It sounded and still sounds like a home recording. But that did not dim the appeal of Ace's young, plaintive voice. The following year yielded two chartmakers for Johnny, "Saving My Love for You" and a No. 1 blues ballad, "The Clock."

Christmas eve of '54 brought senseless tragedy. Sitting in his dressing room in the Houston City Auditorium as a sellout crowd awaited his appearance, Ace whiled away the time toying with a revolver. Reportedly to impress a girl, he began playing Russian Roulette and shot himself to death. "Pledging My Love," released at about the same time, became a posthumous Triple Crown in *Billboard's* charts. He was just twenty-five.

Chuck Willis, a discovery of "Daddy" Zenas Sears of WAOK in Atlanta, was unquestionably the greater talent of the two, a sensitive songwriter as well as an expressive vocalist. The autobiographical "My Story" on Okeh was his introduction to record buyers in '52. It was followed by a series of soft, soulful ballads and recordings that gained Willis a small following but no great renown. It was only after the rock 'n' rollers broke down segregation barriers and Willis moved to Atlantic Records that he came through with "It's Too Late," a moderate hit of 1956. His succeeding two years were good years, filled with numerous personal appearances and chart songs. But they were all too short. When he died in April 1958, he was just thirty. His biggest record came posthumously when "What Am I Living For" b/w "Hang Up My Rock and Roll Shoes" finished as the No. 1 R & B hit of the year.

Three Pioneers

Howlin' Wolf grew up on a Mississippi cotton plantation, on several in fact. Born in 1910 at West Point, near Tupelo, Mississippi, he moved in his teens to Ruteville in the Delta where his parents worked on Young and Mara's plantation.

Country bluesman Charlie Patton lived on Dockey's plantation, near Young and Mara's. "He done taught me," says Howlin' Wolf, who was christened Chester Burnett. "He showed me things on the guitar. . . . At night after I'd get off work, I'd go and hang around. . . . I got the most from Charlie Patton and Lemon Jefferson—from his records. . . . What I liked about Lemon's music was that he made a clear chord."

What Howlin' Wolf provides is a most essential link between the original influentials of country blues and urban rhythm and blues, of which he and Muddy Waters became the two key figures in postwar Chicago. Long before he made his first record in '51, he played (between farm chores) with famous Robert Johnson and the second Sonny Boy Williamson, whose sister he married in the 1930s and from whom he learned the harmonica.

Wolf was living in Memphis when he recorded "Moanin' at Midnight" and "How Many More Years" in '51. Ike Turner, who was a scout for RPM Records of Los Angeles and Sun in Memphis, arranged for the date, and Sun arranged for Chess Records of Chicago to release the sides. They are quite primitive, so primitive it is easy to understand why Chester Burnett became known as Howlin' Wolf. Over a one- or two-bar riff, repeated hypnotically from the beginning to the end of the record, the Wolf growls and moans inchoate lyrics.

"How Many More Years" actually made R & B charts in '51. But in these sides and in "Smokestack Lightnin'," "Killing Floor," and "Sitting on Top of the World," later disks, Howlin' Wolf achieves a sound and a beat that exerted tremendous influence on Chicago musicians—he played in many of the clubs where Muddy Waters performed—and on the first wave of British rockers, including the Beatles and the Stones. To youngsters, bored by the tired sound of pop music, Wolf had a rugged vigor and vitality that was exciting.

In 1952 Fats Domino was not nearly as hot as he soon became. But Art Rupe, head of L.A.'s Specialty Records, was so flipped over his sound that he went to New Orleans looking for someone like him. In the waning moments of a week of auditions, Rupe came upon a singer whose first record sold white as well as black. Southern record dealers reported that white matrons would come into their stores asking for "Lawdy Miss Clawdy"—er, for their colored maid. Naturally, Rupe would not allow anyone to back Lloyd Price in his first outing except Dave Bartholomew, Fats Domino's discoverer, collaborator, and bandleader. If the pianist on the disk is not Fats, then it is someone who imitated him unmistakably. When Price again hit the charts, in '59, he had made the transition from R & B to rock 'n' roll.

The most important bluesman who came to the fore in '52 was Riley B. King, originally a Mississippi cotton picker, later a Memphis disk jockey, whence he acquired the cognomen Blues Boy that led to his being known as B. B. King. Wedded to country blues and an exponent of Delta-blues style, he displayed an unusual ability to take songs associated with other artists and make them his own—"Sweet Sixteen" of Joe Turner and "Everyday I Have the Blues" of Joe Williams. He was not a soft wailer in the Charles Brown tradition or a raucous shouter in a Leadbelly vein. Intensity was his earmark, gospel intensity. Claiming that he could not sing and play at the same time, he used his electric guitar—he called it Lucille—as a responsive voice, playing bluesy, single-string melodies à la Charley Christian or T-Bone Walker.

"Three O'Clock Blues," recorded by Lowell Fulson in '48–'49, was his first chartmaker, followed almost immediately by "You Know I Love You." From '52 on, he wrote and recorded steadily. It was not until after the Beatles that he was able to reach outside the so-called "chitlin' circuit" and a dedicated black following. The latter was agrarian and proletarian, and did not even include Negro college students. B. B. King had to be accepted on his terms. Now known worldwide as the Boss of the Blues and the King of the Blues, King has entrée to the country's glamour showrooms.

B. B. KING INTERVIEW

"My work at radio station WDIA in Memphis started in 1948," he told me during an interview at the Las Vegas Hilton. "It continued until the last of 1952, live every day with a trio plus spinning records for two hours. The live portion was every day, including Saturday, from 12:15 to 12:30 P.M. and I played records from 1:00 P.M. to 1:55 and again from 3:00 P.M. to 3:55. After 1952 I went on the road. Well, I really had been making personals before that, but I would go only so far so that I could return for my next show. I was off on Sunday.

"Although I was known as the Beale Street Blues Boy. I wasn't restricted to playing any particular type of music, as some disk jockeys are today. They left it up to me to play whatever I thought was good. Naturally, I played blues and rhythm-and-blues artists like Lloyd Price, Fats Domino, Little Richard. But I also played Nat King Cole's 'My Mother Told Me There Would Be Days Like This,' 'Now He Tells Me,' and 'Route 66'; Frank Sinatra's 'I'm Walking Behind You,' and 'Lean Baby.' I spun the records of Dinah Washington and Louis Jordan. Why, I even played Vaughn Monroe's 'Ghost Riders in the Sky,' Bing Crosby's 'That Lucky Old Sun,' Louis Armstrong's 'Blueberry Hill,' and many Frankie Laine records.

"One artist I hardly ever played was B. B. King. I had to have a letter or a card requesting a particular song. Didn't want people ever to think I was playing B. B. King just because they were my own records. When I started spinning, my audience was my age or older. It was not the young people that dug me. I tried to play the most soulful things—we didn't use that word then—things that had the most feeling to me as a blues musician. I could feel bluesy things, regardless of whether it was jazz, pop, or rock 'n' roll.

"When I left WDIA, Rufus Thomas took over my show. It's a funny thing about that. Rufus helped me get into show business. They used to have an Amateur Night at the Palace Theatre in Memphis. It started in the '40s and was still going in the '50s. In 1948 I would come down to catch Rufus and Bones, a dance team. Al Jackson, the bass player, had the big band there. It was the best band in Memphis. Al Jackson, Jr., his son, drums today with Booker T and the MGs.

"I had a day job and Rufus did, too. I was working at the Newberry Equipment Company and he was employed at the Memphis Luggage factory. If I was able to go onstage at the Amateur Show, I would get a dollar. And that dollar was carfare for quite a few days. So I'd fight to get on. And Rufus, who was the emcee, would always help me.

"In the '50s I had two shows on WDIA. One was called 'Sepia Swing Club' and the other, 'Heebie Jeebies.' When I left, Rufus took over the 'Sepia Swing Club' and he kept it until a few years ago.

"As for Sonny Boy Williamson, he was indirectly responsible for my going with WDIA. I had been listening to Sonny Boy for years when I was on the plantation in Mississippi. He was like a household word and everybody would try to leave the field and get into the main house to hear him.

"When I came to Memphis to live—this was my second trip from Mississippi—Sonny Boy was at Station KWEM in West Memphis. I asked whether I could play a number on his show. He asked to hear me play, liked what he heard, and agreed to let me play 'just one tune, just one.'

"As fate would have it, he had two jobs that night. One paid $12 and the other, out of the city, $100 or $150. So he called the lady for whom he had been playing the $12 job, a Miss Annie who owned the Sixteenth Street Grill in Memphis. She had heard the program for he advertised the Grill. In fact, it was one of the functions of having your own radio program to talk up the place where you played. She agreed to let me substitute. He told me: 'You better play good, boy, because if you don't, you'll have to answer to me.' I'll never forget that. And that was the first time I played a professional job in the Memphis area.

"I liked it very much because it was my job to entertain the ladies while the fellers went in the back and played cards. [Laughing.] When Miss Annie paid me, she told me that if I would get on the radio as Sonny Boy was, she would give me $12.00 a night plus my room and board and a day off. Man, that was like going to Disneyland. I had been pickin' cotton for 35 cents a hundred, choppin' cotton for $1.50 a day, driving tractors for $2.50 a day. It was unbelievable!

'A little while later, I learned that a black-operated station was starting. WDIA had one black disk jockey, Prof. Nat D. Williams—Nat Dee, as we called him. After I paid for the bus trip from West Memphis to Memphis, I didn't have any money for the ride from the bus depot to the radio station. And I had to walk, guitar on my head, from like No. 1 to the 2700 block. Never forget the station's address: 2724. As fate would have it, it started to rain. But I made it.

'The station had a big picture window on the street, and I could see Nat Dee sitting behind the microphone. I knocked on the window. When he came to the door, I told him I wanted to make a record and play on the radio. He said that he couldn't help with the record. But he was nice enough to call the general manager of the station, a Mr. Ferguson, who was the manager of a station down in Mississippi where I had sung spirituals in a quartet. Mr. Ferguson remembered me and they put me on the air that very day for ten minutes, just me and my guitar. No pay, of course. After that I was on the air regularly and able to advertise the place where I played, the Sixteenth Street Grill.

'I did cut four sides just about this time. They were my very first recordings. And I always said that I put that Bullet label, as it was called, out of business. It did go out of business right after that. The four sides were actually recorded in the studio of Station WDIA.

'When one of the disk jockeys left the station shortly after that, Mr. Ferguson had me take over the show—which I never did learn to talk and still can't today. The general manager said there was no need to try to change B. B. to talk properly because he would never make it. [Chuckling.] But the people trusted me like they did Arthur Godfrey. I spoke what I believed and I would say it as I really felt it. And I became a very popular disk jockey in Memphis.

"Anyway blues and proper English don't go together. That's why some white people can't sing the blues. They don't know the humiliation or the hurt and pride of being black. So they can't give it the rawness, the soul, and the worry. Like the song says, 'Worry, worry, worry, worry's all I can do . . .'

"In late '49 I got a contract to record with RPM, a new label started by Modern Records. Dealt with Jules Bihari, then with Sol Bihari, and later with Joe Bihari. I was one of the first artists on RPM. We made three or four records that did very well in

Memphis and cities nearby, things like 'Woke Up This Morning,' 'B. B.'s Blues,' 'B. B.'s Boogie,' and some songs by Tampa Red and the older Sonny Boy Williamson. Phineas Newborn, who became the well-known jazz pianist, was on these dates, also on the very first sides I made for Bullet. He was under age. Because of my good standing in the local, I was able to get permission to use him.

"In addition to Phineas, I had his brother Calvin on guitar, his father on drums, Ben Branch on tenor sax, his brother Thomas on trumpet, and a guy called Tough Green on bass. It was a pretty big group. I always did like large groups because when you sang spirituals—my first experience with music—you had a chorus behind you. If you had many horns, that was like a chorus.

"Late in '49, around Christmastime, we made one of Lowell Fulson's tunes, 'Three O'Clock in the Morning.' And that was my first hit record—stayed on the R & B hit parade for about eighteen weeks. No. 1 most of the time. Didn't move over to the pop charts, although people in the pop field were aware of the record.

"After that we had one or two big records every year of the 1950s. 'You Know I Love You' was the biggest of them all, a blues ballad. 'Please Love Me' had a Latin feel. When I first started, boogie-woogie was the thing. Later on, mambos and calypso began to catch. 'Woke Up This Morning' has a calypso feel.

'Every Day I Have the Blues' was recorded late in '54. I heard Memphis Slim do it first. I liked it, but it didn't intrigue me. Later on, Lowell Fulson had a hit on it. I was spinning records then. But then I heard big Joe Williams, not with Basie, but with a Chicago band. Most people don't know that Joe recorded 'Every Day' for the first time with King Kolax. That was the record that made me want to cut it. So I went to an arranger who worked with the Bihari brothers, Maxwell Davis. He was a fine sax player and a great arranger. We did it and had a hit in '55. But then Joe Williams did it with Basie and it was bye-bye to my record. [Laughing.]

"Later, I myself recorded it with Basie. Really. As a matter of fact, I did sides with Dorsey and Ellington. The Biharis had bought the rights to a group of masters. Instead of calling in another singer, they had me dub in vocals on the band tracks. In fact, we did 'Yes, Indeed' with Tommy Dorsey. I used to keep copies of these records under lock and key—because people would never believe that B. B. King had recorded with Ellington, Basie, and Dorsey.

"I got the idea for 'Sweet Little Angel' from Robert Night-

hawk's 'Sweet Black Angel,' though I later discovered that the song
had been recorded by someone before Nighthawk. At the time
'black' was not a popular word, as it is now. Instead of using the
old title, I changed it to 'Sweet Little Angel'—and that was a
pretty big record for me.

"I know that some people think of 'Sweet Little Angel' as my
identifying song. It does play a big part. But to me, not as big as
'Sweet Sixteen' and 'Three O'clock Blues.' 'Sixteen' was Joe
Turner's tune. I recorded it in '58. But I had been hearing it
before then. I found that certain artists like Louis Jordan, Joe
Turner, Charles Brown—when they finished with a song, it's not
wise to come up behind them until people have practically forgotten their treatment. And so when I liked a song, I'd hide it and
keep it until I felt that the momentum had died on theirs.

"With the exception of Louis Jordan, the '50s audience of these
artists was black. Late in the '50s, big Joe Turner became a big
pop star with the white teen-agers. This was when he did 'Flip,
Flop and Fly' and 'Shake, Rattle and Roll.' Louis Jordan had
been very big prior to that and was still popular in the '50s. But
Memphis, which was very segregated, if Louis came to town, they
would have two shows, one for white and one for black folks, an
early show for whites and a late one for blacks. This enabled
artists to have somewhat of a double engagement. Louis Jordan
always had to do this because he had a lot of white fans.

"A lot of my early work was influenced by Jordan. Even today
it still is. I have tapes here of his recordings and I'm just about to
do another of his tunes, which I've renovated. His was called
'Jordan for President' and mine's gonna be 'B. B. for President,'
which is his original idea. Jordan should have made it bigger
than he did. Later, when Bill Haley came along, Decca had him
and they had no need to revive Jordan, who was doing what
Haley did long, long before Haley.

"During the '50s my audience was black—99.5 percent black
and that's pretty black. But Fats Domino did break through into
white clubs. Then Lloyd Price and Little Richard began to nibble
at it. But then came Chuck Berry, and he became a big standard
with white people.

"When Lloyd Price was doing 'Lawdy Miss Clawdy,' he was still
in the circle that I was in. But when he did 'Personality' and
'I'm Gonna Get Married,' then he became a white attraction.
Same with Little Richard when he did that movie *The Girl
Can't Help It* with Marilyn Monroe, Edmund O'Brien, and Tom
Ewell. That was the first film I can remember that was accepted
as an A1 movie featuring blacks. It had Fats Domino, Little
Richard, Bill Haley, and several other blacks, and presented them

in a beautiful way. I mean with a lot of class. That really made Little Richard a star.

"During the '50s, I was playing all small clubs. Once in a while, maybe an armory where they would have a Saturday night dance. But no name clubs. Not until the late '50s did we play the 20 Grand in Detroit or Roberts in Chicago where Dinah Washington and the giants of jazz usually appeared. That was because I had a big band then and we were playing quite a number of Basie arrangements. People would comment: 'Sounds like Basie.' And I'd almost bust the buttons off my shirt, I was so proud.

"I think this big band was a kind of smart thing I did, if I ever did anything that was smart. Rock 'n' roll had come in at the time and people weren't digging the blues singers so much. But by having a big band, I was able to play behind many of the rock stars like Jackie Wilson, Sam Cooke, and others. I could go into jazz clubs with the sound. The band would play a set and then I would come on as featured guitarist with my group.

"I always had problems playing and singing simultaneously. I've got stupid fingers and funny ears. They never worked at the same time—and still don't. So I either sing and play between breaths, or play and sing later. Hampton Reese was one of my arrangers and so was Maxwell Davis. Members of the band also wrote.

"The first club that represented a turnaround for me was the Fillmore West after Bill Graham began running it. Before Graham, we played the Fillmore, as it was called, many, many times. Then the audience was 95 percent black. I mean from '57 through '64 or '65. In 1968 when we got there, I saw the change. There were kids everywhere but all of them white, long-haired, white kids. I sung and played, I guess, like I never did before—but only my things: 'Every Day I Have the Blues,' which is my theme song, 'How Blue Can You Get,' 'Sweet Sixteen,' 'Sweet Little Angel'—just my regular things. And were they excited!

"I never used a rhythm guitar, right from the beginning of my career until just about a year ago. I never cared too much about having a second guitar that would overshadow me. The first guitarist I had was Robert Junior Lockwood, who is still my dear friend and taught me a lot about the instrument. And now I have Milton Harper. They each remind me of the other because they're superb rhythm guitarists and they never interfere with me. Just play underneath and give me a smooth pattern.

"In 1956 I did 342 one-nighters. So I was constantly working. Still do about 300 dates a year. But it was at Bill Graham's that I noticed the changeover.

As I left his suite in the Las Vegas Hilton, I heard him flip on the tape recorder into which he had been dictating his book on

Blues Guitar and as I walked slowly down the heavily carpeted hall, I could hear the high-pitched cry and whine of Lucille, his guitar.

End

R & B Goes to Church

Gospel excitement and intensity became the key to black artistry in '53. By then Clyde McPhatter had left the Dominoes and was working with a new group that became the sensationally successful and long-lived Drifters. The son of a Baptist preacher of Durham, North Carolina, McPhatter formed a professional gospel quartet, the Mount Lebanon Singers, while he was still in high school. Two of the other Drifters, Gerhart and Andrew Thrasher sang as children with the Thrasher Wanderers, a sacred family ensemble, and the Silvertone Singers, a gospel group.

Their first release, "Money Honey," was a blockbuster for the Drifters. Vocal simulation of bagpipes, enhanced with a repetitive two-note hook *ah-oom, ah-oom*, gave color to the propulsive four-beat feeling. The realism of Jesse Stone's lyric struck a new note in male-female relationships—no love without *money, honey* said the gal—but also the guy. McPhatter's silvery tenor, almost a falsetto at times, presented the earthy equation with little squeals of delight.

The Drifters followed quickly with "Honey Love," coauthored by McPhatter, and another overnight smash. A Latin beat and rapid triplets on a cymbal added tang to a suggestive lyric, "I want it . . . I need it . . . your honey love . . ." McPhatter histrionics, sighs, squeals, and gasps, emphasized the song's eroticism. Gospel intensity seemed to go hand in hand with ecstasies of the flesh. By the following year, McPhatter was in the army and the personnel of the group began drifting—but not its popularity, which continued into the '60s. Clyde went solo after his discharge, drifted from Atlantic to MGM Records, and died in 1972 at the age of thirty-nine, having failed to achieve the superstar status he sought.

The Five Royales, another hot group of '53, began as a gospel group, the Royal Sons Quintet on Apollo Records. After the Dominoes made it, they changed their name and switched to R & B, imbuing it with a high-roller spirit that made No. 1 records of "Baby Don't Do It" and "Help Me Somebody." Both were written by lead singer Lowman Pauling, whose voice reminded one of Clyde McPhatter—but with more gut. In person, the Five Royales were cutups and wedded the visual dynamism of storefront religion to their vocals, anticipating the polished choreography of the Temptations and other Motown groups. With them, R & B took on the character of secular preaching. In fact, their hit of 1957, "Dedicated to the One I Love," has been called a "secular prayer." Written by Pauling in collaboration with King Records producer Ralph Bass—by then the group had switched from Apollo—the impassioned ballad was a hit for the Shirelles (1961) and later still for the Mamas and the Papas.

R & B reached a peak in '53 with a woman who influenced many rock stars of the '60s and was the source of one of Elvis Presley's biggest noisemakers. A three-hundred-pound, buxom blues shouter. Willie Mae Thornton, had a strong following in Atlanta where she appeared regularly in Snake's Variety Show at Bailey's 81 Theatre; in Chicago at Mike Delisa's Club; in Houston at Don Robey's Bronze Peacock, and in Harlem's Apollo Theatre —in short, on the chitlin' circuit.

Big Mama, as she was known, scored such a sensation in her appearances at Robey's club that the owner of the Peacock label began making records with her, eventually cutting "They Call Me Big Mama," on which he appears as her cowriter. In '53 she recorded a screamer by Jerry Leiber and Mike Stoller. So potent was Big Mama's growl-and-bark delivery from her unaccompanied opening shout that Robey used only a rhythm section to back her. "Hound Dog" shot right up to No. 1 on R & B charts. Three years later, Elvis Presley copied her record for one of his multimillion sellers. No one seemed to notice that the basic concept of the song really made sense only when a woman sang about a hound scraping around her door.

"Our first hit record was in the rhythm-and-blues market," said Mike Stoller, of the team that wrote "Hound Dog" and became one of the great creative combines of rock 'n' roll. "The song was 'Hard Times' and it was cut by Charles Brown on Aladdin. In the early '50s there was really a color line and with the exception of artists like Nat Cole and the Mills Brothers, there was a WHITE pop market and a BLACK pop market, and the records did not cross from one to the other."

Until '54, they not only did not cross. The fields were as separated as American society was segregated. In Manhattan you had to go to One Hundred Twenty-fifth Street if you wanted to buy a best-selling R & B platter. None of the Broadway stores and, certainly, none of the Madison Avenue shops carried Little Esther, B. B. King, or Big Mama. And to hear them on the radio, you had to go searching for the small-wattage stations at the top of the dial. But through the early '50s, young people were searching, and one of the disk jockeys they found and followed was the Pied Piper of rock 'n' roll, Alan Freed.

12

ROCK 'N' ROLL'S
SUPERPROMOTER

In the cool of an early evening in 1954, during a vacation in Bermuda, I went walking. Bicycles were the main means of transportation on the British island, but I managed better on foot. Following a causeway out of St. George where I was staying, I crossed a bridge into Hamilton, the capital city and most populated area.

Before long I found myself on a side street where I heard music blasting out of a speaker. After a moment, I realized that it was a radio turned up so high that it seemed to be playing *into* the street, not in the wooden house from which it came. As the record finished, on came a disk jockey with a machine-gun delivery and a voice whose hoarse rasp was painful to hear.

I was startled. It couldn't be! But the same shout came from a radio next door. By the time I had passed a fourth and fifth house, each tuned to the same station, there was no doubt in my mind. It was Alan Freed on Station WINS in New York. And if I had any doubts that I was in Hamilton's black section, it was put to rest by a small record shop at the end of the block. It carried every American R & B label of the day, and nothing else.

If Bill Haley was the prophet of R 'n' R, Alan Freed was unquestionably its most notorious publicist, a colorful, charismatic man whose intemperate tendencies eventually wrecked his career and, perhaps, took his life.

While he was at WINS, I was in the studio one evening when he took umbrage at something his wife said. We had been chatting pleasantly while recordings were spinning on his turntable. Without any warning he grabbed a glass water pitcher and hurled it at her. It shattered in a hundred fragments, spilling

water and ice cubes as it crashed on a desk at which she sat. She
was not hurt and, perhaps, not surprised. As a studio attendant
rushed to clean up the mess, Freed continued chatting amiably
with me as if nothing had happened.

On occasion when a record wigged him, he would signal his
engineer to open his mike, and accompany the disk by pounding
a heavy, Manhattan phonebook with the open palm of his hand.
Sometimes a record would excite him to such a degree that he
would urge the performers on with "Go, man, go!" or shout his
approval on the air, "Yeah, man, yeah!"

Of Freed, who helped make Cleveland a "breakout" record
town, disk jockey Bill Randle, who was on WERE when Freed was
at WJW, has said: "He was an incredibly involved performer who
lived every beat of every note of the music he played until he got
corrupted by the kind of environment that ultimately destroyed
him."

Because of his unbuttoned style, people generally did not
realize that Freed was an educated man, a student of classical
trombone and music theory, and a trained engineer. He actually
began his career in radio playing classical records over Station
WKST in New Castle, not far from his birthplace in Johnstown,
Pennsylvania. One of his daughters was named Sieglinde because
of his enchantment with the Wagner *Ring* cycle of operas.

Having grown up in Salem, Ohio, he settled in Akron in 1946
(at the age of twenty-five) where he began broadcasting over Station WAKR. Sponsored by a local department store, his "Request Review" climbed steadily in popularity so that in 1950 he
moved to Cleveland, hoping to place the show on TV. Unfortunately, it did not make it on Station WXEL and Freed had no
choice but to emcee the late-night movie, a rather distasteful chore
that allegedly drove him to drink.

It was not until June 1951 that he was able to launch a new
disk jockey show on indie station WJW. The sponsor was a local
record shop whose owner played a decisive role in Freed's career.
Reacting to the trend of sales in his shop, Leo Mintz wanted Freed
to concentrate on R & B disks. Freed resisted until one evening
when he visited the store and watched the reaction, not of black
but white kids, to the tenor saxes of Red Prysock and Big Al
Sears and to the blues-singing and piano-playing of Ivory Joe
Hunter.

"I wondered," he later told a reporter, "I wondered for about
a week. Then I went to the station manager and talked him into
permitting me to follow my classical program with a rock 'n' roll
party."

For his theme, Freed picked "Blues for Moon Dog," a King Record by Todd Rhodes, thereby acquiring the *alter ego* of "Moon Dog," a cognomen he was later forced to drop. And he changed the name of his show from "Record Rendezvous" to "The Moon Dog Rock 'n Roll House Party."

In a liner note for an End album *Alan Freed's Top 15,* Freed claimed that he began using the term "rock and roll" in 1951. He was then actually spinning black R & B disks, not the white derivative that came into being later. Though he did not invent it, as some historians have mistakenly said, he deserves full credit for *naming* the new music and *popularizing* the term.

The phrase "rock and roll" is of blues origin and was used way back as a euphemism for fornication—and how vivid a description of the movements involved! Its evolution from the specific to the general, from sex to having a good time, partying, etc., is quite understandable.

As the market for R & B expanded after World War II, part of the term began to appear in the titles of songs: "Rock All Night" by the Ravens and "Good Rockin' Tonight" by Roy Brown in '48; "All She Wants to Do Is Rock" by Wynonie Harris in '49; "Rockin' with Red" by Piano Red and "Rockin' Blues" by Little Esther in '50. In most of these instances, the word "rock" operated on two levels, sex and revelry, though black audiences and after a time, white) unquestionably read the earthier meaning into it.

The full phrase was heard in the Dominoes' "Sixty Minute Man" (1951) when there was little question as to the meaning of "rockin' and rollin' "; also in the Clovers' "Ting-a-Ling" (1952) where the girls tried you out with "rock and roll." In short, Freed appropriated an already existing jive phrase and, pinning it on a type of music that existed (R & B) helped make the white world conscious of a new sound (to them). As a new generation of singers and songwriters began to appropriate, imitate, and modify that sound, the label stuck.

Time was on the side of Leo Mintz's conviction about the power of the Big Beat, as Freed typed the rhythm. And Freed possessed the personality, the command of jive talk, and even the voice to become its supersalesman. An operation on his vocal chords to remove a polyp left him with a gritty hoarseness that made him sound like a blues shouter. (People who met him for the first time were frequently surprised that he was white.) "The Moon Dog House Rock 'n Roll Party" zoomed in popularity so that several other stations began carrying his WJW broadcasts.

By 1952 Freed began to be nationally known—and not merely because of the success of his show. Renting the Cleveland Arena,

together with Leo Mintz and two other entrepreneurs, he promoted a "Moon Dog Coronation Ball" on his program. So effec-
tive was his salesmanship that eighteen thousand tickets were sold
for a dance hall that could accommodate little more than half.
Inevitably, there was a stampede to get in and a riot. To escape
injury, Freed hid in a broadcasting booth. Although charges of
fraud in overselling were brought against all four promoters, they
were eventually dropped.

The following year, a planned in-person shindig had to be postponed when Freed cracked up in an automobile accident. His
face required plastic surgery. Injuries to his lungs, liver, and
spleen made him susceptible to pneumonia (which he frequently
contracted thereafter), left him with an almost psychotic fear of
automobiles, and may ultimately have contributed to his early
death from uremia. During his heyday at WINS, he arranged to
broadcast from his home in Connecticut so that he could avoid
cars and, during the winter months, the danger of catching cold.
When the "Moon Dog Ball" was finally held in July 1953, again
in the Cleveland Arena, it was again a rocking success.

One year later Freed was ensconced in the key nighttime spot
on WINS and the station was on its way to becoming the major
force in metropolitan radio. Bob Smith, then the program director, had accidentally caught one of his broadcasts over a New
Jersey station—WNJR carried repeats of his WJW show—and he
went running to the station manager for permission to hire Freed.
Paul Sherman, who is still at WINS today (now as a news announcer) and who became associated with the Freed show, has
said: "The kids grabbed him right up. He was hired for peanuts.
But in his first year, he grossed somewhere over $750,000." Within
weeks of his first appearance, Freed's invitation for requests
yielded such a flood of phone calls that he had to restrict requests
to letters and telegrams.

Freed became controversial almost from the moment he hit the
New York airwaves in September '54. Louis Hardin, the blind
New York City poet-musician, widely known to Manhattanites
and tourists as Moondog, immediately sued Freed for appropria-
tion of his professional name. (A Christlike figure in brown Army
blankets, Hardin generally stood statuelike at Fifty-second Street
and Sixth Avenue.) On November 24, the courts supported the
claim—Hardin had used Moondog since 1947 and Freed only since
1951—and Freed was compelled to drop the name under which
his show had grown in Cleveland. Thereafter, his WINS show
was known as "Alan Freed's Rock and Roll Party."

His pyramiding popularity produced an unexpected reaction

in the black community. A mass meeting was held in a Harlem YMCA protesting his style of announcing. Freed was condemned for sounding black and WINS for hiring a white man to play black music. Program director Bob Smith, invited to attend the crowded meeting, later said "Our target was the entire market. . . . It was mostly a black deejay on WHOM who was complaining. He felt he could do it better than Freed, whom we hired without knowing whether he was black or white."

At least one prominent black artist came to Freed's defense. Bandleader Lucky Millinder, acknowledging that Freed imitated Negroes in a jive-talk style, stated: "He has the fire and excitement of a Rev. Billy Graham, but in no way does he burlesque Negroes."

Freed not only did not belittle black people, but constantly refused to play white artists who made cover records of black originals—this, regardless of the sales and popularity of a given platter. Apparently, the black community did not share the animadversions of those at the protest meeting. When Freed ran an in-person dance at Manhattan's St. Nicholas Arena just four months after starting at WINS, he packed the hall mostly with black youngsters. With a seating capacity of six thousand for prizefights, the Arena accommodated fifteen thousand ticket buyers in two nights. Freed's bill was all black and pandemonium reigned from the moment the Buddy Johnson orchestra sounded its first notes at 8:00 P.M. until the doors were shut at 2:00 A.M.

The year of Freed's explosion on the New York scene (1955), Chuck Berry burst on the record scene with "Maybellene." Writer credits on the copyright: words and music by Chuck Berry, Russ Fratto, and Alan Freed. Fratto was a Midwest disk jockey who later removed his name. Now, Freed was schooled in arranging and the solo writer of "Tongue-Tied Blues," recorded by Champion Jack Dupree, and of "Nadine," a solid seller for the Coronets on Chess. But the presence of his name on other songs cut by artists he sponsored suggests that he may have been showered with gifts by writers and/or record companies that wanted the insurance of his turntable.

But Freed was egotistical enough to display his power to people he did not like. Throughout the business, he was known as a friend of the small, independent record companies—some of whom were later exposed as his unpublicized benefactors—and a "foe" of the majors. In part, this attitude was a reflection of the feelings of most black artists. But when RCA Victor, the biggest of the big, released the Isley Brothers disk of "Shout," Freed gave it a tremendous sendoff and a tumultuous ride on his turntable.

Occasionally, when he flipped over an artist or record, as he did over Jackie Wilson's recording of "I'll Be Satisfied," he programed the disk for an entire evening.

When Bill Haley's burgeoning popularity on the heels of *The Blackboard Jungle* led to a film based on its musical theme, Alan Freed's inclusion in *Rock Around the Clock* was a foregone conclusion. By then his recognition as New York City's powerhouse deejay with the youngsters had spread far and wide. Other disk jockeys were imitating him, copying his format as well as slam-bang style, and following his playlists. Naturally the movie company wanted his promotional impact.

As Paul Sherman reconstructs the negotiations: "Freed said he'd take the movie part but he wanted the money up front. Cash. Instead the movie company offered him a percentage. At first he said no. But Jolly Joyce (a Philadelphia agent who was the go-between) was a very smart man and he said: 'Dummy, take a piece.' They settled for a little cash and a generous percentage. They could have bought Freed for $15,000 and instead he made a fortune out of *Rock Around the Clock*."

Within the space of a year. Freed was involved in two other films. By December '56 his *Rock, Rock, Rock* was on release, a production that could have been filmed at one of his in-person appearances. In *Don't Knock the Rock* Freed played himself in a story of a rock 'n' roll singer, acted by Alan Dale, who returns to his hometown, only to be denounced by the mayor as a menace to the country's youth.

Don't Knock the Rock opened at the Times Square Paramount on Washington's birthday in '57. Freed appeared onstage with a stellar lineup of artists. Behind him was an Easter week '56 show at the Brooklyn Paramount that had brought the *Variety* comment: "It was like having an aisle seat for the San Francisco earthquake."

As for the show at the New York Paramount, opening day brought memories of Sinatra's Columbus Day (1944) appearance on the same stage. Over fifteen thousand kids stormed the box office during the first day and poured $29,000 into the cash register. Though there was no fainting, the '57 teen-agers outdid the '44 crowd in one respect. They stamped their feet so hard that the management, fearful of a collapse, cleared the second balcony. Only after building inspectors had examined the structure and its foundations was the area reopened.

By then Freed was heard over WINS every evening, except Sunday, from 6:30 P.M. until 11:00 P.M. for a total of twenty-seven hours of prime time. In addition, he was heard nightly between

9:00 P.M. and 9:30 P.M. over the entire CBS radio network. It was
a transcribed show in which he substituted his own band, directed
by tenorman Sam "The Man" Taylor, for Count Basie's. The programs emanated from his own Connecticut home, which had been
equipped with special remote broadcasting facilities. Freed's
fame had even spread abroad, with Radio Luxembourg in London
arranging for a taped segment as the highlight of a weekly Saturday night "Jamboree."

Christmas week of '57 brought further confirmation of Freed's
hold on teen-agers. Establishing a one-day Paramount box-office
record of $32,000, he grossed over $300,000 in the twelve days
between Christmas and New Year's. The youngsters proved so
restless and inattentive during the film portion of the show that
it was dropped completely after the first few days.

Despite his fantastic and still pyramiding popularity, trouble
was in the offing. A CBS-TV program, "Rock 'n' Roll Dance
Party," came under attack because of its sponsorship by Camel
cigarettes. Curiously, Freed was blamed for encouraging teen-
agers to smoke, rather than the station or the sponsor. And Freed
also took the beating when the camera inadvertently caught
Frankie Lymon of the Teen-agers dancing—horror of horrors—
with a white girl.

But a more serious situation was building as school and church
authorities, unable to stem the increasing interest of juveniles in
R 'n' R, began banning teen-age dances and denouncing the
music with mounting fury. On May 3, 1958, Freed appeared in
Boston as producer and emcee of a show starring the ebullient
Jerry Lee Lewis. Because of riots that had occurred in other cities
and the opposition of the Catholic hierarchy, the police guard was
unusually heavy. Halfway through the show, the police turned *on*
the lights for a look-see at the audience. Freed allegedly sounded
off with the comment: "Hey, kids, the cops don't want you to have
a good time."

It was an unguarded, impromptu statement and potentially
provocative. But to hold Freed accountable for what happened
after the show seems stretching a point. When the crowd left the
theatre, a fracas broke out. It spread to other parts of the me-
tropolis. Apparently one youngster was stabbed and many were
severely beaten. Boston authorities blamed Freed. He was arrested
and charged with incitement to riot and *anarchy*.

When he returned to New York, Freed met with the management of WINS. He was surprised to find the station unsympathetic
to his plight. In a fury, he turned in his resignation. Station
WABC immediately welcomed him as his slogan became, "We

start 'em! The others chart 'em!" Despite the apparent ridiculousness of the charges against him, it cost Freed enormous legal fees before he was able to secure a dismissal. Suddenly, in July 1958 he filed for bankruptcy, claiming that his liabilities exceeded his assets by over $50,000.

From this point on, Freed's career described a steady downward curve. The climax or dénouement came with the payola investigations of '59–'60. More about this later. Although he worked at several radio stations in California and Miami after his ouster by WABC and WNEW-TV in New York, Freed was a broken man. His death in 1965—he was forty-three years old—came as no surprise. The death certificate said uremia, but those close to him, felt he drank himself to a premature end.

He has been called the prince, the king, the dean, and the father of rock 'n' roll. He was certainly one of its most vibrant and explosive personalities, and brought an excitement into disk jockey programing that was little known before him and that was a genuine expression of the music he sponsored. In a sense, he was more a proponent of R & B than R 'n' R, displaying a partiality for black artists that gave him limited national exposure and, by comparison with Dick Clark, restricted sponsorship and revenues. It also made him a more vulnerable target. If he did not invite, he surely did not resist, any more than Clark did, the temptations that came with his power. But in the end, he was a victim of the war of the Establishment against the new pop and its proponents.

13

CONFRONTATION

"Friday night in Smalltown, USA. I was 15. The year was 1954," James Thompson wrote in *Cavalier,* "and I went for the movie. Not excepting much, but what the hell. Natalie Wood had a halfway decent body and I figured to go for popcorn when Sal Mineo came on. . . . Well, I never went for popcorn. When I finally walked out after seeing *Rebel Without a Cause* twice, it came as no little surprise to find the town exactly as I'd left it, the buildings still on their foundations, no cars overturned, just the same as before. But I wasn't. I was changed. James Dean had turned me around. . . . The whole dopey decade was like one big mashed potato sandwich. Except for James Dean. . . . The 50s was Nixon selling a used car and ole Ike standing around looking fatherly . . ."

An awakening of another kind came for young Barry Hansen of Minneapolis, then a seventh grader, and an unwilling student in a dancing class at Mill City's "more proper prep school." Made uncomfortable by an overheated room, an itchy wool suit, and the foxtrots and waltzes of his parents' generation, he was not overjoyed when the dancing master announced that he would teach them the lindy hop—to Hansen, "a dance nearly as venerable as the minuet."

"But when he put on the record," Hansen recalls, "I simultaneously forgot my unfortunate partner, the wool suit, the lindy hop, and Bill Haley, and dashed to the phonograph, goggle-eyed over the red and black label of the spinning 78 and goggle-eared over the music. It was 'Shake, Rattle and Roll,' my favorite song, but it sure wasn't Bill Haley. It was something far more sinister. . . . The dancing master had bought it because he thought that the heavier beat was easier to dance to than Haley's." It was bluesman Joe Turner's original version—and Barry Hansen, today a record annotator and Los Angeles disk jockey known as Dr. Demento, was never the same.

Nineteen fifty-four was a year of confrontations. The most significant, considering its aftereffects, was that of Wisconsin Sen. Joseph R. McCarthy and the U.S. Army. For the first time, the anti-Communist crusader whose name had become synonymous with "reckless accusation without evidence or proof" was up against a formidable adversary, accused of using his senatorial influence to gain special privileges for a former aide. Ignoring the charges, the clever and colorful demagogue resorted to his usual redbaiting tactics, directing them not only at every branch of the government but the Army itself. Clearly, he had not reckoned with his major assailant. Boston lawyer Joseph N. Welch was a master of sarcasm and a gentle, but all-searching inquisitor.

For 36 days and 188 hours of daytime television, millions of Americans watched this classic confrontation—McCarthy constantly interrupting the proceedings with "Point of Order! Point of Order!" when he was not making reckless charges—and Welch patiently probing. When the Senate hearings ended, leaving McCarthy snarling into microphones in an empty chamber— everybody had exited by then—people knew that the Wisconsin senator was finished. Came December of '54 and Joseph R. McCarthy was condemned by a vote of sixty-seven to twenty-two of conduct "contrary to Senate tradition." The McCarthy era was over.

And so it seemed was segregation when the Supreme Court, on May 17, 1954, handed down its momentous decision, declaring unanimously that racial segregation in the public schools was a violation of the U.S. Constitution.

A new climate was in the making. The so-called Silent Generation was dying. It became a time for speaking out—and singing out—and the door was open, however slightly, for the entry of black people into the mainstream of American life. To its everlasting credit, pop music was the first field in which segregation broke down. Black music, until then a ghetto or underground phenomenon, was welcomed by a new generation of record buyers.

1954 Was White Balladry

On the surface, and even in a backward glance, 1954 sounded like a continuation of the "Tin Pan Alley—Your Hit Parade" tradition. Perry Como had the year's top song in "Wanted," or Kitty Kallen in "Little Things Mean a Lot," depending on which survey you accepted. Of course, "Wanted" was a country-flavored tune with a shuffle beat, not a ballad. But that hardly was significant, considering the old-style singers and songs that monopolized the Waspish airwaves.

Doris Day's saccharine and virginal disk of "Secret Love" was the most performed of all, followed by Sinatra's swinging "Young at Heart," Rosemary Clooney's cute duet with herself "Hey There," and Tony Bennett's and the Four Aces' "Stranger in Paradise." The No. 1 publisher of the year was MGM's mammoth publishing combine, the Big Three, followed closely by old-hat giants like the Warner Brothers group, Shapiro-Bernstein, and the Buddy Morris group.

Among the year's Top Twenty-five, four best sellers came from Hollywood films (*Three Coins in the Fountain, Secret Love, The High and the Mighty,* and *That's Amore.*) Broadway shows contributed three: *Hernando's Hideaway, Hey There,* and *Stranger in Paradise.* Foreign countries successfully exported such corn as "Happy Wanderer—Val de Ri, Val de Ra" (Germany), "Oh, My Papa" (Switzerland), "The Little Shoemaker" (France), "Answer Me, My Love" (Germany), and "Skokiaan" (Northern Rhodesia). There was one out-and-out country song, "This Ole House," written and recorded by California-based Stuart Hamblen but given wider circulation by Rosemary Clooney's cover. The rest were tried-and-true Tin Pan Alley concoctions.

There was no sign of a wavering of the popularity of such established artists as Patti Page, Tony Bennett, Doris Day, Rosemary Clooney, Eddie Fisher, or Sinatra, each of whom contributed two chartmakers to the Top Twenty—or of Jo Stafford, Nat Cole, Dean Martin, Como, or Kitty Kallen, each of whom accounted for one. Instrumentals were also well represented in best-selling disks by Hugo Winterhalter, Ralph Marterie, Leroy Holmes, Victor Young, Les Baxter, Henri René, and newcomer Archie Bleyer.

Of the year's most popular disks—"Skokiaan" (Four Lads), "Little Shoemaker" (Gaylords), "I Get So Lonely" (Four Knights), "Stranger in Paradise" (Four Aces), "Three Coins in the Fountain" (Four Aces), and "Sh-Boom" (Crew Cuts)—only "Sh-Boom" represented a departure in style, sound, and age group from typical pop groups. And except for "Sh-Boom," there was not a single small or R & B label to be found in the Top Twenty-five best sellers.

No, the year's top tunes and network radio and TV suggested that it was business and music as usual. Established singers, songwriters, instrumentalists, and record companies seemed in full control of pop.

The Attacks Begin

Nevertheless, there were signs of uneasiness. A group of ASCAP (American Society of Composers, Authors, and Publishers) writers was pressing a $150-million lawsuit against BMI, three networks, and two record companies (Columbia and RCA Victor), charging monopolistic practices. The irony is that they were trying to prevent an impending breakdown of their own monopolistic hold on pop.

Fighting to prevent the increasing play of BMI songs on the air, ASCAP joined an attack on "leerics," as *Variety* typed them. "Such a Night," a song by gifted Lincoln Chase, and recorded by the Drifters became the target of its attack, but only after Johnnie Ray covered the black group and his disk appeared on *Billboard*'s list of records Most Played by Disk Jockeys. So long as the song's spins were limited to R & B stations, ASCAP was unconcerned about its so-called suggestiveness. Its sensitivity was disturbed only after Ray's white version invited plays by pop deejays. Then ASCAP went after the networks—and they banned the Weeper's disk as offensive to good taste. Curiously, censors in Great Britain, long known for their prudery, found nothing objectionable in the Ray recording—and it became a No. 2 best seller, remaining on British charts all through the summer.

The basis of ASCAP's attack was revealed in a statement made to *Variety* by lyricist Billy Rose, then a Board member. "Not only are most of the BMI songs junk," he opined, "but in many cases they are obscene junk pretty much on a level with dirty comic magazines." It was a strange animadversion by the writer of the lyrics of "Tonight You Belong to Me," a song whose words were as free of taint as "Such a Night" but whose subject matter was hardly different.

A more socially oriented attack came from the South. A group calling itself the Houston Juvenile Delinquency and Crime Commission released a list of records they deemed objectionable (undefined) and urged radio stations to place a ban on air performances. Among the more than thirty titles, the overwhelming number was by black artists or groups and recorded on R & B labels. The word was out that teen-agers, and southern at that, were seeking out this segregated material.

Those concerned about such dangerous developments were not

unaware of the crowds flocking to Alan Freed balls. They took
note that he used Negro talent almost exclusively, that invariably
thousands of ticket buyers were turned away at the doors, and
that as early as 1952, a sizable percentage ,of the audience was
white. Having conquered Akron and Cleveland in '52–'54, Freed
ran a Moon Dog Coronation Ball in New Jersey in May 1954.
His first entertainment dance in the East, it attracted a mob of
over ten thousand not counting the thousands who came but could
not get it. Again, it was a mixed crowd. And the shindig had been
advertised exclusively on taped relays of Freed's WJW shows,
aired over Newark's R & B station WNJR.

When *Billboard* covered a late June ball that Freed ran again
in Akron, it not only noted that one-third of the audience was
white but described the group as "the nation's increasingly R & B
audience." The awareness of the major record companies of this
burgeoning market manifested itself in many ways. RCA launched
a new R & B subsidiary, Label X. MGM moved back into the
field with a batch of releases. Decca entered into negotiations with
several indie labels to release their disks. In a Special R & B
Supplement published in April '54, *Billboard* said flatly that "the
R & B field has caught the ear of the nation."

R & B Moves Out of the Ghetto

That it was grabbing the ears of the young was evident to juke-
box operators, many of whom indicated that wherever teen-agers
congregated, R & B disks were being requested and added to boxes
in white locations. Apart from R & B artists who had already
begun attracting white listeners—Ruth Brown, Johnny Ace, the
Dominoes, the Clovers, Four Tunes, Five Royales, the Drifters
et al.—operators noted a demand for Joe Turner, the Midnighters,
and the Penguins, among others.

Big Joe's roots were so deep in Kansas City blues and boogie
of the 1930s that the '50s hardly seemed a time for him. He said
as much when Ahmet Ertegun insisted on signing him to Atlantic
in 1951. But he made Top Ten in R & B that year with "Chains
of Love"—a '56 cover by Pat Boone—the following year with
"Sweet Sixteen" and in '53 "Honey Hush."

His greatest record popularity came during the transition period
from R & B to R 'n' R. With his big, driving baritone, he won
acceptance with "Shake, Rattle and Roll" in '54, "Flip, Flop and
Fly" in '55, and "Corrine, Corrina" in '56. All three were covered
by white artists—"Shake" by Haley, "Flip" by Johnnie Ray, and

"Corrine" by Ray Peterson. The songs proved bigger sellers for the white artists, than for Turner, who could not make the transition from blues shouter to rock 'n' roll.

Turner's disks were not included in the "objectionable" list of the Houston Commission even though Bill Haley blue-penciled "Shake, Rattle and Roll." Neither were the disks of a tough bluesman whose records were quite sensual if not suggestive. In 1954 Muddy Waters, a fixture of Chicago's southside bars and juke joints from the early '40s, attracted listeners with "Just Make Love to Me," "I'm Ready," and "I'm Your Hootchy Kootchy Man."

A Delta bluesman who was master of the whining bottleneck style—in which the guitar was fretted with the neck of a bottle mounted on the pinky—Muddy switched to electric guitar soon after his migration from Mississippi to the Windy City. He became one of the first artists to record for Aristocrat, the Chess Brothers label that preceded Chess, scoring in '48 with the erotic "I Can't Be Satisfied" and autobiographical "I Feel Like Goin' Home." It is likely that his raucous delivery prevented the members of the Houston Commission from understanding McKinley Morganfield, to give him the name with which he was christened in Rolling Forks, Mississippi, in 1915. An amalgam of country, shouting blues, and urban amplification, Chicago-blues style was a black ghetto thing, an in-thing, and a tremendous influence on American and British rockers of the '60s. Connoisseurs like Alan Freed respected Muddy's originality and showcased his talents. But it was the reverence of artists like Mick Jagger of the Rolling Stones and all the Beatles that eventually gained him the recognition and wider audience due his work.

The Houston Commission did come down hard on several disks by a Federal Records group known as the Midnighters. Leader Hank Ballard was to attain fame in the '60s when a '58 tune of his describing a dance caught on and through a disk by another artist (Chubby Checker), created "The Twist" craze, the biggest dance craze since the Charleston and Lindy Hop.

In '54 Hank Ballard and his Midnighters hit with two sensual, shuffle ballads, full of references to teasin', squeezin', meat, etc. "Let's git it while the gittin' is good," Hank sang, and the chorus echoed, "So-oh good, so-oh good, so-oh good . . ." "Annie Had a Baby" was a sequel to "Work with Me, Annie"—and quite inevitable, considering the kind of work Annie did. "That's what happens," wrote coauthors Henry Glover and Lois Mann, "when the gittin' gits good." Glover, King Records' eastern A & R director, was a Lucky Millinder alumnus. And Lois Mann was one of many pseudonyms of Pres. Syd Nathan, a hugely gifted man who was to King Records what A. Nugetre was to Atlantic.

The Commission was outraged, too, by "Sexy Ways," Top Ten for the Midnighters without making No. 1. All of their disks were great dance records, climaxing with "The Twist." At about the same time (1960), they had No. 1 hits in "Finger Pop-pin' Time" and "Let's Go, Let's Go, Let's Go," both written by Ballard.

Many bird groups flew about black charts in the '50s and later, possibly as a result of the success of the Ravens, a pop-slick group on National Records who imitated the Ink Spots. In addition to the Orioles (Jubilee), the covey of bird groups included the Cardinals (Atlantic), Crows (Roma), Flamingos (Gone/End), Falcons (Lupine), Robins (Savoy), Swallows (King), the Jayhawks, and the Pelicans. In '54 the Penguins looked very large on the R & B horizon, with "Earth Angel," a new term for a loved one. To No. 1 went the plaintive plea for affection, provoking a smash cover early in '55 by the group that had made a big nest egg of "Sh-Boom." Apart from their deadpan delivery, which offered an almost humorous contrast to their impassioned plea, the Penguins are remembered inside the business because they led to the Platters. Mercury Records was so anxious to sign them after "Earth Angel" that it also reluctantly signed the other group, managed by the same man. And then the Penguins never winged onto best-seller charts again.

The Charms, a DeLuxe Records group, led a longer life. If the story is to be believed, Syd Nathan, owner of the King subsidiary, found them by looking out of his window. His office and factory were located in a reconverted ice plant on the outskirts of Cincinnati. Nathan had just heard a West Coast tune and was wondering how he could get a quick cover on the market. There, outside his window, a group of black cats were playing softball. On the spur of the moment, he invited the disbelieving group in for an audition. He was looking for one good lead voice, and he found it in Otis Williams.

Into the studio they went and voilà!—he had Otis Williams and the Charms and a million-copy seller titled "Hearts of Stone." The record tells the story. There was Otis doing the lead with a bit of gospel stutter and not too easy to understand. The others kept the up-tempo rhythm going with "doo-doo-WAHs." A series of "No-No-No-No-Nos" by Williams, extended so that the song went out of meter, added tension, and supplied a hook—something to engage the listener's interest and invite replays.

In '55 the Charms maintained their following with "Two Hearts"—a copyright I bought for E. B. Marks Music—and "Ling

Ting Tong," a sound novelty that was covered by another black group, the Five Keys, on Capitol. Like the Penguins, the Charms and Five Keys sang a cool style, which at that moment was becoming the in-thing in Jazz. Tenor saxist Lester Young and trumpeter Miles Davis were the pivots of a school of introverted, unemotional, nonvibrato, lag-along performers in rebellion against frantic bop.

Two years later the Charms were still holding their own with "United." But that year Otis Williams, who was also recording as a single, had "Ivory Tower," a song with a number of white recordings that served as Williams' crossover into pop.

Crossovers—and Roy Hamilton

The year that found Sinatra making a fantastic comeback on wax with "Young at Heart," saw no crossovers, not by black artists, anyway. But curiously, toward the end of the year, a number of white artists crossed into R & B charts. *Billboard*'s R & B tabulation of November 13, shows Bill Haley in the No. 1 slot with "Shake, Rattle and Roll," the Crew Cuts No. 2 with "Sh-Boom," followed immediately by the Chords record they covered, and Patti Page No. 6 with "What A Dream." Just as R & B brought a tremendous change in pop, it in turn underwent changes as a white market opened for it.

On the pop scene, all through the '40s and early '50s, Nat "King" Cole and Billy Eckstine were virtually the only Negro singers of star proportions. In 1954 it appeared that another might join this select company. Roy Hamilton was more of a big ballad singer than an R & B shouter. But he had gospel intensity. In fact, he studied to be a minister after tackling the music scene. His initial impact was, understandably, on R & B buyers, even though his rendering of "You'll Never Walk Alone" from Rodgers and Hammerstein's *Carousel* had an almost operatic quality, also deep, religious overtones.

Jack Schiffman of the family that still owns and runs Harlem's Apollo Theatre recalls that Hamilton appeared on a number of amateur nights. Unlike Sara Vaughan, Ella Fitzgerald, and other Negro stars, Hamilton never won. "His specialty," Schiffman notes, "was 'You'll Never Walk Alone.' But he kept going flat in the last few bars of the song, and he and Porto Rico came to know each other well." Porto Rico was the executioner on amateur nights, a character who danced onstage in outlandish costumes and, wielding a cap pistol, would shoot losers off stage.

Yet Hamilton's disk, cut only months after he was advised by one of the Schiffmans to give up singing, climbed to the very top of R & B charts. The following year, Hamilton, together with another black singer, blind Al Hibbler, accounted for 1955's No. 1 song, "Unchained Melody." Both sold in white and black markets. But Hamilton went to the top of R & B charts while Hibbler did not, seemingly making his greatest impact on white buyers. On succeeding releases, Hamilton's singing turned more in a gospel direction. Neither "Don't Let Go" (1958) nor "You Can Have Her" (1961) commanded the audiences of his two other hits and both featured blues-gospel call-and-release patterns. Then Hamilton, following Little Richard's course, suddenly gave up singing and began studying for the ministry. When he returned to music, even as Little Richard did, he blundered from label to label—and in '69, he died suddenly of a stroke.

Steals and Covers

Year-end '54 Coral Records took full-page ads in the trade papers to announce a new record by the McGuire Sisters. "Sincerely" was the cover of a disk by the Moonglows, a group sponsored by Alan Freed on Chess Records. If the music establishment could reassure itself that the Crew Cuts' "Sh-Boom" was just a fluke, the McGuire disk seemed to suggest a fad, especially since there had also been the Bill Haley cover of Joe Turner's rhythm-and-blueser.

At that moment, however, the record business was involved in an all-out race to capture sales on the first song kicked off by television. "Let Me Go, Lover," sung and recorded by an unknown vocalist, Joan Weber, was featured on a CBS dramatic show involving a disk jockey who murdered his sweetheart. Originally known as "Let Me Go, Devil," it was a song I nurtured as Gen. Prof. Mgr. of Hill & Range Songs, securing a record in '53 by Georgie Shaw on Decca. Although he had sold well on his debut disk, "Till We Two Are One," and seemed on his way to stardom, "Devil" was a bomb, and the country ballad by Jenny Lou Carson appeared to be finished. Then, Mitch Miller approached the firm for a ballad that could be used dramatically in the "Studio One" production.

The "devil" of the original lyric was liquor. I got the idea of changing the title to "Let Me Go, Lover!," and the task of revising the lyric to fit the situation in the play was assigned to three house writers who worked as a team. "Al Hill," the name to whom the special lyrics of the song are credited was a pseudonym for the trio, who rewrote the words to pinpoint the central situation in the play—a girl pleading for release from her former lover.

The morning after the telecast, there were calls for the song and the Joan Weber recording around the country. The word spread like a hurricane wind from dealers to distributors to disk jockeys to record producers. Within days, Mercury was on the market with a Patti Page version, and Coral with a Teresa Brewer rendition.

Mitch Miller reacted sharply to the sudden competition, uneasy that his recording by an unknown did not have enough of a headstart to outstrip disks by powerful, established artists like Page and Brewer. On a platter show he conducted over WNEW, "The Money Record," Mitch charged that the two versions were steals of the Weber arrangement. Patti Page's manager and Coral's A & R chieftain both quickly demanded equal airtime for a reply. They contended that Miller was hardly one to point a finger and proceeded to name two Columbia disks as steals. Doris Day's disk of "If I Give My Heart to You," they maintained, was a copy of Denise Lor's (Majar) recording and Connee Boswell's (Decca) disk, and Rosemary Clooney's "This Ole House" a steal of Stuart Hamblen's RCA Victor recording.

It was an interesting brouhaha, considering that a large phase of recording in '55 was the copying of minor-company records by majors. But then that was white stealing from black, a social pattern apparently sanctioned by tradition.

14

BLACK ORIGINALS
AND WHITE COVERS

Of *The Blackboard Jungle,* the movie that made the music scene explode in 1955, Frank Zappa of the Mothers of Invention wrote in *Life:* "When the titles flashed, Bill Haley and His Comets started blurching, 'One . . . Two . . . Three O'Clock . . . Four O'Clock Rock . . .' It was the loudest sound kids had ever heard at that time. . . . Bill Haley . . . was playing the Teen-Age National Anthem and he was LOUD. I was jumping up and down. *Blackboard Jungle,* not even considering that it had the old people winning in the end, represented a strange act of 'endorsement' of the teen-àge cause . . ."

And the *Encyclopaedia Britannica* noted: "The rowdy element (in pop) was represented by *Rock Around the Clock.* The rock 'n' roll school concentrated on a minimum of melodic line and a maximum of rhythmic noise, deliberately competing with the artistic ideals of the jungle itself."

Nineteen fifty-five was the year when the great prophets of the new music walked the charts and electrified the airwaves—not only Haley but Ray Charles, Bo Diddley, Little Walter, Little Willie John, El Dorados, Nutmegs, Fats Domino, the Platters, and Chuck Berry.

At the beginning of the year, twenty-three-year-old Johnny Ace was "Pledging My Love" in his plaintive, cool, almost flat, nasal style. It was all over the radio dial for months. But Johnny was dead, a victim of his own stupid recklessness. At the same time, Capitol Records became the first major diskery to produce an R & B hit, "Ling Ting Tong" by the Five Keys. And from Memphis, Bob Neal, C & W deejay of Station WMPS, announced that he had "taken over the personal management of Elvis Presley, a nineteen-year-old country singer who in a few short months has catapulted to a top spot on 'Louisiana Hayride' originating in Shreveport." Presley and his supporting team, Scotty Moore (guitar) and Bill Black (bass) plus a "Hayride" show were set for mid-January appearances in Mississippi, Arkansas, Missouri, and Texas—but Neal was "for the time being" continuing his disk-jockey chores at WMPS. Small items in the day's trade papers, they were given only passing notice by the music establishment.

Of course, it was more difficult in '55 to shut one's eyes to a growing accumulation of strange phenomena. But these could be dismissed, and generally were, as a fad rather than a trend. And though established publishers, songwriters, and artists were un-easy—and occasionally saw flashes of lightning as of an oncoming storm—they were reassured by what they heard on their radios and TV, and even by statistics in the trade papers.

Nineteen-fifty-five's top tune, "Unchained Melody," was from a film and the pen of a Hollywood composer. It was a rather odd-ball, folklike melody, and the two records that made it a hit were by blacks. But after all, it lost out in the Academy Awards to a more traditional ballad, "Love Is a Many-Splendored Thing." And the No. 2 song was a good, old, corny, country tune, "Ballad of Davy Crockett" as sung in a dry-as-dust style by Bill Hayes, an unknown who outsold Tennessee Ernie and Fess Parker, the Davy Crockett of the popular TV series.

The No. 3 song was a lovely instrumental, "Cherry Pink and Apple Blossom White," melody by Cuban bandleader Perez Prado. Replete with low, throbbing, pedal tones in the trombones, high-flying trumpets, cowbells, and grunts, it was mambo—a Latin dance that was to the rumba what jitterbug was to the fox trot. Brought in 1950 from Cuba by an American bandleader-arranger, Sonny Burke, in his recording of "Mambo Jambo," the dance became a national craze by 1954. Tin Pan Alley writers created "Mambo Italiano" for Rosemary Clooney, banned by some stations as offensive; "Mambo Baby" for Ruth Brown, No. 1 on R & B charts; and "Papa Loves Mambo," a novelty pop smash for Perry Como. There was even a "Mambo Rock" by Bill Haley. At Christmastime '54, the dance was all over the tree with "I Saw Mommy Doing the Mambo," "Jingle Bell Mambo," and "We Wanna See Santa Do the Mambo." The time was ripe for Prado, who was responsible for the music of "Mambo Jambo," known originally as "Que Rico El Mambo," and who had mi-grated to the States on the strength of Sonny Burke's Decca platter. "Mambo Beat Jogs Santa's Sacroiliac" read a trade paper headline —and it jolted the charts, too.

No. 4 was a rewrite of a Civil War ballad, "Yellow Rose of

Texas," recorded in strict marching tempo by Mitch Miller on Columbia and in an old-style crooning version by Johnny Desmond on Coral. And No. 5 was a tune dating back to 1903, "Melody of Love," revived by Billy Vaughn and his orchestra on Dot—he remembered it as something he heard on the piano when he was a small boy. Refurbished with a new lyric, it was recorded in a duet by Tony Martin and Dinah Shore. But it was the Four Aces who sold the vocal version and David Carroll on Mercury who competed with Billy Vaughn's instrumental treatment.

The balance of '55's Top Fifty was more of the same. But starting with the No. 6 tune, it was not easy to disregard eleven other titles, all redolent of a new sound. To be sure, this passing fad, represented by *Rock Around the Clock*, involved only twelve out of fifty songs—less than 25 percent. And, after all, Sinatra had made a comeback, so that nothing could take the place of "good music." And yet there was this Alan Freed character! He seemed to be shaking up the radio scene, not only in metropolitan New York, but all around the country. And why would he be on the air so many hours if the kids were not listening to him? And he was not playing any of the Top Five, just offbeat labels and artists and songs. Why were so many of the white singers picking up on these songs, instead of finding their own material at the established publishing houses?

The Cover Syndrome

In mid-January of '55 *Billboard* carried a two-page advertisement. On one page RCA Victor shouted, "*Ko Ko Mo* belongs to Como" and devoted the second to a shot of "Perry in Action on a Great Rock-and-Roll Record"—he was snapping his fingers! A few pages later, Mercury presented a Double Smash, by the Crew Cuts—"Ko Ko Mo" in giant type on one page and "Earth Angel" on the next. Well, "Ko Ko Mo" actually belonged to Gene and Eunice, who introduced it on a small, indie label, Combo. And "Earth Angel" belonged to the Penguins on Dooto. But Como took the Jesse Belvin rocker away from Gene and Eunice, whose disk did not appear in the Top Tunes tabulation where Como made No. 25. And the Crew Cuts split sales with the Penguins.

The recording industry had embarked on a pattern for which the Prohibition era provided a colorful term—hijacking. In music circles, it was known euphemistically as "covering." In the Top Tunes tabulation we were citing a moment ago, "Sincerely" at No. 7 was credited to the McGuire Sisters, "Ain't That a Shame" at

No. 10 to Pat Boone, "Dance with Me Henry" at No. 13 to Georgia Gibbs, and "Seventeen" at No. 18 to the Fontane Sisters. But "Sincerely" was originally recorded by the Moonglows, "Ain't That A Shame" by Fats Domino, "Dance with Me Henry" by Etta James, and "Seventeen" by Boyd Bennett. In each instance, the superior pressing, distribution, and promotion facilities provided by a major label—not to mention the reluctance of pop, white deejays to program black R & B disks—put the original recording in a weak competitive position.

But there was something else involved that historians have not previously delineated, largely because they were not conversant with the inner workings of the music business. Let me illustrate.

In the fall of 1955, shortly after I began superintending the song phase of E. B. Marks Music, I approached record producers with a rhythm ballad titled "Dungaree Doll." The very title will tell you that I was trying to capitalize on the dress and fads of the emerging-to-power teen-age crowd. Unfortunately, I could not persuade any of the A & R men to cut it.

Faced with the alternative of shelving the song, I elected to take a rather unusual step—for those days. I set up a recording session in collaboration with King Records of Cincinnati. I created a duo whom I named the Rock Brothers—it consisted of Bernie Nee, a well-known demo singer, and Sherman Edwards, cowriter of "Dungaree Doll" and, later, lyricist-composer of 1776. We cut a session that included two Marks standards and two new songs, the "Doll" ballad and "Living It Up." Marks paid the recording costs and King took care of pressing and distribution. Promotion was a joint enterprise. Fortunately for us, after King released the two new songs, the record showed up on best-seller lists in Cleveland. I took these lists to Joe Carlton of RCA Victor, who immediately cut "Dungaree Doll" with Eddie Fisher—and a chart song 'twas.

Now, was Fisher's record a cover? Yes, but not in the sense in which disks like "Sincerely" and "Sh-Boom" were covers. The distinction inheres in the style and character of the new version. From the time that records became a major exposure device, all publishers tried to get as many versions of a new song as they could. But these versions were different and, what is more significant, in the natural style of whatever artist recorded them. What happened between 1954 and 1956 was a horse of another color. And I do mean "color."

Before Georgia Gibbs went into a Mercury studio to cut "Tweedle Dee," the LaVern Baker recording was carefully studied by an arranger. Since the copyright law does not protect arrangements as such, he was free to copy the bass line, the drum rhythms, and whatever else gave the Baker disk its marvelous drive, vitality, and danceability. In short, the Gibbs version was a copy of the Baker platter. More polished, smoother, but Gibbs in blackface. Likewise with her cover of Etta James's "Wallflower," except that "Roll with Me, Henry," with its inescapable sexual connotation, was softened to "Dance with Me, Henry."

In both instances, Georgia's Mercury recordings were runaway hits, million-copy platters that grabbed the major slice of the market. Exposure was the name of the game—seven hundred R & B deejays vs. ten thousand pop jockeys—and LaVern and Etta were not played on the pop turntables. But there were also the record buyers. In this transition period, young, white listeners were reacting to black records. But having been raised on the polish and varnish, the velvet and satin of big orchestras and syrupy crooning, only a small percentage were ready for the raw and exuberant earthiness of rhythm and blues. The attraction was there but also the edginess. And so along came white producers at the major companies to give them something that caught the lusty quality of the originals but wrapped it in a glossy plastic.

The formula worked for almost two years. To name all the copy disks released between '54 and '56 is unnecessary. Virtually every white artist got into the act. Jim Lowe, a Texas deejay who also recorded, covered "Maybellene." Joe Reisman, an A & R exec and arranger-conductor at RCA Victor, covered "Bo Diddley." And even Sinatra joined the parade with a cover of "Two Hearts, Two Kisses" by the Charms. But it was not long before the white cover had to share sales with the black original and, after a time, white teen-agers rejected the white imitation in favor of the black original. In '56 Little Richard's "Long Tall Sally" outsold Pat Boone's creamy-white version.

The Satellite Companies

Pat Boone's rise to record fame was engineered by a capable southern gentleman who built a million-dollar company on cover records. Smiling Randy Wood started in the music field as the operator of a mail-order record business in a small Tennessee town, Gallatin. Not long after he founded his own record label in 1951, I drove the twenty-seven miles from Nashville to see and audition songs for him.

At that time Dot Records operated out of Randy's home. I went up several steps to a porch and into a rambling, three-story, wooden structure. Randy was auburn haired, soft spoken, and with an expression that always made him look as though he was smiling to himself. He greeted me with typical southern hospitality and insisted that I have a smidgin of lunch with him. Afterward, we went into a smaller chamber behind the dining room where I played several demos for him. Although he was impressed and even amused that a Broadway music publisher would seek him out in Gallatin, he was not really interested in my material, doubtless ersatz C & W. I saw him through the years both in New York and later after he settled in Hollywood (where he sold his company to Paramount Pictures for $5 million in the mid-'60s). He was always polite, pleasant, and polished. And he was obviously a good businessman—rumor had it that he required music publishers to give him seventy thousand records royalty-free (roughly $1,400) as a promotion budget on each side he released.

When he first began making and releasing records, Randy naturally worked with country artists like the Griffin Brothers, Jimmy Newman, and a highly successful vocal group, the Hilltoppers. "Trying," their first hit, was by Billy Vaughn, a local musician who grew as an arranger, conductor, and record producer with the company. (Randy loved recording so much that even after he became chief executive officer of Dot under Paramount Pictures, he still spent as many hours as he could in the studio. I sat with the millionaire one day as he munched a cheese sandwich and supervised a session.)

By 1954 Randy's approach to material had changed so drastically that Pat Boone's first release was a cover of an R & B disk, "Two Hearts, Two Kisses" by Otis Williams and the Charms. Reports have it that Boone, who has a Bing Crosby–type, baritone-vibrato voice, was quite surprised by Wood's choice of material. But Randy's mail-order business supplied an authoritative index to titles for which there was a demand. And as early as '54, it cued him on a growing interest in R & B material among white teenagers, southern, that is.

Most of Boone's early hits were, in fact, covers—from '54 to '56: "Ain't That a Shame" of Fats Domino, titled "Ain't It a Shame"; "At My Front Door" of the El Dorados; "Tutti Frutti" of Little Richard; "I'll Be Home" of the Flamingos; "Long Tall Sally" of Little Richard; and others. In 1957, even after he had cut film themes like the Quakerish "Friendly Persuasion (Thee I Love)" and the ballad-beautiful "April Love," both of which received Academy Award nominations, Boone revived "I'm Waiting Just for You," originally a Lucky Millinder recording on King. By '57 Boone's money-making imitations of black songs had aroused such a furor among black artists that Alan Freed, among other R 'n' R jockeys, refused to play Boone.

But Randy Wood's cover policy extended to his other top artists as well. The Fontane Sisters, who never made it on wax until they left the Como TV show, copied Otis Williams and the Charms disk of "Hearts of Stone," the Marigolds record of "Rollin' Stone," the Boyd Bennett and his Rockets platter of "Seventeen," and the Teen Queens recording of "Eddie My Love." The Sisters were not always as successful as Boone in outselling the originals. However, Gale Storm, then starred on a top-rated TV series, outsold Smiley Lewis on "I Hear You Knockin' " and Otis Williams's record of "Ivory Tower," though Cathy Carr, who also covered Williams on Fraternity Records, gave her keen competition.

The contrast between the white covers and the black originals was a matter of image as well as sound. Boone's publicity emphasized his status as a college student—Charles Eugene Booth graduated from Columbia University *magna cum laude*—as a loving husband, happy father of four daughters, and God-fearing Christian. He always wore white sweaters and white buckskins in his TV appearances to intensify the contrast with the tough rock 'n' rollers in their black denims and motorcycle boots. The Fontane Sisters, who were as good looking as the Andrews Sisters, projected sedate images of decorum and respectability. And pretty Gale Storm looked so healthy and virginal, how could you read sex into a song like "I hear you knockin', but you can't come in."

Unquestionably, these artists contributed an aura of respectability to songs that the music establishment thought belonged in the ghetto and some, even, in the gutter. Disk jockey Peter Potter, emcee of "Juke Box Jury" on a Hollywood station, was quoted as saying: "All R & B records are dirty and as bad for kids as dope." Undoubtedly some adults were exposed to tunes whose audience would have been limited to the high school crowd, white and black. But in giving wider exposure, the white hitmakers appropriated revenues and recognition that might have gone to the black performers who minted the material and originated the style.

The irony is that, except for the artists, everyone else benefitted from the cover syndrome. Charlie Gillett errs when he writes in *The Sound of the City*: "Apart from N. Y.'s Atlantic Records, the company that suffered most from the practice of covering was King of Cincinnati." Covered they were, and not only by Dot, but by Mercury and Coral, two other diskeries that indulged extensively in the practice. But did they suffer?

I doubt it. Gillett and other historians outside the music scene neglect the simple fact that the R & B record companies generally *owned* the copyrights that were covered. What they lost in sales of their own records, their publishing subsidiaries more than made up in royalties received on other records, performance earnings, foreign income, etc. Imperial Records may have lost some sales on Domino's "Ain't It a Shame" but Travis Music, its subsidiary, collected 2 cents from Dot on every Pat Boone record sold. And King Records received 2 cents from Dot on every Fontane disk of "Seventeen."

In '55 when I was at Gen. Prof. Mgr. at E. B. Marks Music, I was constantly approached by indie record companies that wanted to slice, lease, or sell their copyrights—and I made deals on a number with Atlantic, Savoy, and Glory records. These companies were interested in cash advances but also in my getting cover records. For the songwriters, as well as for their publishers, covers meant augmented income. It is also a fact that the competition between the originals and the covers stimulated sales of the original.

It was the artists who suffered, not the R & B record companies, their publishing subsidiaries, or the songwriters. And the copyright law afforded little protection. That is why LaVern Baker, smarting from her experience with "Tweedle Dee," appealed to a Michigan congressman for a bill to halt the theft of arrangements. In 1956 it was the record buyer who temporarily resolved the issue. Just as Alan Freed refused to play white covers, so the young listener began buying the black original. Ironically, it was the cover that led him to the original and helped pave the way for the rise of rock 'n' roll.

Gospel and Rock

Ray Charles came to R & B by way of jazz, having started as an imitator of Nat "King" Cole. In 1954, during an engagement in Atlanta, he returned to his roots, to the gospel music he had heard and sung as a child. In tapping the spiritual resources of his people, Charles performed an alchemy that provoked bluesman Big Bill Broonzy to protest: "He's got a good voice but it's a church voice. He's mixin' the blues with spirituals. That's wrong!"

What Charles did was to rewrite "Jesus Is All the World to Me" as "I Got a Woman." It became the first hit of his career. He took the gospel hand-clapper "This Little Light of Mine" and converted it to "This Little Girl of Mine." The transformation was more than lyrical. It meant fusing the sacred and the secular, the gospel and the blues, two types of music that were as disparate in the Negro psyche as God and the devil. It meant infusing the hungers of the flesh with the ecstasies of the soul. Charles was the preacher man in a gritty baritone, a glittering semicircle of white, clenched teeth, and a style of emotion and commitment that later became known as soul.

It was not until the end of the decade that Ray was able to break out of the black underground with "What'd I Say." In 1955, except for the country's seven hundred R & B deejays and innovators like Alan Freed, pop disk jockeys did not program his records. So Ray Charles had to be content with seeing "I Got a Woman" and a more secular "Fool for You" finish high on the year's R & B charts. But he had broken the ground for the emergence of Little Richard and other ecstasy singers.

A much lesser figure but one who also helped bring soul into black balladry was Little Willie John, a tragic man who died in prison at thirty. Involved in an argument after completing a date in Seattle, John Davenport of Camden, Arkansas, was convicted of manslaughter in '65. Imprisoned the following year, he succumbed in his sleep to pneumonia in Washington State Prison in 1968. Shortly afterward, Soul Brother No. 1, as James Brown called himself, recorded his debt in a memorial album, *Thinking about Little Willie John and a Few Nice Things*. The title told it all, for Brown's LP contained only one song associated with Little Willie, the unforgettable "Talk to Me, Talk to Me." Willie John cut his heart-tearing version in 1958, the year that Peggy Lee took another song introduced (and coauthored) by him, "Fever," and made a pop smash of it. In 1955 Willie made his first appearance on R & B charts with a little-remembered ballad, "All Around the World." In the years that remained, he was responsible for memorable records of "Need Your Love So Bad" (1956) and "Sleep" (1960). The latter was a curious choice, since "Sleep" was a portion of a piano concerto first recorded in 1928 by Fred Waring and his Pennsylvanians and thereafter his signature theme. You can hear him in Sam Cooke although he had a dryer and more brittle, if no less emotional, delivery.

Black Precursors of R 'n' R

Though he influenced the Beatles, Rolling Stones, and other groups of the '60s, Ellas McDaniel was never able himself to make the crossing from R & B to pop. He moved from the chitlin' circuit to white halls only with the rock 'n' roll revival of the late '60s. In '55 he made his raucous appearance on Checker Records under his stage name, Bo Diddley, also the title of his single: "Bo Diddley bought a nanny goat to make his pretty baby a Sunday coat . . ." A fast shuffle, the rocking single embodied a distinctive "shave-and-a-haircut" rhythm, a raspy, barroom vocal, and driving guitar work seldom heard on wax.

The character of his appeal, despite his in-group influence, is indicated by the R & B lists of '55. "Bo Diddley" is not to be found in the Top Twenty-five of disk jockey plays but it rated No. 8 on Juke Box Plays. Bo's raw, bar-blues style was made for high-spirited, noisy scenes. He was an in-person entertainer rather than a record-maker, appearing in loud, striped sports jackets and heavy, black-rimmed shades, and magnetizing the kids with the rhythmic propulsion of his style and the tough, exciting guitar work.

Another Checker artist, Little Walter, is best-known for his lyrical harmonica playing on Muddy Waters recordings. But Marion Walter Jacobs, born in Alexandria, Louisiana, in 1930, also recorded extensively with groups bearing his name from 1947 on. In '55 he struck pay dirt with a Willie Dixon ballad, "My Baby," one of the giant R & B disks of the year.

Little Walter never repeated the feat, although he kept trying. Neither did four best-selling groups of '55 in whose disks one can hear R & B turning into rock 'n' roll. Who can forget the El Dorados and "At My Front Door"?—the instrumental riff at the start in the rhythm of "Crazy, little mama come (pause) knock-in' " that set the pattern for the disk; the foggy tenor solo and the group urging him on with hand claps and "hey, hey's"; the falsetto-voiced, "yi-yi" chorus in instrumental style; the surging, four-to-the-bar rhythm on a ringing cymbal; and the vocal chorus that went "womp (pause) womp (pause) diddily-womp (pause) womp-womp-diddily-womp (pause) womp-womp . . ." It was a happy, boastful tale of the guy who was worried but there was his little mama come "knock-knock-knockin' at my front door." Pat Boone covered the El Dorados in a smooth-as-velvet version that never approached the original for danceability, textural changes, and sheer *joie de vivre*.

Then there were the Four Fellows on Glory with "Soldier Boy" and the Nutmegs on Ember with "Story Untold." The Crew Cuts covered the Nutmegs but they did not make it with this one nor did they capture the appeal of the original.

"Soldier Boy," covered several years later by Presley, was a song on which I negotiated a deal for E. B. Marks with Bryden Music, the publishing subsidiary of Glory Records. Concern over the Korean conflict made it timely among young people, and I was able to secure recordings by Ella Fitzgerald (Decca), Sunny Gale (RCA Victor), Eydie Gorme (Coral), Pat O'Day (MGM),

Burt Taylor (Essex), and Mel Williams (Federal). Despite the
impressive lineup, the song did not make it, nor did any of the
recordings compete too effectively with the original, which made
the Top Twenty in R & B retail sales. But "Soldier Boy" initiated
a relationship with Glory Records, which resulted in my acquiring
"Cindy, Oh Cindy" and "The Banana Boat Song" for E. B.
Marks. Cut by a short-lived group, the Tarriers, whose personnel
included the now-famous Alan Arkin, both songs contributed
significantly to the calypso craze of '56.

BO DIDDLEY INTERVIEW

He sat in the coffee shop, the Appian Inn, of the Flamingo
Hotel, a large black Stetson on his head. It was a bizarre sight but
no one bothered to ask him to remove it in a hotel where once
they had emptied the swimming pool because a black entertainer
had dunked his black skin.

The backstage for the rock concert was at the far end of the
kitchens and the massive roasting ovens. Three men surrounded
Diddley as I found the spot. They were blue eyed, blonde, and
crew cut, dressed in khaki, and wore large revolvers. On their
left shoulders a patch shaped like the state of Nevada bore the
words *Nevada Security Police.* Once, they might have been
searching a black man for something that might embarrass or
harass him.

Today, they were asking for Bo Diddley's autograph! After he
gave it to each, one of them handed him a card the size of a
driver's license. It had Diddley's real name typed on the back, Ellas
McDaniel, his height, and his weight. On the front, it bore a
legend stating his membership in the Nevada Security Police.

Diddley was laughing heartily when he saw it, his mouth open
in a grin that showed an upper row of uneven discolored teeth.
On the request of one of the khaki-garbed man, he took off his hat
and gave it to him, not without some reluctance. When it was
returned to him, it bore a silver star, like a western sheriff's
badge. He grinned like a kid with a new toy.

Later in the afternoon—this was a Sunday matinee performance
—he sneaked up behind Chuck Berry, who was also on the bill.
Tapping the thin, lanky, loose-jointed rock 'n' roll colleague on
the shoulder, he said with a growl: "I've been lookin' for you."
When Berry turned from the table over which he was leaning
and examining his guitar, he could see only the silver star on the
black hat. For a moment, he was startled. Then, Diddley raised
his head—and both broke into infectious laughter.

"The '50s were a rather tough period," said Bo Diddley. "But then it seems to be getting together now as far as the current entertainers. I can dig being out here still being able to do my thing. I don't feel that I have lost very much. . . .

"Several people have asked me whether I got started as a disk jockey. Don't know where they got the idea. I was a prize fighter and goofed around a bit. I'm glad I quit, because today I could be half crazy. I'm doing something that I really like to do. Perform for people and see them be happy, and during the time that they're happy, I'm happy along with them. . . .

My music got its start on the streets of Chicago. Then I started working in a club, around 1945 to '46, in the real, rough part of town, the 708 Club. It wasn't too far from my house. But two or three blocks was another territory. If I was on Forty-seventh Street and went down to Forty-third, I might lose a leg. [Chuckling.]

"My guitar got me through a lot of hassles. All the other kids were hassled by the tough gangs that used to run the streets of Chicago. They'd just as leave strip you naked on the street as look at you. I would walk up to them—there was no way to get around them—and they'd say, 'Hey, man, whatcha got there?' They were the same age I was, but I couldn't fight fifteen or twenty of them. When they saw the guitar, they'd say, 'Let us hear somethin'.' So me and my two cats, Jerome and a cat named Roosevelt Jackson who played Brownie Bass—the washtub bass— would play a little bit. And they never bothered us. All the gangs got to know us. . . .

"I came to make my first records by going into Chess. They told me to go home and rewrite 'Bo Diddley.' It was called 'Uncle John' then. And I went back and changed the name of it and started using the name I was fightin' under. . . . And boom!— up come a hit. Thanks to my public, they dug it. It's really groovy.

"But, you know, something really hurt me. When I was coming along, all of my black following kinda dropped off. When the segregation thing started—I don't know what happened—everybody was saying: 'Well, wow, he's playin' music that's puttin' us back fifty or seventy-five years." It hurt. I couldn't see it. I was only playing music that was native to me. I don't play blues. . . .

"I was a Muddy Waters fanatic. But I wasn't a cat that was trying to play like Muddy Waters. I wasn't even thinking about making a record. That was an accident in the first place. I got mad at my wife and went to Chess Records and took a little piece of dub. And Phil Chess say: 'Wow! That's different!' And that's how I got in. If I were playing like Muddy, they'd say, 'Naah!

You ain't got nothin' no different. We hear that all day.' That's why I'm considered a cat in my own bag.

"Lately, I began to pick up a few more of the brothers. It took them a time to figure out that I was really doing *our* music. It's something that I felt out of my background, of my bringing up. But nobody recognized it because I got two or three things all mixed up together, two or three rhythms. My one aim is to make people be happy. And when I see them happy, I'm happier.

"They were doing all kinds of dances to my rhythms. I don't even know what they were, to tell the truth. They had some dances they called the Dish Rag, the Chicken, the Slop. I never danced except on stage.

"In addition to Muddy, the artists I admired were Johnny Hooker, Jimmy Reed, Louis Jordan. I always wanted to be like Jordan. I dug his style. But I just couldn't blow no saxophone. So I had to jump off that kick and jump on something else. See, I'm a string lover. I love string instruments. I played the violin for like twelve to thirteen years, before the guitar. I played the classics. Lotta people don't know that. Took lessons for years with Prof. O. W. Frederick who lives in Chicago. He took me under his wing. I wasn't able to pay for lessons; we were on relief.

"Professor Frederick said to my mother: 'Mrs. McDaniel, with your permission, we'll get together with the church and take up a collection, and buy him his first violin. All I ask you to do is see that he gets it.' And he taught me until I was able to pay that seventy-five cents a lesson. It was the hardest seventy-five cents to get hold to back then. People that pay $1.25 a lesson now think they're paying too much money—they don't know. They're having it easy now because there's a lot of money floating around. But when I was growing up, there was no money. There was nothing but food stamps and war-ration books."

Leiber and Stoller

The Cheers were another one-hit group. But their disk, covered by the Diamonds and Vaughn Monroe (!), is historically important. "Black Denim Trousers" embodied the image of tough youth, previously projected on the screen by Marlon Brando in *The Wild One. . . .* It caught the imagination of the young and the song climbed into the Pop Fifteen on the Honor Roll of Hits. Apart from image, it introduced the team of Jerry Leiber and Mike Stoller, two white California lads (originally from the East)

who produced the record and became one of rock's most successful, versatile, and prolific writer-producer combines.

"I was brought up in Baltimore in a mixed black-and-white
neighborhood during World War II," Leiber said recently, "and
I was exposed to a lot of country music and delta blues. . . . My
family moved to Hollywood when I was twelve. When I was about
sixteen I was working in a record shop, and I started listening to
a lot of the blues records that were coming out on Specialty,
Aladdin, Modern, Savoy, and King—and that became my music. I
decided I wanted to be a songwriter, and naturally those sounds,
the subject matter of blues material, jokes in the blues vein, the
kind of backhanded social commentary in the blues were the elements of my work . . ."

Stoller, who was also attending Los Angeles high school,
imbibed the influences that came from a student body that was at
least 85 percent Mexican. Six months after the two got gether,
they had their first hit with Charles Brown on Aladdin. In this
period, 1952–54, they worked with Johnny Otis and the Coast
office of Federal Records, writing songs for and producing records
with Little Esther, Mel Williams, and Big Mama Thornton.
"Hound Dog" and "Kansas City," both later smashes for Presley,
came out of this activity.

By 1953 they felt confident and enterprising enough to start
their own R & B label, Spark Records. With the Robins they
produced a series of local best sellers, among them "Cell Block
Number Nine" and "Smokey Joe's Cafe." As a result of the latter,
late in '55, Atlantic Records bought the Spark masters and signed
Leiber and Stoller to an independent production deal. It was the
first of its kind and initiated a development in which eventually
creative control of recording was taken out of the hands of company A & R executives and vested in outside indie producers.

Coda

Considering the degree to which R & B figured in the pop scene
of '55 and the noise that R 'n' R was making—like a volcano before an eruption—you would imagine that the pop music world
sensed what was in the wind. Certainly some publishers, artists,
songwriters, and record men did. But the music establishment
regarded the interest of young people in R & B and that new-
fangled thing as a fad that would pass, like belting, the mambo,
or calypso.

15

"ROCK AROUND
THE CLOCK"

If one had to pick the recording session at which rock 'n' roll was born, it would be the date on April 12, 1954 at Pythian Temple on Manhattan's West Side at which Bill Haley and the Comets cut "Rock Around the Clock." It would not be an easy choice because the '55 session in Chicago at which Chuck Berry recorded "Maybellene" could not be dismissed. Neither can one minimize the importance of "Ain't It A Shame," cut in New Orleans by Fats Domino, or of "Only You," recorded in Los Angeles by the Platters. I mention the localities to suggest that the development was beginning to assume national proportions. In the final analysis, Haley's disk would get the nod because of his style and impact.

All of these songs were pop hits and not merely R & B. While one of them made it on a cover, "Maybellene," "Only You" and "Rock Around the Clock" hit on the original disks. "Maybellene" finished lowest and "Rock" in the top six of the year's Top Tunes. Also in the Haley record and rendition, we had that unique mingling of two regional streams of music, R & B and C & W, that gave R 'n' R its distinctive character. In essence, Haley was the forerunner of Presley, the Memphis crowd, and rockabilly.

There will always be the lingering suspicion that without *The Blackboard Jungle*, "Rock Around the Clock" might have been a bomb. The song was actually written in '53 by two white, middle-aged, part-time Philadelphia songwriters. An R & B disk by Sonny Dae was a dismal flop. Haley's record, first released in May 1954, made less of a stir than his cover of Joe Turner's "Shake, Rattle and Roll," released two months later. Only after the film hit the screen in '55 did its popularity zoom—and not only in this country but wherever the film played. It is conceivable that time worked in its favor. Nineteen fifty-four was, perhaps, too early.

Although Haley was born and raised in Highland Park, a suburb of Detroit, he began by fronting a hominy-grits, C & W combo known as the Saddlemen. They broadcast over Station WAPA of Chester, Pennsylvania, where Haley was musical director. An admirer of Red Foley and Hank Williams, Haley retains his hayseed appearance—the spit curl on the forehead, the unfocused eyes, and the field-hand's hulk.

While his work on a small-time radio station paid for little more than groceries, it gave him contact with the world of recordings, including those of black musicians like Lucky Millinder and Louis Jordan. Nevertheless, his first releases on Essex Records were conventional C & W. I did not meet Dave Miller, the wiry, hoarse-voiced, sandy-haired owner of Essex until some years later. But like most indie record men, Dave was an aggressive, adventuring and alert disk producer. Sometime in '51 he persuaded Haley to cover Jackie Brenston's "Rocket 88." Brenston made No. 1 on R & B charts. Haley did not show but he took something from the experience that proved a turning point in his style.

In '53 Haley took a then-current jive expression *Crazy, man, crazy,* wrote a song, and made a record. An Essex ad in the April *Billboard* claimed a sale of over one hundred thousand in fifteen days. By June, the song was in the Top Fifteen in the Honor Roll, though it was said that Ralph Marterie's cover on Mercury, rather than Haley's disk, accounted for its popularity. Nevertheless, the buzz was sufficient to attract the attention of a major record company. By '54 Haley was signed to Decca, the diskery that been recording Louis Jordan since the early '40s.

The move of covering Joe Turner on "Shake, Rattle and Roll" was sound—also instructive. Turner's tempo is slower than Haley's, with a persistent, heavy afterbeat and a rippling, whorehouse piano in the background. It was "Shake (sock) Rattle and Roll (sock), Shake (sock) Rattle and Roll (sock) . . ." And the first line placed the singer and his partner in an appropriately sensual setting—"Get outa that bed, and wash your face and hands . . ."

Haley's up-tempo, four-to-the-bar was addressed to a younger crowd for whom he felt it necessary to bowdlerize the lyric. The first line became: "Get out in that kitchen . . ." without the slightest reference to bed. A subsequent reference to a transparent, revealing dress—"I can't believe that all of this belongs to you"—was deleted. Turner's earthy R & B version had turned into exuberant, teen-age R 'n' R.

The country twang remained in Haley's voice even when he sang a blues. Like blues singers, he shouted rather than vocalized, but his voice lacked the bluesman's burden of time and frustration. Yet he made it with black record buyers in '55 with "Dim, Dim the Lights . . . I Want some Atmosphere," written by a black man and a white woman. In the spring of '56 Haley had another best seller, based again on a jive expression, "See You Later, Alligator." A cover of a Chess disk by Bobby Charles, it was an R 'n' R hit, rather than R & B.

The significance of "Rock Around the Clock" is much greater than its fantastic sale and acceptance would suggest, for it became an international hit, the *first* international rock-and-roll hit. And yet even this achievement does not sound the depth of its impact. It was the film that freighted it with a meaning hardly intended by its middle-aged writers and surely not by Bill Haley.

Using a shuffle figure—a rhythm sequence of dotted eighth and sixteenth notes—in ascending and descending thirds and an old-hat swing riff, "Rock" was simply a song about having a good time: "Put on your glad rags . . . and we'll rock till broad daylight . . ." But its role in *The Blackboard Jungle* elevated it into the "Marseillaise" of the rock revolution. An unintended association was established between rock 'n' roll and teen-age alienation and hostility. Riots that attended the showing of the film in Princeton, New Jersey, and several foreign cities made it appear that the song was a tocsin of rebellion. The ground was unwittingly laid for the older generation to associate the new music with rowdyism, violence, and juvenile delinquency.

Inevitably, "Rock Around the Clock" became the title of a '56 film featuring Haley, Little Richard, Chuck Berry, and Alan Freed. Haley also starred in a counterattack film of '57, *Don't Knock the Rock*. After 1956, his power on wax seemed to disappear, even though in '57 he rode in state from Southampton to London and drew sellout crowds in personal appearances throughout Europe.

Haley's combos of five and six pieces have always included tenor saxist Rudy Pompelli whose frantic antics hark back to the early days of Dixieland. His string bassist also indulges in the lying-on-the-floor and swinging-and-rotating the big fiddle bit of early jazz. Once Presley and the Memphis rockabilly crowd appeared on the scene, Haley's R 'n' R had the ersatz quality of any forerunner. He remained a favorite of those who could not take Presley. And today, with the revival of rock 'n' roll, he has found a new audience in his native land.

BILL HALEY INTERVIEW

"A number of people have asked me about Louis Jordan's influence," said Bill Haley, as we talked offstage in the Flamingo Hotel. Haley was part of Richard Nader's "Rock 'n' Roll Revival" show.

"I would honestly have to say," Haley continued, "that I wasn't consciously influenced by Louis Jordan at all. But I have thought about it and I would say that there is a possibility that I was influenced and didn't realize it. I was originally from Michigan, but we moved to Chester when I was a kid. My mother was a piano teacher. My dad, who was from Kentucky, played mandolin. And I suppose that was where the country influence came from. I started to play guitar at the age of seven and I was a country-and-western fan. I used to go around entering amateur contests in an outdoor country-and-western park near my home in Chester.

"I yodeled as well as played the guitar. And the day that I won the contest, Hank Williams was appearing there. . . . He took me into his dressing room and talked to me. After that, every time he appeared in Chester, I tried to get on the same show. We became very good friends. Hank taught me a few chords and he did influence me. He was a great blues singer and he stimulated my interest in rhythm-and-blues music, race music, as it was called then.

"I got my first job singing professionally when I was fifteen or sixteen, on Station WDEL in Wilmington, Delaware, singing with a group called Cousin Lee. Left home after that and traveled around, ending in New Orleans about which I had heard a lot from Hank Williams. There, I listened to Dixieland and boogie-woogie type of music. Some years later, I traveled with a medicine show and finally landed at Station WOWO in Fort Wayne, Indiana, where I got my first network show with a group called the Down Homers.

"I was trying then to become America's champion yodeler. But the influence of rhythm and blues had taken effect, I suppose, during the New Orleans period. And I would imagine that a lot of the groups were playing Louis Jordan music. In that way, probably Louis Jordan did influence me.

"Then I traveled and was with the WLS 'Barn Dance' in Chicago. There I met Red Foley and he became another idol of mine. Also met Lulu Belle and Scotty, who were big then with a song called "Have I Told You Lately (That I Love You)." (Parenthetically, they wrote it and it became the first song that Arnold Shaw promoted when he became Gen. Prof. Mgr. of Duchess Music Corp. in 1950.) After this, I worked at Station WTIC in Hartford, Connecticut.

"And then I decided to give up show business. I had been roaming around for four or five years, had made three or four records that did not set the world afire, and I went back home to see my mother and dad in Chester, Pennsylvania. Fortunately for me, a man named Lew Pollard had just started a radio station. It was just a 250 watter. At my father's urging, I went to see him and I became record librarian, sports announcer, and did a live show for three or four hours a day with my own group.

"On the station there was a show called 'Judge Rhythm's Court,' a record show, run by a man called Jim Reeves (not the country singer-writer). . . . He was a character. His show, an hour of rhythm and blues, ended just before I came on live for an hour with my band. All of this led me to think: 'Why shouldn't a country-and-western act sing rhythm-and-blues music?" It was unheard of in those days. . . . I didn't see anything wrong in mixing things up. I liked to sing rhythm-and-blues tunes and I sang them.

"Shorty used as his theme a tune called 'We're Gonna Rock This Joint Tonight,' and I began doing it. About this time, Dave Miller of Essex Records in Philadelphia came to see me. He and his sister and mother had been listening to my radio programs and he thought I had something different: singing rhythm and blues with a country-and-western background. So I agreed to make some records. And the first side we cut, 'Rocket 88,' an R & B hit, did quite well for us.

"For about a year, I kept having what we used to call territorial hits—disks that broke in Cleveland, Baltimore, Washington, or other individual cities. And that was it. We sold enough records to keep Dave Miller interested and making money. After about a year, we did 'We're Gonna Rock This Joint Tonight' backed with 'Icy Heart,' a country-and-western tune. The next I knew, Dave Miller was on the phone telling me we had a hit—a real hit—and that he wanted me to go on a promotion tour. I agreed and went out on the road with Jack Howard as our advance man. We saw Bill Randle in Cleveland, Robin Seymour in Detroit, and key jockeys in many cities, mostly C & W jockeys. When I reached Nashville, I was real proud because I got an offer to go with the 'Grand Ole Opry.' Having known the show from the time I was a kid, it was the greatest thing that could have happened to me.

"That night I called Hank Williams at his home. He was just leaving on a tour. It was the last time I spoke to him because he died right afterward. He told me how proud he was of me and my acceptance by the 'Grand Ole Opry.' This must have been in October '53.

"As I was leaving Nashville to go to Richmond, I received a phone call from Dave Miller, who told me that it wasn't 'Icy Heart' that was selling but the other side of the record. By the time we returned home, there was no question. It was 'We're Gonna Rock This Joint Tonight,' and we sold about four hundred thousand copies. That was a big figure in those days.

"And now we had a problem. We were a country-and-western act doing R & B. Joe Glaser took over our management. This was before Jolly Joyce came into the picture. Glaser found it tough booking us. But he finally got us into the Preview Lounge in Chicago. It was a Dixieland-jazz room. The people didn't know what we were playing. It wasn't rhythm and blues and it wasn't country and western. And even though we were selling records, it was a very difficult time for us. . . .

"Soon we got rid of our cowboy boots and we shaved off the sideburns. We bought tuxedos and became a pop act. Then we decided we had to have a name for this. I had written a song for the Treniers called 'Rock-a Beatin' Boogie.' The opening lyric went 'Rock, rock, rock everybody/ Roll, roll, roll everybody,' and they recorded it on Okeh Records, I think it was. Also a group called the Esquire Boys recorded it. . . .

"At that time, there was a disk jockey in Akron/Cleveland, Ohio, getting started, Alan Freed, who began using one of these records as his theme song. He used to start pounding the desk along with the record and holler: 'Rock, rock, rock. . . . Roll, roll, roll''—and the name *rock and roll* was born there. Of course, we didn't realize what we had until 'Crazy, Man, Crazy,' our next record, went over a million.

"Then we were off with 'Dance with the Dolly with the Hole in the Stocking,' 'Stop Beating Around the Mulberry Bush'—and enter Mr. Milt Gabler of Decca Records. By then our contract with Dave Miller and Essex had expired. I believe that it was Jimmy Myers, a Philadelphia publisher (later of 'Rock Around the Clock'), who got us with Decca. Of course, by then, several of the major companies were interested in us. When we went with Decca, we were also mulling offers from Mitch Miller at Columbia and Steve Sholes at RCA Victor. I hit it off well with Milt when I went to see him in New York. And I guess I liked Decca because Red Foley was on the label.

"There never was a first session like ours. . . . We worked well with Milt. On that first date, we did 'Rock Around the Clock,' which has now sold over seventeen million copies. 'See You Later, Alligator' racked up two million and a half. It was our moment and our time. So many people have said, 'You were a genius.' There was no genius involved, just something that had to be. We were just a bunch of kids from Philadelphia. And suddenly we were the idols of the world. . . .

"The Sinatra phase had faded. Glenn Miller was gone. And there was nothing happening, except modern and progressive jazz. Stan Kenton and Dave Brubeck, and of course, bop. It was wide open and we offered a simple beat that the kids could dance to. We used to go to assemblies and do free shows and record hops all over the Philadelphia area. Bob Horn and Dick Clark were friends of mine. In a way, I kind of helped Clark get his job on the 'Bandstand.' Jack Step, who was the program director of Station WFIL, was a friend of mine. Bob Horn had just had his problem and they were looking for a replacement. Dick Clark was a part-time announcer whom I liked. And when Jack Step asked me, as he did others, I was one of the people who recommended Dick. . . .

"We did nine motion pictures: one in Italy, one in Germany, two in Mexico, and five here. They've been a great help since they're always playing the late shows somewhere on TV. We've worked hard but we've also had a lot of luck. You can work hard and without luck, you don't make it. Rudy, who has been musical director of the group all these years, and I always say: somebody up there must like us. And obviously, as you've said, somebody down here must like us, too.

"I always liked Bob Wills and his Playboys. He certainly was tops in western swing, along with Tex Williams and Spade Cooley. But they did not influence me. My influence in the country field came from Hank Williams, largely because of the good songs he wrote, the heart songs and blues. Later, I became good friends with Marty Robbins and Hank Thompson. Now, Hank also had a western swing band and I think he had a little influence on me because he used fiddles. . . .

"I did 'Caldonia' in the latter part of my career at Decca largely because Milt Gabler was a cowriter. He once played Louis Jordan's record for me and I liked it, and I liked the idea of doing Milt a favor. It sold records. Louis Jordan was great and never realized the potential that he deserved. I think that possibly he did not have more effect on me because he was at his peak when I was wholly in country-and-western music. Later, when I became interested in the blues, Louis's time had passed. But I am sure that some of the groups I listened to, were influenced by him.

"I'll tell you a fellow who had a tremendous influence on my career. I just saw him in Los Angeles at the Hollywood Bowl—and that's big Joe Turner, the boss of the blues. Joe and I became great friends on a tour we did together in Australia in 1957. . . . Joe Williams is great but Joe Turner is the boss.

"When I was growing up, Chester was a nice, small, industrial town. A suburb of Philadelphia. It was a musical town; the climate was good for musicians. The Four Aces came from Chester—Frankie Avalon, Fabian, Mario Lanza, and others. Then we had Philadelphia and 'American Bandstand.' Chester had a lot of night clubs where musicians would work and the people were very responsive.

"Chester had a black section. But there was no tension. . . . Back then, we worked colored night clubs and there was no problem either with the musicians or the patrons. And I worked on the same bill at Pep's Musical Barn with B. B. King, Fats Domino, Lloyd Price, Ray Charles, Nat King Cole—no hang-up whatsoever.

"The current rock 'n' roll revival is a strange thing. We did go through a period when the excitement died down, certainly here in this country, though we continued working steadily abroad. Then in 1967 we went to Europe, as we had been doing, and we were fourth on the bill at the Alhambra Theatre in Paris. At that time, the big attraction was an English combo, the Spencer Davis group. We were sitting in the dressing room and we could hear this racket going on in the theatre. Then, we heard them shouting: 'Bill Hah-lee . . . Bill Hah-lee!' We were even a bit sceptical as to how we would go over. We went out there and killed them. And that was the beginning of the revival for us. Later, the same thing happened in Amsterdam and in other parts of Europe. Before we went on, they'd start singing 'Rock Around the Clock.'

"Then in 1968 they had the big 'Rock 'n' Roll Revival' in England. And in '69, it was Richard Nader at Madison Square Garden. The only answer I have is that nothing is happening right now and the kids went back to rediscover the original music."

The Platters

Four guys and a girl, the Platters were the first '50s black group to go it in pop without a white cover to power the process. They established themselves, not with a jump tune or humorous novelty but with a ballad. "Only You" was a corny tune that could have come from the 1930s. But the Platters' styling was black.

How black is suggested by their version of Jerome Kern's standard, "Smoke Gets in Your Eyes." Shortly after it was released in '58, a representative of Kern's widow was on the phone with the publisher demanding that he get an injunction and stop its circulation. According to reports, publisher Max Dreyfus—venerable, venerated, and patron of all the show-music greats—had solicited the recording and even offered a promotion budget or a percentage of royalties to assure it. But the estate representative was adamant—Mrs. Kern thought the Platters' version would do irreparable harm to the copyright. All counterarguments having failed, the publisher mentioned that the record could sell as many as a million copies. Apparently, the prospect of wide circulation among a new generation of buyers—not to mention the sizable royalties—mollified Kern's widow, and the Platters' disk went on to earn a Gold Record.

When "Only You" was scaling the charts in '55, a Manhattan disk jockey overdubbed the clucking of hens to mock the style and to suggest that the Platters were short-lived, one-shot birds. How wrong can you be? In '56 they scored two of the three top songs of the year with "My Prayer," a revival of a '39 hit, and "The Great Pretender," a new song by their manager that soothed the egos of young people with inferiority feelings. Again in '58, it was revival time with "Twilight Time," once the theme of the instrumental group known as the Three Suns, who wrote it with Buck Ram, the Platters' manager.

After "Smoke Gets In Your Eyes," the disk popularity of the group began to wane with "Harbor Lights," another best-selling revival, this time of a ballad popularized by Rudy Vallee in 1937. It was clear by then (1960) that the Platters were reinterpreting songs of the past in terms of the present, and that they had a large, loyal following. However, success apparently went to their heads and several of the group were busted in a Cincinnati hotel on charges involving prostitutes and pot. The attendant publicity was destructive.

As with the Four Aces, the downfall of the group came when lead singer Tony Williams, who had a distinctive, piercing sound, decided to go it alone. It was disastrous for both. Williams worked with Herb Abramson, cofounder of Atlantic Records, who also went out on his own. Triumph Records did not prove true to its name either for Williams or Abramson. The Platters did not make it on wax, although with new personnel, they have continued making personal appearances into the '70s.

Chuck Berry

Chuck Berry has been called "folk poet of the '50s," "the major figure of rock and roll" and "the single most important name in the history of rock." All of these epithets are well deserved, not only because of his own achievement but because of the influence he exerted on later super-rock artists like the Beatles, Rolling Stones, Bob Dylan, and the Beach Boys (whose surfin' music was based on his "Sweet Little Sixteen").

He was tall, wavy haired, looked a bit like young Abe Lincoln, walked with a crouch—and he sang about "Maybellene," who took off with a cat in a Coup de Ville and he went *motivatin'* after her in his Ford—*nothin' outrun my V-8 Ford*—and though Maybellene might be untrue, he drove his way truly into the heart and psyche of school kids in '55. Today, it's motorcycles but back then, hot rods and stock cars and anything that moved fast on four wheels meant romance, adventure, and sex—and Chuck Berry felt it and told it like it was.

As for the contribution of the other two men whose names appear as coauthors, Berry has only recently spoken out clearly: "Alan Freed grabbed a third," he told his biographer. "Actually, there were two grabbers. Russ Fratto, another deejay, was on it, too. I got it back from Fratto but I didn't get it from Freed. It went to his estate—and they do still get a third—Freed actually didn't sit down with me at all or write anything."

Working the Cosmopolitan Club in East St. Louis and studying at the Poro School of Beauty Culture, Chuck was six months a practicing cosmetician when he brought "Maybellene" to Chicago. Muddy Waters allowed him on the stand of a southside club and urged him to see the Chess Brothers. At his audition, Berry performed "Maybellene," then known as "Ida Red," in a country style. Legend has it that Leonard Chess added the rock beat of Chicago blues. Chuck has said that the only Maybellene he ever knew was a cow and that his work as a cosmetician did not influence his choice of name. He tends to be contrary in discussing himself or his work. Helped by the excitement of Alan Freed's exposure, the song went to No. 1 on R & B charts, succeeding "Rock Around the Clock," as it in turn was superseded by "Only You." On the pop Honor Roll of Hits, it made Top Fifteen but limited plays on the country's white radio stations caused it to finish almost at the bottom of a tabulation of fifty of the year's Top Tunes.

In the year (1956) that brought the emergence of Presley, Chuck Berry created a number of teen-age classics. "Too Much Monkey Business" caught the "botheration" of kids working in a filling station and being burdened with all the menial little tasks. Like "Thirty Days" in its comment on judges and "No Money Down" in its putdown of car salesmen, this song embodied criticism of the establishment to which Chuck was sensitive as a Negro and which incorporated the new generation's beefs against authority and conformity.

In "Roll Over Beethoven" and other songs, Berry beautifully captured and expressed the feelings of the young about things they enjoyed or "disenjoyed." Here it was R & B music and he was for their digging it freely "if you feel it and like it . . ." The words and images were unexceptionable but they had sex in them. Not being a teen-ager, Berry did not write as one identifying with the young but as an observer. But what an observer and what empathy!

"School Day," "Johnny B. Goode," and "Sweet Little Sixteen" of '57–'58 were minor masterpieces of insight and understanding. "School Day (Ring! Ring! Goes the Bell!)" pinpointed the teen-ager's feelings from his arrival in school where "the teacher is teachin' the golden rule" to the three-o'clock bell that spelled release and the rush to the juke joint around the corner: "Hail! Hail! Rock 'n' roll/ Deliver me from the days of old . . ." But in "Baby Doll" he also sensed the nostalgia of young people, looking back after graduation and summertime, and remembering how they walked to school "when the weather was cool" and stopped to catch the newest song on car radios passing by.

In "Sweet Little Sixteen" he described sympathetically a girl's joy in collecting autographed pictures of singing stars, her excitement in seeing them in person—"Oh Daddy, Daddy/ I beg of you/ Whisper to Mommy/ It's all right with you . . ."—acting grownup in tight dresses and high heels, and then the letdown of being "sweet sixteen back in class again . . ."

"Almost Grown" of '59 defined maturity in teen-age terms—I ain't never been in dutch and don't browse around too much—and in a throwaway line, caught the loneliness, introspection, and abstraction of adolescence: *Don't bother me, leave me alone . . .*

Of historians who have read autobiography into "Johnny B. Goode" and other songs, Berry has said: "Everything I wrote about wasn't about me, but about the people listening to my songs. Like I didn't write 'School Day' in a classroom. I wrote it in the Street Hotel, one of the big, black, low-priced hotels in St. Louis."

Musically, Berry came from the opposite direction of Presley to meet almost at the crossroad of rockabilly. As Presley was a Memphis white singing guttural, bluesy black, Berry was a St. Louis black singing country white. When he came to Chicago, he was singing, in his words, "Nat and Eckstine with a little bit of Muddy." In fact, his clean-cut enunciation occasionally caused him to be taken for white as Presley was taken for black.

Berry was rocking high until in '59 he did what any foolish, arrogant kid might do. On a tour in Mexico, he picked up a

Spanish-speaking, Apache-Indian girl and transported her to St. Louis where he gave her a job in his Bandstand club. When he fired her, she ran to authorities with a tale that brought news headlines: "Rock 'n' Roll Singer Lured Me to St. Louis, Says 14 Year Old." Berry was arrested and charged with violation of the Mann Act. In the war on teen-age music, the Establishment had an easy victim. Even though it was proved that the girl was a prostitute, he was convicted. The first trial was thrown out because of the judge's patent prejudice. But he was convicted in a second trial and entered the Federal Penitentiary at Terre Haute in February 1962.

Despite prison records, Berry has on occasion denied that he spent time in jail. Contradicting himself, he also has claimed that he was framed by business interests in Wentsville, Missouri, where he has a half-million-dollar estate, country club, pool, night club, and motel. In any event, he was out of circulation during the early '60s. But toward the mid-'60s he made a triumphal tour through Europe where all the British groups showered him with affection and adulation, besides recording his songs. Of his post-Beatle recognition, he has said: "Sometimes kids hear a record by me and they go, 'Wow! that dude is doing a Rolling Stones record!'"

The "Rock 'n' Roll Revival," popularized by Richard Nader and others, has opened the country's top showplaces to him, including the Las Vegas Hilton. But he plays the Lounge whereas Elvis plays the Main Showroom. Some critics feel that it should be the other way around and that if skin pigmentation were interchanged, it *would* be the other way around. The thought has occurred to Berry, who has said: "It's obvious that Presley's road was free and mine had to be paved."

Onstage, Chuck can be cute and inviting, as when he tickles an audience into singing response lines in "My Ding-A-Ling," his Gold Record of 1972. He has never approached the Pelvis's charisma, the duck waddle (which he first performed at the Brooklyn Paramount in 1956) being the height of his in-person shows. But when it comes to sheer creativity, wit, and imagination as a songwriter, he has few peers. Except for Leiber and Stoller, possibly Otis Blackwell, no songsmith has done more to body forth the rock 'n' roll experience and the outlook, feelings, put-downs, and hang-ups of the teen generation of the 1950s. He was and is its song laureate.

III

THE ROCK 'N' ROLL YEARS

1956-1960

16

THE GOD OF R 'N' R ARRIVES *Elvis*

In 1956 President Dwight Eisenhower went to Walter Reed Hospital for an operation on an intestinal obstruction. Film actress Grace Kelly went to Monaco and became a twentieth-century princess. Soviet troops went to Poland and to Hungary to suppress revolts. The Swedish-American liner Stockholm went to sea and the Italian luxury ship Andrea Doria went to the bottom. Archie Moore went into a New York ring and Floyd Patterson became the youngest world's champion in boxing history. Tommy Dorsey went to bed and choked to death in his sleep. Milton Berle went into retirement after reigning eight years as Mr. Television. And a young, black woman, Autherine Lucy, went to the University of Alabama, backed by a court order and bayonets.

In 1956 Elvis Aaron Presley, ex–truck driver, went into an RCA Victor studio, recorded "Heartbreak Hotel" and emerged the god of rock 'n' roll.

Hysteria had marked the advent of Sinatra in the '40s and accompanied the rise of the Beatles in the '6os. Presley's emergence was as explosive and more controversial. The Beatles were a generation image. Sinatra was a sex image. Presley was a stud, too, his low growl of a voice suggesting a hound dog pawing a bitch's door. But unlike the others, his initial image was that of a hood. By year-end, it softened into the perennial adolescent, sometimes shy, sometimes vain, sometimes vulnerable, but always respectful to his elders, sir.

In December of '55 RCA released five Presley disks acquired from Sun and previously issued by the Memphis company. The move was made because of a concern that Presley's unique quality might be lost in the more sophisticated atmosphere and machinery of a major record company. These disks sold so poorly that RCA executives wondered about the $40,000 it had taken to acquire him. Then came "Heartbreak Hotel," cut in Victor studios under the supervision of Steve Sholes, the executive who had bought and fought for the deal. By late April, trade-paper headlines told a different story: "Sholes Has Last Laugh? As Presley Rings Up Sales." The disk had, in fact, passed the million mark and was at the top of the Honor Roll of Hits. And all the other Presley disks were selling at such a rate that he alone accounted, unbelievably, for almost half of Victor's entire pop sale.

When he made his second appearance on the "Milton Berle Show" early in June, Presley was presented with two *Billboard* crowns. Not too many artists achieved No. 1 on three pop charts, Retail Sales, Juke Box Plays, and Disk Jockey Plays. The Pelvis had made it also on C & W charts. At the time, "Heartbreak Hotel" was in the Top Ten also of two R & B charts. His first album was the No. 1 best seller of all pop LP's. And a new single, "I Want You, I Need You, I Luh-huh-huh-huv Yew-hew," broke simultaneously into the Top Twenty, pop, and C & W, on its first appearance.

Presley's tumultuous acceptance by teen-agers, black, white, and redneck, was hardly shared by the adults. "He can't sing a lick," wrote Jack O'Brien in the *Journal-American*, "and makes up for vocal shortcomings with the weirdest and plainly planned, suggestive animation short of an aborigine's mating dance. . . . He wiggled and wriggled with such abdominal gyrations that burlesque bombshell Georgia Sothern really deserves equal time to reply . . ."

The venerable radio-TV critic of *The New York Times,* Jack Gould, described him as a "rock and roll variation of one of the most standard acts in show business, the virtuoso of the hootchy-kootchy."

To John Crosby of the *New York Herald-Tribune,* generally libertarian in his views, Presley was "an unspeakably untalented and vulgar young entertainer. . . . Where do you go from Elvis Presley, short of obscenity—which is against the law?"

Even a New York disk jockey, Jerry Marshall of WNEW, joined the outcry. Before playing Presley's new disk on his "Make Believe Ballroom" turntable, he said: "If the future is important, Elvis will have to stop the 'hootchy kootchy' gyrations or end up as 'Pelvis' Presley in circus side shows and burlesque . . ." A Chicago radio station made a more dynamic comment: daily it smashed Presley records to pieces while on the air.

To all the panning, NBC-TV replied with a statement that the Pelvis's appearance, wriggles and all, had given Uncle Miltie a rating superior to the competitive "Phil Silvers Show" on ABC-TV. Nevertheless, when Presley guested in July on the "Steve Allen Show" on NBC, he appeared in a tuxedo and was, in the words of a critic, "painfully subdued." When he sang his new single, "Hound Dog," Allen substituted, for the pelvic gyrations, shots of a sad-faced beagle hound. Once again, as with Berle, Allen's ratings forged ahead of the competitive "Ed Sullivan Show" on CBS. But the kids were not pleased. When Presley cut some new sides in New York, youngsters picketed the RCA Victor studios on East Twenty-fourth Street with signs reading, "We want the real Elvis!"

On seeing the Trendex that put him below Steve Allen, Ed Sullivan reportedly sniffed, "Presley is not my cup of tea," and added that he would not have the gyrating groaner on his "family-type show at any price." But the following week, when Allen without Presley dropped below Sullivan, Ed quickly forgot his disdainful dismissal and signed Elvis for three fall appearances at $17,000 per show.

During the second half of '56, statistics supplied ample testimony to Presley's pyramiding impact. "Hound Dog" b/w "Don't Be Cruel" was a two-side hit, rare enough in music business, with each side making No. 1 and racking up a sale of over a million disks.

"Love Me Tender," the September release, had advance orders for over eight hundred fifty-six thousand copies a week before issue. A soft ballad, sung low and slow, it was the title tune of Presley's first picture—the first of a series of thirty so-so, ho-hum films that were substantial box-office successes. A measure of the singer's popularity and of Colonel Parker's managerial muscle, was their coup in acquiring publishing rights to the score of the picture. Presley also received credit—and royalties—as "cowriter" of the songs.

Presley's September release on RCA Victor included, in addition to the title song of his film, seven other single disks. It was an unheard-of maneuver that was instantly seized upon by the anti-Presley brigade as a move to "take the money and run." Music pros argued that anything that went up so fast, had to come down faster. RCA Victor execs admitted that theirs was a saturation gimmick but that it was based on the apparently insatiable demand for Presley recordings by teen-agers.

Sales of "Love Me Tender" seemed to bear out their contention. In its first appearance on the Best-Selling Singles chart of *Billboard,* it bounced into the No. 2 slot. No other record in the trade-paper's history had ever accomplished this. Simultaneously, it smashed into the Top Ten in both the C & W and R & B fields, demonstrating that "rockabilly" was indeed a fusion of these two styles with pop impact.

By year-end, those who wanted to denigrate Presley's appeal as being limited to depraved American youngsters were faced with figures that came flying down from Canada. In a country where a hundred thousand seller was considered a smash, "Hound Dog" and "Don't Be Cruel" aggregated a total exceeding two hundred twenty-five thousand and "Love Me Tender" soared over the one hundred thirty-five thousand mark in six weeks. More impressive even was the report of music stores in Toronto and Montreal that Presley mania had enormously upped the sale of guitars. RCA of Canada not only named "Don't Be Cruel" as the biggest single in the company's history, but asserted that Presley was the only American artist who had ever appealed to the French population as well as English.

In a midyear ad, Dot Records made the claim that Pat Boone was "the only artist in the history of music business to be on 'Best Selling Retail Record Charts' thirty-eight out of fifty-two weeks in his first year on records." Boone's was a formidable achievement, including hits like "Ain't That a Shame," "I Almost Lost My Mind," "I'll Be Home," "Friendly Persuasion," "Tutti Frutti," and "Long Tall Sally." But in an overall view, the young man in the white buckskins came second to the Tupelo troubadour. Presley was Hound Dog of the year by a wide margin.

"I saw a cousin of mine dance when I was very young," said David Bowie, the English rock star. "She was dancing to Elvis'

'Hound Dog' and I have never seen her get up and be moved so much by anything. It really impressed me. The power of music. I started getting records immediately after that. My mother brought me Fats Domino's "Blueberry Hill" the next day. When I got older, I heard about Chuck Berry and that led me into R & B, jazz, and blues."

17

KNOCKING
THE ROCK

From Cincinnati came reports that a used-car dealer jacked up his
business with a sign that read:

WE GUARANTEE
TO BREAK 50 ELVIS PRESLEY RECORDS
IN YOUR PRESENCE
IF YOU BUY ONE OF THESE CARS TODAY.

In one day, he sold five cars.

Presley's fanatical acceptance by teen-agers brought attacks by
Establishment forces that had first leveled their guns at Alan
Freed. All through 1956, these barbs were directed not merely
at the Pelvis but at rock 'n' roll as such. The motivation was at
times economic (when old-time publishers, songwriters, and entertainers were involved), at times a matter of "moral" indigna-
tion, and not infrequently, racist in origin.

"Rock and roll inflames and excites youth," the Very Rev. John
Carroll told a Teachers Institute of the Archdiocese of Boston,
"like jungle tom-toms readying warriors for battle. Inject a wrong
word of misunderstanding and the whole place blows up. The
suggestive lyrics are, of course, a matter for law-enforcement agencies. But the first line of defense must be the disk jockeys."

In Buffalo disk jockey Dick Biondi was fired on the air by
Station WKBW for spinning an Elvis Presley disk. Later at a
show where Elvis autographed his shirt as a token of regard,
Biondi made the mistake of moving into a crowd of excited girls.
They promptly tore the shirt off his back.

But *Billboard* reported in its first issue of the year that R & B,

or as the teen-agers call it, R 'n' R, had "achieved respectability."
Cited as tokens of acceptance were a "Rock 'n' Roll Ice Revue" at
New York City's palatial Roxy Theatre; the scheduling of a rock
radio show emceed by Alan Freed on CBS; the presentation on the
"Ed Sullivan Show" of a revue emceed by Dr. Jive, an R & B deejay; use of the Big Beat on a Pall Mall cigarette commercial;
booking of an R & B revue at Carnegie Hall; and the release by
MGM Records of a "Rock Around Mother Goose" disk. R & B
was enjoying a *boom*, the trade paper observed, "in spite of wistful
obit-prophesying by chauvinistic pop music characters."

The chauvinists were not in music alone. In the South, the
White Citizen's Council of Birmingham, Alabama, formally
announced a continuing campaign to rid all local juke boxes of
rock-and-roll disks. In Hartford, Connecticut, a three-day appearance of Alan Freed's rock 'n' roll show prompted a move by the
police to revoke the license of the State Theatre. The gendarmes
received moral support from a Hartford psychiatrist who characterized the new pop as "a communicable disease with music
appealing to adolescent insecurity and driving teen-agers to do
outlandish things."

Three older-generation musicians came to the defense of R 'n'
R. In an open letter, Sammy Kaye of swing and sway fame condemned the psychiatrist's comments as "thoughtless and in bad
taste." Agreeing that youngsters who misbehaved should be pun-
ished, Kaye stated: "Some years ago when teenagers began to
Lindy Hop there were persons—among them, perhaps you—who
called them lunatics and delinquent. I have no doubt that the same
reception greeted those who first danced the Fox Trot years ago."

Terming the nationwide assault on R 'n' R a "conspiracy," Alan
Freed announced that bandleaders Benny Goodman and Paul
Whiteman had both invited him "to compare scrapbooks." These
would reveal that attacks had been made on them for sponsoring
music that "corrupted the youth of their day."

April brought a new onslaught, this from the large circulation
New York *Daily News*. In a two-part feature, the tabloid castigated
R 'n' R as an "inciter of juvenile delinquency" and blasted Alan
Freed as a prime offender. CBS used the occasion for a special
news program moderated by commentator Eric Sevareid. Film
clips of an R 'n' R show at Camden, New Jersey, were followed
by interviews with teen-agers. All denied that it was a bad influence. Several psychiatrists queried by Sevareid exonerated the
music of evil influence and attributed riots to shortcomings in the
home environment of the rioters. A & R man Mitch Miller,
known as a critic of rock, made a surprise appearance during

which he stated: "You can't call any music criminal. If anything is wrong with rock and roll, it is that it makes a virtue of monotony."

Climax of the Sevareid inquiry was an interview with Alan Freed, who denounced press stories of riots at his other rock shows as "grossly exaggerated." He reminded "mom and dad" of their own (and his) teen-age years when the Big Swing Bands were to them what rock 'n' roll now was to their children. Denouncing the *Daily News* for failing to mention his welfare activities, he noted that eleven thousand youngsters appeared for him on a rainy Saturday, to distribute 500,000 fund-raising circulars to fight nephrosis. His was a good performance.

The controversy continued. In Boston, Station WBZ presented an hour-long documentary, with Duke Ellington appearing for the affirmative. The anti view was represented by the director of the Catholic Youth Organization of the Diocese, who stated: "There is no doubt but that the by-product of rock and roll has left its scar on youth."

Even while Freed and the *Daily News* were throwing karate chops at each other, the ABC network launched "Rhythm on Parade," an R & B program originating at Detroit's famous Flame Bar and hosted by deejay Willie Bryant. NBC-TV was making plans for a Saturday afternoon show aimed at teen-age rock 'n' rollers. And CBS-TV, sponsor of Alan Freed's "Rock 'n' Roll Dance Party" was considering use of the deejay in a half-hour segment on Jackie Gleason's "Stage Show."

A similar change was occurring among C & W listeners. Despite opposition to the new style, partly because of its Negro origins, an increasing number of C & W disk jockeys were yielding to listener demands and programing R & B and rock 'n' roll records. As for the record companies both in the South and North, there was a widespread search for another Presley.

In the midst of the raging brouhaha, a flanking attack took shape in Chicago. In an effort to divert teen-age interest in dancing from R 'n' R to the polka and schottische, ABC-TV began telecasting nationally Station WKBY's "Polka Time Show." ABC-Paramount Records joined the drive by releasing a series of Polka albums by Steve Wolowu, the featured bandleader. Later, *Billboard* headlined: "Polkas Fade from Milwaukee Juke Boxes/ Beer City's Favorite Folk Music Bows to Pop Hits and Rock 'n' Roll Records."

Pearl Bailey tried to inject some humor in the situation by recording "I Can't Rock and Roll to Save My Soul" b/w "The Gypsy Goofed." But in the fall, the battle raged on a new front.

Before a congressional committee investigating monopoly in the broadcasting industry, came a group of outstanding songwriters, mostly of show tunes, headed by the president of ASCAP. Their charge: BMI, the competing performance-rights society, was a conspiracy by the broadcasters to control the nation's songs.

Accusing BMI of "muddying up the airwaves with rock and roll and other musical monstrosities," songwriter and theatrical producer Billy Rose claimed that a songwriter had little chance of being heard unless he was associated with BMI. But even as he made the charge, his own song, "Tonight You Belong to Me" was No. 6 on *Billboard*'s Honor Roll of Hits, the result of a new teen-age version by Patience and Prudence, aged eleven and fourteen.

An unusual number of ASCAP standards were, in fact, then available in new rock 'n' roll versions. Among Presley's seven newly released singles were "I Love You Because" and Rodgers and Hart's "Blue Moon." Fats Domino was on R & B and pop charts with "When My Dreamboat Comes Home," introduced in 1936 by Guy Lombardo. He had previously made a smash of Walter Donaldson's "My Blue Heaven," vintage 1927, and was about to do the same for "Blueberry Hill," sung originally by Gene Autry in a 1941 oatuner. "My Prayer" (1939) was then an R & B and pop hit for the Platters.

There were in addition new releases of "Candy" (1944) and "Mean to Me" (1929) by Big Maybelle on Savoy; "Yes, Sir, That's My Baby" (1925), "Ain't She Sweet" (1927), and "My Heart Cries for You" (1950) by the Sensations on Atco; Irving Berlin's "White Christmas" by the Drifters; "I Don't Care If the Sun Don't Shine" (1949) by Presley; and "I Wanna Be Loved," a Billy Rose ballad of 1932, by Ruth Brown on Atlantic. It was no wonder that several top echelon ASCAP executives dissociated the organization from statements made before the Celler House Committee, claiming that charges by Rose and others were their own personal opinions.

One ASCAP standard that did not go very far in '56 was an R & B version of Cole Porter's "I Love You" from *Mexican Hayride*. Originally a hit for Bing Crosby in '44, it was cut by the Robins. Chappell Music, publishers of most Broadway show scores, took up arms. Contending that the new version ridiculed the song and tended to destroy the value of the copyright, they forced the Robins disk off the market. A few years later, the same company manifested an entirely different attitude when it came to the Platters recording of another show standard. "Smoke Gets In Your Eyes."

The Celler Committee itself came under fire as the result of a

telegram from Frank Sinatra that was read into the record. Sinatra's blast was directed mainly against Mitch Miller, whom he
blamed for his decline of the early '50s, but it also lambasted BMI.
The Swooner claimed that as A & R head of Columbia, Miller
denied his right to choose material and "by design or coincidence
began to present many, many inferior songs all curiously bearing
the BMI label." Adverting to his phoenixlike rise of the mid-'50s,
Sinatra stated: "It is now a matter of record that since I have
associated myself with Capitol, a company free of broadcasting
affiliations, my career is again financially, creatively, and artisti-
cally healthy. My career as a successful recording artist was based
on material from the catalog of ASCAP . . . and will always be
based on the catalog of ASCAP."

This "kiss by wire," as *Billboard* ironically termed it, led a
tradester to observe that "Frank didn't know his ASCAP from his
BMI." Columbia Records quickly supplied the supporting evidence. It pointed out that of the fifty-seven songs recorded by
Sinatra under Miller's direction, only five were in BMI and of
the remaining fifty-two, eleven were in Sinatra's own ASCAP
firm, Barton Music. (It so happened that the five were hits for
other artists: "Goodnight Irene" for the Weavers and Red Foley
and Ernest Tubb; "I Hear A Rhapsody" for Jimmy Dorsey;
"Chattanooga Shoe Shine Boy" for Bing Crosby; "That's How
Much I Love You" for Bing Crosby; and "Poinciana" also for
Bing Crosby.) Columbia also noted that Sinatra's early rock 'n'
roll hit "The Hucklebuck" was in ASCAP while his first hit on
Capitol, "Young at Heart," was in BMI. Adducing additional statistics, it disclosed that during his forty-five-month tenure at
Capitol, Sinatra had recorded, apparently of his own volition,
eleven BMI tunes, including the hit, "Learnin' the Blues."

Hank Sanicola, Sinatra's personal manager, tried to emphasize
that Sinatra's wire was not directed so much at BMI as Mitch
Miller, and he admitted that he was then negotiating a new
contract with BMI for firms owned by Sinatra.

The ASCAP attack on BMI, meanwhile, proceeded on another
front. By way of pressing a $150-million lawsuit initiated by a
group of ASCAP writers against BMI, broadcasters, and diskeries,
attorney John Shulman subpoenaed a group of BMI publishers
for pretrial hearings. Rumor had it that a writer's committee was
being formed to discuss dropping the suit with BMI if broadcasters would divest themselves of their control. About which
some BMI publishers raised a corollary question: Would the big

film companies, MGM, Warner Brothers, and Paramount, divest themselves of the ASCAP firms they owned?

When ASCAP publishers and writers met for their annual conclave just a few weeks after the monopoly blast against BMI, they learned that for the first eight months of 1956, the Society had distributed over $11 million, an increase of 5 percent over the preceding year.

The statistics led a Hollywood song plugger to pen an open letter to the ASCAP warriors around the theme "You Ain't Nothin' but a Big Hog," paraphrasing Presley's recent hit. Noting that several thousand publishers and songwriters were able through BMI to earn a livelihood and advance their creative careers, Don Genson observed: "As for the charge that BMI songs are aiding and abetting juvenile delinquency, I think it best to remind them that they were writing the songs when the delinquents of the 1920s were annihilating themselves with denatured alcohol to the tune of 'Barney Google,'" which, incidentally, was a novelty song by Billy Rose.

During a visit to New York in December, ASCAP composer Dmitri Tiomkin, whose recent film scores included *High Noon* and *Friendly Persuasion,* leveled an attack on musical snobbism. "Some like Bach," he said, "some like Benny Goodman and some like rock 'n' roll. . . . These are all good for certain moods and they are all aspects of American music." Then he raised a point that did not seem to concern anyone except the record buyers: that there should be "freedom not only for the creators but also for the audience."

According to the disk buyer of Liberty Music Shops in Manhattan, adult record buyers then were "purchasing decibels not music." Although they denounced young music as noise, they themselves were buying train records, band records, recordings of motorcar races, etc., in fantastic quantities. In short, not unlike the younger generation, their search was for "excitement, sensationalism, and plain noise."

As the year of conflict drew to an end, the National Guard Armory of Washington, D. C., was declared off limits for rock 'n' roll shindigs. The Armory Board blamed disturbances *not* inside but outside the Armory. About the same time, disk jockey Tom Edwards of Station WERE in Cleveland, appearing at a local church dance, was not allowed to play any Presley records, give out any Presley pictures, or show five pictures of him as part of a color-slide show he had planned for the dance's intermission.

One of the year's most disturbing incidents occurred toward the end of April. Because it involved a singer who was not even remotely associated with R & B or rock 'n' roll, it suggested the irrational character of the attacks on the music, also the prejudice frequently at the bottom of such onslaughts. The scene was the Municipal Auditorium in Birmingham, Alabama, on the evening of April 23. Four thousand whites were in attendance since a city ordinance forbade mixed crowds. Star of the variety troupe that included comic Gary Morton and Ted Heath's orchestra was a singer who had been born in Montgomery, Alabama, Nathaniel Adams Cole, better known as Nat "King" Cole.

He had just completed singing "Autumn Leaves" and was in the middle of "Little Girl"—hardly R 'n' R fare—when five men came charging down the aisle, leaped onto the stage, and attacked Cole. Police, who had been forewarned of a demonstration, charged out of the wings of the auditorium and freed Cole from his attackers—but not before he had been knocked off the piano bench and mauled. Arm-locking the five hoodlums, the police marched them out as the Ted Heath band played "America."

After order was restored, comic Morton explained that Cole could not continue the performance because of an injury to his foot. Nat managed to limp back onstage for a five-minute ovation. Arrested with the five goons was a sixth man whom the police found in a parked car, loaded with a cache of brass knuckles, a blackjack, and two rifles.

One of the men arrested was later identified as a director of the White Citizen's Council, a group promoting a boycott of "bop and Negro music" in its effort to maintain a segregation of whites and blacks.

The attack on Cole had repercussions in Charlotte, North Carolina, where Bob Raiford, a disk jockey, was fired from Station WBT. Raiford had toured the city with a tape recorder, getting comments from citizens about the attack on Cole and he had aired some of them on his program. Station management denied that the deejay had been fired for his opinions on race relations, or that these even figured in the dismissal. No, he had been dismissed for disobeying orders—he was instructed not to play the interviews —and for criticizing the station on its own facilities.

Bill Haley's final record release of '56 sounded a tonic chord. One could take it as a plea, warning, or advice. Its title: "Don't Knock the Rock."

Perry Como

Frank Sinatra

Bobby Darin

Patti Page

Bill Haley

Johnny Ace

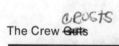

The Crew Cuts

Fats Domino

Howlin' Wolf

The Kingston Trio

Hank Williams

The Drifte

Johnny Mathis

La Vern Baker

B. B. King

eil Sedaka

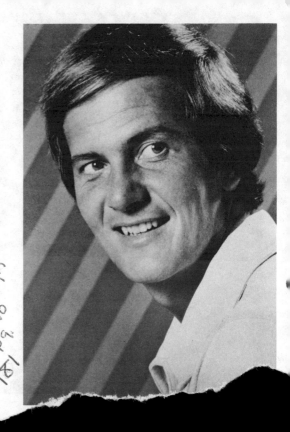

turn to pg. 181

nway Twitty

The Coaste

Ray Charles

Little Richard

Buddy Holly

he Everly Brothers

Jerry Lee Lewis

Paul Anka

Frankie Avalon

Connie Francis

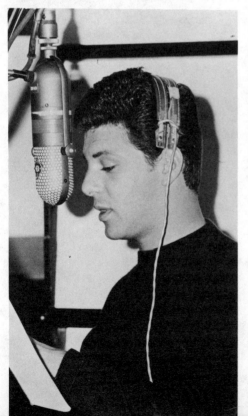

18

TEEN-AGE
ERUPTION

"Little Richard, man, was the god!" said Marty Balin of the Jefferson Airplane. "I grew up on Little Richard."

When Jerry Lee Lewis hits the piano keyboard with his butt, bangs the keys with the boot heel of an outstretched leg, and leaps on top, it's Little Richard. When Presley chokes-gasps-gulps his words and swivels his pelvis, it's Little Richard. When the Beatles scream "Yeah, yeah, yeah" and gliss into a high falsetto, it's Little Richard.

They all grew up on him. So did Bill Haley and the Rolling Stones, who also recorded his frantic songs and imitated him in varying degrees. So did Pat Boone, who didn't grow up but grew fat, tenderizing his style for white, teen-age consumption.

"Gonna rock it up! Rip it up! Shake it up! Ball it up!" Little Richard was a revivalist preacher of the gospel of joy. "I call it the healing music," he has said, "the music that makes the blind see, the lame, the deaf, and dumb hear, walk, and talk. The music of joy, the music that uplifts your soul. I said, because I am the living flame, Little Richard is my name . . ."

He sang with an intensity and frenzy and commitment that marked the outer limits of rock 'n' roll "Ohhh! My Soul!" was one of his favorite exclamations, and later, they called his style soul. He was excitement in motion, a whirling dervish at the keyboard, showmanship royale in eye-dazzling costumes topped by a high, slick pompadour of hair.

In 1955 he was working as a dishwasher in his hometown. "Oh my God, my God," he exclaimed, "I was working in the Greyhound bus station in Macon, Georgia, oh, my Lord. I was washing dishes. I couldn't talk back to my boss man. He would bring all those pots back for me to wash, and one day I said, 'I've got to do something to stop that man bringing back all those pots to me to wash,' and I said, 'Awap bop-a-lop bop-a-wop bam boom, take 'em out!' and that's how I came to write 'Tutti Frutti.' And so I wrote 'Good Golly Miss Molly' in the kitchen. I wrote 'Long Tall Sally' in that kitchen."

Long Tall Sally was a girl in his hometown, way back, he later said. "I used to call her Slim. Long Tall Sally and my Uncle John used to drink a lot on Saturdays, you know, you had to get paid on Saturday in the South. And he would go off with his women, you know, and get drunk, and when he'd see my aunt coming, he would duck."

In 1951 Little Richard, just fifteen, recorded some bland blues for RCA Victor. In 1953 he recorded some crying blues for Peacock. Roy Brown had done it better. In 1955 he recorded for Specialty, and that was Little Richard. Gospel blues, and an agitation and effervescence approached by few singers.

"Tutti Frutti" came first, a hit for Pat Boone rather than Little Richard. But they all really came at once. On 1956's R & B charts, Richard Penniman, to mention his Christian name, had no fewer than five records in the Top Fifty: "Tutti Frutti," "Ready Teddy," "Slippin' and Slidin'," "Rip It Up," and the biggest of all, "Long Tall Sally." But except for "Sally," Little Richard did not really cross over into pop.

Apparently, he was a bit too much, not for the nation's teen-agers, but for the white knights of the turntable. They were overwhelmed, if not repelled, by his violent emotionalism and sweat-pouring expenditure of energy. Inevitably, this opened the door for imitators to enter—and they did. But his unique and extreme style attracted the attention of show-biz people, and Little Richard appeared in several of '56's rock 'n' roll movies, stealing *The Girl Can't Help It*, regarded as the most realistic and best plotted of the group.

In '56 Fats Domino did cross into pop, scoring with "Blueberry Hill," "I'm in Love Again," and "My Blue Heaven." Since two of the three were revivals of standards, the fat man's appeal may have encompassed adults. Though he sang in a high nasal voice to a boogie-shuffle accompaniment, his New Orleans, Cajun accent had no black identity. Even the tenor-sax solo by Lee Allen or Herb Hardesty were more melodic and not as raucous as on typical R & B disks. The young found him irresistible. His voice was bright, good humored, and youthful enough to establish an infectious camaraderie. He provided an easy transition from rhythm and blues to rock 'n' roll.

The third giant seller of the year was, of course, the young southerner who served as a guide to black song and styling. Like the Beatles with rock of the '60s, Pat Boone brought a measure of respectability to rock 'n' roll of the '50s with his well-mannered and warm baritone.

These three major figures of '56 span the spectrum of R 'n'R— Little Richard at the black extreme, Fats and Chuck Berry as middlemen, and at the white rock extreme, Pat Boone.

Black Rock

James Brown, known as Soul Brother No. 1 and recently as the Godfather of Soul, came from the same red-clay hills of Georgia as Little Richard. Instead of washing dishes, he shined shoes in front of a radio station in Macon he now owns. When King Records released his first side in '56, it could not have realized that it had a legend in the making. "Please, Please, Please" appeared as another title in a one-column ad of ten other King/ Federal releases.

But it was an unusual record, opening cold with four, hoarse-voiced repeats of the title word, after which an off-harmony group came in against hammering triplets. The song was not structured but consisted of four lines repeated again and again with the mounting intensity of a revivalist preacher: "I love you so-o-o-o," "You done me wrong," "Please don't go-o-o-o," and the title word, "Please . . . please . . . please." All the devices of gospel preaching gave the disk a rare emotional incandescence: the stuttering, the slashing outcries, the hoarse and catlike screeches. It was the beginning for "Mr. Dynamite." And it would take time for white audiences to go with the unbuttoned emotionalism.

Having wedded gospel and the blues, Ray Charles turned to a more secular song in "Drown In My Tears," a black ballad by Henry Glover that grew in stature through the years. In "Halle-lujah I Love Her So" Ray gave new evidence of the power of his sacred-secular style. It was a song that Peggy Lee recorded in '59 after she had scored with Little Willie John's version of "Fever," a '56 R & B chart song.

Oreo Rock

More tractable than either Charles or Brown were the vocalists who were black on the outside but white on the inside à la the popular cookie. Gifted, bespectacled Ivory Joe Hunter was in the

black-and-white school of Chuck Berry and Fats Domino, though
he never made it as big as either. In '56 he had a Top Ten song,
and one of the year's Top Tunes in his own blues ballad "I Almost Lost My Mind." He sold to white as well as black, but lost
out in record sales to Pat Boone, who copied his tempo, phrasing,
and intonation, and got the airplay denied to Hunter.

"Since I Met You Baby," a December release, graphed a change
in taste as well as Hunter's own appeal. His record outdistanced
cover versions by Molly Bee on Dot and Mindy Carson on
Columbia. Also, his recording came out on Atlantic, more potent
in its promotion than MGM Records. And record buyers were
beginning to go for the original rather than the copies by the end
of '56.

The White Teen-age Crowd:

Carl Perkins/Johnny Cash/George Hamilton IV/Gene Vincent

Trooping behind Boone, Presley, and Haley, there was a long
line of teen-age vocalists, among whom Carl Perkins was the most
creative and Johnny Cash the longest lived and most successful.
John Lennon, ex-Beatle playing a live performance for the first
time with the Plastic Ono Band, announced that they would do
only songs they knew—they had not had time to rehearse new
repertoire—and he and guitarist Eric Clapton immediately took
off with "One for the money, two for the show, three to get ready,
now, go, cat, go!" What rock 'n' roll star of the '50s did not do
"Blue Suede Shoes"?

"It was the easiest song I ever wrote," said Carl. "Got up at
3:00 A.M. when me and my wife Valda were living in a government project in Jackson, Tennessee. Had had the idea in my
head, seeing kids by the bandstand so proud of their new city
shoes—you gotta be real poor to care about new shoes like I did—
and that morning I went downstairs and wrote out the words on
a potato sack—we didn't have reason to have writing paper
around."

More, perhaps, than any other of the day's teen-age songs,
"Blue Suede Shoes" epitomized the mood of the new, rising generation—the determination to create and protect its own identity.
The blue suedes were a symbol. You can do anything you want to
my house (burn it), my car (steal it), my liquor (drink it), but
"Don't you step on my blue suede shoes!" Perkins's own recording of his song raced ahead of a group of covers that included
country disks by Pee Wee King, Jim Lowe and Cliffie Stone; and

instrumental platters by Boyd Bennett, Sam (The Man) Taylor, and Lawrence Welk. Statistics verify its wide appeal since Perkins's Sun disk made the charts in all three areas, strongest in C & W where it was in the Top Four, next in R & B, and weakest in pop, though even here it was in the Top Twenty.

Unfortunately for Perkins, Presley recorded the song in '56 and made it the first track in his first album, with the result that many associate "Blue Suede Shoes" with him rather than its creator. Perkins also had the misfortune to be in a car crash when he and his group were driving to New York to appear on the Perry Como and Ed Sullivan shows. David Stewart, a Memphis deejay who was his manager, fell asleep at the wheel—and the only appearance they made was in a Dover, Maryland, hospital. Perkins was unconscious for three days—with four broken ribs and three breaks in his right shoulder—and in traction for eight days with sixteen pounds of lead to pull his neck out. The accident was on the night of March 22, and Perkins was not able to give thanks to all his well-wishers until mid-May.

Ex-Beatle George Harrison, who became a disciple of Ravi Shankar, has said that he was originally inspired by Perkins's guitar playing—a debt he shares with Jerry Garcia of the Grateful Dead. In '64 and '65 Perkins was one of three American song-writers whose songs the Beatles recorded—the other two were Chuck Berry and Little Richard. Their early LPs include "Match-box," "Honey Don't," and "Everybody's Trying to Be My Baby." Perkins was more of an original, if not as charismatic a figure as either Elvis or Cash.

On May 12, 1956, Sun Records ran a trade-paper ad in which Perkins expressed the gratitude of himself, his brother Jay, and the rest of the band for the friendship displayed by fans and disk jockeys while they were recuperating from the car crash. In the bottom half of the ad, Sun announced a two sider "by one of the truly great talent finds"—Johnny Cash. Cash spoke rather than sang, in a low, low, vibrant voice that communicated integrity and commitment. "I Walk the Line," which he wrote, was one of the big disks of the year, but only in the C & W field. Unlike Perkins's "Blue Suedes," it did not sell pop or in R & B. But it led to Cash's moving in July of '56 from the "Louisiana Hayride"—Presley's springboard show—to the prestigious "Grand Ole Opry."

Cash later explained that he wrote "I Walk the Line" out of frustration with a job he could not stand. He was a refrigerator salesman in Memphis. As for its motivation: "When you live close to the earth," he said, "you learn to understand the basic

things about love and hate and what people want from life. Don
Gibson, Hank Williams, and I came from the same poor dirt
farms. We were all raised in little shacks, learned to pick cotton
and work the ground."

After the passing of the Presley furor that gave Sun artists and
rockabilly singers a special aura, Cash continued to work in
C & W traditions, little altering his low-voiced, declamatory style.
When rock returned to its roots in the late '60s, the rising tide
carried him to superstar status, a starring TV series, and international fame.

Another country singer who made the "Grand Ole Opry" as a
result of a '56 hit was nineteen-year-old George Hamilton IV of
Winston-Salem, North Carolina. Thin-voiced and adenoidal,
George captured the imagination of young record buyers with "A
Rose and a Baby Ruth," a song by a top country writer, John
Loudermilk. It was a corny story of a lovers' quarrel and the
boy's effort to patch it up with the flower and candy bar. But the
two items projected an appealing and identifiable image of teen-
age romance, heightened by Hamilton's own youthful face. Although the disk reportedly sold close to a million, George never
did it again, making him possibly the first of a long line of one-
hit teen-age singers.

Gene Vincent's image was tougher and more in the black
leather, motorcycle-boots syndrome of Presley. Capitol Records
thought, in fact, that they had found an answer to RCA Victor's
god of rockabilly in the young sailor from Norfolk, Virginia. Like
Presley, Vincent was originally a country singer. Through the use
of flutter echo, Capitol engineers were able to distort his gentle,
high-pitched voice to give it a raspy, driving rockabilly sound.
"Be-Bop-a-Lula," written by Vincent and an Atlanta deejay, Sheriff
Tex Davis, made it big in pop and bigger in C & W.

While his paean to the woman with a beat was still a smash
single, Capitol released a new disk designed to enhance Vincent's
aggressive image. But "Race with the Devil" b/w "Gonna Back
Up Baby" bombed, and though he had quite a number of releases,
Gene and his Blue Caps never had another record hit. However
"Be-Bop-a-Lula" was remembered abroad even after American
fans had forgotten him. Early in the '60s, he toured England with
a group whose drummer was Richard Starkey, later better known
as Ringo Starr. In April of '60, he was in a tragic car crash. Young
rock star Eddie Cochran was killed instantly and Vincent was so
badly hurt that a leg was amputated. He went back to work after
a time, but did not have a new record release in this country
until 1970 when he cut two albums for Buddah.

The Black Groups

"Now, they often call me Speedoo," he sang, to an uptempo background of *boom-boom-diddliums'*, "but my real name is Mr. Earl." His name was, in fact, Earl Carroll, and he was part of the Cadillacs, who had an R & B smash in "Speedoo" on Josie Records. It was a mildly funny record, and they tried a follow-up in "Zoom." But it was too much like the tale of the man whom some called Moe, others called Joe, but who was never slow—and "Zoom" did not make it. In '58 they had a moderate hit in "Peek-a-Boo" and that was it. But the Cadillacs were forerunners of one of the most unusual groups in rock 'n' roll history—and "Mr. Earl" was featured for a time with the Coasters.

Humor is a rare quality in popular song and it was even rarer in rock 'n' roll. The Coasters were the brilliant exception, a group that emerged from the Robins when Leiber and Stoller signed an indie production deal with Atlantic Records. Two of the Robins, lead singer Carl Gardner and bass Bobby Nunn, joined with tenor Leon Hughes and comedy singer Billy Guy to form the new group, named for their beginnings on the West Coast.

In '56 they had their first release, "Down in Mexico" b/w "Turtle Dovin'." "Down in Mexico" was a narrative song, a genre that Leiber and Stoller were to develop to a high level of perfection. It was also implicitly satirical, poking good-natured fun at the colorful come-ons of south-of-the-border vendors. The café owner wore a red bandana, played a cool pianner, wore a purple sash, and had a black moustache—and you hear him only at the close of the record, under the Mexicali instrumental rideout, delivering a typical "come-on" pitch.

"Down in Mexico" did not have the zing of "Smokey Joe's Café," an earlier Robins' tale of a café owner whose cutlery collection cooled a beanery customer interested in his girl. But lead singer Carl Gardner handled end words with a rising inflection that was suspenseful, sprightly, and sportive. The accompaniment was not only danceable. It underscored and hyped the narrative like film music. "Down in Mexico" was a moderate R & B hit, but it gave more than a hint of what one might anticipate. The Coasters' explosion came early in '57.

A number of R & B groups whose existence was ephemeral, if not conjectural, contributed sound memories to 1956. These included the Satins with " (I'll Remember) In the Still of the Night" on Ember; the Cleftones with "Little Girl of Mine" on Gee; the Turbans with "When You Dance" on Herald; and the Cadets, with "Stranded in the Jungle"—they were also the Jacks

of "Why Don't You Write." Aladdin, a West Coast label responsible for Gene and Eunice and "Ko Ko Mo," came up with another duo that created an R 'n' R classic. Shirley and Lee's "Let
the Good Times Roll" attracted white buyers even though the
disk was proscribed by many pop deejays for its alleged suggestiveness. Lee, who wrote the rocker, sang in a sad-sack drawl that was
an appealing foil for Shirley's piping little-girl voice.

During 1956 the word "teen-age" became a catchword and a
banner. Groups blossomed with names like the Teen-Queens, the
Teenagers, and the Six Teens. Recording on the West Coast RPM
label, the Teen-Queens more than held their own on "Eddie My
Love" against a more polished and better promoted cover by the
Fontane Sisters.

The most popular group of '56 after the Platters was the Teen-
agers, an R & B quartet whose lead singer had just entered his
teens. Frankie Lymon also wrote " Why Do Fools Fall in Love"
although George Goldner is listed as a coauthor. Goldner, who
owned the Rama, Gee, Gone, and End labels, prowled the ghetto
sections of New York City and found the Teenagers as well as the
Crows singing on a street corner. "Why Do Fools Fall in Love"
was a curiously adult concept for a kid of thirteen to deal with.
But it was Lymon's sound—choirboy sweet with a thrust and a
beat—that put the record near the top of all R & B charts, as high
as No. 15 on the Honor Roll, and in the Top Thirty among the
big tunes of '56—this despite the formidable competition of the
Diamonds' cover on Mercury and Gale Storm on Dot. The kids
bought the kid.

During the year, Lymon and the Teenagers maintained their
popularity with "I Want You to Be My Girl," a song he did not
write. But it did not approach the million-copy sales of their
debut hit. Neither did "I Promise to Remember" or "ABCs of
Love," a contrived effort to trade on Lymon's youth. The joke
inside the business was that Goldner said a prayer each night, lest
Frankie's voice change. But the hits stopped before then.

As the "Rock 'n' Roll Revival" began to take shape in 1967,
"Why Do Fools Fall in Love" became a hit again with the
Happenings. The following year, Lymon was found dead in a
cold-water flat in Harlem, apparently from an overdose of drugs.

At the pop end of the sound spectrum, one of the most successful groups was the Four Lads on Columbia. Although they sang
"mature" ballads like "Standing on the Corner" from the
musical *The Most Happy Fella*, "No, Not Much," and "Moments
to Remember"—all among the Fifteen Most Played Records of
'56—their robust, belting style and raucous harmonies gave them
contact with young record buyers.

The "Flying Saucer" Caper

One of the oddest record developments of 1956 was "The Flying Saucer," a disk on which two young men effectively exploited the talk and rumors about UFOs (Unidentified Flying Objects). Pretending that a flying saucer was paying a surveillance visit to Earth, Buchanan and Goodman strung together excerpts from fifteen recent song hits, dubbing directly from available commercial records. There was no structure or logic to the ten-second excerpts. But youngsters loved it, not only because it appealed to their sense of fantasy, but because it became a game to identify each dubbed record, artist, and song.

The reaction of the music business was something else, especially since "The Flying Saucer" took off in mid-July like a jet-propelled rocket. Record companies and publishers were up in arms threatening lawsuits on piracy of recordings, failure to obtain a license, violation of copyright, etc. The jokesters at Lindy's had a field day needling publishers—"What? You're not on 'The Flying Saucer'? You're nowhere!" Much mystery surrounded the Luniverse label under which the disk appeared: who the principals were, the financing, who pressed the records, etc.

Despite the many threats, "The Flying Saucer" soared into the Honor Roll of Hits—in fact, into its upper regions. Eventually, the publishers whose copyrights were involved made an out-of-court settlement with the two perpetrators of the weird three-minute anthology. But by the time this occurred, there were three new unlicensed compilations on the market: "The Answer to the Flying Saucer" on Cosmic, "Marty of Planet Mars" on Novelty, and "Dear Elvis" on Plus. None of these attained the popularity of the original "Saucer."

However, Buchanan and Goodman did open an office at 1650 Broadway, upstairs over Hanson's drugstore, a show-biz hangout. One of the store's phonebooths had served as headquarters from which Buchanan, a good-looking Irishman, reportedly wrote most of the orders on the "Saucer."

Their second disk, released at the end of September, was "Buchanan and Goodman on Trial" b/w "Public Opinion." Both sides employed their gimmick technique of brief excerpts, like a sound montage, from recent hits. Instead of dubbing directly from commercial records of other companies, as they had done on their original coup, they used live imitations and copied backgrounds. The new Buchanan-Goodman opus never got off the ground.

A second oddity that became part of music biz's midsummer madness was a record titled "Transfusion," released on Dot and recorded by someone who billed himself as Nervous Norvus. This disk caught on, too, and made its bloody way to the Honor Roll, though not as high as "The Flying Saucer." The lyric dealt with an auto accident—sound effects of the crash were included—and with one of the injured crying "Transfusion." It was sick humor that quickly provoked outcries of bad taste and motivated many radio stations to ban the disk, but not before it had been covered by the Platters on Mercury.

Although neither disk had anything to do with rock 'n' roll, the music-business Establishment, not to mention the older generation, pointed to them as tokens of the low level to which taste had sunk.

"Rebel Without A Cause"

Late in '55 just after he shot the last scene for the epic film *Giant*, actor James Dean, who loved to drive at high speeds, was killed when his sportscar crashed. He soon became the subject of an eerie posthumous cult. James Dean was an oddball, the iconoclastic star of *Rebel Without a Cause*, an offbeat actor of genius proportions (conceded even by his detractors on the release of *Giant*), and a young man who enjoyed living dangerously—and whose self-destructive tendencies led to an early, violent death.

In March '56, RCA Victor released a folksy disk, "The Ballad of James Dean" by Dylan Todd. Although the movie fan magazines were on a Dean kick, it made nary a ripple. But as the hoopla preceding the November '56 release of *Giant* began to gain momentum, the James Dean cult took on fanatical proportions —and music business went into high gear.

MGM released a two-sided "Tribute to James Dean" by Art Mooney and his orchestra, the themes of two of his films, packaged in a special sleeve—unusual at that time—with a picture of Dean "suitable for framing." At that moment, a fan magazine devoted entirely to Dean professed to have "an exclusive message from beyond." Forest Records, an indie label, had a more mundane message. Releasing a disk by Nathan Russell (who he?), it employed actress Veronica Lake on a promotional tour of radio deejays and TV talk shows.

Soon there were singles on Jubilee ("Ballad of James Dean"), on Mecca ("His Name Was Dean"), and on Mercury ("Love Theme from *Giant*"). Two LPs and an EP later, the effusive elegies reached a climax with a maudlin, monster Coral LP. For *The Story of James Dean*, as it was called, TV's Steve Allen wrote and recited a special prologue. Disk jockey Bill Randle narrated

Dean's life story and introduced the musical selections. Jimmy Wakely warbled "James Dean," "Jimmy Jimmy," and "His Name Was Dean." Gigi Perreau recited "We'll Never Forget You."

Musically, the supersaturated effort to exploit Dean's posthumous popularity yielded nothing. There was no question that for thousands of young people—rebels without a cause, except their own identity and loneliness—he was a larger-than-life figure. Considering the animadversions about teen-age taste by the older generation, its readiness to trade on genuine adolescent feelings provided its own cynical commentary.

"Let's Go—Calypso"

That was the title of an early '57 recording by West Coaster Rusty Draper. But the cauldron of Caribbean sounds known as calypso had been bubbling since 1953 when Perry Como hit with a Tin Pan Alley concoction, "Pa-paya Mama." The following year, Eartha Kitt was in a three-way race with Georgia Gibbs and Ella Fitzgerald on another ersatz calypso, "Somebody Bad Stole de Wedding Bell . . . Who's Got de Ding Dong?" And that Christmas, pidgin English and Caribbean rhythms were heard in many yuletide songs.

Apparently, the crowd that had been running from New York and Chicago winters to Miami was now flying to the leeward and windward islands where trade winds filled their nostrils with the exotic scent of bougainvillea and where they were buying hilltop homes in a vain effort to escape the rat race. They returned to their high-blood-pressure world with the sound of marimbalike steel drums, pidgin English, and off-key harmonies in their ears. Calypso was nostalgia. It was escape.

And in '56 calypso came in strong with "Cindy, Oh, Cindy," an adaptation of a Georgia Sea Island chantey, which I took over from Glory Records on a Vince Martin disk, and converted into a vehicle for Eddie Fisher—his last big single. Calypso gained momentum with the Glory Records follow-up, "The Banana Boat Song," an adaptation by Erik Darling, Bob Carey, and Alan Arkin, who recorded it as the Tarriers. Their disk had just begun to rise when Harry Belafonte covered them with his version, "Day-O," which he himself published.

It was a natural for Harry whose first RCA Victor recording in '53 had been a calypso, "Matilda, Matilda." Glory Records owner Phil Rose sued RCA Victor, the company that pressed his Tarriers disk and released the Belafonte cover, on the ground of unfair competition. (He lost the suit.) Belafonte soon established his hegemony with "Mama, Look a Booboo," an authentic calypso novelty by Lord Melody, which led to two giant album sellers, *Jump Up Calypso* and *Belafonte Sings of the Caribbean*. By then it was 1957 and Rosemary Clooney was trying to catch the updraft of the trend with "Mangoes" and "Who Dot Mon, Mom?," both out of cubicles in the Brill Building. And choral director Norman Luboff was back from Haiti with a West Indian folk song ("Chacoun") that became known as "Yellow Bird." The older generation was dancing the calypso while the kids who were also attracted to the exotic sound and Caribbean rhythm, cavorted to the chalypso, a combination of the cha-cha and the calypso.

You Can't Stop This Rocking and Rolling

Though the sound of the steel drum was in the air, providing a seductive background for the emergence of Belafonte and his navel—he wore V-neck shirts open to his midriff—1956 was the first rock 'n' roll year and it belonged to Presley and his undulating pelvis. As personality disk jockeys erupted into powerhouse figures à la Alan Freed, record hops became a way of life for the young, an exciting way of bringing artists and audiences together, and a moneymaker for the deejays who ran them (and got talent free in return for air promotion of their records). Despite the hostility of church, school, and civic authorities, who tried to associate them with juvenile delinquency and banned them, record hops became bigger and bigger business through the year.

A measure of the advance of R 'n' R in '56 was to be found not only in the extensive cover pattern pursued by older-generation artists, but in the growth of ersatz rock. Tin Pan Alley creations like "Juke Box Baby" (Perry Como) and "Dungaree Doll" (Eddie Fisher) appealed to the more tentative teen-agers and became solid sellers. The biggest of these was Kay Starr's "Rock and Roll Waltz" with a schmaltzy melody and an all-in-the-family concept that doubtless attracted older as well as younger listeners.

Despite the apparent teen-age cast of the record scene, year-end polls and recaps reflected only limited acceptance of the new sounds. In a survey of 179 station managers, *Billboard* found an intransigent group who made comments like, "We do not consider rock and roll music," and "It is the worst influence ever to hit the music business—a disgrace." However, almost half of the station managers indicated that they were compelled to alter their programing practices in the direction of more R 'n' R records.

A poll of disk jockeys disclosed a conflict between their personal preferences and playlists. Morris Stoloff's "Moonglow and the Theme from *Picnic*" emerged as Favorite Record, and only three platters in a list of twenty-one were R 'n' R. But the list of Twenty Most Played Records contained eight R 'n' R disks. A similar discrepancy appeared between Favorite Male Vocalist (Sinatra) and Most Played Male Vocalist (Presley). Again, the Favorite list had only one R 'n' R artist (Pat Boone) among ten while the Most Played included four out of ten (Presley, Boone, Haley, and Domino).

Perhaps it was no surprise then that the recap of Top Tunes revealed a ratio of three to two on the side of Easy Listening, as it came to be known later. The year's biggest was "The Wayward Wind," a folklike, poetic song by two West Coast writers, with a record by a young unknown, Gogi Grant, on an indie label, Era. Next came "Poor People of Paris," a British instrumental with a Les Baxter disk; "Memories Are Made of This" in a slurping ballad version by Dean Martin; and "Moonglow and the Theme from *Picnic*," the revival of a ballad of the '30s, fitted with a lovely new countermelody by screen composed George Duning and recorded by Morris Stoloff, a film-studio conductor. Elvis Presley's "Don't Be Cruel" was the No. 5 song.

Three more Presley tunes showed in the next fifteen: "Heartbreak Hotel," "Love Me Tender," and "Hound Dog." Although the Platters ("My Prayer" and "The Great Pretender"), Otis Williams ("Ivory Tower"), and Pat Boone ("I Almost Lost My Mind") appeared in the Top Twenty, Easy Listening tunes led by a margin of twelve to eight. Doris Day, Patti Page, and Perry Como were still top favorites.

In the field of instrumental music, the scales were also weighted on the side of the old-timers: Dick Hyman with a harpsichord-piano version of the haunting "Theme from the Threepenny Opera," Hugo Winterhalter and pianist Eddie Heywood with a boogie-inflected version of "Canadian Sunset," and Mitch Miller with "Song for a Summer Night."

The big surprise of the year was a rhythm-and-blues instrumental by Bill Doggett, a pianist-arranger who had worked with the Ink Spots, Lionel Hampton, Louis Jordan, and Ella Fitzgerald and who had organized his first band in 1938. "Honky Tonk" featured a tenor-sax solo in the shrilling sound of a Screamin' Jay Hawkins. A shuffle-gaited, hand-clapping blues, it was embroidered with traditional boogie styling on a heavily echoed bass guitar. There was occasional shouting in the background of the two-sided disk as if it had been recorded live and not in a studio.

An R & B Triple Crown, it placed in the Top Thirty of pop. If King Records' claim that it sold four million disks is reliable, then "Honky Tonk" outsold every tune on the entire pop chart.

In '56 the record scene was a battleground of "Two Different Worlds," to use the title of a romantic hit of the year. Young and old were, in Matthew Arnold's memorable words, "on a darkling plain/Swept with confused alarms of struggle and flight/ Where ignorant armies clash by night." But "Honky Tonk" was a semaphore of future developments in pop.

19

THE AMERICAN BANDSTAND

In 1957 Americans were chattering about Sputniks, the Edsel, Maverick, and Palladin, words that had special connotations. Sputnik I was the first earth satellite launched by the Russians, exploding the frantic race in space. The Edsel, a new car introduced by Ford, bombed—as did the Vanguard, the first U.S. rocket cum satellite. "Maverick" was a new, hot TV series, and Palladin the new knight of the West, a bookish gunfighter of "Have Gun Will Travel." "Adult westerns," they called these and others, like "Tombstone Territory" and "Wells Fargo." And millions of Americans missed hours of their sleep watching the "Tonight Show" with Jack Paar or old movies on the "Late Show"—as twelve hundred theatres closed their doors.

In '57 Eisenhower sent federal troops into Little Rock to protect black school children from Gov. Orville Faubus of Arkansas while white citizens bombed black churches and homes in Montgomery, Alabama, as reprisal for the desegregation of buses. Arturo Toscanini, the great conductor died but so did Sen. Joseph McCarthy, conductor of another kind of chorus. Kids were dancing the calypso and chalypso while their elders were doing the mambo and cha-cha-cha.

In '57 the big news for teen-agers—"Young Love" was the first smash hit of the year—was "American Bandstand," a Philadelphia TV show that went network (ABC) and became to young people what "Your Hit Parade" was to their parents—only more so. For "American Bandstand" was the cement of a generation, setting its dress, dances, pop heroes, and modes of behavior. A vehicle, it was also a symbol of victory for teen-agers—a program that was *theirs* and that was soon imitated by hundreds of local shows around the country. And Dick Clark, the youthful, debonair host with the Dentyne smile, became the ballast to Alan Freed, representing cool, white rock as Freed was the avatar of hot, black rock. At its peak, "American Bandstand" went out over one hundred five TV stations, reaching the eyes, ears, and hearts of at least twenty million youngsters.

Dick Clark described himself as "too old to be a playmate and too young to be a father." Big Brother might have been a good designation, but he never used it. Unlike the screamers and exciters, the Dr. Jives, Jocko Hendersons, and Alan Freeds, Richard Augustus Clark II (to give him his full name) was calm, reserved, and somewhat removed. "I'm an observer and a presenter," he said, in his most august manner. And with becoming modesty, denied that he was a hitmaker or even an interpreter. His affable loftiness served to restrain the kids.

Clark was, in fact, the great tranquilizer of the era, reassuring parents by his suave manner that rock 'n' roll was not bad and transforming the youngsters on his show into sunshine biscuits. (Smile but don't laugh.) There was much milk in his baking, no yeast, and the kids "danced apart," bobbing up and down like expressionless zombies.

Billboard's reaction to the premiere of the show on August 5, 1957, was none too favorable: "As a sociological study of teenage behavior," the reviewer wrote, "the premiere was a mild success. As relaxation and entertainment, it wasn't." And here the reviewer, without realizing it, had stumbled on what was to be the "American Bandstand's" great appeal to the teen-ager: it was *not* entertainment basically but a *happening* in which he could participate. If it did not attract the seasoned, middle-generation viewer, so much the better. It was not his program but *ours* and helped create an identity for us.

The reviewer continued: "The bulk of the 90 minutes was devoted to colorless juveniles trudging through early American dances like the Lindy and the Box Step, to recorded tunes of the day. If this is the wholesome answer to the 'detractors' of rock 'n' roll, bring on the rotating pelvises.

"Dick Clark, a handsome and personable host who deserves a better network debut, chatted briefly with two guests before they mimed their own platters."

The show had really had its start five years earlier when it was known simply as "Bandstand" (modeled, perhaps, on Al Jarvis' and Martin Block's "Make Believe Ballroom" on radio). Its presiding maharajah was Bob Horn. No live artists appeared. Visual appeal was achieved through filmed performances of artists, supplied by managers, publishers, etc., and used in conjunction with records.

In July 1956 Horn came a cropper. While the *Philadelphia Ledger* was waging a vigorous campaign against drunken drivers—it owned WFIL—Horn was arrested on just such a charge. There previously had been rumors of an affair involving a young fan of the program. Now, management felt that it had no alternative. Horn was suspended. Angry teen-agers picketed the station with signs that read, "We want Bob Horn back!" and "Doesn't Roger Clipp drink?" (Clipp was WFIL's manager.) To succeed Horn, he selected young Dick Clark, who had come to WFIL in '52 from Bronxville, New York, Syracuse University, and an announcing job on a Utica, New York, station.

According to Clark, dancing became part of the "Bandstand" quite accidentally. The station was located near a Philadelphia high school. After school kids would drop in to watch Horn and then Clark as they announced records and read commercials. "When recordings were played," Clark recalls, "the kids got up and danced quite spontaneously." In short, "Bandstand" became a record hop, as it were, with entertainment almost incidental.

Taking the stance of an almost detached observer—and there were frequent shots of Clark viewing the proceedings almost as if he were a teacher—he never acted or dressed like a youngster. Like a teacher, he set down strict requirements for those who wanted to be part of the studio audience, watching or dancing. Boys had to wear jackets and the girls, skirts not jeans or dungarees. Tight-fitting sweaters or T-shirts were out. During Philadelphia's autumn and winter months, the girls wore heavy sweaters and heavy, rolled, white socks, a form of dress that was copied even in Atlanta, Miami, and the warm South. "American Bandstand" was creating a life-style and one that pleased parents. Clark later "wrote" a book on etiquette.

The following story may be apocryphal, but it illustrates how crucial a consideration appearance was when it came to record artists booked on the show. When Fabian walked into a record hop being emceed by Clark, the girls reacted the way they once had to young Sinatra, more recently to Presley. "That was enough for us," Clark reportedly has said. "You don't look for a singer. The person who is the star has that magic thing, and that's all that counts."

Well, quite a number of the record stars who broke big in '57 were most assuredly *not* singers. Certainly Fabian and his Philadelphia *paisano,* Frankie Avalon, would be high up on a list of nonsinging record stars. But Avalon told a reporter: "When I recorded "Venus," Dick got behind it and it sold a million and a half copies. He's the greatest!"

There were other Philadelphians who could duplicate Avalon's statement, and not surprisingly, they also recorded for local labels like Chancellor, owned by Bob Marcucci, one of Clark's many *sotto voce* partners. Other companies that "were well-placed to promote their product," as one scholar put it, were Swan Records of Philadalphia, who had Top Ten stars in Freddy Cannon and Billie and Lillie, and Cameo-Parkway under whose aegis Bobby Rydell, Charlie Gracie, the Rays, and John Zacherle became record sellers. The tangled skein of Clark's relationships with the owner of Cameo-Parkway surfaced during the payola probe.

Over and above life-style, Dick Clark created record hits and stars as well as several dance crazes. During the peak years of his reign (1957 to the Beatles), all of music business converged on Philadelphia's Thirtieth Street Station and WFIL-TV—record promoters, managers, song pluggers, publishers, songwriters, record artists, and even A & R men. You could not just walk in on *the man*, as you might on most disk jockeys. No, you had to make an appointment in advance, even if you came from another city.

I once made the ninety-minute train ride from New York's Pennsylvania Station to Philly to promote a new recording. Although I arrived at the appointed time—a week or two after I phoned for an appointment—I was advised that Clark was unavailable, due to some unavoidable top-level, station conference. When I offered to wait, I was told that Clark was booked solid with appointments, one after the other, and there was no telling how long this meeting would last. Later, I discovered that many out-of-town record promoters and publisher's representatives encountered similar stalls—and ended, as I did, by seeing Tony Mammarella, producer of the Clark show and his partner in sundry outside undertakings.

Recording artists seldom faced the same hurdles. But they also approached the man with care and consideration. On his birthday in 1958, little more than a year after the local "Bandstand" became the ABC network "American Bandstand," Clark arrived at the studio to a surprise gathering. Among those present were Bobby Darin, Connie Francis, Sal Mineo, Danny and the Juniors, Little Anthony and the Imperials, and Pat Boone, in addition to the local contingent. And that year, Chuck Berry opened a club in St. Louis, which he named The Bandstand as a tribute to the Clark show.

In his first appearance on the "Bandstand," Chuck Berry had

a fight with Clark. Because teen-age records were so frequently "engineered" and not just performed, artists on the Dick Clark and other TV shows did not sing but merely mimed the lyrics to the playing of their records. There was also a financial factor involved. "Lip-syncing," as the faked singing was termed, was promotion. Singing was a performance requiring payment.

When Berry was informed that he was to "lip-sync," he declared: "Chuck Berry is not gonna open his mouth and have nothing come out." But then Leonard Chess, head of Chess Records, came over and they had a little talk. As Berry latter explained: "Leonard said, 'There are some things you gotta do in this business that you don' want to do.' So we made friends, because Dick Clark was held in esteem and he had a lot of power."

How much power was indicated by Bill Randle of Station WERE in Cleveland, who was something of a powerhouse himself and who readily admitted that Clark's network TV show was more formidable competition to local disk jockeys than any rival radio station. In the period that the Clark telecast appeared in Cleveland, Randle veered from programing single disks to selections from albums. The "Bandstand's" success was so phenomenal that over one hundred video stations around the country introduced record-hop shows in the postschool hours.

New dance steps were, of course, an integral part of the teenager's life-style. All of music business worked at devising and incorporating them in new songs. And "American Bandstand" became the vehicle for transforming them into national, if short-lived crazes. As an instance, take the Stroll, devised by the teenage daughter of a music man, recorded by the Diamonds on Mercury, and diagramed in trade-paper ads in December '57. Shortly after their record was released, the Diamonds made an appearance on "American Bandstand" and taught the studio audience how to do the dance. In succeeding days, local TV record hops, anxious to be in on something new, repeated the dance lesson. Within a matter of weeks, the Diamonds' song and disk were in the top group of the Honor Roll of Hits. And the Stroll was being danced at teen-age hops around the country.

Not all dance steps previewed on "American Bandstand" did as well. But during the late '50s, teen-agers were doing the Fish, the Walk, the Madison, the Slop, the Circle, the Chalypso, and the Philadelphia, many of which they first saw on the Dick Clark program. In these, the partners danced apart, not touching or talking at all. (To dancer-choreographer Agnes de Mille, the dance floor was then "not a group of couples but a crowd of

individuals. . . . These dances are the expression of total, persist-
ing loneliness and desperation. They are dances of fear.")

According to music men I knew in Philadelphia, and who hung
around the studio, there were occasional flare-ups of temper and
square-offs between teen-age participants, usually as a result of
dancers who tried to hog the tube. Regulars knew about the two
little red lights that lit up when a given camera was sending out
pictures—and some of the exhibitionists sometimes maneuvered
a little too quickly to get into the scene. None of the fracases ever
was seen by the viewing audience. Clark's staff was well trained to
avoid controversy just as he worked constantly to keep the natives
cool and unruffled.

Even "Your Hit Parade" tried to arouse a feeling of excitement
and worked at creating suspense about the No. 1 song of the
week. Not Dick Clark. He was the great pacifier, working, as he
told a reporter not too long ago, "to reflect what's going on early
enough to make a profit on it." And that he did for others as well
as himself—so enormous a profit that at the height of the "play for
pay" congressional investigation, Rep. Peter F. Mack of Illinois
called him "top dog in the payola field."

It was a phase of his existence that his bland and affable image
on camera never betrayed or even hinted at. What you saw was
an older brother, viewing with curiosity, interest, and sympathy
the doings of his younger sisters and brothers. At a much later
date, after he had settled in Hollywood and was appearing as a
dramatic actor in a number of films, he told a reporter: "I always
seem to play the nice, clean-cut fellow, who turns out to be a
louse."

The kids never saw him as that—and many refused to believe
what they read in the papers and heard on radio and TV regarding his conflict-of-interest holdings in publishing and recording.
Others were deeply disillusioned, feeling that what they had regarded as *their* program might have been much manipulated by
Big Brother and his business associates. But from '57 until the
end of the decade, his image was that of the all-American boy who
helped nice young people savor and enjoy their own kind of
music in a wholesome atmosphere. It had nothing in common
with the sensuality of Presley, the vulgarity of an Alan Freed, or
the dirty suggestiveness of rhythm-and-blues records.

If rock 'n' roll had a rebellious, defiant, or anti-Establishment
side, it was not in evidence on "American Bandstand." In place
of the antiheroes of Marlon Brando's *Wild One* and James Dean's
Rebel Without a Cause, you saw well-mannered, nicely-dressed,

well-behaved teen-agers spending a pleasant afternoon under the scrutiny of a gracious chaperon. It was a scene that made it difficult for the critics of R 'n' R to find grounds for attacking the music. Of course, it did not stop them, as we shall see.

turn to pg 193

20

THE AUDACIOUS AMATEURS—
AND THE COUNTRY ROCKERS

In April '57 a *Billboard* editor received an inquiry from a young man of Delphos, Ohio, who wrote: "Altho I have never acted or sung with music, I can truthfully say I can sing just about as good as Como, Crosby and Boone. . . . I think also that I could make another John Wayne altho I am not as big as he and don't look like him, but I can play it calm and cool. My shoulders and arm muscles are quite prominent and if handled right I think a big thing could be built up. Any suggestions would be appreciated."

Quite recently, composer-arranger Alec Wilder wrote in *Popular Music:* "When you get to rock, that's the age of the amateur." When one thinks of Leiber and Stoller, Chuck Berry, Kris Kristofferson, Carole King, John Lennon, Curtis Mayfield, Bob Dylan, Jimmy Webb, Paul Simon, Isaac Hayes, Neil Diamond, Harry Nilsson, to mention a few, it is apparent that the generally perceptive Alec could not be wilder in his generalization. But it is true that the early years of rock 'n' roll, as with any new art style, were years of the audacious amateurs.

They sprouted from every corner like children leaping from the brow of record Zeuses, and some of them made it big for a brief moment. You didn't have to know how to sing and you didn't need a voice. You just had to have the cool to try. The more awkward and unprofessional you were, the better. Showmanship, poise, and polish were older-generation criteria—and suspect. If anything suggests the fear and trembling of the new generation, it was the glorification of mediocrity and primitivism. "Why I can sing as well as he does—I must buy his record!"

Fabian/Sal Mineo/Charlie Gracie/Bobby Helms

Fabian did not appear until the end of the '50s. But the manner of his discovery and buildup tells it like it was. One day a South Philadelphia cop, Dominick Forte, had a heart attack on the street. Bob Marcucci, manager of Frankie Avalon, happened by and offered help. Then he noticed Forte's fourteen-year-son, Fabian. Marcucci was struck instantly by a resemblance to Presley—the high, black pompadour, duck-ass hairstyle, olive skin, and the sultry look. If only he could sing!

Marcucci took Fabian Forte, not without some reluctance on his part, to a voice teacher, who refused to accept him as a pupil. This did not deter Marcucci. He found an opportunist (several in fact), who did give Fabian voice lessons, an ex-actor who tried to teach him how to talk, an etiquette teacher who instructed him in dress and manners. The grooming took two years. Then Marcucci began running full-page ads in the music trade papers. Finally, Chancellor Records of Philadelphia, in which Dick Clark had an interest, released "Turn Me Loose." This was followed by "Tiger." Computerized Fabian—the surname had been dropped —made a number of appearances on "American Bandstand." The first disk sold three-quarters of a million copies and the second reportedly a million. From wax, Fabian leaped to the screen. He appeared in *Hound Dog Man* and later with John Wayne in *North to Alaska*. There were two things wrong—he could neither act nor sing. He sold on his looks. (He was still selling on his looks in 1973 when he posed nude for *Playgirl* magazine.)

Sal Mineo on the other hand, could act. But he could not sing either. He had two disks in 1957 that were noisemakers, if not chartmakers—"Start Movin'" and "Lasting Love." Mineo was one of a number of young movie stars who sold records without being anything more than amateur singers. The most successful of these was blue-eyed, blonde-headed, pearly-toothed Tab Hunter, who covered Sonny James' version of "Young Love," and garnered a Gold Record. just as James did. They demonstrated, as Ed Byrnes of the "77 Sunset Strip" TV series later did that personality and image counted more than vocal ability, not to mention the mammoth visual exposure of mass media like the movie sceen or TV tube.

Nineteen fifty-seven's flashes in the pan included the Tune Weavers, who sang "Happy, Happy Birthday, Baby" with such misery in their voices, and the Bobbettes, who hiccupped "Mr. Lee" into the Top Fifty. (Mr. Lee turned out to be the principal of the high school the four girls attended.) Other "one-shot"

artists were Jodie Sands on Chancellor with "With All My Heart,"
coauthor Bob Marcucci; the Rays on Cameo with "Silhouettes,"
an interesting and imaginative ballad by Frank C. Slay, Jr., and
Bob Crewe, owners of Swan Records; and Charlie Gracie, also on
Cameo, with "Butterfly." All three were part of the rocking, criss-
crossing Philadelphia scene.

"Butterfly," the biggest song in this group, was the work of
Bernie Lowe and Kal Mann, who founded and launched Cameo
Records with it. On the back was a song titled "99 Ways" by A.
September, a pseudonym of Dick Clark's producer, Tony Mam-
marella.

To record "Butterfly," Lowe and Mann selected Charlie
Gracie who was known as a fine guitarist. Andy Williams quickly
covered the song on Cadence while Tab Hunter covered "99
Ways" on Dot. Powered by two disks, "Butterfly" sailed to the
top of the Honor Roll of Hits where it remained for three consecutive weeks in April '57. The week that it dropped to the
No. 4 position, "99 Ways" climbed to No. 11. Although Williams
and Hunter received a major share of the credit for the success
of the songs, Charlie Gracie obviously had a monster of a disk.

"Fabulous," a follow-up and an obvious imitation of Presley's
panting-gasping-choke style, was a severe letdown. Gracie had no
style of his own. And though he appeared the following year in
Jamboree, a quickie and shoddy rock movie, he was one of R 'n'
R's flashes in the pan.

For Bobby Helms, a twenty-two-year-old from Monroe County,
Indiana, 1957 yielded three solid sellers that promised a substantial future. He had the background, having begun singing
professionally when he was only eleven on his father's radio
show, "Monroe County Jamboree." His first and biggest hit was
"Fraulein." Helms actually outsold Kitty Wells, who also recorded
the song, in the C & W field by a wide margin. "My Special
Angel," Bobby's second hit did not do as well as "Fraulein,"
though it scored No. 15 in the year's C & W disks and became a
standard and a much-performed song in the revival of tunes of
the '50s. And "Jingle Bell Rock," his third noisemaker, ran far
behind the other two. Apparently, Bobby had too much of a
country sound to make it in teen-age pop.

But 1957 did bring a flood of pop talent. Tommy Sands, born
in Chicago in 1937, came from a show-biz family. His mother was
a dance-band singer and his father, a well-known eighty-eighter.
Appearances on the TV shows of Ted Lewis and Tennessee
Ernie Ford led to a vocal-dramatic debut on the "Kraft Music
Hall" in a role turned down by Elvis Presley. Tommy played a

Presley-type rocker in "The Singin' Idol." Out of the appearance came his first record smash, "Teen-Age Crush," a country ballad that took a stronger position on youthful romance than either "Young Love," then at the top of the charts, or "Too Young," a Nat Cole ballad of the early '50s. Chiding the older generation for forgetting how they once felt, the lyric pleaded. "Don't try to keep us apart."

When "The Singin' Idol" was made into a film late in '57, Sands played the lead in *Sing Boy Sing*, as the teleplay was re-titled. He moved quickly into the nightclub scene, starting at the top in a major Las Vegas hotel. A short-lived marriage to Nancy Sinatra opened the door to a role in a Sinatra movie. Observers feel that his misfortune was that he succeeded too fast.

The Tex-Mex Sound

From another country area, the Southwest, came three young singing minstrels, one of whom turned into a major, albeit short-lived, figure. The first of the three to hit the charts was Buddy Knox, born in Happy, Texas, in 1933. And he hit hard in March '57, making No. 1 on the Honor Roll with "Party Doll," a rockin' ballad he wrote with Jimmy Bowen. Remember? He needed a chick when he was feeling wild, to be ever loving and run her fingers through his hair, mmmm, mmmmm. Jimmy Bowen, the second of the Southwesterners, was born in Santa Rita, New Mexico, in 1937 and was the bass player of the Rhythm Orchids, a group formed by Knox when they were attending West Texas State College. He was on the charts with "I'm Stickin' With You" at the same time as Knox, with whom he had also written this tune.

Like "Party Doll," "Stickin' " was released originally on Triple D, a record label launched by the two in Dumas, Texas, in association with the two other members of the Rhythm Orchids. When the sides began making noise in West Texas, Roulette Records, then owned by Hugo and Luigi, bought the masters and, after re-recording the songs, released them nationally.

Unlike the rockabilly style of the Memphis crowd, the Tex-Mex sound of Knox and Bowen revealed no black influences. Buddy Knox later indicated that he did not recall hearing a black singer until he went to New York to re-record "Party Doll." Both Texans sang a western country style, adding a rock beat that was an extension of western swing.

Buddy Knox followed "Party Doll" with "Rock Your Little Baby to Sleep" and "Hula Love," both of which he wrote. Despite the title of the latter, American Indian rhythms, not Hawaiian, were used. Neither song achieved the popularity of his debut disk. Although Knox continued to record and perform, and made a comeback during the country revival of '69 with "Gypsy Man," he never attained star status. After a series of so-so records, and even a featured appearance in the film *Jamboree*, Jimmy Bowen became a producer at Chancellor Records, then at Reprise, and finally at Amos, his own company.

Bowen and Knox cut their debut disks at a recording studio in Clovis, New Mexico, a town with a population of just over twenty thousand. Norman Petty, an organist-pianist with a background in show and film music, was the owner—and the sponsor-guide of the most important of the Tex-Mex rockers. I was so curious about Petty and his studio that during a trip to Los Angeles in '58 or '59, I made a side trip to Clovis. Clovis had no airfield then and the nearest airport was at Albuquerque. Petty met me and we drove one hundred and seventy-five miles, due east, almost to the border of Texas, through a cold, wood-scented night. I was amazed at the sophistication of his recording equipment (in this far-out place) and impressed by the elegance of his style of living.

By far and away the most important proponent of the Southwest school of rock 'n' roll, sometimes identified as the Tex-Mex sound, was Charles Hardin Holley of Lubbock, Texas. Better known as Buddy Holly, he was fired by an Elvis Presley appearance in Lubbock in 1955 to leap onstage and give an impromptu performance. He was then working as part of a duo, Buddy and Bob (Montgomery), that had a conventional Nashville country album on the market. Decca quickly signed him as a single and made some unimpressive disks with him. On the termination of the deal, Holly went to Norman Petty, and working in the Clovis studio with a group that became known as the Crickets, developed the style that put "That'll Be the Day" high on the Honor Roll in the fall of '57.

The song, by Holly, Petty, and drummer Jerry Allison, explored the ambivalent emotions of a young man, worried that his girl would not return, and confident that she could not stay away. Petty's contribution was managerial and in the recording studio. In fact, there was an earlier Decca recording of the song by Holly in which he and Allison were listed as the sole writers. But it was the version on Brunswick by Holly and the Crickets that was the hit.

"Peggy Sue," the follow-up disk, exploded Holly on the pop scene. In style it was closer to Bo Diddley, who influenced Holly's songwriting, than to rockabilly, derived from western swing rather than Nashville country. Petty played a jangling piano. The ringing chords of a hi-amp electric guitar rolled over each other like a vibrating cymbal. The flowing rhythm had pulse rather than a hard beat. It was the Tex-Mex sound. Against the heavily echoed, metallic sound, Holly sang a nasal, high-pitched kind of Hank Williams vocal, replete with hiccups, stretched syllables, and a feeling of nervous excitement that almost seemed foreign to the ballad.

An older school of singers found this disregard of lyrics rather disconcerting. But Holly's admirers were unconcerned that his performance bore no relation to the woeful words of pleading. What counted was the agitation, tension, and energy of Holly's delivery. Here in a large sense was the dividing line between the eras of the Big Ballad and the Big Beat. For the rock 'n' roll singer, the song was not a medium but a springboard. He was not an interpreter but a stylist. His performance was the song. His record was the song. What was amateurville in the eyes of the "good music" advocates was a new esthetic to teen-agers.

Holly's biographer, Dave Laing, sees in Norman Petty's work with the Crickets and the man with the heavy, black-rimmed glasses and open-mouthed smile, an early instance of "studio rock." It was not that the singers and instrumentalists came to the studio to record a song as that the song emerged in the process of recording. The Tex-Mex sound was not planned or arranged. It developed as the result of the interaction of songwriters, singers, musicians, record producer, and the instrumentalities of the studio itself.

How Holly would have fared in the '6os is an open question. Like Anka and Bobby Darin, he was moving, under Petty's guidance, in an adult direction. On "It Doesn't Matter Anymore," an Anka song, he experimented with strings. But Holly's career was cut short by a plane crash early in '59, and like James Dean, Johnny Ace, and Hank Williams, he became a legend. Bobby Vee, who imitated him in his early recordings, was one of a number of young singers whose tributes (*I Remember Buddy Holly*) converted the Texan into the stuff that myths are made of.

The Everly Brothers

From Nashville country, sounding like adolescent choirboys, came the Everly Brothers. "I didn't think Presley was as good as the Everly boys," says Chuck Berry, "the first time I ever laid eyes on him. . . . And I didn't think the *Beatles* were as good as the

Everly Brothers either." In truth, before they became the Beatles, John Lennon et al. called themselves the Everlys—and you can hear the sound of Phil and Don as well in the Beach Boys and the Mamas and the Papas.

Sons of Kentucky country singers, Phil and Don became troupers when they were still kids. In '57 they burst on the record scene via Archie Bleyer's Cadence Records. They had two giant sellers in "Bye Bye Love," a rocking shuffle that went to No. 2 on the Honor Roll, and "Wake Up Little Susie," which shot up to No. 1 in four record weeks. Both were the work of resident Nashville writers Boudleaux and Felice Bryant, who supplied the duo with many of their subsequent hits. For a country songwriter, Boudleaux came out of a curious background, having been a member of the string section of the Atlanta Symphony Orchestra in his twenties.

"Wake Up Little Susie" got itself banned in Boston. Too suggestive, said several radio stations. This even though Susie and her boyfriend just fell asleep over a dull picture in a movie house. The ban was probably more extensive than reported, for "Bye Bye Love," recently revived by Donny Osmond, made the year's Top Tunes, while "Susie" did not. But it effectively portrayed the worldwide predicament of the teen-ager overstaying curfew and being compelled to face irate, not to mention suspicious, parents.

The Everlys were able to maintain their hold on the under-thirty generation through the rise of acid rock and the British invasion, and to stage a comeback when rock returned to its country roots in the late '60s. At the height of their popularity, country comedienne Minnie Pearl was asked when "hillbilly" music became "country" music. Cackling chicken-style in a way familiar to viewers of the "Grand Ole Opry," she patted an expensive blue-mink stole she was wearing and said: *"Hillbilly* becomes *country* when you can buy one of these."

From Presley's old stable, at least two record stars burst forth. Like many aspiring singers who came flocking to Sun Records, Jerry Lee Lewis journeyed from Natchez, Mississippi, where he performed at a local club, the Wagon Wheel, from the time he was fifteen years old. It took a little doing to get an audition in '56 by the much-harried Sam Phillips, and Lewis had to settle for Jack Clements, an associate. "Crazy Arms," his first record, meant nothing since it was a cover of a Ray Price hit. But it did introduce Jerry Lee Lewis and his Pumping Piano—that's the way the label read.

Carl Perkins, who worked with Jerry Lee at the time of

"Crazy Arms," claims that he was "people shy. . . . He'd sit at the piano with just one corner of his face showing . . ." But there was nothing shy about the driving singer-pianist one heard in '57 on "Whole Lot-ta Shakin' Goin' On." It zipped to No. 1 on R & B charts as well as country and pop.

"No group," John Lennon has said, "be it Beatles, Dylan, or Stones has ever improved on 'Whole Lot-ta Shakin' Going On' for my money."

As a youth, Jerry Lee studied to be a preacher. In its frenzy, his style is closest to another singer who also studied to be a preacher, Little Richard, many of whose dynamic, onstage gambits he has copied. More boisterous onstage than Elvis, he has a heavier southern-white accent but vocalizes with the gospel excitement of a hell-and-brimstone black preacher.

"Great Balls of Fire," another '57 hit for Lewis, was also a raging, up-tempo number. It was the work of Jack Hammer and Otis Blackwell, whom Lewis has described as "a little colored feller in a black derby." The gifted Blackwell was the writer of "Don't Be Cruel" and "All Shook Up"—Presley smashes on which Presley appeared as cowriter—and the sole writer of "Breathless," a panting hit for Lewis in '58.

That year, Lewis married his fourteen-year-old cousin, Myra Brown, an event that brought such scandalous publicity that it halted and almost destroyed his career. He was touring England when the news broke and made the mistake of bringing Myra onstage in a London theatre. The curtain had to be rung down. He was asked to leave the hotel where they were staying. And the tour had to be curtailed. In the United States, "High School Confidential," his new record release, was virtually blacked out by the stations.

"The parents wanted to kill rock 'n' roll," said Judd Phillips, who handled promotion for brother Sam's Sun Records in the Presley era and who today heads Jerry Lee Lewis Enterprises. "They found that they could throw this marriage to Myra up to the world and say, 'Look what kind of image you kids are idolizing'. . . . Mothers and fathers used to be able to call the radio stations and say, 'I don't want you to play that record' and it'd scare the hell out of the station. . . .'"

It was not until the late '6os that Lewis was able to resume his career and recapture the acceptance that gave him a hit album in '73. After Presley, he was the most exciting and explosive of young, white performers. Many feel that, had he not been the victim of the anti-Presley hysteria of the time, he might have outclassed the Pelvis in the late '50s.

JERRY LEE LEWIS INTERVIEW

"When I was about twelve," said Jerry Lee Lewis, who is now older and wiser but still talks with a heavy southern accent, "I walked into a theatre in Ferriday, Louisiana, where I was born. (Sept. 29, 1935.) Before the picture went on, they played a record. I never stayed for the picture. That record hit me so hard I rushed out, ran all the way home, sat down at the piano, and tried to sing 'Down Among the Sheltering Pines' exactly as Al Jolson had done it. And would you believe it? Although I heard the song just once, I knew every word. The way Jolson did it, each word stood out like an electrified stop sign. I've never forgotten those words—and I've never stopped admiring Al Jolson.

"Jolson is still the No. 1 showman-singer to me. And you know who's No. 2? Jimmie Rodgers, the Singing Brakeman. No. 3 in my book is Hank Williams, the Hillbilly Shakespeare. And No. 4 —take my word—is Jerry Lee Lewis. I would gladly follow Presley onstage and I'd hold my own. I respect Johnny Cash, Merle Haggard, and Tom Jones. But they don't bother me. Now, Al Jolson is a different story. If he were alive today, he could take tonight's audience and make them beg and beg and beg for more. I wouldn't want to follow him.

"I started to play when I was eight years old. My first instrument was a six-string guitar. It belonged to my father, Elmo Lewis. He was a giant of a man, six feet four inches tall, and worked as a carpenter-contractor. When I was nine, the family went out and bought an almost new Stark Piano. Guess they were impressed by my quick way of picking up chords and learning songs.

"Four years later, I made my first public appearance. It was unscheduled and occurred in a car lot. The Ferriday Ford Agency was introducing its new line of cars and the entertainment was furnished by a country-and-western band. Like a young bullfighter charging into a Mexican ring, I just got up and did an impromptu version of 'Drinking Wine Spo-de-o-de.' The crowd was amused and they passed the hat. I walked away from that car lot with the most money I ever had in my jeans. But I was even more excited at hearing my voice for the first time over a PA system.

"I played my first professional engagement when I was fourteen at the Blue Cat Club in Natchez. It was a short gig. Going to school during the day and performing at night didn't work out. So I settled for weekend appearances at the Hilltop and later at the Wagon Wheel. Played drums or piano and sang with a trio led by blind Paul Whitehead, who could play accordion, piano, and trumpet.

"In February '56, right after Sam Phillips sold Presley to RCA, I drove three hundred miles to see him. Every southern youngster who wanted to sing was there. And I never did see Sam but I cut some tapes with Jack Clement, who now has his own big studio in Nashville. I got a better reception on my second trip to Sun several months later. My record of 'Crazy Arms' didn't shake up the world but it sold enough to get me Bob Neal, Presley's first manager, as my booker. After 'Whole Lot-ta Shakin' Goin' On.' I was on the Steve Allen and other TV shows, and my price went up to four figures a night. 'Shakin'' eventually sold six million copies. So did 'Great Balls of Fire.' You better believe it."

Lewis opened his blue eyes wide and nodded his head of wavy, blond hair for emphasis. When I asked whether he had come to Sun as a country singer and adopted a blacker style as a result of Phillips's influence, he said:

"I don't know. I always liked Moon Mullican, Merrill Moore, a lot of them old boogie-woogie piano players. All those old records I used to listen to 'Drinkin' Wine Spo-de-o-de,' 'House of Blue Lights,' 'Hey Ba-ba Re-Bop'—I heard back home in Ferriday when I was growing up. And I liked blues singers like B. B. King and Ray Charles.

"I played a lot in church. . . . That was the Holiness Church, Meeting of God Assembly, and I went to Southwest Bible School near Dallas in Waxahatchie (don't ask me to spell it). . . . I done some preaching. Sang it with a beat, always sang with a beat.

"When I was a young man, I used to go to Haney's Big House, a local dance hall where Negro bands and combos played. Afterward, I'd try to do the songs I heard and pick up on their styles. But I also liked singers like Hank Williams and Red Foley, who was my favorite. I created my own style from all of these, I'd say.

"As for boogie-woogie, I was doing it long before I recorded for Phillips. Knew 'Cow-Cow Boogie' and all the boogies you can name. And what's 'Whole Lot-ta Shakin'' if not boogie-woogie?

"Even though my folks belonged to the Assembly of God Church, I listened to what I wanted and played what I wanted at home. My parents never held me back. They told me what they thought was right. But they never interfered with my music or what they thought I should do.

"My daddy had all of Jimmie Rodgers's recordings. He was like any southern farmer who'd go to the general store and order bread, eggs, potatoes, 'and the latest Jimmie Rodgers record.' We used to listen to them all the time when I was a kid. And Rodgers was a great blues singer, a great, great blues singer. He had a lot of Negro, spiritual-type blues to his voice. What a talent! I knew every one of his songs. A lot of people didn't like Hank Williams's singing. But you listen to his records and he can class-sing when he wants to. And the songs he wrote—the greatest in the world. His whole career was only four years old. He was only twenty-nine when he died. He was just startin'—a young man—don't know why it happened—can't understand it—terrible thing—and a lotta people got cheated out of a great, great talent."

Of the change that his marriage in '58 produced, Lewis said: "Myra was my second cousin. And she was fourteen, not thirteen as the papers kept saying. I believe that if the record company had stuck by me and really been on the ball, I don't think I would have the decline that I did have. A certain decline, maybe. But if it had been handled right, all that bad publicity wouldn't have meant a thing. Tom Parker made the statement that if he had had me, he could have made a zillion dollars out of it. And I don't doubt it. But nobody else had enough sense to do it. Everybody wsa runnin' scared. And I was a twenty-one-year-old kid, and I didn't know whether I was comin' or goin'.

"But I don't regret any of it. If I had to do it, I'd do it again. I've got a lovely daughter, eight years old, I wouldn't take a zillion dollars for. So, therefore, I really came out a winner.

"We were married for thirteen years and one day, Myra just upped and walked out. Thirteen years right out the window— just like that. I accept the fact but I can't get over it. Thirteen years is a large chunk of a man's life—and to blow it off like that! I can't help getting angry every time I think of it. But I don't regret it. It was a good relationship. I don't blame anybody but myself. I always liked the ladies a bit too much. Apparently, marriage didn't work out after thirteen years. [Chortling.] A terrible thing, I'll tell you."

As the interview was coming to a close, I apologized for asking Lewis about a Band-Aid over one of his eyes. Laughing, he said: "It's a helluva way to treat a guest in Las Vegas. Happened in front of the Landmark Hotel here, almost under that giant sign with my name on it. Guy beatin' on the hood of my car. I asked him to quit. He got real smart—and I got the Band-Aid. In San Antonio back in the '50s, I was just sittin' and not even lookin' at this guy. I was talkin' to a friend and this guy hauls off and hits me. Twelve stitches. The women love me, but these damn bruisers—they don't like me at all. I'm stitched up all over.

"That phone call a minute ago . . . that was Fats Domino on

the way over. He's one of the great talents in the world. So is Little Richard, but he has problems. 'I'm not a Negro,' he says. 'I'm an Indian.' Was on a tour with him and he used so much paint that the piano keyboard had to be wiped with a towel before I could play on it."

Fats enters. They greet each other warmly. "Sauterne," Fats says, as Jerry Lee holds up a Bloody Mary he is drinking.

They clink glasses and Jerry says: "Appreciate your comin' over. You'll stay for the show?"

Smiling, Fats nods.

"I've got a little of God on my side," says Jerry Lee.

"That's right," says Fats Domino.

turn to pg. 222

Raunchy Guitar

In addition to Jerry Lee Lewis, the other Sun Records discovery of '57 was a guitarist who labored as a studio musician and producer. Before, and after, he established himself as a recording artist, Bill Justis served as Jerry Lee Lewis' producer—also Roy Orbison's and of Johnny Cash's follow-up hits to "I Walk the Line," including "Ballad of a Teen-age Queen." Late in '57, Justis experimented with a slowed-down vibrato and an exaggerated echo on his electric guitar. Collaborating with a funky tenor saxman, he produced a wailing instrumental that caught on. "Raunchy," capitalizing on a new teen-age expression, kept nudging Pat Boone's "April Love" for the top spot on the Honor Roll and finally made it in December '57.

It was the forerunner of a series of guitar instrumentals, all of which traded on tension and toughness. In May '58 Link Wray and his Ray Men took another teen-age word, "Rumble," and used distortion and a blues-styled melody to evoke the roughhouse mood of a street gang angling for a fight.

Within a matter of months, "Rebel Rouser" was vibrating the charts. Released by Jamie Records of Philadelphia, it was made in Phoenix, Arizona, by Duane Eddy, working under the guidance of Lee Hazelwood, later Nancy Sinatra's rejuvenator. Employing the newly developed fender bass—it looked like another electric guitar but sounded like an amplified, stand-up bass—as well as an electric tremolo (also new), Eddy achieved a provocatively ominous sound. On his boss guitar, as it came to be called, Eddy also scored with "Ramrod" while Link Wray followed "Rumble" with "Rawhide" (not the theme of the TV series).

The electric guitar was on its way to becoming the king of rock, and rock 'n' roll was on the road to psychedelia.

21

WE'RE SO YOUNG—
AND THEY'RE SO OLD

In '57 four white teen-agers attained record prominence. Paul Anka, aged fourteen, was the most precocious and a gifted writer as well as performer. His "Diana," the woeful tale of a lad in love with an older lass, captured the travail of a generation eager to grow up fast. In France there were a dozen versions of the song with the memorable line: "I'm so young and you're so old . . . Di-i-i-ana . . ."

Before the decade was over, Anka's list of best-selling records included "Put Your Head on My Shoulder," "You Are My Destiny," "(I'm Just a) Lonely Boy," and "Puppy Love." He was still writing hits—for others—when his own flow of Gold Records stopped. Displaying a brash confidence and show-biz savvy—later displayed by Boby Darin—he quickly made the transition from teen-age record star to adult entertainer. He was only twenty when he began playing the main showrooms in Las Vegas as well as expense-account clubs like the Copa, once the stomping ground of old boozers like Joe E. Lewis, Sinatra, and Dean Martin.

PAUL ANKA INTERVIEW

Of Lebanese descent, Anka was born in 1943 and raised in Ottawa, Canada. Like most World War II babies, he grew up listening to Chuck Berry, Fats Domino, the Platters, Frankie Lymon and the Teenagers, etc. He managed to hear these and other R & B artists through broadcasts by platter spinner George "Hound Dog" Lorenz out of Buffalo.

The artist who most interested him was Sammy Davis, Jr., largely because he was doing impressions of him at amateur shows and shindigs at the Fisher Park High School. He became seriously concerned with music when he was thrown out of a shorthand class and substituted a course in music.

"A story has frequently appeared in print that I walked into the offices of Paramount Records at 1501 Broadway without an appointment, wangled an audience with the head of the A & R department, and landed a record contract. It's only partly true. You see, I knew the Rover Boys, who had just had a big hit on Paramount with "Graduation Day." I knew them from Canada and a club where they worked. I used to get them drinks, take walks with them, and hang around them. They put in a good word for me with Don Costa, who was in charge of A & R. I was living in the bathtub of one of the executives of the President Hotel. He phoned Costa about me.

"Don deserves credit for making the appointment and taking the time to hear me. I was a kid in the raw. Never made a record. I did three or four songs. He must have heard something because he immediately said that he wanted to record me. And he was responsible for all of my early hits. He arranged and conducted "Diana," "Lonely Boy," "My Destiny"—all of them. Later, Sid Feller took over.

"On the record of "Diana," we used just five pieces—piano, bass, guitar, sax, and drums—plus three voices. We recorded in the Capitol Studio on West Forty-sixth Street, just across the street from *Variety*. "Diana" was finished in Ottawa. But it wasn't finished when I got in the studio. That's why I used those 'uh-oh's' that every rock group was soon doing. I just didn't have any words for those notes. And the 'uh-oh' became the gimmick of the record. The three background voices, all male, were used for padding. They yelled footballs (whole notes) and sang a couple of licks. Don used girls to back me when he wanted interesting vocal effects.

"After my first session, I used to call Don Costa from Canada whenever I had an idea. That's how we got the sound on "You're My Destiny" in '58. I was thinking that I wanted to go from a small-band background to a big band. I heard a record of "Star Dust" by Billy Ward and the Dominoes, one of the first R & B disks with strings. I immediately called Don and asked him to pick up a copy. When I recorded, he used a big-band backing. I finished the song on the plane ride to New York.

"Lonely Boy" was a very personal song. Nowadays, my songs are frequently based on observation. But then they came from inside. I was eighteen and in the middle of everything that goes with success. I was getting away from the teen-age thing into the young manhood scene. And my mother was dying at the time. I can't even put the emotional pattern into words. But 'Lonely Boy' tells it like it was.

'Put Your Head on My Shoulder' is my favorite of the early recordings. I was hung-up at the time on a girl called Annette Funicello. We were both in that bikini-blanket-beach bag. It was my first real hookup and my writing took a romantic turn. "Puppy Love" also came out of that frame of reference. It was a hit for me in '60 and now it's a Gold Record for Donny Osmond.

"I did appear in a number of films, with Mamie Van Doren and Tuesday Weld. And I did some pictures with Annette at MGM and Allied Artists. But these came about because I was writing music for the films. Since I was a hot record artist, the studios tried to capitalize and wrote parts in for me. I knew that I wasn't a Rock Hudson. But I wanted to give it a shot. *The Longest Day* was the last thing I did in Hollywood.

"I had left Paramount and was with RCA Victor when the Beatles came along. That's when we became aware of what limited airplay can do to you, regardless of how good your records and songs are. The British groups grabbed so much airplay we just couldn't break through. I suffered like most Americans that came up with the Presley wave.

"But I was able to ride out the British tidal wave because I expected the drop-off. I'd had a very good run of records but I was aware of the cycles in the business. I am an individualist but I was surrounded by some very smart business people—my father, who ran Spanka Music and my other publishing companies; my manager, Irving Feld; and Buddy Howe at CMA (Creative Management Associates). Eventually, their savvy sinks in. I didn't accept the turnaround easily and I was a bit defiant. But I did accept it.

"And I went into my next ego transition. Because of my father and where I came from, I knew other values. I was not really taken in by the big-success thing. I got married and found a new outlet for my emotions, and that took care of some things.

"I did save when I was young and I had financial stability. That took care of other things. Now, if I had just been a singer, I might not have weathered the transition as well as I did. But I was a songwriter and earning income as a writer. The toughest part was to make the transition from kid songs for kids—that was my success—to make it in your head as a writer.

"It took some figuring. I'd gotten into the rut of writing for myself, which put me in a terrible groove—like if I didn't want a song for myself, who else would? One night, I came to the simple idea: I've got to design songs to fit other people. When the melody of "My Way" came my way, I wrote it for Sinatra and sent it to him. That was the turning point—in '68—for me as *From Here to Eternity* was for him in '55. Suddenly, after years of sending out songs and demos, I was accepted and recognized as a writer—I mean, for others . . ."

Ricky Nelson/Jimmie Rodgers/Eddie Cochran

Anka had nothing more than his talent and audacity to kick open record doors. Eric Hilliard Nelson, better known as Ricky Nelson, had his parents' TV soap opera "Ozzie and Harriet" as a springboard and exposure medium. Ricky struck pay dirt with his first disk. In his singing debut on his parents' show, he introduced one side, "I'm Walkin'," a cover of the Fats Domino hit. But it was the flip side, "A Teen-ager's Romance" that earned the Gold Record.

Imperial, the label for which Fats recorded, quickly signed Ricky when it was discovered that he had no contract with Verve (on which he had made his record debut). Together, Fats and Ricky transformed Imperial into a million-dollar label. "Be-Bop Baby," Ricky's first Imperial release, was followed by six other Gold Records: "Poor Little Fool" and "Stood Up" in '58; "Lonesome Town," "Never Be Anyone Else But You," "Sweeter Than You," and "Just A Little Too Much" in '59.

More youthful-looking than Pat Boone and with less of a voice, he served the same function as Boone and, later, the Beatles. The kids loved him but the parents did not hate him, as they did Presley. His brand of R 'n' R was distinctly white and embodied a juvenile sweetness that made his records a bridge between young and adult listeners. Although his parents' TV show contributed tremendously to his popularity, he himself had star quality. Next to the Pelvis in blue suedes and Pat in white buckskins, Ricky was unquestionably the most popular of the white, teen-age vocalists.

Jimmie Rodgers was a lumberjack in Seattle before he became a record artist. Yet his style and sound were tender enough to make him a singing pitchman for Kellogg's cereals. "Honeycomb" was the vehicle and one of the big disks of 1957.

Rodgers's route to this record success was both circuitous and fortuitous, having its beginnings in the Air Force during the Korean war. A sympathetic sergeant encouraged him to entertain at camp shows. On his discharge, a series of disappointments led him to roam the Pacific Northwest—he was born in Camus, Washington, in 1933—working farms and lumber camps. Eventually, he found his way to Nashville where a music-business friend, who heard him in a small club, urged him to tackle the New York recording companies. The day he wandered into Roulette Records, the offices were occupied by electricians and carpenters busily transforming a Tenth Avenue tenement into a business building.

"I sing," he told Hugo and Luigi, who were trying to work in the din. "O.K., sing," they said. Unpacking his guitar, Jimmie sang two numbers, one of which was "Honeycomb."

"Call us in a few days," they said. Accustomed to disappointments, Jimmie took the statement as a brush-off and promptly disappeared.

It took six months of searching before Hugo and Luigi located him, sent him money to bring him to New York, and brought him into a recording studio for his first session.

"Honeycomb" was quickly followed by Rodgers's rendition of a folk tune, "Kisses Sweeter Than Wine," adapted in the early '50s by the Weavers from an old Irish folk song. Apart from the appeal of his soft-sweet style, Jimmie had a two-syllabled hook, "Uh-oh!" that became his trademark. He endured the letdown of most Americans rockers when the British invasion occurred in the '60s. Afterward, he found record outlets, first at Dot and after suffering a skull fracture that almost took his life—he was in an altercation with police on a Hollywood freeway—at A & M Records.

What Eddie Cochran might have achieved, had he lived beyond the age of twenty-one, it is impossible to guess. But he had the makings of a stellar showman. Before he moved to Hollywood and began recording for Liberty, he attained recognition as a guitarist in his native Oklahoma and recorded for Ekko, a local label. His first Liberty hit was "Sittin' in the Balcony," the work of John Loudermilk of Nashville, and a realistic recognition of one of the best places for a teen-ager to smooch. It was followed by "Summertime Blues" and "C'mon Everybody," on both of which Cochran collaborated with Jerry Capehart, his manager and record producer. Domineering parents concerned him in one and teen-age fun in the other. In the songs he recorded in an all-too-brief career, teen-age problems were Cochran's paramount concern, particularly the inner conflict between young desires and parental castigation.

Cochran was a Presley imitator, affecting his hoarse, panting vocals and his choked rhythms. At moments, his toughness turned into tension à la Little Richard. Between his breakout in '57 and the end of the era, he acquired a large enough following to invite an English tour. On April 17, 1960, he was riding in a London taxi with performer Gene Vincent and Shari Sheeley, his girl-friend and writer of Ricky Nelson's "Poor Little Fool." There was a collision and Cochran was killed instantly.

As with Buddy Holly, a cult developed and there were record tributes both here and in England.

Johnny Mathis

Sometime in the spring of '57 Mitch Miller phoned me. I sprinted from my office in the RCA Building to Columbia Records at 799 Seventh Avenue to hear a new recording. I was anticipating a Four Lads disk—they were hot then—on a rhythm ballad that had gone through a number of rewritings. Miller liked the Sherman Edwards–Ben Raleigh song when I first auditioned it for him. But he thought it was too wordy and lacked warmth. Eventually the second and third stanzas were revised and the bridge or release was shortened. It took three months of work by the writers and many conferences, with me acting as the go-between.

What I heard in Miller's office was not a group, as I had hoped, but a strange, new voice. It was young with chesty tenor tones and heady high notes almost falsetto in character. It had no sex or real warmth, but it had lift and a sensuous feeling of ex-hilaration. And when the singer got to the arching, terminal phrase, "oh . . . so . . . won-der-ful, my love," the tender and mature love of which he sang became a very palpable reality.

The singer was, of course, Johnny Mathis and the song, "Wonderful, Wonderful." Except for a marked guitar afterbeat, it had little in common with the summer songs that were being heard on the nation's beaches. But the record had a distinctive, wave-like sound in a sinking cello figure and rising fiddle reply. And the song had a loveliness of melody and concept that made it Johnny's first hit recording, a status that it developed slowly as "It's Not for Me to Say" leaped over it on the Honor Roll of Hits and "Chances Are" quickly became his third consecutive best seller of 1957.

H. Kandy Rohde, a writer who was growing up in the Mathis days, recently referred to him as "king of necking music." It was curious to me since the words of Mathis's hits, with the exception of "Wonderful, Wonderful," had a cute ambiguity and were de-void of the thrust and emotional directness of songs like "All Shook Up" or "Bye Bye Love." But Rohde explained: "As much as we loved to be rocked by our music, we found that there were those quiet times when only Mathis would do. Only he could say those tender things we were too shy or too inexperienced to think of . . ."

At the height of the rocking Presley–Jerry Lee Lewis–Little Richard era, there was room and a feeling for innocence and tenderness. Pat Boone gave expression to it in "April Love" and "Love Letters in the Sand," as did Debbie Reynolds in "Tammy" and Jimmie Rodgers in "Honeycomb." All of these were No. 1 Honor Roll songs of the year.

Nineteen Fifty-seven was a white year, with more white singers breaking into R & B charts than black singers into pop. In rhythm-and-blues charts, one found Jimmie Rodgers, Paul Anka, the Everly Brothers, Jerry Lee Lewis, Ricky Nelson, Buddy Knox, Presley (of course), and even Guy Mitchell (with "Singing the Blues"). Also a white group from Canada named the Diamonds, who covered "Little Darlin'," originally cut by the Gladiolas on Excello, a Nashville indie label. The Diamonds employed all the devices of black groups, the low-low, bass voice, the comical, falsetto, high-pitched voice, and even a spoken segment à la the Mills Brothers. "Little Darlin' " not only finished as one of the Top Ten pop songs of 1957 but it was the Diamonds' disk that made R & B charts—and high up. The group hit it big again in '58 with "The Stroll" and in '59 with a novelty ballad, "She Say (Oom, Dooby, Doom)."

Among black singers who maintained their hold on pop, Fats Domino continued his winning streak with "Blue Monday," "Blueberry Hill," and "I'm Walkin'." Chuck Berry rang the bell—and how—with "School Day." Belafonte sold pop with "Banana Boat," "Day-O" as did Nat "King" Cole on "Send for Me" and Billy Williams with a revival of "I'm Gonna Sit Right Down and Write Myself a Letter." But none of these were rockers. Neither were two new black hitmakers.

Sam Cooke

Sam Cooke, son of a Chicago Baptist minister, spent his formative years singing with a gospel group known as the Soul Stirrers. While they were recording for Specialty Records, Sam made some pop sides. Specialty would not release them, fearing with good reason that these might hurt the acceptance of the Stirrers. When Bumps Blackwell, who cut these pop sides, left Specialty, he was able to take them with him. "You Send Me," which Cooke wrote, was released on another offbeat West Coast label (Keen) and sent listeners to the tune of over two million copies. Teresa Brewer, who covered the sensuous ballad, found herself hopelessly outdistanced, despite the superior distribution and promotion of her Coral disk.

To pop balladry, Cooke brought a rare fervor and intensity. Yet he was a crooner rather than a screamer. Singing softly and tenderly, he effused a sensuousness, gospel in its roots, that Otis Redding later tried to put into hs singing. (Redding always sang Cook's posthumous hit "Shake" as a tribute to him.) After "You Send Me" Cooke was quickly grabbed up by RCA Victor where he had a succession of best sellers into the '60s, many of them No. 1 songs like his "Chain Gang." At the height of his career, he was shot to death by a white motel owner, who claimed he tried to attack her. In his clarity of diction and the timbre of his voice, Cooke reminded many of Nat "King" Cole—and he did have Cole's pop appeal. But whereas Cole had polish and finesse, Cooke had depth of feeling. He was Cole with sex and soul.

Della Reese, another new black hitmaker, started ostensibly as an R & B singer, playing clubs like the famous Flame in Detroit. But her repertoire and style were much broader than the label would connote. Her first recordings appeared on Jubilee, the New York indie. In '57 she demonstrated her power in a horse race on "My Heart Reminds Me," a vocal adaptation of "Autumn Concerto," an Italian import. In a field of ten starters, Della ran neck-and-neck with Kay Starr on RCA Victor. "Don't You Know," her follow-up hit—after she had moved from Jubilee to Victor—was an adaptation of "Musetta's Waltz" from the Puccini opera *La Bohème*. It, too, tapped the resources of a rich contralto voice that sounded more operatic than pop, and certainly not R & B or R 'n' R.

DELLA REESE INTERVIEW

"I guess Detroit is a good starting point," said Della Reese. "I had a job as a hostess in a bowling alley that had a trio. It was the first suburban entertainment. Everything had been in the heart of town until then. One night I sang with the trio and the owner offered me an additional $5 a week if I would sing occasionally. I continued working and 'singing' there for two or three months.

"At that time—about 1954—the Strolls Brewery was having a coupon contest. You cut the coupons out of the paper. The prize for the one who sent in the most was a week at the Flame Show

Bar. It had nothing to do with talent, just with coupons. I had many friends who helped me assemble a bushel of the slips. After one week, the 'engagement' was extended so that I stayed there for eighteen weeks. The pay was sensational—$85 a week. And that was my start in show business.

"Prior to that, I sang gospel music. From the time I was six years old. I sang with Mahalia Jackson, with the Ward Singers, with Roberta Martin, Beatrice Brown and her Inspirational Singers—and I even had a group of my own called the Meditations. The Flame was my first departure into popular music. I sang three jazz songs. I thought they were jazz songs but later found out that they were standards. 'Fine and Dandy' was one. But I considered myself a great jazz singer, this departure from 'Jesus, Keep Me near the Cross.'

"My mother was a very religious woman, and music other than gospel was a no-no. We heard Bing Crosby and Kate Smith. That was it. Kate came on at noon in between 'Ma Perkins' and 'Helen Trent.' My mother loved to listen to those radio soap operas and we got to listen to Kate Smith since she came on between them. Bing Crosby was in the movies that we got to see on Saturday afternoons. Although they were both very good singers, they didn't make me want to leave the gospel because they sang a plain, bland kind of music. And gospel was driving and forceful. I was very happy with it—it wasn't as if I was suffering with it.

"But when I went into the Flame, I had an opportunity to hear Ella Fitzgerald. I was the opening act. I worked with Dinah Washington, Billie Holiday, Billy Eckstine, Count Basie, Erroll Garner, and just everyone who came to town. The Flame was the place to be. Television was then a thing that only an exclusive group of people had. Live entertainment was really the only form of entertainment—stage shows, nightclubs, and bars. In Detroit, in an area of five or six blocks, there wasn't one without spots of live entertainment. Friday and Saturday nights were get-up-and-go nights, get dressed and go out.

"Wayne University was in Detroit and so a lot of the young people came in, particularly on Saturday nights. But every night was nightclub night. The Flame was considered the hottest spot in town and we had a mixed audience, black, white, blue, and green. The Flame was letting your hair down.

"Maurice King, who has since become associated with Motown, had the house band at the Flame Show Bar. He made me arrangements on 'April in Paris' and 'With These Hands.' My program consisted entirely of standards.

"I did some recording at this time. Tony Vance, who was a

Detroit personality, had a label called Great Lakes Records. On this, I recorded a song called 'Blue and Orange Birds and Silver Bells,' 'There'll Never Be Another You,' and some other titles.

"Before I found Lee Magid—the beginning of major things for me—I worked through Canada quite a bit. I also worked towns like Chicago, Buffalo, and other cities within a two-hundred fifty-mile radius. The Pete Iodice office in Detroit booked me and Steve Massey was the agent I used.

'In the Still of the Night' was my first release on Jubilee Records, the New York company. 'And That Reminds Me' was such a big hit, it led to my association with RCA Victor. That happened when Hugo and Luigi were running the A & R department—and, incidentally, I am now working with them on Avco-Embassy Records. 'Don't You Know,' based on Puccini's *La Bohème,* was my first release of RCA and that was really a giant seller. I remained with RCA for over six years.

"In the '50s, I was in my twenties and now I'm in my forties. Naturally, my outlook is different. In the '50s, we were just over the war and there was a kind of affluence. The boys were coming home and it was a reconstruction period. There was no hydrogen, atom, or cobalt bomb. There was a happier atmosphere and the main struggle was existence, personal existence from day to day, and not world existence as we have now, not knowing who's going to push the button when. It was a lighter society, a society seeking enjoyment to a great extent.

"Some of the young people's music of today is very good and very exciting to sing and listen to. But the music of the '50s was a different kind—a spoon-moon-June, I love you, you're dear to me, you're the sweetest, let's go look at the moon and the mountains and watch the reflection on the water—that kind of atmosphere. Now, it's more driving, it has to do with messages, pollution, love your brother.

"There's another way that things are different. Now, everywhere you go, you can dance. In the '50s, people wanted to be entertained. They hung on every word, and were interested in every syllable.

"I had the 'Autumn Concerto' in '57, which was called 'And That Reminds Me.' I like to sing all types of music. In my dinner shows, I include something classical, something spiritual, something in the modern rock vein, something old. I don't consider myself a jazz or pop singer. Back then, I sang semiclassic through the rock and roll phase and sold a million and a half copies right in the middle of Bill Haley and the Comets, Elvis Presley, and Fats Domino. . . .

"Lee Magid and I have an agreement that he doesn't tell me what to sing and I don't tell him how to run the business end, and we've been together twenty-one years. I've been fortunate in that I have not had very many people directing me because that wouldn't really have worked. Lee has been very instrumental in seeing that I could do whatever I wanted to do.

"Back in those days, they tried to sell black artists to black people. I was fortunate in that I didn't have a voice that was typically black nor did I have a voice that was straining to be white. When I did 'Don't You Know' there were people who thought I was a baritone who had tenor qualities. They kept expecting a man when I showed for a personal engagement. And there I was. There were people who thought I would be the size of Kate Smith or Mahalia. And when I arrived, they were surprised. You couldn't classify my voice just by listening to it—and maybe that had a lot to do with the freedom I enjoyed.

"I don't have any vivid memories of Billie Holiday. I was always anxious to see her because she had one of the most ardent followings I know of. Everybody who loved her, loved her as if they were under some kind of spell. I wanted so much to see her to try to understand this magic. It never came through to me on records and I could not understand what was so exciting about her.

"She had no influence on me at all. I think that Dinah Washington did the things that Billie got the credit for doing. Dinah had more fire. She was more my kind of singer. Dinah pierced you. Billie was a crooner to me, kind of a sad wailer. I have never had that much sadness to wail about. Dinah even in sadness was a bit bitchy, which is basically my attitude. When sorrow comes, it makes me angry. It doesn't make me pitiful so that's why I relate to Dinah more. Carmen McRae, who is my dearest friend and is an entirely different kind of person than I am, feels a great empathy with Billie. I enjoyed Billie but I was never under her spell.

"When I came into show business, I had no background for it. Every time I got paid, I kept looking over my shoulder for the man to come and take the money back. I sang three songs a night. I got $85 for it. I had so much fun and he paid me for it. I was not impressed that you could make a career or that you could do well financially from it. I had been singing gospel for sixteen or seventeen years and starving to death. Singing was something you did just to have a good time. I had a series of other jobs because I had absolutely no faith that this man would be idiot enough to keep giving me $85 a week. I drove a truck, I drove a taxi, I was a secretary to a real estate broker, I was a receptionist for a dentist. I never expected the singing thing to last so I didn't get involved in the excitement of 'I am in show business.' I was quite a few years into the business before I began trying to establish myself and decided that I could make it my life's work.

"But I guess I began to sense the potential during the eighteen weeks at the Flame. Gradually, I listened to the people who came through, and saw the entertainment that people derived and the feelings that they generated, I saw the possibility of a career. LaVern Baker happened to be very hot at the time, with 'Tweedle Dee Dee.' Her manager was Al Green, who was also the manager of the Flame Show Bar. He felt that I had something but he was handling just race groups. So he sent me to New York to see Lee Magid—and that's when the pieces fell into place . . .''

But there were several artists with blacker sounds that attracted pop buyers. Mickey and Sylvia on Groove Records, a Victor subsidiary, made the lists with "Love Is Strange." But the calypso craze may have accounted for this. Larry Williams, originally Lloyd Price's valet, became a recording artist when his boss left the Specialty label. Sounding a lot like Price, he found a market with "Short Fat Fannie," a humorous novelty that made the Top Twenty of the Honor Roll. Williams also wrote "Bony Moronie," which remained in R & B, as well as "Dizzy Miss Lizzie," an obvious takeoff on Price's classic "Lawdy Miss Clawdy."

"Short Fat Fannie," whose title reminded one of "Long Tall Sally," was a tour de force in which Williams told of how he tired of the latter and came to meet and love the former. Within this framework, he used a gimmick, which appealed to teen-age record buyers. Into five stanzas, he squeezed the titles of as many rock 'n' roll songs as he could work into the so-called story line. The lyric read like a roll call of recent hits, including "Slippin' and Slidin'," "Rip It Up," "Work with Me, Annie," "Heartbreak Hotel," "Fever," "Tutti Frutti," "Hound Dog," "Blue Suede Shoes," "Honky Tonk," "Mary Lou," "Jim Dandy," and "Blueberry Hill."

The Stroll—and Chuck Willis

In 1957 the kids began to stroll. That was the name of a new dance that caught on quickly and reached its peak the following year with the Diamonds disk "The Stroll." The dance produced an unanticipated bounty for a soulful balladeer who had been recording and writing for a number of years. Suddenly, there he was onstage in Arab-styled turbans, a colorful figure with a royal title, *king of the stroll.* Chuck Willis had nothing to do with the dance. But it so happened that a disk he cut of an old blues, Ma Rainey's "C. C. Rider," had an easy, swinging tempo that was just right for the dance.

Produced by Atlantic's Ahmet Ertegun and Jerry Wexler, the record opened with a sweet-sounding marimba that set down a standard boogie figure (I-IV-V-IV). The figure became an ostinato with a female chorus and then a mixed group. The standard tenor-sax solo was expressive rather than raucous. And Willis's voice was clear not gritty, emotional not aggressive. The record went pop although it finished higher on the R & B charts.

Chuck was able to capitalize on his sudden popularity with his own version of another traditional blues, "Betty and Dupree." Personals were bringing him before large audiences who had never heard of him during his years on Okeh, Columbia's R & B subsid. In February of '58 he cut two sides, fully revealing that he had made the transition from a rhythm and bluesman to pop singer—"What Am I Living For," which he did not write, and "Hang Up My Rock and Roll Shoes," which he did.

Both sides have a strangely prophetic, if not ominous aura, although "What Am I Living For" is more of a love ballad than its philosophical title would suggest. Less than two months after he left the Atlantic studio in New York, he died on an operating table in an Atlanta hospital.

The Coasters

When Atlantic Records celebrated it tenth anniversary early in 1958, it was stated that the company's "biggest record of all time" was "Searchin' " by the Coasters, originally a West Coast group known as the Robins. Backed with "Young Blood," it was one of the Top Three records in R & B, a substantial hit though not as big in pop, and the most important of the black disks that crossed over in '57. With it, the group and its gifted writer/producers burst out of black ghettoes into the pop teen-age world.

"Searchin'," as its title suggests, dealt with a lover's effort to locate his errant girl. It was not a ballad but a comedy song. This cat was going to use the techniques of all the great detectives of films and TV—Charlie Chan, Bulldog Drummond, Sam Spade, and the Northwest Mounties—to bring her in. Baritone Billy Guy, who was a natural comic singer, took the lead on a song that set the pattern for the group and writers Leiber and Stoller. Call it situation comedy or three-minute comic skits. The songs were humorous narratives and the singers, comedians on wax.

In "Young Blood," the underside, the four lads spotted this chick on a corner and each said, "Looka there," with a different inflection, all lecherous and funny. "What's you name?" each asked, playfully but with one thought on their collective minds. And then they met Dad, played by bass Will "Dub" Jones whose voice told what he had on his mind. It was not friendly. But they still couldn't get "Young Blood" outa their minds, so maybe lust would develop into love. It was clever and imaginative.

In '58 Leiber and Stoller and the Coasters produced two gems of satire and humor and social comment. In a driving, up-tempo meter, enhanced by the exuberance of the voices, "Yakety Yak" sounded the tension between generations, the older critical of the younger's laziness and neglect of responsibilities, the younger resentful of parental officiousness. The form of the song was unusual in that the title came in as a throwaway, but told it all. And then there was the rasping voice of baritone Buddy Guy urging, "Don't go back." (Incidentally, King Curtis's chicken-stuttering tenor was undoubtedly the inspiration of Boots Randolph's yakety-sax style.)

"Charlie Brown" had nothing to do with his namesake in the Peanuts cartoon. He was a roguish cutup who called the teacher "Daddy-O," set fire to the auditorium, and indulged in other bits of mischief. But in Dub Jones' bass voice, he asked innocently, if not slyly: "Why is everybody always pickin' on me?" And while two of his classmates thought he was a clown, they had mixed feelings of admiration and suspicion.

Before the decade ended, the Coasters had "Poison Ivy," "The Shadow Knows," and the celebrated "Along Came Jones," a brilliant satire on TV westerns. Focusing on the old-hat situation of the villain seeking the deed to the mortgage, they built each threat of destruction to a pyramiding series of "And then. . . . And then . . ." And the dénouement was the arrival of Jones, slow talkin' and slow walkin'. We never learned what he did, but it was clear that you could rely on Jones in his baggy pants.

Leiber and Stoller were consummate craftsmen—as adept in creating evocative melody for their concepts as in choosing the right tempos, the expressive arrangement, the amusing interplay of voices—all to project a tale for fun and insight. They were superb songwriters, artful arrangers, inventive record producers, and knowledgeable studio men. If rock 'n' roll had produced nothing but the Coasters and Leiber and Stoller, it would still have commanded attention as the sound embodiment of a time and generation. They reflected the world of the young with understanding, good humor, and social insight. This was rock 'n' roll at its best—ebullient, energizing, entertaining, expressive, and danceable. And what could the detractors of the style say to that?

On December 1, 1957, a southern black seamstress refused to yield her seat to a white man when ordered to do so by a white bus driver in Montgomery, Alabama. Rosa Parks' arrest led to a boycott that lasted for 369 days. "I was just tired. My feet hurt," she said. The Rev. Martin Luther King, who emerged as a leader from the bus boycott, said: "I have a dream."

"Hail! Hail! Rock 'n' Roll," Chuck Berry sang, "deliver me from days of old." In '57 music became a persistent search of the young for identity. The songs dealt with their clothes: "Short Shorts" (Royal Teens), "Black Slacks" (Joe Bennett and the Sparkletones), "A White Sports Coat . . . and a Pink Carnation" (Marty Robbins). They dealt with their meeting places, "At the Hop" (Danny and the Juniors) and their dances, "The Stroll" (the Diamonds). They probed their adolescent feelings: "First Date, First Kiss, First Love" (Sonny James), "The Ballad of a Teen-age Queen" (Johnny Cash), "Cool Baby" (Charlie Gracie), "High School Romance" (George Hamilton IV). Their lingo produced song titles like "All Shook Up" (Elvis Presley), "Raunchy" (Bill Justis), "Rumble" (Link Wray). Parental attitudes and animosities were explored in "Teen-age Mother, Are You Right?" by Bill Haley, in "Get a Job" by the Silhouettes, in "Why Don't They Understand" by George Hamilton IV. Chuck Berry described the learning grind and the after-hours release in "School Day" while two youngsters attending a high school in Queens, New York, made a record of their own and achieved a mild noisemaker in "Hey, Schoolgirl." Tom and Jerry, as they called themselves, came to be known as Simon and Garfunkel.

To the question "Who am I?" a generation fighting alienation and loneliness answered *a teen-ager*. And that commonplace word became freighted with special emotions almost as, at critical moments, "worker" did in Russia and "citizen" did in France.

What they were rebelling against musically was around them in the work of the polished performers and dedicated interpreters of the older generation. Patti Page made it to "Old Cape Cod" and Sinatra went "All the Way" with the Academy Award song of the year. You could hear the sounds of old in Dinah Shore's

"*Chantez, Chantez,*" the Ames Brothers' "*Melodie d'Amour,*" Jane Morgan's revival of a *valse tzigane,* "Fascination," and in Victor Young's schmaltzy waltz ballad "Around the World." The velvet buzz of the big baritones was present in Vic Damone's "An Affair to Remember," Nat Cole's "Send for Me," and Perry Como's engaging novelty, "Round and Round."

As the Top Tune of the Year, *Billboard* named "Tammy," a movie theme with recordings by Debbie Reynolds and the Ames Brothers, and the list of Top Ten included older-generation songs like "Around the World," "So Rare" (a fluke hit for Jimmy Dorsey), "Round and Round," and the calypso-folkish "Mari-anne," with records by Terry Gilkyson, Burl Ives, and the Hill-toppers. In short, the list was split evenly between old and new. But when it came to Best Selling Records, the No. 1 was Presley's "All Shook Up," and seven of the ten were rock 'n' roll.

The year had its curiosities ("The Green Door"), and their appeal was to the young, even when the proponent was a middle-aged deejay from Texas, Jim Lowe. "Little Bitty Pretty One" achieved its effect through performance, rather than the lyric, which was really nonexistent. Vocalist Thurston Harrison Aladdin simply kept repeating one line, "Little bitty, pretty one, won't you come with me?" while a vocal group hummed and chanted something that sounded like *mm-mm-mm-muh-muh-mm* in the background. The record had an erotic-seductive quality that made it a solid R & B seller. More of a dance disk, despite its humorous title, was "Rockin' Pneumonia and the Boogie Woogie Flu" by Huey Smith and the Clowns. Released on the short-lived Ace label of Jackson, Mississippi, the disk rocked to a healthy, New Orleans shuffle. The biggest of the curiosities was the strangely titled "Come Go with Me," a disk by the Del Vikings on Dot. It was a whopper, as was the follow-up, "Whispering Bells," in-triguing for its sound effects. The Del Vikings were the most successful of all of these, but even their run of hit disks never made three.

Perhaps the most bizarre happening of the year involved Little Richard. In October as he was sailing on Sydney's Hunter River during an Australian tour, one of his musicians dared him "to prove his faith in God." The ecstasy singer loved showy jewelry and his fingers were adorned with four rings valued at $8,000. Little Richard's response was to tear them from his fingers and throw them, one by one, into the river. Then he announced that he was finished with the devil. No more shimmering, silk suits, piano pounding, or the oily pompadour and rocking it up, ripping it up, shaking it up, or balling it up. He was through with record-making and show business.

"If you want to live with the Lord," he told an Australian reporter, "you can't rock 'n' roll it, too. God doesn't like it." He was returning to L.A. immediately to be baptized in the faith of the Seventh Day Adventists.

By January 1958 Little Richard was enrolled at Oakwood College, a Seventh Day Adventist school in Huntsville, Alabama. Noting that he had earned nearly a million dollars in the preceding two years, he paid for his four-year tuition in advance. He indicated that he was quitting show business because of a dream in which he "saw the world burning up and the sky melting with heat." He confessed that he was motivated in part by an experience in the Philippines when his plane caught fire and the flames went out in answer to his prayer.

Art Rupe for whom Little Richard recorded on Specialty Records traced his conversion to the first earth satellite. "He thought that the Sputnik," Rupe has said, "was a sign from Heaven: that was it."

Call it "seeing the light," religious fervor, cosmic terror, or what you will, could anyone make a gesture that better bespoke the youthful idealism and romanticism of the time?

Little Richard kept to his vow for a number of years. When he began recording again, he cut only gospel songs. But the spirit that infused rock 'n' roll with its euphoric excitement, its high-flying sense of fun, and its ecstatic elation could be contained only for a while. After a time, Richard Penniman was back hammering feverishly at the keyboard, exploding with ebullient scat syllables, "Wop/bop-a-lou/bop-a-lop, BAM BOOM" and shouting "Shut Up! I'd rather do it myself."

22

GET PRESLEY!

In 1957 the Establishment was still gunning for Presley and fighting to shore "good music" against the rising tide of rock 'n' roll, a wave that now could not be dismissed as a passing craze.

At Station CHWK in Chilliwack, British Columbia, a disk jockey was dismissed for programing Screamin' Jay Hawkins' "I Put a Spell on You." Bob Friesen had taken literally an Epic Records advertisement in which the company stated: "Deejays, give this one a spin. If you get fired, we'll get you a job." Friesen wrote of his plight to Epic. No one seemed to know what to do and the letter wound up at the Bridgeport pressing plant of Columbia, the parent company, where it was bucked to the trade papers.

Top ASCAP songwriters fought to stem the inroads of new, rock writers, generally associated with BMI, on several fronts, As their $150-million lawsuit against BMI, broadcast networks, and record companies owned by broadcasters made its slow way through pretrial proceedings, they ran to Congress for help. In June '57 their hopes that the Celler House Anti-Trust Committee would recommend dissolution of broadcast ownership of BMI came to naught. Instead, the Committee merely requested that the Department of Justice undertake a complete and extensive investigation into the music field.

Working through Songwriters Protective Association (SPA), the ASCAPers, not without the protest of BMI members of the organization, turned their attention to the Senate Commerce Committee. To pressure this committee into holding hearings, as requested by SPA's Washington representative, the top ASCAP songwriters brought an over-thirty name artist into the conflict.

Bing Crosby lent his name to a letter charging that "a monopo-
listic trend in music on the part of the broadcasters is certainly
apparent" and that the deteriorating quality of music on radio
and TV was "the result of pressure exerted by BMI."

In turn, BMI released a letter in which older-generation name
artists denied that they were subject to pressure from either BMI
or ASCAP. Included among the signatories were Eddy Arnold,
Gene Autry, Nat Cole, Percy Faith, Benny Goodman, Sammy
Kaye, Dinah Shore, and Lawrence Welk.

Came August and the efforts of the ASCAP songwriters bore
fruit. Senator Smathers introduced a bill requiring that broadcasting stations divest themselves of recording and publishing interests. BMI quickly responded with a statement in which it announced that it would prove that it was "organized and is operated
to create competition in the music-licensing field, formerly entirely monopolized by ASCAP; that the overwhelming majority
of phonograph records . . . and performances . . . are of com-
positions licensed by ASCAP, not BMI; and that composers and
publishers are better paid and have more opportunities now than
before BMI was founded."

Newspaper stories on the Smathers bill had hardly hit print
than SPA released a letter from Frank Sinatra. Claiming that the
bill would clear up much "skullduggery," the Swooner expressed
strong support of the attempt to break broadcaster-diskery affilia-
tion. Sinatra also used the occasion to fire a new barrage against
his unfailing target. This time he accused Mitch Miller of ad-
mitting under oath that he "took large sums of money from
writers whose songs he recorded." Miller countered with the claim
that Sinatra had distorted his testimony by taking isolated portions
of statements made by him at pretrial hearings of the ASCAP
songwriters' suit against BMI.

Appearing on an "Entertainment Press Conference," a weekly
feature of Station WABD in New York City, the Beard found
himself the unexpected target of three critics, all of whom vented
their animosity toward teen-age music by attacking Miller—who
curiously was on their side. Later in the year, during an appearance on the "Barry Gray Show" on WMCA, Miller found himself
in the strange position of having to defend rock 'n' roll, or at least
of denying that the big beat contributed to juvenile delinquency.
"There isn't a piece of music written or recorded," he said, "that
can do to a child what the home has not already done" He
suggested that teen-agers went for the new music because "my
parents and teacher don't like it" or "Nobody likes it but us."
Yet he felt that "good music" lovers had reason to feel encouraged

for some stations were programing other types of music than Top Forty.

About a week later, Miller appeared on an interview show with three other A & R executives. Miller and Sammy Davis, Jr., who was host, were outspokenly anti–rock 'n' roll, with the Beard dismissing it as "the comic books of pop." Arnold Maxin of MGM Records attributed the rise of R 'n' R to the increased pocket money carried by teen-agers.

"They have the money," he said, "but they also have untrained ears. The only thing they have is a feel for the beat and the sound." Maxin added that he did not foresee an end to R 'n' R in the near future, at which point Davis announced: "I might commit suicide."

Asked why Eddie Fisher had not been able "to get arrested in the last year on records," Hugo Winterhalter of RCA Victor responded: "I know that the past year or two—not only to Fisher and a lot of other established recording stars—has been more or less of a nightmare to me as an arranger."

Milt Gabler of Decca was the only A & R man who evinced a positive attitude toward R 'n' R. "It was Louis Jordan's baby," he said, not without regret, "and it's too bad that he missed the boat. Bill Haley is one of my children and I love him, but I know Louis started it, and if I had a chance to get back with him, we could do it all over again."

The over-thirty musical Establishment seized upon every available statistic to buoy up its spirits and energize resistance to change. When Pulse and Neilsen surveys revealed that grown women, not teen-agers, constituted the bulk of radio's listening audience, a number of station managers announced that a counter-trend to Top Forty programing was taking shape.

To demonstrate how transitory rock trends might be, reference was made to the skiffle craze. A type of fast shuffle, it had come roaring in on "Freight Train," introduced in England by the Clyde McDevitt Skiffle Group, vocal by Nancy Wiskey. Margie Rayburn quickly covered on Liberty, as did Rusty Draper, who had the best-selling disk. Dick Jacobs of Coral got into the race with a skiffle band. Within a matter of weeks, the sound had faded from the musical horizon like a fast passenger train.

In July 1957 *Harper's* magazine threw its weight on the side of "good music" in a heavily promoted article, accusing American disk jockeys of "going steady with baby sitters." According to the writer, a Chicago trade paper reporter, the tie-up between tot sitters and deejays was "obstructing the development of a truly popular music culture." Stations that switched to adult programing, he claimed, achieved astonishing success with advertisers and audiences.

Nevertheless, by September *Billboard* announced in a shattering headline: "Demise of R & R Just So Much Wishful Thinking." An examination of pop charts disclosed that twelve titles were identical with those on R & B charts and eleven of these were in pop's Top 15. Three rock 'n' roll tunes appealed to listeners in all areas, pop, C & W as well as R & B: "Teddy Bear" (Presley), "Whole Lotta Shakin' Goin' On" (Jerry Lee Lewis), and "Bye Bye Love" (Everly Brothers). For the proponents of "good material," it was a sad confirmation that the record-music market was succumbing more and more to the necromancy of R 'n' R.

By year-end Ray Anthony, a swing-era bandleader, announced that he was incorporating a rock 'n' roll library in his repertoire: "I have come to the conclusion," he said, "that a whole generation of dancers has grown up around us. The only thing wrong is that bands haven't been playing their kind of music." Anthony's solution soon became a commonplace. At weddings, confirmations, etc., there was a sweet-styled, tenor band playing medleys of show tunes, film themes, and standards for the older people and a small rock 'n' roll combo socking it over for the teen-agers.

Throughout the year, Presley continued to be the center of antirock attacks, a circumstance that did not hurt his popularity at all. In the course of '57, three of his disks zoomed to the top of the Honor Roll: "All Shook Up" in April, "Teddy Bear" in August, and "Jailhouse Rock" in November. By the time "Teddy Bear" was No. 1, he had amassed eight Gold Records while "Bear" sold a million within two weeks after its release.

One result of his continuing sales was a shakeup in RCA Victor's chain of command. In August Steve Sholes, who had stuck his neck out by signing Presley, was elevated to the top A & R spot previously occupied by Eddie Fisher's hitmaker, Joe Carlton. Shortly after he assumed control, Sholes signed writer-producers Leiber and Stoller, who had written "Jailhouse Rock," "Hound Dog," and other Presley hits, as independent record producers. One of the first disks they cut was Georgia Gibbs doing "Great Balls of Fire," which hardly gave any competition to Jerry Lee Lewis's own original recording. In an effort to meet the challenge of small independents like Sun, other major companies began adding young, indie producers to their staffs. Mercury, for example, retained twenty-four-year-old Nat Tarnopol, who had discovered Jackie Wilson. The majors were trying to achieve the raw sound that seemed so appealing to youngsters on the indie disks.

While the management of RCA Victor was more than happy with Presley's popularity, the elation among civic authorities and broadcasting management was rather tempered, if not nonexistent. During a two-day appearance at the Pan Pacific Auditorium in Los Angeles, the police issued an edict that he "clean up the show or else . . ." The vice squad was to stand by and monitor Presley's elimination of "all sexy overtones." The newspaper reviewers were likewise severely critical of the Pelvis's movements and his groan-and-grunt, pant-and-choke vocals. Nevertheless, Presley attracted a young audience of over nine thousand who dropped $60,000 into his coffers.

In Chicago, Station WCFL issued a ban on plays of all Presley disks. The station was immediately surrounded by a huge picket line of his fans. Before things got out of hand, a movie press agent advised that both actions were a publicity stunt for Presley's new film *Jailhouse Rock*.

But in Portland, Oregon, Station KEX was not making believe. It fired one of its deejays for playing Presley's disk of "White Christmas." The management felt that "the treatment was in extremely poor taste." Disk jockey Dick Whittingill of KMPC in Los Angeles agreed and refused to program the platter and remained adamant despite listener requests. "No, I won't play it," he announced. "That's like having Tempest Storm [a stripper] give Christmas gifts to my kids."

In Canada, likewise, a large percentage of stations banned Presley's *Christmas* album. When a disk jockey on CKWS of Kingston, Ontario, asked for listener reaction to Presley's singing of hymns and Christmas songs, the results were quite different. As he played cuts from the album late one December night, eight hundred listeners called in, among whom there were a number of ministers and priests. Ninety-three percent said amen to the pious Presley.

Sacred or profane, kneeling or twisting, Elvis was a symbol of something that was reshaping the entire music scene *and* the life-style of the young.

23

GOING STEADY

In January 1958 Beverly Ross, cowriter of "Dim, Dim the Lights,"
came to my office with a young, black lad of thirteen or fourteen.
Beverly had been doing volunteer work at the Harlem YMCA
and she had worked up an arrangement with the youngster on a
new song, written with Julius Dixon, her cowriter on "Dim." In
the lingo of the day, I was so *flipped* by the rhythm ballad
Beverly sang with Ronald—I cannot recall his surname—that I
had my secretary instantly phone a recording studio and book
time for us to cut a demo. All I wanted was four back-up musicians, piano, bass, guitar, and drums—and I did not want to wait.

When we arrived at Associated Recording—the studio was then
in a squat, three-story building adjoining the Brill and next door
to Hector's cafeteria—there were only three musicians. No pianist.
I did not care. I wanted that demo as fast as I could get it and I
felt that the song was strong enough to register with any background, even *a cappella*. We cut the demo in the allotted hour.
Studio cost—$15.00. Musicians—$30.00. Young Ronald—$10.00.
Beverly waived a fee as the writer of the song. Total cost—$55.00.
Dubs were then cut for $2.00, perhaps $2.50 a side. And so for
$65.00, I was set to submit the new song to record companies. If
memory serves me, I heard the song and cut it on a Friday. I spent
a restless weekend, exulting in what I heard on the demo—played
over and over and over—and fretting that I had to wait two days
before I could audition it.

By Tuesday afternoon, all of my hopes had mounted to a
feverish peak. But I had a problem. Archie Bleyer at Cadence
liked the demo so much he wanted to release it as a master. So did
Steve Sholes at RCA Victor. There were three hang-ups: 1) I did

not have Ronald under contract as an artist and therefore could not license the demo as a master; 2) young Ronald was underage so that a contract would have to be worked out with his parents or guardian; and 3) he was black and Beverly was white, and neither record companies nor disk jockeys were then too receptive to mixed duos.

A day or two later, as I was trying to nail down a contract with Ronald, Archie Bleyer was on the phone. Archie had what he regarded as an infallible sounding board at home: his wife's teen-age daughter and her friends. Apparently their reaction to "Lollipop"—that was the song—was so strong that he wanted me to come over that day and sign a licensing agreement. I had no recourse, except to stall. Bleyer was one of the most honorable men in the business. But I could not afford to let it be known that young Ronald was then up for grabs as a recording artist.

Late that afternoon, I met with Ronald's manager. He suddenly had two, Julius Dixon, cowriter of the song, and a Chicano friend. It was not until the following week that they had a firm commitment from Ronald's parents and that Edward B. Marks Music Corporation in turn had a signed contract with Ronald. My memory is that we bought Ronald a winter coat in order to persuade his parents and then gave him a small advance on the the signing of the agreement.

In the meantime, Archie Bleyer was on the phone with me at least once a day. Before I was able to knot things up at Ronald's end, Bleyer lost patience and finally indicated that unless he had a licensing deal on the master by the following day, he was going to record the song with the Chordettes. And that was exactly what he did.

I was hardly upset by this turn of events. My primary interest and responsibility were to find and create hit songs. If one could develop a recording artist and add the income from a master in the process so much the better. But the chart song was the *sine qua non*. Bleyer was apparently so edgy about the potency of my master or the possibility that he might be scooped by another record company that he rushed copies of the Chordettes disk to jockeys overnight. What recording men did in such a situation was to make a duplicate master tape and have individual copies dubbed directly off the tape, instead of being pressed from a metal stamper. It was a slow and costly process but one that worked in emergencies.

I had no problem in negotiating a deal with Steve Sholes at RCA for release of the Ronald and Ruby master, as we dubbed the duo. Instead of using photographs in promotion and advertising—as would have been done with a new artist—RCA employed a cartoon approach. Their trade-paper advertising scooped Archie Bleyer's ads—recall the old lady leaning out a window. However, Cadence moved much faster, as independents did when it came to disk-jockey promotion and getting records into retail outlets.

When "Lollipop" crystallized on *Billboard's* Honor Roll of Hits on March 17, it was No. 14. Two weeks later, it made No. 2. It was the fastest-breaking record in my career. It remained there for two weeks, unable to displace "Tequila" (ugh!) in the No. 1 slot. The Best Selling Record was, of course, by the Chordettes. But Ronald and Ruby made enough of a showing for RCA Victor to invite me to cut a session with them. The new sides did not make it, partly because the songs were not strong enough but also because Victor was not too successful in promoting rock material (except, of course, Presley).

"Lollipop" was a simple "I love him" song, couched in teen-age, really bubblegum, terms. To the more sophisticated youngster, it might have had erotic overtones. What it did have for all was on-the-nose aural evocation of the title word. "Lol-li-pop, lol-li-pop (pause) lol-li-lol-li-pop" perfecty fitted the jogging and bobbing type of rhythm the kids were then dancing, like the Chicken. The song became an international hit. We discovered afterward that the word *lollipop* was used in Spanish, Portuguese, Italian, and other foreign languages, and the title never had to be changed.

January 27, 1958   Honor Roll of Hits

No. 1.   **AT THE HOP**
         Best Selling Record: Danny and the Juniors, ABC-Paramount 9871

On Monday, January 20, Station KWK of St. Louis, Missouri, announced a complete ban on rock 'n' roll. During the preceding week, each disk jockey gave an R 'n' R disk a farewell spin and proceeded to smash it to smithereens on the air. The management designated the seven days "Record-Breaking Week." Pres. Robert T. Convey characterized the dramatic gambit, typed "platter-pillory" in a trade paper, as "simply weeding out undesirable music."

The warfare waged by adults on young music was still on. But in a January editorial commemorating Atlantic Records' tenth anniversary, Paul Ackerman wrote in *Billboard:* "American pop music today, despite the attacks upon it, is in its most vital period. It most broadly reflects the diverse elements making up musical America. It is rich and fresh in sound and in content."

And January's Honor Roll did display diversity: "At the Hop" was No. 1, "April Love," a "good-music" film theme No. 2, and Sinatra was in the Top Ten with another film ballad, "All the Way," Oscar song of the year. Como had two disks in the Top Thirty, which included schmaltzy melodies like "Tammy," another film theme, and revivals of "Fascination" and "Sail Along Silvery Moon." While R 'n' R disks seemed to have an edge, middle-generation music was well represented. Apparently, it was the mere presence of teen-age records that caused such petulant outbursts as KWK's on-the-air smashing of disks.

Reacting to adult hostility, Danny and the Juniors followed their hit disk of "At the Hop" with a reassuring "Rock and Roll Is Here to Stay." And so it was, though the four white lads from Philadelphia were not. But their second best seller was revived by the Sha Na Na early in the current "Rock 'n' Roll Revival" and became the title and theme of their first album.

The Silhouettes on Ember were another one-hit group whose "Get a Job" had the sounds then used by vocal groups as rhythm devices. It had "yip-yip's" and "mum-mum's" and "sha-da-dada's." Unfortunately, it was also hardly intelligible. But when the lyrics written by the group were deciphered, "Get a Job" was indisputably a social document. Its cameo drama embodied the story of a man being unrelentingly nagged by his girlfriend to find a job.

Both "At the Hop" and "Get a Job" were Philadelphia-produced recordings. The former was the creation of local deejay Larry Brown and vocal coach Artie Singer, who owned Singular Records, managed Danny and the Juniors, and arranged for the release of the disk on ABC-Paramount. "Job," as cut by the Silhouettes, was the product of another local deejay, old-timer Kae Williams, who leased his Junior Records master to Ember. As the year progressed, the production of masters by disk jockeys and their sale/leasing became a widespread practice. At one point, four disk jockeys at Station WBR in Dallas even formed their own disk company. They called it White Rock Records.

From Philadelphia, too, came a duo, Billy and Lillie, who recorded for Swan and enjoyed extensive exposure by Dick Clark. Their "La Dee Dah" was in the groove of Larry Williams's "Short Fat Fannie," a play on current titles. Its use of a chalypso background helped make it extremely popular. Larry Williams was himself on the charts with his own "Bony Moronie."

No. 1.   SUGARTIME
Best Selling Record: McGuire Sisters, Coral 61924

In February veteran disk jockey Martin Block, then on WABC, shelved Top Forty programing and adopted a format "to cover all musical preferences." To select his records, he used something called Teen-Age Survey, with a coverage of sixty thousand listeners. The nub of the change was that it would permit Block to "personalize his show." Through '58, Top Forty programing remained highly controversial, almost as volatile as rock 'n' roll itself with which it was temporarily associated. Top Forty carried the threat of "automation," a new dirty word.

Returning from a trip to the Near East, Walter Cronkite reported that rock 'n' roll had been banned in Iran. Ostensibly, it was against the precepts of Moslem religion. Additionally, Iranian doctors claimed that hip injuries resulted from rock dancing. R 'n' R had also been banned in Egypt where it was "against public morals."

Among the middle-aged, a new musical fad took shape. Originated by Lester Lanin, a bandleader who had been playing society dances for two decades, it was known as Medley Time. On LPs, the bands offered—as they did at weddings, etc.—single choruses of twenty to forty tunes. The music was continuous and all tunes came from the '20s and '30s. The success of a Lester Lanin LP on Epic led to a rash of albums by other bands. For songwriter Irving Berlin's fiftieth anniversary, Jay Blackton adopted the Medley Time concept for an Epic album.

The big news of February was the debut of "Dick Clark's Saturday Night Show" on ABC-TV. The trade papers saw an analogy with radio's first "Hit Parade," then in a wobbly stage on TV. Clark followed the formula of his weekday shows but concentrated on bigger names. The debut lineup of lip-syncers included Pat Boone, Johnnie Ray, Connie Francis, and Chuck Willis, who died two months later. Performing live with his own combo, Jerry Lee Lewis scored the wildest reception.

"They're screaming for a new Frankie," Chancellor Records announced. Young Frankie Avalon was Italian, dark, good looking, and an average singer. But through exposure on "American Bandstand," his record of "Dede Dinah" became a best seller. Despite his vocal limitations, he achieved a Gold Record with

"Venus" in '59. Then he went on to make a series of grade-B *Beach Party* flicks.

March 17, 1958   Honor Roll of Hits

No. 1.   CATCH A FALLING STAR
         Best Selling Record: Perry Como (Victor 7128)

A keynote speech made on March 8 by Mitch Miller served to crystallize widespread discontent among the nation's disk jockeys with Top Forty programing. Speaking at the First Disk Jockey Convention in Kansas City, Miller accused the platter spinners of abdicating their responsibilities to "the commercial record shop; to the eight- to fourteen-year-olds; to the pre shave crowd that make up 12 percent of the country's population and zero percent of its buying power once you eliminate the ponytail ribbons, popsicles, and peanut brittle." Adverting to Longfellow's famous poem "The Children's Hour," Miller said: "On much of today's radio we're lucky to get a grown-up hour anywhere before midnight. Adults all over the land are yearning for a pause in the day's cacaphony. I, too, believe that youth must be served but how about some music for the rest of us. . . ." Accorded the convention's only standing ovation, his remarks received major coverage in the nation's press.

Outspoken condemnation of the restrictiveness of Top Forty programing was immediately voiced by many deejays. Others criticized the depersonalization of simply serving as announcers for records selected by station management. The outcries made little impress on executives of the Plough, Balaban, and McGlenndon chains, all of whom followed the Top Forty formula, pioneered by Storz, sponsor of the convention.

While Miller's attack was directed as much at R 'n' R as it was at Formula Radio, a panel discussion of "Is Rock and Roll a Bad Influence on Today's Teen-agers?" produced a strong negative response. "Parents should quit blaming rock and roll," said Robin Seymour of Detroit's Station WKMH, "and be more concerned in getting a good brush, a bar of soap, a nail clipper, and a good home life to get the kids in line."

Commenting on Miller's speech, Dick Clark said: "I find it very interesting that Columbia has used Otis Blackwell for writing and arranging plus other creative rock-and-roll talent and that Columbia has also just started the Date label for rock-and-roll records."

Alan Freed observed: "It sounds like sour grapes. Mitch knows little about R & B and native American music. He's always been classical minded and my feeling is that he's a musical snob." Noting that Miller had tried unsuccessfully to purchase rock-and-roll masters, Freed said angrily: "Let's face it. Rock and roll is bigger than all of us. And as my personal protest, I'm hereby banning all Columbia and Date records from my show."

On another front, hearings of the Senate Commerce Subcommittee on Communications, the attack on R 'n' R continued unabated. A group of top ASCAP songwriters appeared once again to reiterate charges they had previously made before the Celler Committee on how the interlocking interests of BMI and broadcaster-owned record companies stifled ASCAP songs. Appearing on behalf of the Songwriters Protective Association, author Vance Packard (*Hidden Persuaders*) claimed that conniving disk jockeys and BMI foisted cheap music on passive teen-agers. Asked to define "cheap music," Packard led with his chin and said he meant hillbilly, Latin American, and rhythm and blues or rock 'n' roll.

A California attorney, Seymour Lazar, brought the bristling word "payola" into the hearings with a charge of the widespread passing of coin to deejays, a form of corruption (he contended) that originated in BMI's easy handout of promotional funds. Unable to supply precise details requested by Committee Chairman Pastore, the attorney leveled a broadside against a group of Los Angeles record companies that owned BMI publishing subsidiaries —Aladdin, Checker/Chess, King, Modern, and Specialty.

Lazar's blast brought a storm of protest not only from California but from disk jockeys in other areas. "It's a damn lie," said Peter Potter of KLAC. "Except in three isolated cases, 97 percent of the deejays here in L.A. are honest."

Meanwhile, the trade papers noted two types of record payola that had become rampant. As a result of Top Forty programing, record companies were giving away freebees to dealers, who then reported these titles on best-seller lists to stations, who in turn added these titles to their playlists and included them on "Top Forty" circulars distributed free by the stores to record buyers.

A more localized merchandise payola had developed in Philadelphia. Record companies, desirous of getting their artists on the "Dick Clark Show," turned for help to the distributors in the area: Cosnat, Nelson Verbit, and the three Harry's—Chipetz, Finfer, and Rosen. Inevitably, there was a gush of free disks into the city of Brotherly Love for this fraternal assistance.

Considering the raging hullabaloo over R 'n' R, March's Honor

turn to pg. 252

Roll supplied its own commentary: four of the Top Ten were "Who's Sorry Now?" revival of an old-time ballad of 1923; "Swinging Shepherd Blues," a jazz instrumental with a piping flute lead; "Sail Along Silvery Moon," a Billy Vaughn revival of a nostalgic 1937 ballad; and at the head of the list, Perry Como with "Catch a Falling Star," a title taken from a John Donne poem.

Connie Francis had been cutting so-so records at MGM for several years when, in desperation, she recorded a tune that was one of her father's favorites. "Who's Sorry Now?" was just right for the country cry and sandpaper tears in her voice. With Dick Clark's assistance, it launched her on a hit streak that lasted into the '6os. The tear-stained tune of the '2os was followed in the late fall by "Stupid Cupid," a petulant teen-age torcher in a driving up-tempo by Howard Greenfield and Neil Sedaka, who himself joined the roster of recording stars about the same time. Connie remained the leading female vocalist from '58 almost to the rise of the Beatles.

"Twenty six miles . . . across the sea," a paean to California's offshore island (Catalina) brought the Four Preps to the fore. The four Hollywood High School alumni were not really a rock group so much as a youthful-sounding, gentle-voiced, cool-jazz quartet. But they had a fresh, arresting sound that caught on with young listeners and sent "Twenty-Six Miles" into the Top Three. Bruce Belland and Glen Larson, the two Preps who wrote the Catalina ode, repeated their success with "Big Man" two months later.

The Champs were an instrumental combo with a feeling for Latin-American material. "Tequila," they shouted during pauses, and the kids bought it as if it were Pepsi. For their follow-up, they rocked a Mexican ballad of 1934, "Alla en El Rancho Grande," which became "El Rancho Rock." Glen Campbell was part of the combo in the days when he was trying to find himself and played one of the guitars on "Tequila," which made No. 1.

Among the pioneers of rock, Chuck Berry made the Top Five with "Sweet Little Sixteen" in three swift weeks. The Beach Boys later used the rhythm pattern as the basis of their first surfin' hit. Elvis Presley, who was about to be drafted, scored with "Don't," a Leiber-Stoller song, which was unusual in that it did not go to No. 1. The surprise artist of the month was Andy Williams, then on Cadence Records, who was able to penetrate the Top Five with "Are You Sincere?," a Nashville song and a distant sound from the Hollywood film ballads that later became his basic repertoire.

No. 1.   HE'S GOT THE WHOLE WORLD IN HIS HANDS
Best Selling Record: Laurie London, Capitol 3891

April '58 brought a shower of religious recordings. Also in that month rock 'n' roll and Top Forty programing faced the most concerted attacks of the decade.

Following an announcement of a switch to Top Forty format by station management of Station KLAC in Hollywood, five key disk jockeys turned in their resignations. These included such popular personality spinners as Dick Haynes, Gene Norman, Earl McDaniel, Duke Norton, and Jack Smith. The president of the station told the local press: "The day of the disk jockey is over with." Veteran deejay Peter Potter, who had already left the station, asserted that KLAC's new program format spelled the demise of the personality disk jockey in radio. Automation was on the way.

Now, a chorus of voices rose in protest. "The biggest cancer," said Stan Dale of WAIT in Chicago. "Top Forty completely suppresses all individuality." "It defrauds the advertiser," said Doug Pledger of KNBC in San Francisco. "Lists are valuable as a reference," said Bob Landers of WNEW in NYC, "and for watching trends, but not as a basis for format." "It appeals to juveniles and the juvenile-minded," said Doug Arthur of WIBG in Philadelphia, "to delinquent station management, and to rating-happy ad agencies who don't mind wasting clients' money."

Unanticipated at ASCAP's annual dinner was an outright attack on R 'n' R by Congressman Emanuel Celler seated on the dais together with executives of the major networks. Celler predicted that the broadcasters and BMI would be divorced. Speaking of his fondness for Jerome Kern and Vincent "Yeomans," as he pronounced Youmans, he recalled the legend that a swan sings before it dies. "There are those who should die before they sing," he observed.

Celler's belligerence found a reflection in the tactics adopted by an increasing number of stations to dramatize their rejection of R 'n' R. A new San Francisco station opened its programs with the slogan: "I Kicked the Junk Music Habit by Listening to KSFR." Resentment was expressed by fans who felt that the station was sneakily tieing R 'n' R to dope addiction.

Using reverse English, Station WISN of Milwaukee programed nothing but R 'n' R for five consecutive hours. After six hundred phone protests, the station returned to its normal, nonrock format. But to emphasize its rejection of R 'n' R, deejay Charlie Hanson destroyed two hundred records at a public burning in the station's courtyard, depicted in the city's newspapers. Despite a furor of protest, the station circulated an advertising brochure whose theme was "We gave them what they were told they wanted—but they hated it!" A picture of Hanson at the disk burning bore the caption: "WISN finds a good place for Top 40 records."

WPIN of St. Petersburg, Florida, used a more charitable device to advertise its ban on R 'n' R disks. As it received such recordings, it gave them away gratis to children. And for the Easter Seal campaign, deejay Chuck De Witt auctioned off the station's entire R 'n' R library and contributed $500 to a fund for crippled children.

In Denver, Station KDEN deejays chanted during station breaks: "Help stamp out rock and roll. Patronize KDEN advertisers and KDEN, Denver's first station now busily engaged in stamping out rock and roll." A window poster distributed by the station to Denver stores spotlighted Whistler's mother sitting near a radio with the slogan: "Music for Reading—KDEN."

Nevertheless, the two best-known exponents of the Big Beat basked in the limelight of not unfavorable publicity. Dick Clark made an appearance with his wife, son, and dachshund on CBS's prestigious "Person to Person" program, sharing the hour with Dr. James B. Conant, ex-president of Harvard. And Alan Freed appeared on NBC-TV's early morning "Today" show. As teenagers danced properly to his orchestra, he answered queries put to him by host Dave Garroway.

A sign of the times, and harbinger of more dismal developments in '59, was the indictment of former WFIL disk jockey Bob Horn on charges of income tax evasion. As reported by the U.S. attorney handling the case, the ex-Philadelphia deejay was accused of receiving in '54–'55 at least $50,000 in unreported payola on which he failed to pay a tax of about $9,500. The IRS had arrived at its figures by subpoenaing the books of Philadelphia record distributors. By then, the former "Bandstand" host was working in Houston. Although no other names were mentioned, the U.S. attorney would not deny that evidence had been found in distributor books of payola to other disk jockeys.

There were signs that the attack on rock was having its impact. ABC-TV announced that it was cutting Dick Clark's ninety-minute show to an hour. It was claimed that "American Bandstand" was "strong in ratings but not in sponsors"—and a giveaway "bingo" show was to fill the vacated thirty minutes. Of greater significance: Three touring rock 'n' roll shows were experiencing box-office difficulties. While the Alan Freed package was described as "not losing yet," Irving Feld's Biggest Show of Stars was known to be "just about breaking even" and the Rhythm & Blues Cavalcade of '58 was scheduled to be pulled off the road.

The spreading recession also was held accountable for a marked influx of religious recording that occurred in April '58. An awareness of the trend came as a result of a recording by an English teen-ager, which became the No. 1 song of the nation in four short weeks. It was a strange occurrence since in the 1950s, unlike the Beatles era, the import-export balance between England and the U.S.A. was heavily weighted on our side.

"He's Got the Whole World in His Hands" was a reversal of trend. The recording was by a fourteen-year-old British lad, Laurie London, who had never had a music or singing lesson in his life and who was almost as new to English audiences as American. Unquestionably, London's high-pitched, choirboy sound won him acceptance among young record buyers. But American disk jockeys were not known to be too receptive to hand-clapping *religioso* disks. "It Is No Secret (What God Can Do)," a song that I sponsored, was extensively recorded and a best seller without ever making the big charts or being heavily played. Obviously, "He's Got the Whole World in His Hands" carried a sense of reassurance that Americans, young and old, seemed to crave at the time.

The search and need became more apparent as more and more disks appeared with "the sanctified beat." Pat Boone, who was tops in a poll of high school kids in a *Scholastic* magazine poll of eleven- to fourteen-year-olds, caught the spirit in a Top Ten disk, "A Wonderful Time Up There." and Johnny Mathis scored a best-selling album in *Goodnight Dear Lord*. Harlem's Apollo Theatre found that "the spirit was really on them" when it presented an all-gospel show. "A number of women collapsed," said theatre manager Frank Schiffman, "and we were obliged to have two nurses stand in at all the evening performances with smelling salts."

At the other end of the sound spectrum, a novelty titled "Witch Doctor" zoomed into the Top Ten, put a spell on all competing disks, and was No. 1 in three record weeks. Ross Bagdasarian, co-writer of "Come On-A My House," was the author-composer and David Seville had the hit disk on Liberty. But they were one and the same man. Before 1958 modulated into the final year of the decade, many other novelty songs captured the public imagination. The April charts included "Dinner with Drac" and "The Little Blue Man."

In the Army as of March 24, Elvis left his languishing fans with a sentimental ballad, "Wear My Ring around Your Neck." It was a mark of going steady, a burgeoning teen-age practice that aroused as much opposition among adults as R 'n' R. Adults were not sensitive to the subtle differences between "going steadily," "going together," and "going steady." An exchange of I.D. tags was a form of commitment. The kids who were not yet old enough, traded friendship rings, and to make these fit their fingers, wrapped the ring with brightly colored yarn or string, held together by clear nail polish.

On April 10 Dick Clark devoted an hour of his show to songs associated with one singer-writer. Chuck Willis had died that day on an operating table in Atlanta, his hometown. Clark programed records by the Clovers, the Five Keys, the Cadillacs, the Hilltoppers, and Patti Page, all of whom had recorded Chuck Willis songs: "Close Your Eyes," "From the Bottom of My Heart," "It's Too Late," "Search My Heart," and "The Door Is Still Open." Willis was then at the peak of his recording career, delivering ballads with a gospel fervor much like Johnny Ace, who also died young.

May 19, 1958   Honor Roll of Hits

No. 1.   ALL I HAVE TO DO IS DREAM
         Best Selling Record: Everly Brothers, Cadence 1348

In May the sound of pop was merry for a number of old-timers. Perry Como nestled once again in the flowering fields of the Top Ten with "Kewpie Doll." So did fuzzy-voiced Dean Martin with "Return to Me," cowritten by Carmen Lombardo and recorded by brother Guy's Royal Canadians on Capitol. Nat Cole and his satin baritone were also high on the Honor Roll with "Looking Back," a ballad written by a trio of black musicians soon to make their mark as a team: singer Brook Benton, arranger Belford Hendricks, and songwriter Clyde Otis who became the first black man to head the A & R department of a major company, Mercury.

May brought an intensification of friction between personality disk jockeys and station management. In Des Moines, Iowa, Station KIOA dropped $30,000-a-year, top-rated deejay Don Bell, who had made the station No. 1 in thirty days after coming to it from competitive KRNT a year earlier. In Denver, Colorado, Joe Flood of KTLN, whose salary was $32,000 a year, became the third of the city's key jockeys to walk out on Top Forty programing. Previously, Ray Perkins had left KIMN and Ed Scott, KMYR.

The most newsworthy and unexpected departure was that of Alan Freed, who suddenly walked out of WINS because of the station's refusal to back him in his controversy with Boston authorities. Freed had been indicted for inciting to riot after a theatre appearance. But within a week of his departure from WINS, Station WABC grabbed Freed for a six-day-a-week show from 7:15 P.M. to 11:00 P.M. Nevertheless, Shaw Artists canceled a projected tour by Dick Clark, feeling that the "second Boston Tea Party," as Freed's indictment was typed, might have cooled arena and auditorium owners on R 'n' R shows.

As an aftermath of the Boston riot of May 3, an Alan Freed show scheduled at the Newark, New Jersey, armory for May 10 was canceled. In Washington, D.C., the city fathers withheld a permit for a "Biggest Show of Stars for '58," scheduled for June 1 at Griffith Stadium. Although promoter Irving Feld pointed out that Paul Anka, one of the show's headliners, had been chosen to highlight the recent Cherry Blossom Festival, a family-type tourist attraction, the Washington officials remained adamant.

The Boston melee itself became the subject of acrimonious debate on Capitol Hill. As a number of congressmen attacked rock 'n' roll, Senator Fleming declared: "I don't think that rock 'n' roll music was the primary cause. I have been informed that certain products—narcotics—were sold."

As hearings began on the Smathers Bill to terminate broadcast ownership of BMI, rock 'n' roll was vigorously defended. "The same people who screamed and rioted when Sinatra sang in '43," said the music director of WARL in Arlington, West Virginia, "are now damning such actions as 'horrifying' today."

A letter from a New York justice of the Court of Domestic Relations was read into the record by BMI veep Robert Burton. It advised the public to stop ranting at a musical fad when the true cause of outbreaks by "our damaged children" lies much deeper. The justice noted that, despite their musical fads, "the jitterbug generation" had grown into solid citizens.

May Axton, a Jacksonville schoolteacher and cowriter of "Heartbreak Hotel," rejected the idea that rock 'n' roll was a factor in juvenile delinquency. "It is an outlet for tensions of today's teen-agers, not the cause," she said. Mrs. Axton, a BMI writer, created a stir at the hearing when she stated that two letters of application had never been answered by ASCAP. Subcommittee Chairman Pastore observed: "If a contention is being made of the danger of monopoly (by BMI), we must make sure we would not have a monopoly overall if BMI lost its advantage in being broadcast owned."

Rejecting the charge of a broadcaster conspiracy to promote any one type of music, BMI veep Burton argued that technological changes altered the character of pop music as well as old-style promotion via name bands and singers. The introduction of tape, decentralization of radio outlets, and development of unbreakable vinylite records all contributed to overturn "the tightly held monopoly" of Tin Pan Alley and Hollywood songwriting and recording centers. As records could be made anywhere and hits could develop anywhere, a democratization took place that opened the door to hundreds of new songwriters and publishers and made it possible for BMI to compete with ASCAP. New styles were the inevitable concomitant. As for the broadcasters, their ownership in the early years (1940s) made it possible for BMI "to get off the ground."

At a subsequent committee session, Goddard Lieberson, president of Columbia Records, noted that the recording of full scores of ASCAP musicals by net-owned record companies had resuscitated the shows and stimulated performances. He accused the ASCAP writers suing CBS and NBC of biting the hand that fed them since "the overwhelming proportion of music heard on these stations year in and year out is ASCAP."

In broadcast circles, the debate over Top Forty programing raged unabated. There were those like Lanny Ross of WCBS in New York City, who felt that Top Forty was "predigested food for the ears, with others doing the chewing; the public does the swallowing." Others like John Scott of WSOP in Boston, contended that "adults like Top Forty, too." Henry Busse, Jr., of KOWM in Omaha viewed Formula Radio as "a challenge to the personality of anyone in maintaining his individuality. . . . I try to use gimmicks of clipped delivery, personal appearances, and a weekly teen hop to build a complete identity for myself." Regardless of the debate, Top Forty stations across the country were thriving.

In May, George Wein, producer of the Newport Jazz Festival, announced that for the first time in its history, one evening would be devoted entirely to the blues. Among the artists scheduled: Chuck Berry, Big Maybelle, and Joe Turner. Even the prestigious Newport Jazz Festival found the impact of R 'n' R too widespread to ignore.

"All I Have to Do Is Dream," the biggest song of the month and one of the three most popular of the year, was the third consecutive hit for the Everly Brothers, but not their last of '58. "Bird Dog" came running in the fall to make it four in a row for the Kentucky lads who sang simple, two-part, country harmony.

"Oh, Lonesome Me," another country ballad published by Acuff-Rose of Nashville, made its imprint in pop. No. 1 song of the year in C & W, it was the work of North Carolina singer/ writer Don Gibson, who labored in a Shelby textile mill as a teen-ager before he moved to Knoxville, Tennessee, formed his own band, and performed on WNOX for almost eight years. On the back of his own record was another ballad by Gibson, "I Can't Stop Loving You." Pop listeners did not find it until 1962 when Ray Charles helped transform it into one of the great country classics.

Nineteen fifty-eight was turning into a substantial year for Chuck Berry who was now on the charts with "Johnny B. Goode." Nothing preachy, despite the title, but a tale of a country boy who made good in the city. Berry denied that it was autobiographical.

June 14, 1958   Honor Roll of Hits

No. 1.   THE PURPLE PEOPLE EATER
         Best Selling Record: Sheb Wooley, MGM 12651

"Witch Doctor" was still hypnotizing listeners when "The Purple People Eater" flew onto the disk scene and devoured everything in its way to reach No. 1 in three fast weeks. It was a fluke like most novelty songs. Sheb Wooley, who wrote and recorded it, was a man who had been making westerns for years and was almost as well-known to TV and film audiences as Chill Wills or Walter Brennan. He was a leading country writer with a wry sense of humor, responsible for a Tex-Mex song, "When Mexican Joe Meets Jole Blon" and a curious ballad, "Peeping through the Keyhole," about a feller who learned how to "dance and kiss" by watching his friend through a keyhole.

Capitalizing on contemporary interest in UFOs and the imaginative involvement of youngsters with monsters, "The Purple People Eater" became and remained Wooley's only pop hit. His dry, talking style was really more country than rock.

Country music was also the strength of newcomer Jack Scott, who came to Carlton Records from Windsor, Ontario. "Leroy," a song he wrote, caught public fancy but not for long as disk jockeys discovered the other side, "My True Love," another ballad by Scott. By August it was in the Top Ten and paved the way for the success of "Goodbye Baby," another Scott opus.

Two new black singers became best sellers in June. Ed Townsend sounded like a cross between Sam Cooke and Roy Hamilton. He was not as warm as Cooke nor as gospel-big as Hamilton. "For

Your Love" sweetened the summer for many lovers. Like Townsend, Bobby Freeman recorded his own song. "Do You Want to Dance?" with its Latin rhythm, served to break the ice for many youngsters on their first date.

Among older rock 'n' rollers, Jimmie Rodgers sold well on "Secretly," a Tin Pan Alley ballad whose writers included Hugo and Luigi under the *nom de plume* of John Markwell. Before the end of the year, Rodgers was on his way to "Bimbombey."

Three of the Memphis crowd demonstrated their continuing power, Jerry Lee Lewis with "High School Confidential," Johnny Cash with "Guess Things Happen That Way," and Tommy Sands with "After the Prom." Playing a rock 'n' roll singer who returns to a cold reception in his hometown, Sands introed "After the Prom" on a "Studio One" production *The Left Hand Welcome*.

CBS-TV explored the controversy raging over teen-age music also in a debate between Alan Freed and Art Ford on "Right Now!" But Ford who was supposed to be anti, refused to blast the style. And the third member of the panel, executive director of the Child Study Association, instead of representing a middle-of-the-road position, flatly condemned censorship of music. His position was that adults allowed their own anxieties to affect their thinking about the so-called dangers of R 'n' R to their youngsters.

In discussing his own situation in Boston, Freed noted that he had recently played forty-two other cities without incident and rejected the idea that anything he said onstage could have prompted the altercations that occurred outside. He took umbrage at a comment of moderator Ron Cochran regarding the "moral responsibilities" of R 'n' R artists, which he interpreted as a slap at Jerry Lee Lewis. (The rock 'n' roller's marriage to his teen-age cousin was then a highly combustible subject.) Observing that Lewis was a southern boy "and Tennessee boys get married quite young," Freed suggested that the example set by Hollywood film stars and jazz musicians were hardly as acceptable as those of the rock 'n' roll crowd.

24

HULA HOOPS, CHIPMUNKS, AND THE KINGSTON TRIO

The second half of 1958 witnessed the rise of several remarkably creative youngsters and the emergence of a folk trend that came to fruition in the early '60s.

July 29, 1958   Honor Roll of Hits

No. 1.   PATRICIA
Best Selling Record: Perez Prado, Victor 7245

Having tasted "Tequila" and rocked to its mambo rhythm, now the public took a huge fancy to "Patricia," written and performed by the master of the mambo. Perez Prado, an intense, mustachioed, little man who wore high, elevator-heeled shoes, had come from Cuba, long the source of rhythms that intermittently helped to freshen pop and provide American dancers with new steps. They liked "Patricia" so much they bought two million copies of Prado's platter.

One of the most recorded songs of the month was the film ballad, "A Certain Smile." Written by Paul Francis Webster and Sammy Fain, two Oscar winners ("Secret Love" and "Love Is a Many-Splendored Thing"), it was a natural for Johnny Mathis. However, in the balloting for the Academy Awards, "A Certain Smile" lost out as Best Song to Lerner and Loewe's "Gigi."

Elvis was back at the top of the charts with a rockin' blues, "Hardheaded Woman." And Ricky Nelson had a best seller again in "Poor Little Fool," a song suffused with self-pity. Elvis fans were buying a dog tag featuring his Army serial number, blood type (O), a facsimile signature, and an etched-out portrait. Merchandised by two Boston disk jockeys, the tag was marketed to coincide with the release of *King Creole,* the Presley starrer based on Harold Robbins' novel *A Stone for Danny Fisher.*

But in July '58 the big news was brash Robert Waldon Cassatto, better known as Bobby Darin, who came "Splish Splash"-ing onto the record scene after kicking around Tin Pan Alley as a demo singer and tyro songwriter. Two years earlier, Darin had quit Hunter College in New York City, where he was a freshman major in drama, and gone on the road with a young people's theatre group. A meeting with Connie Francis's manager, George Scheck, led to an appearance on the Tommy Dorsey TV show immediately after Presley's third controversial debut. Club work in the Midwest followed and then a dead-end Decca contract.

It was the mother of disk jockey, Murray Kaufman, later known as Murray the K, who suggested the idea of "Splish Splash" to Darin. And it was Kaufman who published the tunes that Bobby wrote during '58, including several that were recorded by Gene Vincent and LaVern Baker. By the time that the tale of the exposed and embarrassed bath-taker was high on the Honor Roll, it became known in the trade that Darin was the unbilled lead singer on a Brunswick recording of "Early in the Morning" by the Ding Dongs. Since Darin was then under contract to Atco, Brunswick turned the Ding Dongs' disk over to Atco, who released it under the name of the Rinky Dinks. Having lost Darin, Brunswick covered "Early in the Morning" with Buddy Holly. But Holly was unsuccessful in challenging Darin's priority.

"As far as 'Early in the Morning' goes," Darin said, at the time, "I admit it was a mistake to do what we did. I had cut 'Splish Splash' but there was a chance that Atco wouldn't pick up my option. So we made 'Early in the Morning' under another name (the Ding Dongs) figuring that if Atco didn't come through, at least we would have a record we could sell to somebody or maybe bring out ourselves. Well, it was sold to Brunswick and meanwhile 'Splish Splash' became a hit. We were accused of all kinds of underhanded tricks, but no kidding we didn't mean to hurt anybody . . ."

Bobby early displayed a propensity for shooting off his mouth and managed to grab space almost as readily as Sinatra whom he soon sought to engage in a verbal slugfest. His comments about other singers revealed sensitivity: "I put Ray Charles on a pedestal," he said, arguing that the blues are the basis of great artistry. "Charles's blues are right out of the church. And there's Fats Domino. A great artist with sort of the sound of the Delta. Little Richard's a wonderful church-type blues artist, too. The top artists of our day and age are all influenced by the blues. That's true of Sinatra and Ella and Peggy Lee and Presley, too. I'm crazy about Presley's understanding of what he does." Darin's own feeling for the blues put both "Early in the Morning" and "Splish Splash" high up on R & B charts.

By the end of the year Darin had another raucous Gold Record in "Queen of the Hop," a song cowritten by him. Coming from an impoverished background—his father died when he was a kid and the family was on relief—he hungered to be a show business legend before he was thirty. He made it at twenty-six in '59.

On the same label as Darin (Atco), the comedians of rock 'n' roll, the Coasters, made July memorable with Leiber and Stoller's "Yakety Yak." Its huge acceptance by young record buyers—it was No. 2 on the Honor Roll—suggested a deepening of the gap between generations. Teen-agers were moving beyond a search for identity to a confrontation.

July saw the axing of the Smathers Bill. At the committee session when its negative attitude became manifest, the chairman concluded that Congress could not and should not be asked to legislate against a musical fad.

Correspondents of *The New York Times* confirmed the world-wide impact of and interest in R 'n' R. "Rockabilly rules Japan's hit parade," was the word from Tokyo, where Paul Anka's "Diana" and "You Are My Destiny" and Presley's "Don't" and "Jailhouse Rock" were at the top of the lists. From Peking a correspondent reported that strains of "Rock Around the Cook-house Door," heard at a Czech Electronics Exhibition, attracted teen-age Pioneers who indulged in a forbidden forty-five-minute R 'n' R session. Communist authorities had shuttered all dance halls when they discovered in '57 that rock 'n' roll records were being smuggled into China aboard ships arriving from Hong Kong.

The death of the Smathers divorcement bill saw no abatement of the American war on rock. Now, NBC spot sales took the offensive with an album *Music to Buy Time By,* released in behalf of WRC of Washington, D.C. Sampling excerpts from R 'n' R disks, a commentator introduced each with derogatory comments. Buddy Holly's "Peggy Sue" was described as "mood music for stealing hub caps." Of "Yakety Yak" the commentator said: "Well, let's see what other garb—uh—rock and roll music we have. This one is by the Coasters, four fugitives from the hog-caller seminar . . ."

Noting the curious discrepancy that not one Presley excerpt was included—Elvis recorded for NBC's own record subsidiary—Ahmet Ertegun of Atco said: "That little opus ('Yakety Yak') was written by two writers who penned many of Presley's biggest Victor hits, including 'Hound Dog,' and who are currently under contract to produce records for Victor."

Todd Storz, president of the radio chain that pioneered Top Forty format, also locked horns with NBC on the issue of Formula Radio. Citing market after market where the Storz-affiliated station outclassed an NBC affiliate in audience size, Storz quipped: "Knowing that the Top Forty is doomed, RCA Victor will probably want to drop the $1,000-a-week contract with Elvis Presley (perhaps the greatest of the Top Fortyers) and put him up for grabs. Even Mitch Miller might be interested."

In Buffalo the area's most influential disk jockey, George (Hound Dog) Lorenz, took a walk when Station WKBW switched to Top Forty. "This concept of radio programing," he said, "is helping to kill the single-record business, is lowering radio listening, and is decreasing a new artist's chances of making it. . . . Stations are programing twenty-four hours a day with no more than fifty records. When they change only ten or so a week, it begins to get pretty monotonous. . . . A dealer tells me: 'Do you think any kid is going to buy what he can hear on the radio till it's coming out of his ears?'" By year-end, Lorenz was barking his announcements over Station WHAY in Hartford, Connecticut.

On another front, the Catholic Youth Center of Minneapolis fired a broadside at the nation's disk jockeys, urging them not to spin certain disks whose lyrics "lowered the moral standards of teenagers." Presley's "Wear My Ring around Your Neck" and Jimmie Rodgers' "Secretly" were named because they sanctioned going steady. George Hamilton IV's "Why Don't They Understand" was rejected because it "challenges youngster attitudes toward parents." Sinatra's "All the Way" and "Witchcraft" were included as Don't Spins because of "the suggestion in the lyrics."

Contacts, newspaper of the Catholic Youth Center, set forth a code of action: "Smash the records you possess which present a pagan culture and a pagan concept of life. Check beforehand the records which will be played at a house party or a school record dance. . . . Phone or write a disk jockey who is pushing a lousy record. Switch your radio dial when you hear a suggestive song. . . . Some songwriters need a good swift kick. So do some singers. So do some disk jockeys." Inciting to violence?

Among the records that were listed as "up to the standard": "Witch Doctor," "The Purple People Eater," and "Kewpie Doll." Also surprisingly, "Rumble." No objection to teen-age gang fights?

Meanwhile, stations were changing their formats and disk jockeys were being fired. In Pittsburgh NBC's new outlet, Station

WAMP, banned all R 'n' R disks as well as "other raucous tunes in the so-called Top Forty charts." Play only dogs? In Cincinnati WZIP and in Lubbock KSEL both followed similar courses, with the Ohio station adopting an "all mood music format" and the Texas station concentrating on "good old-style pops."

Reacting either to his Boston indictment or to the coaching of WABD management, Alan Freed turned to polite rock and roll. In addition to Chuck Berry, who did a lip-sync on "Johnny B. Goode," Freed's guests included the Four Lads, who presented their new disk, "Enchanted Island." Tradesters saw in the programing and Freed's subdued announcing style an attempt by WABD to develop a record-hop format that would appeal to adults as well as teen-agers. Freed played it all very straight, even to the point of introducing a Little Richard rouser as a memory-lane song.

The end of July brought a strange turn of events. Alan Freed Enterprises, theatrical promotion firm headed by Jack Hooke, filed a voluntary petition in bankruptcy. It listed liabilities of $51,985 and assets as nil. According to the petition, the firm owed Shaw Artists Bureau $24,665 and a disk jockey named Alan Freed $15,000.

August 18, 1958   **Honor Roll of Hits**

No. 1.   VOLARE (Nel Blu Dipinto di Blu)
          Best Selling Record: Dean Martin, Cap. 4028; Domenico
          Modugno, Dec. 30677

One of the year's most competitive wax races began shaping up early in the summer when Robbins Music, an ASCAP firm, imported an Italian rhythm ballad and Decca Records released a disk (in Italian) by cowriter Domenico Modugno: *"Volare (Nel Blu Dipinto di Blu)."* Everybody rushed to get into the act. There were vocals, instrumentals, English versions, Italian, accordion disks—you name it.

The American steeplechase was kicked off by what happened in Italy, where in the words of Arnaldo Cortesi of *The New York Times,* "Nel blu dipinto di blu exploded with the violence of a bomb. For once at a San Remo Festival (an annual song competition), everyone was in agreement—public, press, and jury. Even the other competitors recognized that Modugno's and Migiacci's song was the best."

"Volare," as it came to be known here, was lyrically unusual. A song about a dream, it was filled with surrealistic dream

imagery—he was painting his hands in blue and suddenly flying and singing . . . in the blue painted in blue (*nel blu dipinto di blu*) . . . and dreaming in her beautiful eyes, blue as the skies. Yet it is doubtful that the words received much attention. The hook of the song was in two melodic phrases: *Volare . . . oh-ho. . . . Cantare . . . oh-ho-ho-ho*. The catchy melody expressed a feeling of joy and freedom so complete and infectious that people burst out singing whenever and wherever they heard it.

By mid-August *Volare . . . oh-ho, Cantare . . . oh-ho-ho-ho* was virtually monopolizing the airwaves. It remained No. 1 on the Honor Roll for more weeks than any other song except "It's All in the Game," as *the* song of the year. Dean Martin was the only American who gave any real competition to writer-singer Modugno. And yet despite the magnitude and quality of the song, Modugno never was able to duplicate or even approach its popularity with another record or ballad.

In the period that record companies were frantically cutting, releasing, and seeking disks of the Italian import, more than one American publisher was racing around Italy in search of hit songs. A relatively obscure publisher, situated in Milan's Brill Building in the Galleria del Corso, reported visits from four American publishers in one morning.

Peggy Lee, who had an enormous in-group following, paid one of her rare visits on the charts with "Fever." Her version of Little Willie John's original had the finger snapping and the voice stark against rhythm accompaniment. But it contained a jazz feeling and licks that made it a permanent part of Peggy's repertoire. During August, another older-generation artist, Doris Day, found acceptance with a sunny ballad, "Everybody Loves a Lover," and Tony Bennett reached all too small an audience with a lovely ballad, "Young and Warm and Wonderful."

The summer charts were full of new, young artists many of whom never saw the limelight again. There were the Elegants who took a nursery rhyme, "Twinkle, Twinkle, Little Star," and sang it with a rocking rhythm. "Little Star," as they called it, appeared on one of the numerous offbeat labels (Apt) that proliferated in the '50s. But it skipped into the upper reaches of the Honor Roll to become the No. 2 song in September.

The Poni-Tails, three attractive eighteen-year-olds from Cleveland, were also unable to go beyond one smash platter. With Toni Cistone singing lead, and LaVerne Novak and Patti McCabe, high and low harmony, the girls began performing at high school functions in Lynn, Ohio. They failed to make it with "Que La," a song they wrote, and "Just My Luck to Be Fifteen." But "Born

Too Late," a ballad I published by Fred Tobias (of the Tobias songwriting clan) and Charles Strouse (later the composer of *Bye Bye Birdie, Applause,* and other musicals) did it for them.

Little Anthony and the Imperials came out of the same stable that bred Frankie Lymon and the Teenagers. Like the Lymon group, they had one selling voice and it was that of Anthony Gourdine of Brooklyn Boys High. Possessed of a winning, nasal falsetto, Little Anthony was able to give "Tears on My Pillow," a unique, lachrymose sound that made the group hugely popular. Coached by George Goldner, owner-producer of End Records, Little Anthony employed a staccato delivery and freighted pauses with great emotional impact. A year later, they were able to repeat their record success with a rhythm rouser, "Shimmy Shimmy Ko-Ko Bop."

Not too long ago, Clarence Collins, a long-time friend of Little Anthony and an original Imperial, recalled the record session at which "Tears on My Pillow" was cut: "We made it at the old Bell Sound on West Fifty-fourth Street in Manhattan. Remember the old-style four-track recording console? The session was sort of like an audition with lots of groups waiting to use the studio. The engineer would come out and say, 'All right, your group next.' One of the groups that was there that day was the Dubs, another of George Goldner's street-corner finds, and they came outta there with 'Could This Be Magic?' We used five pieces. Buddy Lucas on sax was the leader on a lot of peoples' dates. He would say, 'O.K., it's in G' and then the band would learn it. Fast. And we worked out our harmony in the studio."

This was a style of recording that explained the success of the independent record companies of the day. The majors, with their rehearsals, charts, and schooled arrangers, could never achieve the spontaneity, immediacy, or raw vigor—and not even the crude but dynamic sound.

A more gutsy group than Little Anthony's was that headed by veteran R & B performer Johnny Otis and that accounted for a dance novelty, "Willie and the Hand Jive." It was written by Otis, who was white and who became record-worthy when he recorded with Little Esther back in the '40s. Early on the road with an R & B show, he was able to find and showcase talent. His own singing had the detachment of the pioneer bluesmen but he had a dictional clarity unapproached by them. Otis's gifts were as a producer and popularizer. But he was responsible for a number of humorous novelty songs, of which "Willie and the Hand Jive," employing the Bo Diddley rhythm, was the biggest.

When you first heard "Just A Dream," you could have mistaken the singer for Johnny Ace. Jimmy Clanton, who came from the Deep South, was more of an oreo singer, black on the outside but white inside. He won quick acceptance among the country's teen-agers with his viable blues style, and even went on to achieve a second best seller with "Ship on a Stormy Sea." His disks were released on Ace Records, an indie operated in Jackson, Mississippi, by Johnny Vincent, whose training had been as a producer at L.A.'s Specialty label.

August saw a continuation of the attacks on rock 'n' roll even as its appeal broadened and its style matured. As a group of ten disk jockeys were about to depart for Europe, under the auspices of the State Department, to stage typical American record hops abroad, a Manchester, New Hampshire, deejay wrote a number of senators warning that the venture could be "at best a boondoggle and at worst, a serious blow to our already low prestige." The WFEA deejay contended that teen-age record hops were "powder kegs" and that it would be the easiest thing in the world for a few Communist plants to touch off a riot.

Sen. Norris Cotton immediately registered a protest, with the result that the State Department withdrew its stewardship. Murray Kaufman, president of the National Council of Disk Jockeys for Public Service, persuaded the State Department to query its field offices and promised that no R 'n' R records would be played. Pending replies, Murray the K (as he became known in the Beatles era) indicated that the ten platter spinners would confine their record hops to Army bases under the auspices of the USO. Some wags wondered how one could present a typical American record hop without playing disks by Presley, Darin, and Ricky Nelson, not to mention the Platters and Chuck Berry.

In the meantime, a second network (Mutual) joined NBC in excluding R 'n' R disks from its turntables. Not all, but those in the words of the network's musical director, that were "distorted, monotonous, noisy music, and/or suggestive or borderline salacious lyrics." Said musical director was to be the sole judge and censor. Mutual was also changing its format from Top Forty to "Pop Fifty," thereby hoping to add to its teen-age audience adults "comprising the buying public."

While the State Department and Mutual fulminated against teen-age music, a "Salute to Dick Clark" at the Hollywood Bowl attracted an overflow crowd of twelve thousand teen-agers. And ABC-TV, the only network that had not spoken out against R 'n' R, tacked an additional half hour to Clark's "American Bandstand." During Clark's trip to the West Coast, fifteen deejays from other stations took over his chores. But producer Mammarella daily read letters from the absent Clark, provoking June Bundy's comment in *Billboard:* "Out of Sight But Not Out of Mind."

"One of the most attractive qualities about 'American Bandstand,'" she concluded, "is the frankly adoring attitude displayed by teenagers in the studio toward Clark, who emerges as an idealized father figure. Consequently the visiting dee jays—limited to one-day appearances and haunted by constant on-the-air references to Clark—registered at best as distant uncles."

September 8, 1958   Honor Roll of Hits

No. 2.   LITTLE STAR
         Best Selling Record: Elegants, Apt 25005

In September the country was suddenly in the grip of the Hula Hoop craze. Apparently it started, as many crazes do, in California where the Wham-O Manufacturing Company began marketing a plastic hoop, adapted from an Australian game. The fad spread with hurricane force. In no time at all, adults as well as kids were swinging their fannies to keep the hoop rotating around the hips. Hoops sold for seventy-nine cents to $2.50. But one company planned a giant-sized hoop at $4.95, designed as a tandem toy for couples. Terming it the hottest craze since the demand for Davy Crockett chapeaux, *The New York Times* estimated that over twenty millions hoops were bought for a retail gross of approximately $30 million.

The impact on music business was violent. The first to cut a Hoop disk was Atlantic. Over a weekend Trinity Music publisher-songwriter Charlie Grean wrote "Hoopla Hoola" with Bob Davie (cowriter of "The Green Door"). On Tuesday, September 2, Grean flew to Chicago where he recorded Betty Johnson, later his wife. Atlantic rushed out deejay acetates the following day while a pretty Trinity secretary visited New York disk jockeys to demonstrate Hoop swinging. Through its distributors, Atlantic set up giveaway contests on stations in Akron, Kansas City, and other areas.

Meanwhile, Georgia Gibbs, who was switching from RCA Victor to Roulette—following Hugo and Luigi, who were responsible for her Mercury hits—recorded a ditty titled "The Hula Hoop Song." La Gibbs beat Betty Johnson to the TV tube, introducing her Roulette disk on the "Ed Sullivan Show" on September 6 and on Clark's daytime show on September 9. Roulette followed the Atlantic pattern of cutting one day (Friday, September 5) and having copies in the hands of deejays and distributors by Monday, September 8.

On the same day that Gibbs was recording at Roulette, Teresa Brewer was cutting the same song at Coral. The Decca subsidiary did not wait until Monday, but had copies on the turntables of New York disk jockeys the same afternoon. While Gibbs was lip-syncing her record on "American Bandstand," Steve Allen was in a Dot studio recording a Hula Hoop song he had written. Allen himself kicked off his song on September 14 with a mammoth production number on his NBC-TV show.

"Hula Hoop" was the title not only of Allen's opus, but of another Hoop song cut by Imperial Records. That made four different songs and five different disks racing in a breakneck competition to cash in on the craze. Who picked up the money? The manufacturers of Hula Hoops. The craze was much bigger than any of the recordings, and all of them put together.

The Olympics were another of the day's one-record giants. Their good fortune was to encounter a song titled "Western Movies." It was a comic novelty in the vein of the Coasters' humorous playlets. The guy never could get to first base because his gal could not get her fill of western films—the record was graphic in its use of rifle shots. The group itself displayed talent for comedy. All it needed was a team like Leiber and Stoller to produce material. Lacking which, it had to be satisfied with one noisy hit.

Jerry Wallace was white but he had a black-ballad sound. "How the Time Flies" not only launched him but Challenge Records of L.A. for which he recorded it. He was able to come up with a repeater in "Primrose Lane." Then he moved into the never-never land of record artists, performing in local clubs and night spots.

Like Wallace, Dion Di Mucci helped start a record company. Laurie Records of New York City was so impressed by a demo that they signed three of his friends from Roosevelt High School and *violà!* they had Dion and the Belmonts. The group's (and Laurie's) first release, "I Wonder Why," sold well enough to put motive power behind "No One Knows." But their big disk did not come until '59 with "A Teen-ager in Love." Lead singer Dion had a high-pitched, sad-sounding voice that appealed to youngsters, but was rejected by adults as whiny—a sound that most

parents find repellent. Like Tony Williams of the Platters and
Al Alberts of the Four Aces, Dion eventually split from his
paisanos, except that he made it in the '60s as a single-o.

Two novelties caught the public's ears in September. One was
"The End," a rocking organ number by Earl Grant, an ebullient
personality and flamboyant dresser who died in a tragic accident,
but not before he recorded over two dozen albums for Decca.
Grant paved the way for Baby Cortez and his "Happy Organ" of
'59. The other novelty was a hit disk for the Tommy Dorsey band
sans Tommy with a revival of a great show tune. It was the tempo
and dance rhythm that made "Tea for Two Cha-Cha" a best
seller.

Having automated many of the country's stations, enterpreneurs
now tried record hops without disk jockeys. It worked in Chicago
where a veteran bandleader ran successful afternoon dance-to-the-
record sessions at the Boulevard Ballroom. Two other promoters
converted defunct theatres into ballrooms and ran successful Sunday afternoon, Sunday night, and Wednesday night hops. The
absence of live talent made it possible to keep the gate charge
as low as ninety cents. The entrepreneurs thought the secret was
that kids could practice dancing at home to the record played in
the ballroom.

Labor Day weekend proved a bonanza for Alan Freed, who
took his annual "Big Beat Show" into Fabian's Fox Theatre when
the Brooklyn Paramount nixed him as being "too hot" (because
of the Boston rap hanging over his head). Opening day (Friday,
August 29), the line of waiting teen-agers extended, four across,
a block and a half around the theatre. Excitement ran to fever
pitch but the audience was quite orderly. Freed could not resist
making the comment: "My critics said that rock and roll would
last six months. That was four years ago when I was appearing
at the Brooklyn Paramount. Here I am today and we'll still be
here another four years." (He was not prophetic.) At the conclusion of the engagement, he took full-page ads in the music trade
papers, simply citing the gross: $207,000. His own take was about
$84,000.

During September Dick Clark ran a contest on his "Saturday
Night" show to "Name nameless," a little puppet-type doll. Teen-
agers were then flocking to see a science-fiction film *The Blob.*
It starred young Steve McQueen and dealt with a disgusting
gelatinous mass that swallowed half the cast. The musical theme,
recorded on a number of labels, curiously was by Burt Bacharach
and Mack David. Lyricist David was the older brother of the man

who became Bacharach's permanent collaborator in the 1960s–
'70s, Hal David.

October 6, 1958   Honor Roll of Hits

No. 1.   IT'S ALL IN THE GAME
         Best Selling Record: Tommy Edwards, MGM 12688

October's No. 1 smash, "It's All in the Game" was a curious
song, and Tommy Edwards, who had the blockbuster, was a
curious artist. The song was the brainchild of a Vice-President
of the United States, a claim that no other song can make. Gen.
Charles G. Dawes, who served during Calvin Coolidge's second,
disastrous term, composed the "Melody," as he called it in 1912.
Words were written in 1951 by Carl Sigman, a top ASCAP lyric
writer. And Tommy Edwards recorded it then and had a hit.
Although he had quite a number of releases after that, there were
no best sellers and Tommy dropped out of sight.

Then in '58 once again he cut "It's All in the Game." His voice
had not changed much in the six years. He still had an arching,
sandy quality that reminded one of Frankie Laine's dramatics.
The second time around, "Game" held the No. 1 spot on the
Honor Roll for six consecutive weeks, tying *"Volare."* It garnered
a Gold Record and established itself as one of the three most
popular songs of the year. After that, Tommy's career once again
described a downcurve. For a time he made demo disks for Tin
Pan Alley publishers, including me. Then, again, he disappeared.

When he died in 1969, he was in his early '40s. He obviously
had problems. Whatever they were, he did not share them with
people in the business—and his early death was a sorrowful
surprise.

The tremendous acceptance of "It's All in the Game" set off
a chain reaction. Other artists began re-recording their hits of the
early '50s, flavoring the arrangements with a contemporary beat
or sound. Fran Warren tried to repeat with "A Sunday Kind of
Love," her '48 hit. Johnny Desmond recut *"C'est Si Bon,"* vintage
1950 with a cha-cha beat. Guy Mitchell tried again with his '51
hit, "My Heart Cries for You." None of them made it.

But a revival of an old-hat ballad of the late '40s did become
a best seller. "Near You" was composed by patrician-looking
Francis Craig, who led the band for many years at the Hermitage,
one of Nashville's oldest hotels. In '47 Craig cut his melody for
a local label (Bullet), using a western-gaited boogie and shuffle

accompaniment. In '58 another pianist, Roger Williams, famed for his version of "Autumn Leaves," tackled the oldie. Dot, the cover company par excellence, located Craig and had him re-record his composition. It became a chart climber and Williams had the best-selling disk.

"Susie Darlin' " was a Gold Record of the year on which Dot "produced" the original. It sounded like a disk and song that came from Nashville. But in actuality it was recorded in Hawaii by a handsome, sunny-haired teen-ager, Robin Luke, who also wrote it. Dot's island distributor persuaded the Hollywood office to purchase the master. But Luke became one more of the era's one-hit wonders, even though he later recorded for Liberty.

It was an unnamed disk jockey who informed a record promoter: "Don't tell me about your record. I collect pictures of dead Presidents." *Billboard*'s reaction was summarized in a headline: "Payola Grows Faster Than Jack's Beanstalk."

Free artists were reportedly considered more valuable than outright cash—meaning artists who appeared without fee at deejay record hops or stage shows. One record company exec stated that payola sometimes backfired. He cited a station where the record of the week was picked on the basis of a cash payment. Other stations knew and curved the given record.

The No. 4 disk on October's Honor Roll was a novelty titled "Rockin' Robin" that flew to No. 1 in the R & B field. Many felt it owed its popularity as much to a rocking flute that suggested a bird in flight, as it did to a heady, nasal vocal by Bobby Day. He was another one-hit disk artist on a one-hit record label, Class. But this fact does not tell the entire story of Bobby Day, who apparently recorded as Bobby Garrett, as Bob and Earl on Mirwood Records, as one of the Hollywood Flames on Ebb Records, and who cut the original disk of "Little Bitty Pretty One," a '57 hit for Thurston Harris. Some say he also wrote the Harris hit although the name to which it is credited is Robert Byrd. Bobby was versatile, which may be another way of saying that he had no identity of his own.

November 17, 1958   Honor Roll of Hits

No. 1.   TOM DOOLEY
         Best Selling Record: The Kingston Trio, Cap. 4049

In a backward glance, "Tom Dooley" assumes a historical importance far beyond its achievement as the No. 1 song of November–December '58. The ballad of the Civil War veteran hanged for the murder of his cheating sweetheart, triggered a simmering folk revival that lasted well until the rise of the Beatles in '64. Having established its identity in clothes, lingo, mores and music, the rock generation was now tapping the past in a search for its values.

"Tom Dooley" also introduced the Kingston Trio, a group that got together at Menlo College and had its start at the Purple Onion in San Francisco. Capable performers on guitar, banjo, and ukulele—Dave Guard and Bob Shayne were raised in Hawaii —the trio, with the addition of Nick Reynolds, was able to follow "Tom Dooley" with a series of folk hits: "Tijuana Jail," "It Takes a Worried Man," "M.T.A.," and Pete Seeger's anti–atom bomb ballad, "Where Have All the Flowers Gone?"

The trio had a lusty, vigorous, rollicking sound that made it a great favorite in collegiate circles. But as the folk movement gained momentum, controversy developed as to their authenticity and purity. They answered their critics by calling themselves *urban* folk singers who were reinterpreting the literature of the past in contemporary terms.

The No. 2 song in November was a ballad of self-pity, "It's Only Make Believe" by a "new" singer named Conway Twitty. Born in the tiny town of Friars Point, Mississippi, in 1934, he was christened Harold Lloyd Jenkins, after the silent film comic with the black, horn-rimmed glasses sans lenses.

"I played and sang in the Army," he explained. "My act was called Harold Jenkins and his Rockhousers. Strictly rock. When I got out, I figure I needed a name that sounded more like show business. So I looked over a map of the South and picked two towns—Conway (Arkansas) and Twitty (Texas)."

Before going into the Army, Jenkins had considered becoming a minister—he had preached at Baptist youth revivals. But having attained some prominence as a high school athlete in Helena, Arkansas, he had an offer to go with the Philadelphia Phillies. He was about to accept a contract when the Korean conflict made him an Army draftee.

When Presley became the teen-age singing idol, Jenkins (now Twitty) journeyed to Memphis like hundreds of other southern youngsters. He managed to interest Sam Phillips in cutting some sides but not sufficiently, in competition with Jerry Lee Lewis, Carl Perkins, Johnny Cash, and Roy Orbison, to have them re-leased. For a time he appeared on Red Foley's "Ozark Jubilee," originating in Springfield, Missouri. But he was working in Canada where he wrote "It's Only Make Believe" with Jack Nance when MGM Records beckoned.

Twitty copied and exaggerated Presley's panting-growl style. The kids loved it, also the toughness-on-the-outside, softness-on-the-inside of his realism—"myself I can't deceive . . . it's only make believe . . ."

Twitty, who earned a second Gold Record with "Lonely Boy Blue," faded with the waning of the rockabilly phase of R 'n' R. But his name served as the inspiration for Conrad Birdie in the Broadway musical *Bye Bye Birdie.* When rock returned to its country roots in the '60s, he enjoyed a revival.

Another newcomer was the singer-writer whose name was J. P. Richardson, sometimes Jape Richardson, and who achieved fame in tragedy. The Big Bopper, as he called himself, was a disk jockey and program director of Station KTRM of Beaumont, Texas. He wrote songs in his spare time. At least one, "White Lightning," became a best seller for country singer George Jones on Mercury. But that was after he himself had hit with "Chantilly Lace," the No. 7 song on November 17's Honor Roll. (The backup side was a little opus titled "Purple People Eater Meets the Witch Doctor.")

Performing, the Big Bopper wore a wide-brimmed Stetson and a striped jacket that reached below his knees. With his deep, booming voice, he was a natural as a country comic. On the night of February 2, 1959, after an appearance at the Surf Ballroom in Mason City, Iowa, he, Buddy Holly, and Ritchie Valens decided to fly to their next date in North Dakota.

When they awoke the next morning, the weather was bad. But they chartered a Beechcraft Bonanza, and took off in festive spirits. The small plane was only five miles from the airport when it crashed. All of its occupants were killed. Mythic cults of idolatry developed around all three figures—Holly, Ritchie Valens, and the Big Bopper—and tribute songs were written about each.

One of the most unusual best sellers of the year was "Topsy II," accomplishing the rare feat for a jazz disk of hitting No. 4 on November 17's Honor Roll. Considering that its featured soloist was a drummer, it was a fantastic achievement. Cozy Cole, who had his start with Cab Calloway and worked with Benny Goodman, Artie Shaw, and Louis Armstrong, was then heading a Gene Krupa–Cozy Cole Drum School. "Topsy I" and "II" were based on a 1939 composition, "Uncle Tom's Cabin," by Edgar Battle and Edward Durham. To those who criticized the vulgarity and monotony of teen-age musical taste, the two Topsies, as well as "Tom Dooley," offered a thundering rebuttal.

The popularity of ballads like "It's All in the Game," of cha-chas like "Tea for Two," and of a jazz drum disk like "Topsy II" created a feeling, as Bob Rolontz observed in *Billboard,* that "the great rock and roll wave which has engulfed the entire record business for the past five years, is slowly receding." Rolontz urged caution upon those who thought that rock 'n' roll was dead or dying.

"What it does mean," he suggested, "is that rock and roll is moving closer to Pop in style and content, and that Pop is absorbing the rock and roll beat." By way of contrasting generation attitudes, Rolontz noted: "To some people, especially the kids *It's All in the Game* was a rockaballad in the rock and roll genre. To others, especially adults, the record was a pop hit with some rock and roll figures." The coalescence or merger of the two styles meant that rockabilly, as the first stage of rock 'n' roll, was approaching a terminal point.

When it came to Dick Clark, however, there was no recession in his appeal or impact. Young & Rubicam, the giant ad agency, revealed that since Beech-Nut Gum had assumed sponsorship of his "Saturday Night Show," its sales had risen 100 percent. Solely on the strength of "Bandstand" plugs, Clark sold more than six hundred thousand copies of his annual yearbook at one dollar a piece in a two-month period. A premium deal for Bosco chocolate flavoring—send fifty cents and a wrapper for an EP of all-time hits—drew two hundred sixty-two thousand replies.

As a result of these demonstrations of his pulling power, the TV superstar was planning to expand his tie-ups to a line of Dick Clark teen-age dresses and blouses. He was also negotiating for a third network TV show, a panel program. In mid-November he began "writing" a syndicated column of advice to teen-agers for *This Week,* a Sunday magazine with a circulation of twelve million.

Meanwhile, from Great Britain came a new onslaught on the "pop rot" exported by the U.S.A. Writing in *Melody Maker,* bandleader Vic Lewis asserted: "We've all noticed the deterioration in the field of popular music. Any thinking person knows the teenage idols are largely the creation of self-seeking wire-pullers with little principal and less artistic discernment. . . . Teenagers don't really know what they want. Musical worth rarely enters their heads. How ridiculous it is when a cockney singing American folk songs in a fake accent can become a star! Are the stars of the future to be drawn exclusively from the three-chord guitar bashers and bawlers of gibberish?"

An executive of the British Musicians Union quickly backed up Heath's outcry against "the overdose of importations from the jungle of American entertainment" and the "rubbish forced

upon the kids." So did a representative of the Songwriters Guild
of Great Britain, who suggested that parents and youth groups
should "demand that recording and broadcasting companies stop
this poisoning of youth immediately."

I cannot help wondering how all of these middle-aged defenders of "musical worth" felt when the balance of trade shifted
in the mid '60s and British rock groups inundated the American
market.

November '58 was a month in which Sam Cooke and Lou
Rawls, then still a member of the Travelers Quartet, were injured in a Chicago auto accident—both recovered. Milt Gabler
shuttered his famous thirty-two-year-old Commodore Record Shop,
a legendary part of the American jazz scene, really international
jazz scene. Alan Freed's Boston trial on a charge of inciting to
riot was postponed until next year. And disk jockeys Bill Randle
and Martin Block, speaking at a Columbia Records conclave,
warned somewhat belatedly, though not for the first time, that if
present trends continued in the broadcasting field, the name disk
jockey would be as extinct as the dodo bird.

But in Cincinnati, Sunday, November 30, was proclaimed "Bob
Braun Appreciation Day" by the mayor of the city. And Braun
was just a disk jockey on Station WLW radio and TV. Despite
freezing weather and a record snowfall that blocked roads leading
to the city, seven thousand teen-agers from the Greater Cincinnati
area, Northern Kentucky, and Southeastern Indiana, braved the
storm to pay homage to Braun. The mayor attended the hop at
Cincinnati Gardens to present Braun with an official scroll, as
did a judge of the Juvenile Court, who praised Braun for his
work among teen-agers. Three thousand dollars realized from the
event was turned over to various juvenile charities. The personality disk jockey was not yet extinct in Cincy.

December 22, 1958   Honor Roll of Hits

No. 1.   TO KNOW HIM IS TO LOVE HIM
   Best Selling Record: Teddy Bears, Dore 503

One of the most novel sounds of '58 was heard in December
when something called "The Chipmunk Song" skittered like a
fleet-footed squirrel up the tree of hits to the very top in three
short weeks. It was the work of the highly talented and imaginative Armenian, Ross Bagdasarian, writer-producer of "Witch
Doctor."

Now, he accomplished the unusual feat, not only of writing and singing but of *engineering* an ingenious novelty in which he worked with three different voices, all his own. Using speeded-up tape and other electronic devices, he appeared on his best-selling platter as David Seville, also as Alvin, Theodore, and Simon, three chipmunks whom he created and individualized. Alvin was the recalcitrant one and as popular for a time as Donald Duck, Snoopy, or Charlie Brown. It was a masterful feat, intriguing the imagination of old and young. The trade papers termed his disk the fastest-moving record of the year and possibly in the history of record business. Clocked at a supersales pace of two and one-half million disks in two weeks, "The Chipmunk Song" gave a merry cast to the yuletide season, also to the early weeks of 1959, a year that proved quite dismal for rock 'n' roll.

The song that displaced it in the No. 1 spot on December 29 was the work also of a highly gifted, if strange man. Phil Spector, born in the Bronx in 1940, came to California with his mother when he was nine, shortly after the death of his father. The title and idea of his first song were the result of a visit to his father's grave where he found inscribed on the headstone: To Know Him Is to Love Him. Forming a group with two classmates of Fairfax High School, Annette Kleinbard and Marshall Lieb, he produced the record that became a hit for the Teddy Bears, as they were called. Annette was just sixteen. Marshall Lieb was then a student at Los Angeles City College, majoring in law and music. Spector was eighteen, planning to become a court reporter, and very much under the musical influence of Leiber and Stoller.

Despite the tremendous success of the Teddy Bears with "To Know Him Is to Love Him"—they cut some follow-up disks for Imperial Records—Spector was restless and soon launched his own label. On Philles—the word was a combination of Phil and Les(ter) Sills, a man who had worked with Leiber and Stoller on their Spark label—Spector developed the Crystals, Bob B. Sox, the Blue Jeans, the Ronettes, and the Righteous Brothers into hit groups. When a fabulous record he made with Ike and Tina Turner, "River Deep, Mountain High," failed of acceptance, he announced his retirement from the record business. By then, he was one of rock's young, new millionaires. He returned later as producer with the Beatles and then with ex-Beatle John Lennon, among others.

In a year of novelty hits, "Beep Beep" came chugging along at the year's end. The race was between a Cadillac and an old but brash, second-hand jalopy. As with any little guy, its pride was at stake and it went beep-beep and beat the Caddy. The hit record was by the Playmates, three guys from Waterbury, Connecticut,

who met at the University of Connecticut. All musicians, Donny
Conn, Morey Carr, and Chic Hetti gigged their way through
college. Afterward, they formed a group called the Nitwits who
combined comedy and music. Signed by Roulette Records in '57,
they made some noise with "Jo-Ann." But "Beep Beep" was their
big record. In '59 they had another chart climber in "What Is
Love," after which they apparently became solid citizens, one in
psychology, another in business administration, and the third, in
engineering.

As seemed appropriate in the final month of the year, a number of the recognized artists asserted their priorities. Presley
registered in the Top Ten with "I Got Stung" and "One Night."
Ricky Nelson also demonstrated his staying power with two
Honor Roll songs, "Lonesome Town" and "I Got a Feeling,"
back-to-back hits. The Everly Brothers were present, too, with
"Problems," another country ditty by the Bryants, Felice and
Boudleaux. And Duane Eddy continued to make ears stand up
with his reverberating guitar treatment of "Cannon Ball."

Clyde McPhatter came through with the biggest disk of his
career in the million seller, "A Lover's Question," a rocking
ballad by Brook Benton and Jimmy Williams. Fats Domino, for
whom '58 was not a banner year, returned to the charts with
"Whole Lotta Loving," another song by himself and his New
Orleans arranger-producer, Dave Bartholomew.

December's freak hit was a revival of a great standard, Harold
Arlen's "That Old Black Magic." Old-timer Louis Prima did it
with his wife, Keely Smith, in a fast-paced, jazz-scat version that
was ear arresting.

The holiday season brought a fresh-sounding Christmas song,
"The Little Drummer Boy" in a sparkling, imaginative, choral
version by its composer, Harry Simeone. It quickly established
itself as a permanent and charming addition to the yuletide repertoire.

But the Christmas season brought no cessation of hostilities in
radio's format fracas. In Pittsburgh, as WAMP switched from
Top Forty to a "sweet-music format," veteran Barry Kaye announced his resignation. This was a reversal of the usual development but Kaye had been the top-rated deejay in town as a result
of his strong teen-age following.

Despite the move of the NBC-operated station away from Top
Forty, Formula Radio continued to thrive in ratings and sponsors.
In a public announcement, the manager of KWK in St. Louis expressed the increasingly prevalent view that programing was a
management responsibility and the disk jockey's function one of

selling on the air. They were not pleasant words to the rapidly decimating body of personality deejays.

The continuing ambivalence of the record-broadcasting scene and its central figures asserted itself once again in *Billboard*'s annual survey of disk-jockey preferences. Favorite Male Vocalist once again was Frank Sinatra, followed by Como and Nat Cole. Among the entire group of eleven names, only Pat Boone and Elvis Presley represented the dominant style trend. Favorite Female Vocalist was Doris Day, followed by Patti Page and Peggy Lee. There were no rock chirpers in the list.

Favorite Singing Group was the Four Freshmen, followed by the Ames Brothers and Four Lads. Only one rock group appeared in the ten choices—the Platters. The discrepancy between what deejays played on their turntables and what they liked was as stark as an off-center record. It was a schizophrenic world.

About pop music in 1958, the eminent musicologist Sigmund Spaeth wrote in an *Encyclopoedia Yearbook*: "The incubus of rock 'n' roll continued to weigh down the popular music of the year, with a majority of the music representing some form of the illiterate, savage noise. . . . The violence of this juvenile concentration on aboriginal rhythms actually led to several cities eventually barring rock 'n' roll from public performance." Dr. Spaeth, who broadcast as "The Tune Detective," a show in which he uncovered the origins and sources of contemporary songs, revealed something of his bias when he wrote: "One of the biggest sensations of the 'Hit Parade' was a definitely Negro exaltation, *He's Got the Whole World in His Hands.* . . ." Reflecting the older generation's effort to pray the new music out of existence, he concluded: "The recent history of popular music in America may be summed up in a series of comparatively meaningless titles such as *Tequila, Lollipop, Sugartime, Diana, Kewpie Doll* [but that was Como!], *At the Hop, Honeycomb, Chances Are, Short Shorts, The Stroll* [more meaningless than *The Charleston?*] *Get a Job* [meaningless?], *Raunchy* and *Silhouettes.*"

How cum the good doctor left out "Purple People Eater," "Witch Doctor," "Hula Hoop Song," and "The Chipmunks?"

25

WHAT A DIFFERENCE
A DECADE MAKES

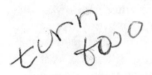

Nineteen fifty-nine was the year that Castro took over Cuba, Eddie Fisher took temporary possession of Elizabeth Taylor, and Telephone Box Squash, as the booth-crowding craze was called, took hold of the college generation. During a highly publicized visit to the USA, during which he viewed the filming of *Can-Can*, Soviet Premier Nikita Khrushchev complained bitterly that he was not permitted to visit Disneyland! Toward the end of the year, the nation was shocked by news of the wanton slaughter of the entire family of a quiet Kansas farmer, Herbert Clutter. (*In Cold Blood* later was the title of a bestselling documentary novel by Truman Capote.)

Can you recall the No. 1 song of the year? How about Lloyd Price's "Personality," Frankie Avalon's "Venus," the Fleetwoods' "Come Softly to Me," the Browns' "Three Bells," or Bobby Darin's "Mack the Knife"? All of these were No. 1's—and not swifties. "The Three Bells" rang best-seller registers for six weeks. And the Darin revival of the *Threepenny Opera* theme occupied the top spot for ten. But when all the tallies were in, the year's No. 1 song and record was an old fiddle tune, embellished with new words by an Arkansas schoolteacher, and sung by an East Texas honky-tonk singer.

The Saga Songs

"The Battle of New Orleans" was a narrative ballad, not a love ballad, as top pop songs usually were. (For that matter, the top three songs of the year were *not* love ballads, suggesting that the teen generation was growing and sobering up.) Originating in the early nineteenth century, "The Battle of New Orleans" was based on "The Eighth of January," a fiddle tune written to celebrate America's 1815 victory at New Orleans. It had the same American appeal, perhaps, as the Kingston Trio's "Tom Dooley," the Civil War ballad that launched the folk-song revival of the '60s.

Singer Johnny Horton's dry-talking style was more country than folk, a product of work in the swinging dance halls of East Texas and as a star of Shreveport's "Louisiana Hayride." Before "New Orleans," Johnny had a hit in "I'm a Honky Tonk Man." But that was in '56. Now, it seemed that he was on the way to a superstar career. It never happened. In November 1960, just about a year after the sensational success of "New Orleans," he was in an auto crash near Milano, Texas, and left the second wife of Hank Williams a widow for the second time.

Jimmy Driftwood—his name seems just right—was the author-composer of "The Battle of New Orleans." A native of Timbo, Arkansas, he was a schoolteacher around the Snowball, Arkansas, area with twenty years seniority. During much of those years, he moonlighted as a writer-performer and was under contract to RCA Victor as a folk recording artist. Two years elapsed between the time that Warden Music of Nashville published his rewrite of "The Eighth of January" and Johnny Horton covered his own recording of the broadside ballad. In that period, Driftwood contributed "The Tennessee Stud" to Eddy Arnold's repertoire and gave the Tennessee Plowboy his first big record hit in a number of years.

The popularity of "The Battle of New Orleans" enhanced Driftwood's career as a record artist and songwriter, motivating his departure from the Arkansas educational field. As the country prepared itself for a visit from the then-premier of the Soviet Union, Nikita Khrushchev, Driftwood signalized the occasion by writing and recording "The Bear Flew over the Ocean." A composite of two folk songs, "The Bear Went over the Mountain' and "Skip to Mah Lou," it failed to catch popular fancy.

Driftwood's smash led to an upsurge of recordings of historical ballads, some of them inspired by the Civil War Centennial. Johnny Horton's saga-song records included "Johnny Reb," "The Battle of Bull Run," and "Sink the Bismarck," a song inspired by the film of the same title and written by him and his manager, bassist Tillman Franks. A North Carolina log trucker with the name of Stonewall Jackson, apparently his real name, achieved a resounding hit with "Waterloo."

With another country singer, Marty Robbins, the saga songs

took a western gunfighter direction, a genre he explored effectively as writer, publisher, and Columbia recording artist. The most successful and the first of these was "El Paso," one of '59's tremendous C & W and pop hits, along with Johnny Cash's own cowboy-badman ballad "Don't Take Your Guns to Town." Marty sang more and Johnny talked more. And Jimmy Dean, delivering in the deep-bass, talking style of Cash, scored with his own narrative ballad "Big Bad John." But by then, we were in the '60s.

The climax of this development, as unexpected and unusual as it was revealing, came in September of '59. Onto the singles pop charts moved a recording made by the Philadelphia Symphony Orchestra and the Mormon Tabernacle Choir. The surprising entry was the traditional "Battle Hymn of the Republic," performed without frills. Eventually, the disk became a Top Fifteen best seller, suggesting that the interest in saga songs and folk ballads involved something more profound and basic than the chance appeal of a tune or singer.

A signpost was raised by the program director of a Dayton, Ohio, radio station (WONE), who spun "Battle Hymn" frequently during Khrushchev's visit as a reminder of "the sound of freedom." Whether the impulse was patriotic, pride in America's past, or a feeling for the times that try men's souls, the popularity of the saga songs betokened a concern with roots, values, and directions. The search was a prelude to the '60s, a time of commitment and involvement for the seekers and the rebels without a cause of the '50s.

The Search for Values

The two runners-up to "The Battle of New Orleans" were profound and analytical songs. "Mack the Knife," with a mordant lyric by German playwright Bertolt Brecht and American composer Marc Blitzstein, depicted man as a predator, a schemer, and a killer—all qualities that earned him respect in a society based on force and moved by greed. It was a far cry from the early rockabilly songs and years away from "Dream Lover," Bobby Darin's other '59 hit. That he was able to make the leap was a testimonial to his growth and that his record was accepted by youngsters, a token of theirs. Modeled on Louis Armstrong's swinging version, Darin's handling of "Mack the Knife" had ebullience and drive. His interjection of the name of Lotte Lenya, composer Kurt Weill's wife and the celebrated Pirate Jenny of the cast, indicated his familiarity with *Threepenny Opera*, then in the fifth year of its record-breaking, off-Broadway run.

Obviously, the older generation bought Darin's disk, too, giving him an entrée to the badge of adult acceptance, a booking at New York's Copacabana—vaunted bastion of Sinatra, Joe E. Lewis, and all the old boozers. Darin was the first of the rock 'n' rollers to make the crossover, an assurance of career longevity and a mark of maturing showmanship.

The other runner-up to "The Battle of New Orleans" was a rather morbid song. Of French origin, "The Three Bells" suggested the brevity of man's existence in the image of the bells that toll at his birth, his marriage, and finally, his death. Implicit was a critique of man's vanity, almost in the vein of *Ecclesiastes*. Recorded in Nashville and sung by the Browns, "The Three Bells" was hardly an oatuner and certainly not rock 'n' roll. Nor was it a religious song although the record had the prayerful sound of people in a church. Originally titled "Les Trois Cloches," it was introduced in the U.S.A. in the late '40s by Edith Piaf and Les Compagnons de la Chanson. The version by the Browns was a revival. Its tremendous acceptance proved an index to the sombre and existential, fatalistic or depressing mood of the times. It said something for young people as well as old, remaining the No. 1 bell ringer on the Honor Roll from late August until early October.

Teen Scene

The first shock that the younger generation was to suffer in '59 came early-in February with the plane crash that took the lives of Ritchie Valens, the Big Bopper, and Buddy Holly. The least known of the three was Valens whose style was similar to Holly but more Latin inflected. Holly's stardom was just two years old. Jape Richardson became known in the latter part of '58. Ritchie Valens had his two hits posthumously. In the three weeks after his death, "Donna," a plaintive ballad he wrote, flew up to the No. 2 spot on the Honor Roll. "La Bamba," which did not do as well, was more characteristic of a Mexican-styled rock with which he was experimenting.

Although the fans were shocked, the tragedy did not disrupt or halt the tour, headlined by the three. The performance at Moorehead, Minnesota, the destination the three failed to reach, went on as scheduled. The following night, at Sioux City, Iowa, Frankie Avalon, who was flying high with "Venus," joined Dion and the Belmonts, Frankie Sardo, and the Crickets, as a replacement.

Neil Sedaka, a Brooklyn-born boy who had started as a songwriter ("Stupid Cupid" for Connie Francis, etc.), blossomed as a

teen-age record favorite in '59. It was a strange change for a man
who had studied at Juilliard and was planning to become a concert pianist. "The Diary," his first release, replete with his own
overdubbed harmony, was a modest seller. But by the time it
made the charts early in '59, Sedaka had supplied Clyde McPhatter with "Since You've Been Gone" and LaVern Baker with "I
Waited Too Long," both substantial sellers. His succeeding release, "I Go Ape," was a bomb, but "Oh, Carol," Top Ten in
December, marked the beginning of a hit parade that included
"Breaking Up Is Hard to Do," "Happy Birthday, Sweet Sixteen,"
and others. Howard Greenfield, a friend from his high school
days in Brooklyn, was his constant collaborator. Unlike Ricky
Nelson, Frankie Avalon, and other teen-age artists, who manifested an appealing kind of shyness, Sedaka looked confident and
was as egotistical as Bobby Darin, if not as brash.

For three Philadelphians, '59 was a triumphal year. This,
despite the somewhat negative reactions of adult reviewers.
Fabian, one of the three, was described by John Crosby of the
New York *Herald-Tribune* as "reeling like a top, snapping his
fingers and jerking his eyeballs, with hair something Medusa had
sent back, and a voice that was enormously improved by total
unintelligibility." Apparently, the kids understood him and
bought two of his records in quantities that made best sellers of
"Tiger" and "Turn Me Loose." He had the look and image, if
not the voice.

His confrere on Chancellor Records, Frankie Avalon, had
"Dede Dinah" behind him when the year began. During the
year, he had a steady stream of sellers in "A Boy without a Girl,"
"Just Ask Your Heart," and "Bobby Sox to Stockings." But the
biggest was "Venus," a ballad that floated at the top of the Honor
Roll all through March and finished the year just behind the
three blockbusters discussed earlier in this chapter. Like Fabian,
Avalon owed more than a small share of gratitude to Dick Clark
on whose shows he made frequent appearances.

Ditto for Robert Louis Ridarelli, better known as Bobby
Rydell, who had more vocal ability than his two South Philadelphia colleagues. Rydell was a discovery of bandleader Paul Whiteman, who changed his name and arranged for him to join Rocco
and his Saints, a rock group that included Avalon. With "Kissin'
Time" he became a record seller in '59 but ran a weak third to
the other two Philadelphians. His star rose precipitously in the
early '60s, burning brightest with a leading role in the film
version of *Bye Bye Birdie* after which he became a rapidly falling
star.

Freddy Cannon really belongs to the Philadelphia crowd, except that he came from Massachusetts and had a pronounced Boston accent. But he recorded for Swan Records and exposure on "American Bandstand" helped give him a Top Ten platter. "Tallahassee Lassie" was cowritten by the owners of Swan, Frank Slay and Bob Crewe, who, like many Philadelphia entrepreneurs, seemed to have easy access to Dick Clark. Cannon's disk had a solid dance beat and a mannerism that was mimicked by teenagers. "Whew" he exclaimed periodically.

Except for Connie Francis, rock 'n' roll was singularly devoid of female soloists. But in '59 a tiny girl from Nashville with a piercing voice made her first, tentative step onto the charts. Her name was Brenda Lee and she did it with a whispered song, "Sweet Nothin's." Her real sendoff came the following summer with "I'm Sorry," after which she was seldom without a hit disk for years.

For Connie Francis, whose sound was like hers though more strident and less country, '59 was a felicitous year. At the beginning, she had "My Happiness," a ballad that she delivered with an appealing sense of sadness. Then came a rocking "Lipstick on Your Collar." And before December was torn off the calendar, she had "Frankie," a ballad by Neil Sedaka and Howard Greenfield.

Teen-agers still showed their fondness for Paul Anka, who scored giant sellers with "Lonely Boy," sopping with self-pity, and the strong, arching melody of "Put Your Head on My Shoulder." Ricky Nelson remained a great favorite with four best sellers, including the didactic "Never Be Anyone Else But You." The Everly Brothers continued their journey on the charts with two hits, and Elvis Presley with three. But after four years, it appeared the Presley was beginning to show his age: three songs in the year's Top One Hundred including "A Big Hunk o' Love" and "A Fool Such As I," but none above No. 30.

Car Groups and Such

As bird names once were popular, groups now seemed to favor car names—Impalas, Falcons, Fleetwoods, Fiestas—reflecting the generation's emotive response to automobiles. But hardly any of the year's record sellers were longer lived than the Cadillacs, who had a runaway hit in '55 in "Speedoo" and swiftly vanished in the night. Let's go cruisin'.

The Fleetwoods? Three teen-agers from Seattle made a whispery, sweet sound on "Come Softly to Me"—*Doom-doo-be-doo*. . . . *Dahm-dahm-da-ahm-boo-da-ahm* . . . *oo-doo-be-doo* . . ." The boy continued "doobydoo"ing as the two girls cooed the title. It was gently erotic and it finished among the ten hottest records and tunes of the year. So did the follow-up, "Mr. Blue."

The Impalas? Four eighteen-year-olds from a Canarsie candy store, they had "Sorry, I Ran All the Way Home" and never made it again. The Falcons, five blacks from Detroit, had "You're So Fine" and the Fiestas, four blacks from Newark, "So Fine," a different song. Memorable echoes all of the sounds of '59 but of groups that did not make it into the '6os.

Remember the Crests and "Sixteen Candles"? It became a Gold Record. Toward the end of the year, they had "The Angels Listened In." But the public did not after that.

R 'n' R seemed to be going soft in '59. People said teen-agers were tiring of the Big Beat or maturing musically. Yet a number of groups rolled off small-company assembly lines with a simplistic brand of R 'n' R that attracted buyers. Long forgotten are Johnny and the Hurricanes, who came from Toledo, Ohio, and hit with "Red River Rock," made it with "Reveille Rock" and disappeared as swiftly as even the most violent of hurricanes. But then there were Santo and Johnny, a wailing guitar and an organ, and "Sleep Walk," gentle and melodious balladry. Written by the three Farinas, Santo, Johnny, and Ann, it was followed by "Teardrop. Both made it, the former garnering a Gold Record, and then silence.

Black Is the Color

Perhaps the most significant aspect of 1959's sound spectrum was its change in color. It was a year when numerous black singers crossed from R & B or gospel into pop—or just made it after paying their dues.

In '52 Lloyd Price created a rhythm-and-blues classic in "Lawdy, Miss Clawdy," a song that influenced the Hollies, Johnny Rivers, Sandy Nelson, the Dave Clark Five, and other British rockers, most of whom recorded the gospel-guided, boogie-bouncing jumper. In '59 it was "Stagger Lee," adapted from an old, folk blues, that rocketed Price into pop. Two other Price-written songs, "Personality" and "I Wanna Get Married," helped to confirm his status as a record star of '59. But that was it, as far as big disks went for "Mr. Personality," as he became known.

When she was not recording rhythm and blues, former Lionel

Hampton thrush, Dinah Washington, served as Mercury Records' black interpreter of pop hits. In fact, when I persuaded Clyde Otis to record "What a Difference a Day Made"—she sang it "makes"— I was told by Mercury executives not to waste my time trying to bring her into white pop markets.

But I had a hunch. For the first (and last) time in years, I traveled for nine weeks, visiting pop jockeys from New York to Los Angeles, via Chicago, Denver, and Salt Lake City, and then moving through Texas along the southern rim of the U.S.A. into Miami. I was able to sway pop deejays to help effect a crossover. I received tidings of the development at the Americana Hotel in Miami when I attended the opening of the Second Annual Disk Jockey Convention late in May. At a poolside cocktail party, hosted by Mercury Records, one of the executives who had advised me not to waste my time, made the announcement that Dinah's disk had gone pop. By mid-August it had climbed into the Top Ten of the Honor Roll.

To reward me for my efforts, Mercury Records put "Broken-Hearted Melody" on the back of "Misty," which they pulled on the urging of deejays, from *Sassy*'s album. They had had so little faith in the bossa nova–inflected song by Sherman Edwards (later lyricist-composer of 1776) and Hal David (later Burt Bacharach's lyricist) that the side lay in the can for months after it was recorded. It was, in fact, a "leftover" side, since Sarah Vaughan was then on the verge of leaving Mercury. A singer's singer, Sarah had been making efforts to transfer her vocal elegance from the jazz field into pop with songs like "Make Yourself Comfortable" and "Experience Unnecessary." These allowed expression of Sassy's coyness and sly eroticism, but they were too sophisticated for mass appeal. It was "Broken-Hearted Melody" that won her wide acceptance in white pop even though (perhaps because) she improvised freely. Her disk climbed even higher than Dinah's, reaching No. 5 on the Honor Roll early in September. But Dinah's was a bigger seller, perhaps because it commanded a larger adult market as the revival of a standard.

Nineteen fifty-nine was pivotal also for Jackie Wilson, who combined the tantalizing eroticism of Billy Daniels with the gospel excitement of Little Richard. Curiously, like Daniels, and Sam Cooke, too, he was shot by a female admirer, and like Daniels, recovered. Immediately after graduating from a Detroit high school, Wilson became lead singer of one of the best R & B groups of the early '50s, Billy Ward and his Dominoes. After he left the group, he spent two years trying to make it on his own before he hit the Top One Hundred. "Lonely Teardrops" and "That's

Why" were both written by a trio of fellow Detroiters, Berry
Gordy, Jr., Gwendolyn Gordy, and Tyran Carlo. Yes, it was *the*
Berry Gordy who borrowed $700 in 1960 and founded the multi-
million-dollar black entertainment combine known as Motown
(a contraction of motor town).

Like Gordy, Brook Benton was a successful songwriter before
he became a hit record maker, cowriter of Clyde McPhatter's
memorable "A Lover's Question." As a singer, Benton brought
into pop music a bantering male egotism that stemmed from folk
blues and Negro culture. It attained its fullest expression in two
million-copy duets with Dinah Washington, "Baby (You've Got
What It Takes)" and "A Rockin' Good Way (To Mess Around
and Fall in Love.)" Dinah's own brand of sly sexuality was a per-
fect foil for his playful, male smugness. Both of these came in the
early '60s. In '59, after he had made pop-slanted R & B disks on a
smaller label, Benton broke through on Mercury with the sardonic
and vengeful, "It's Just A Matter of Time," and "Endlessly."

Nina Simone tapped and exposed an unsuspecting vein in the
taste of young buyers. An ex-piano teacher from North Carolina,
who had studied at Juilliard and was heading toward a concert
career, Eunice Kathleen Waymon—she changed her name not to
offend her parents when she was playing in a bar—became a singer
by accident. It happened in the summer of '54 when she took a
job in an Atlantic City bar while her private students were away.
She did not realize that for $90 a week, the owner expected her
to sing—but sing she did.

Her acceptance as a recording artist came with her first release.
For Bethlehem of New York City, she cut "I Loves You Porgy"
from the Gershwin–Du Bose Heyward opera *Porgy and Bess.*
It was hardly the type of song that one expected to find on the
charts. And Nina's style was closer to jazz than R 'n' R, R & B, or
pop. Ditto for her virtuoso piano playing, which was harmonically
and melodically sophisticated. But Simone had an intensity, involvement, and a searing emotionalism that overwhelmed listeners. Young and old. Call her style soul, because that's what it was.

And 1959 was the year in which soul music spread its wings and
began to transport young whites as well as blacks. Until then
Ray Charles had displayed his genius in several genres—as a
Nat Cole–type vocalist, as a rhythm-and-blues singer, as a jazz
instrumentalist. In the mid-'50s he had begun mixing two categories of song that were traditionally as far apart for blacks as God
and the devil, wedding blues and gospel. But now in '59 he
brought the new genre to a peak of expressiveness.

In "What'd I Say" the spiritual glorification of God is transformed into an ecstatic exaltation of love. We have here a secular revival meeting with Charles in the profane pulpit and the congregation responding antiphonally to his outcries. The preacher is praying for fleshy gratifications, pretending at moments to be concerned about his concern. "What'd I Say," he asks slyly. The song was a turning point for black music, also for pop, auguring as it did the widespread acceptance of soul. It was a turning point for Charles, too, whose apotheosis as a pop superstar was in the making.

The Isley Brothers made a lot of noise in '59 without making it. But "Shout," a two-sided disk on RCA Victor, eventually became a classic and the foundation of careers that brought them into the Motown fold and climaxed with the establishment of their own record company. "Gospel music was our beginning," said Kelly Isley, "and our faith in God strengthened us to accomplish what we as a group have done. It helped carry us through a trying time when our brother Vernon, who was the fourth member of the group, was killed in a car accident." The singing Isleys are Kelly, Ronnie, and Rudolph, but they have always had the support of two other brothers, Ernest and Marvin, who play in the back-up band and arrange.

In '59 the market for an increasing number of R & B artists widened tremendously. LaVern Baker, who had been outsold by charlotte-russe versions of her mid-'50s hits, now had "I Cried a Tear" to herself and the acceptance that gave her a Top Ten position on the Honor Roll. The Platters achieved top position, as they had in the past, but with a revival of a Jerome Kern standard, "Smoke Gets in Your Eyes," whose sales suggested adult buyers as well as teen-age. Perhaps the most revealing indication of the shift in taste was "Kansas City," a rocking blues that made No. 1 on a disk by an unknown, Wilbert Harrison, on an offbeat R & B label, Fury Records.

"Kansas City" was the work of Leiber and Stoller, for two of whose groups '59 was a rocking year. They had nurtured the Coasters from the start and had already had the magnificent "Yakety Yak" with them. Now, everybody was singing, "Fee, fee, Fi, fi, Fo, fo, fum. . . . I smell smoke in the auditorium" from "Charlie Brown." And it was hard to forget "Poison I-i-vy," with the warning against the eternal female that'll make you scratch like a hound the minute you start messin' around—you'll be using "oceans of calamine lotion."

Leiber and Stoller inherited the Drifters when their manager, George Treadwell, sacked the entire group and changed the name of a group called the Crowns to the Drifters. A change of style

seemed in order, and Leiber and Stoller were called in as producers. For the first time, they added strings to a typical R & B
combo and brought in a white studio arranger, Stan Applebaum.
Use of the *Baion* rhythm also was innovative and contributed a
fresh feeling. "There Goes My Baby" went to No. 2 on the Honor
Roll and finished in the Top Thirty of the year's hot records.

Having altered the character of pop, R & B was now undergoing
changes in its new milieu. It was also giving the lie to those who
saw rock 'n' roll simply in white, teen-age terms and dismissed the
late '50s as a period of the doldrums.

The Adults Were Buying Albums

Early in the year, record business went through one of its
periodic frenzies. All the companies were suddenly rushing
combos into their studios to cut the theme and music of a hot
television show. "Peter Gunn" was the "Mannix" of its day and
the score was by composer Henry Mancini. What generated the
excitement was the underground info that the Ray Anthony
single on the theme and the Mancini album of the music were
both turning into runaway hits. No one caught up to Anthony on
the Honor Roll and Mancini's LP finished as *the* top album of
the year.

It was a strange development, considering that both the theme
and score were jazz-inflected. "Peter Gunn" was, in fact, a break-
through for the use of jazz in television scoring. It also demonstrated the power of the TV tube to sell records, a fact that was
confirmed a month later when a nonsinger named Edward Byrnes
and pert Connie Stevens had the No. 3 song in the country,
"Kookie, Kookie (Lend Me Your Comb)." Byrnes played a hip-
talking, smug, and smiling parking lot attendant who was constantly combing his hair in "77 Sunset Strip," another popular
TV whodunit.

In a backward look at the album charts of the year, the cleavage
in generation tastes becomes most apparent. Of the Top Fifty
LPs, only six were by such teen-age favorites as Pat Boone, Ricky
Nelson, Duane Eddy ("Have Twangy Guitar, Will Travel"),
Fabian, and the Kingston Trio. The remainder were sound tracks
(*Gigi, South Pacific, The King and I, Oklahoma, Porgy and Bess*),
original-cast albums (*My Fair Lady, Flower Drum Song, The
Music Man, Gypsy*), and collections by armchair artists. The
Mantovani Strings were represented by three albums of film
music. Mitch Miller had no fewer than five Sing Along an-

thologies, dear to the heart of the older set. Young Johnny Mathis also had five best-selling albums. Despite his youth, the titles of two of his LPs provide an index to his audience: *Open Fire, Two Guitars,* and *Warm* (not hot!). Sinatra maintained his own unique place with three autobiographical—emotionally speaking—albums: *Only the Lonely, No One Cares,* and as he came out of his torch-for-Ava stage, *Come Dance with Me.*

In the late '50s, albums were for adults. When Station WZIP of Cincinnati, Ohio, decided to further its image as programers of "good music," it began billing itself as the hit-album station.

The Top Forty Brouhaha

Early in the year, one of radio's best-known personality disk jockeys, Ed McKenzie, quit Station WXYZ in Detroit in protest against Formula Radio. "I would sooner dig ditches or sell hot dogs," said McKenzie, who had been known countrywide as Jack the Bellboy on WJBK before switching to WXYZ in 1952.

McKenzie's criticism was seconded by his strongest competitor in the Detroit market. Robin Seymour, who occupied the time slot opposite McKenzie on his old station for eleven years, commented: "It's a shame when one of the men who made the disk jockey a major factor in programing, has to bow to the dictates of a program director." At the time, Seymour's station (WJBK) was the only one in the area not following a Top Forty rock format.

McKenzie's exit, followed almost immediately by the resignation of Eddie Chase from Detroit Station CKLW, sparked a furor. Formula Radio became a hotly debated subject in the city's newspapers. Some record executives criticized Top Forty programing on the ground that the public tired too quickly of a disk because of overexposure. But one of WXYZ's radio-TV jockeys argued that Formula programing led to "fast-paced production, station identification, less talk, more music." He should have added more commercials.

Dick Biondi of Station WKBW in Buffalo urged personality disk jockeys not to quit. "At this moment," he opined, "the greatest deejay is the one who can live within the formula or Top Forty list, and make it sound not only happy and interesting but as if he is producing and pulling the music all by himself." Biondi felt that if the deejays used their talents as molders, they could in time retrieve "a little of the freedom that has been taken from us . . ."

Addressing the Second Annual Convention of the Disk Jockeys

in May in an atmosphere of upheaval and conflict, the president of the Broadcasters Association told the assembled deejays: "You are none of these—personalities, names, or characters. You are the station and all of the people that make it possible for you to be on the air."

The apparent resignation of the deejay fraternity to the shape of things was indicated in a statement by an L.A. disk jockey: "I am format and I have personality." And Jim Hawthorne of KDAY added: "I was brainwashed about three years ago." He had modified his show to cut down on chatter and speed up the pace.

The following month, Baltimore's most influential deejay announced that due to the number of new records released each week, he was eliminating the Best Bets portion of his Top Fifty show. He hoped thereby "to turn the tide of pressure from overanxious record firms, cut to a minimum the unethical trade hypoing of new disks, and the unnecessarily inaccurate listings." The last was a reference to the tie-up between record stores and radio stations in which dealers prepared and distributed Top Forty lists, ostensibly based on sales, which served as playlist of the cooperating station.

Came July and the exit of another of the nation's key personality jockeys from Station WERE in Cleveland added fuel to the raging controversy. "I did not resign," wrote Tom Edwards, an eight-year veteran, in his longtime weekly newsletter. "I was fired." And he pleaded with the record companies: "Don't drop me like a hot potato just because I can't do you some good for a period of time," offering his home address for a continued flow of new record releases.

"You'll have very few spots to expose new records in Cleveland," he warned. "WERE is going into the Format. . . . Where will adults turn for music now?"

The move to Top Forty programing continued apace, as WKLO of Louisville, Kentucky, and WBBM of Chicago announced their switch to Formula radio. In Atlanta, the Plough chain bought WAGA and converted it into the third Formula station in the area.

Fighting both the Plough and Storz chains, a Balaban executive denounced the abandonment of programing "to the corner record shop and the preshave crowd." Addressing a Conference of American Women in Radio and TV, the Balaban chieftain predicted the demise of Top Forty. And as he did so, Station KWK of St. Louis announced that it was switching to Top Forty. "Programing from a current playlist is not as bad as it sounds," the station's manager averred. "If you were radio management and concerned with corporate realignment, you too would adopt a 'safe play' policy."

As the defenders of what later became known on radio as Easy Listening continued to retreat before the spreading flow of hot-lava rock, some of their cohorts struck back angrily. In Baltimore one morning in April, disk jockey Jack Gale started his show at 7:20 A.M. with a new rock record. The station's program director cut in and announced: "Mr. Gale is no longer with us." And Gale never returned to the microphone. Reminiscent of Arthur Godfrey's on-the-air firing of singer Julius La Rosa, the incident ignited the local press.

Late in September, Station WLEV of Erie, Pennsylvania, indulged in a more ceremonial expression of its distaste for teen-age music. Loading seven thousand rock 'n' roll disks into a hearse, rented for the occasion, the station's personnel mounted a funeral procession that proceeded to Erie Harbor where the disks were unloaded and dumped into the river.

The dean of rock deejays, Dick Clark, revealed his sensitivity to the attacks in a TV Special, "The Record Years," which he produced and emceed in June. Highlight of the show was a scene that was readily recognized as a defense of teen-agers and their music. Clark presented renditions of some of the more ridiculous songs of yesteryear, among them "Ta Ra Ra Boom De Aye" and "Three Little Fishes," and depicted some of yesterday's more idiotic fads, like college boys gulping goldfish, dancing in theatre aisles, wearing zoot suits, and sloppy-Joe sweaters, etc. Then, he introduced a group of neatly dressed, well-behaved youngsters dancing calmly to a current R 'n' R tune. To take the edge off his takeoff, Clark concluded with a tongue-in-cheek presentation of the then-current craze of kids-crowding-into-a-telephone booth.

In a follow-up trade-paper ad, Clark boasted that the show had scored an average share of audience rating of 50.6 in a twenty-three-city Trendex. The amazing size of the audience, among other things, led *Billboard* to comment in an August headline: "Rock and Roll Ain't Ready/ For Ol' Rockin' Chair Yet." Noting that the charts included hits by many non–R 'n' R singers and hybrid pop-country-rock numbers, and that the Big Beat was being softened by the addition of strings and woodwinds, the trade paper observed that the pioneer R 'n' R artists still retained their popularity and that hits were still being churned out by the recognized R 'n' R record producers—this, despite the vociferous opposition of educators, columnists, musicians, and politicos.

When the Dick Clark Caravan played the Hollywood Bowl in

August, it not only attracted a sellout audience, but five thousand fans were turned away at the gate. Loud speakers were set up five blocks away to discourage additional thousands from pouring toward the Bowl. General Amusement Corporation, bookers of the tour, also bragged that the Caravan had smashed all attendance records in the one-hundred-and-ten-year history of the Michigan State Fair.

Two related media served to emphasize the expanding appeal of R 'n' R. Motion pictures were more and more featuring rock stars like Fabian, Frankie Avalon, Paul Anka, Pat Boone, and even lesser figures like Dodie Stevens and Connie Stevens—and not merely in rock musicals but dramatic roles. And an increasing number of fairs were presenting rock performers as a means of drawing teen-age attendance.

As Leiber and Stoller wrote in a Coasters' Song: "You say that music's for the birds/ And you can't understand a word/ But, honey, if you did, you'd really blow your lid/ 'Cause, baby, that is rock and roll . . .'"

The End of a Decade and an Era

On April 24, "Your Hit Parade" presented a nostalgic salute to its debut show of April 12, 1935. Warren Hull, the announcer of that initial program, appeared and joined Dorothy Collins and Johnny Desmond in singing the first group of songs heard on the "Hit Parade": "Lookie, Lookie, Here Comes Cookie," "Lullaby of Broadway," "When I Grow Too Old to Dream," "Isle of Capri," "(It's So) Easy to Remember," and "Lovely to Look At." When the final note was played and the final word sung, "Your Hit Parade" passed from the scene. It had been on TV for nine years and on radio for twenty-four.

In '59 there were two other symbolical deaths—Billie Holiday, the most significant and influential voice in pop music of the '30s and '40s, and Jack Robbins, the most colorful and one of the most powerful publishers of the Tin Pan Alley era. In an unrelated act, RCA Victor terminated the recording contract of Eddie Fisher, the young man responsible for its biggest sales before the appearance of Presley. All of these departures served to emphasize the end of an era.

Billboard made the same point in a survey-comparison of the pop picture of 1959 with that of 1939. Although the number of hits and songwriters for the first nine months of each year were virtually the same—seventy as against seventy-two songs, and one hundred four as against one hundred and eighteen songwriters—

there was a tremendous geographical dispersal. Whereas the publishers of Top Ten songs in '39 were all located in New York, in '59 they were distributed in eight states. The songwriters now came from eighteen states instead of three. In '39 Top Ten disks were made by only three companies; in '59 by thirty-nine companies. And these companies, instead of all being located in New York, were distributed in ten states.

The conclusion was inescapable: music business had broken out of Broadway, and Tin Pan Alley was gone as a shaper of trends and styles.

Year-end, Ohio State University announced the results of a survey it had made. The statistics contained no surprises. Among youngsters of fourteen to eighteen, eighty-two percent preferred R 'n' R over seventeen other categories of music. As for adults (nineteen to seventy), R 'n' R was more actively disliked than any other category, with 35 percent indicating that they flipped to another station if as much as a half hour of the Big Beat was programed.

In Seattle the general manager of Station KAYO announced: "The listening public is turning off rock and roll music." Henceforth, the station would play only cuts from best-selling albums and the "sweet side" of Top Fifty singles.

But by the time these conflicting viewpoints were aired, teenagers, the entire music business, and a large sector of the general public were deeply embroiled in the payola scandal.

26

PAYOLA

Nothing shook up the youngsters of the 1950s as much as the revelation of payola among some of their favorite disk jockeys. Many just wouldn't believe it. Others felt ashamed, as parents of juvenile delinquents frequently do, suffering the onus of guilt instead of feeling betrayed.

"All shook up" was the phrase used by a trade-paper reporter in describing the impact on music business. "There's a complete cessation of the normal, fraternal spirit that once animated all levels of the business," Bob Rolontz wrote. "No longer are the lobbies of the Brill Building or its annex thronged with music business men, wildly ecstatic over a newly recorded song or a newly released disk. The crowd that used to stand in front of the Turf and Dempsey's [restaurants] or Hanson's Drugstore have faded away. Disk jockeys cannot be reached by phone, distributors are out of town, A & R men are suddenly vacationing, and many record company officials answer their phones in soft, whispering voices. . . .

"There is an eerie silence about; and the lack of gaiety in a usually happy industry was evident at the annual NARAS dinner at the Waldorf last Sunday [November 29]. All eyes are turned toward Washington and toward the Subcommittee on Legislative Oversight hearing that is due to take place on December 9. In New York all eyes are turned toward the office of the district attorney . . .

"Jokes about payola made the rounds from Al & Dick's to Lindy's and down to Klube's Restaurant [on Twenty-third Street near RCA Victor]. The most common was the one about the

268

promo man frustrated by the refusal of a jock to play his new record who blurted out—'Listen, you, if you don't play my record, I'll send you money . . .' "

To the general public of the late '50s, and even to some of the legislators and law enforcement officers involved in its investigation, payola was a new word. But inside music business, play-for-pay dated back at least to the vaudeville era. Then publishers bought scenery, costumes, railroad tickets, and paid hotel bills and hauling charges in return for onstage performances. The more important performers like Al Jolson were "cut-in" on a song's royalties.

"It was an era of outright payola," Abel Green, editor of *Variety* wrote recently. "From the opening acrobatic act, which plugged *Japanese Sandman, Dardanella* or some other instrumental while making with the hand-to-hand gymnastics, through the rest of the bill, there was little that the then powerful Vaudeville Managers Protective Association and the Music Publishers Protective Association could do to kayo it."

With the advent of radio, the play-for-pay gambit shifted mainly to bandleaders with airtime. But there were outstanding stylists like Harry Richman who, according to Green, "made no bones about charging a flat fee per plug, even though it was over a local Loew's station." Again, when there were not outright cash payments, there were dodges like Paul Whiteman acting as a musical adviser to publisher Leo Feist, Inc., advances for the use of a performer's name on a folio collection, subsidies for orchestral arrangements, etc.

In the early '40s, the industry was startled by a crackdown of the song pluggers' union on five of its members. All five had no way of denying that they had violated the Contactmens' Union rule against paying for plugs. The Three Suns, recipients of the coin, themselves named the men who had bought their cooperation.

In January 1950 the union tackled the problem once again by penalizing a bandleader instead of its own members. Vincent Lopez of "Nola" fame, who led the band at the Hotel Taft grill in New York City, was placed on the Unfair List. Lopez denied receiving money for plugs but readily admitted that he accepted fees for new arrangements he added to his library.

Claiming that "payola to disk jockeys is at an all-time peak," *Billboard* detailed some of the forms it took in December 1950. Without naming names of the spinners involved, it indicated that some took a percentage on all local sales of a given disk while others worked on a flat-rate arrangement, $50 to $100 for a drive of specified duration on a new record. An outbreak of deejays opening record shops was noted, in which case quantities of free platters figured as the consideration. In all these instances, local record distributors bore the brunt of the cost, though sometimes manufacturers contributed a share.

"But publishers do considerable subsidizing," the trade paper reported. "Much of the money they used to set aside for live remote broadcasts now goes for the spinners. In addition to cash, they send gifts, cut jockeys in on tunes and entertain them on lavish New York junkets—a tour deluxe of the big city, with rail fare, hotel room, eats, drinks, night clubs, theatre tickets, etc."

In 1954, Jack Robbins, who ran MGM's pubberies, told *Variety*: "In the old days, by cutting in such-and-such singer and this-and-that bandleader, we had at least 100 shots at a hit because these maestros and singers were great plugs and by concentration could help put a song over. Now, it's limited to a handful of payola characters at the record companies." The statement came at a time when the *sine qua non* for making a hit was the record and the *sine qua non* for getting records was the A & R executive. It was two years before the advent of Elvis Presley, and the situation was so bad that Abel Green wrote a series of editorials headed: "Payola—Worse Than Ever."

I have sketched this history of play-for-pay because during the scandals of '59–'60, the public gained the impression that payola was associated specifically with rock 'n' roll, if it was not generated by it. Obviously, it was a way of life in music business, if not in American business generally.

All of this was known inside the entertainment world when a young Columbia University professor, Charles Lincoln Van Doren, answered a subpoena of the House Special Subcommittee on Legislative Oversight in mid-November 1959. Van Doren was a member of a distinguished family of university professors, writers, poets, and literary critics. He had already been suspended by NBC from a $50,000 job as a consultant and "Today" commentator for refusing to accept an invitation to appear before the Committee. Now he was under subpoena and had no choice. The Committee wanted him to testify on how he had come to win $129,000 on NBC's "Twenty-One" quiz show. There were rumors that he had been given the answers in advance.

In actuality, the explosive situation had passed beyond the rumor stage. The man defeated by Van Doren, winning a mere $49,500, had already stated that he had taken a dive. Corroboration had been supplied by another contestant who dramatically opened a registered letter, postmarked May 10, 1957, containing not only the questions and answers for the May 13 quiz but also instructions for dramatizing the answers. And the producer of "Twenty-One," Dan Enright, had testified that on many quiz shows, "the fix has been in force for many years."

Van Doren's opening sentence, after he had nervously gulped a glass of water, told the story: "I would give almost anything I have to reverse the course of my life in the last three years." As he made a full confession, "he was the anguished soul torn by struggles of conscience," *Time* reported, "and when he was finished, there was barely a dry eye among the Congressmen." The troupe of former contestants that followed Van Doren all served to confirm that the TV quiz shows were rigged, the producers had corrupted the contestants, and the contestants were quite willing to be corrupted.

It was a dark hour for television. NBC bounced "Tic Tac Dough" and "The Price Is Right," and put all shows under strict supervision. In one swift move, CBS eliminated all quiz shows from the tube, and fired the president of the CBS-TV network, whose rise had been associated with "Quiz Kids," "Stop the Music," and the mammoth "$64,000 Question." (Eventually in '62, Van Doren and nine other "lucky" contestants pleaded guilty to charges of perjury in a New York County Court and received suspended sentences.)

The TV quiz-show scandal quickly overflowed its banks into the record field. The most immediate result was the disclosure that a certain number of music publishers had been playing hanky-panky with quiz-show producers, kicking back percentages of money they received for performances of their copyrights. The interesting fact was that these publishers were all old-time owners of standards—the performance payoff, because of ASCAP seniority weighting, was larger than on new songs. In other words, play-for-pay was not limited even in the rock 'n' roll years to current teenage songs.

Early in '59, before Van Doren's self-abnegating confession, hearings held by another congressional committee created a furor in the record field. The name of a former manager of singer Tommy Leonetti cropped up during an investigation into the attempts of gangsters to strong-arm juke-box plays of recordings by singers they controlled. As newspapers and TV news reports bandied Leonetti's name about, Dick Clark cancelled a scheduled appearance of the young singer. Steve Allen was one of many who felt that Leonetti had been treated unfairly and immediately offered him a spot on his show.

The music trade papers also came to his defense. Noting that

Leonetti was now managed—and had been for three years—by a man whose word was his bond, Bob Rolontz of *Billboard* wrote: "I signed Tommy to the Vik label when I was on the A & R staff of the late RCA Victor subsidiary in 1957. I certainly would not have signed him if he had been connected in any way with the mob. Leonetti was not responsible for the acts of his first manager who tried to get his early records on the boxes by using muscle. It is even more unfair to tar him with something that took place four years ago."

A week later, Dick Clark announced that Leonetti, who had been scheduled for a February 21 guest shot, would appear on March 2. It was a minor brouhaha but an augury of the fireworks about to explode. If Van Doren's singing did not set them off, they came at about the same time.

Suddenly, a probe of disk jockey payola by the Federal Communications Commission and a House Subcommittee, seemed imminent. Radio stations from coast to coast were in a dither. Two New York dailies, the *Journal-American* and *Post* began readying exposés as troubled station managers began interrogating their staffs, "Have you ever . . .?" They were running scared over an FCC announcement that stations could lose their licenses if payola existed *even* if they were unaware. At stations where record-promo men had always had a warm welcome, they suddenly were confronted by No Visitors signs. And, "frantic on-the-take dee jays were calling distributors and/or labels asking them to hold off on payments," according to the trade papers.

Station WNEW in New York City put four of its deejays on the air on Sunday, November 15 to face the $64,000 query, "Have you ever?" Deejays William B. Williams and Peter Myers both stated that they had been approached but had turned down the offers—Myers: because "maybe I was afraid of being caught" and Williams: because "I would then not have control over my show." However, Williams indicated that he had heard from quite a number of song pluggers of a network disk jockey who weekly notified each one as to when he expected to be taken out for lunch or dinner. "The boy never went for a check."

Paul Ackerman, a member of the panel and music editor of *Billboard,* brought up the matter of *freebees*, records given as bonuses to distributors by manufacturers. He contended that these violated the copyright law since writers and publishers seldom received royalties on them. Pete Myers agreed and added: "If there is any immorality in payola, it is in the siphoning off of money in front of the artists' anticipated royalties. He doesn't get anything until this whole thing is washed out."

In Chicago, as the result of an on-the-air-discussion, Paul Lind of WAIT requested police protection. He claimed that he had received anonymous threats because of a tape he had cut with the owner of a small West Coast record label. Citing instances (but no names) of deejay demands for weekly retainers, the label owner claimed that it would cost him $22,000 to get a record adequately exposed in the Windy City.

Howard Miller, the city's leading jockey, told the *Chicago Tribune*, "Everyone in the industry knows payola is running rampant," and stated that he possessed an affidavit given to him by a record distributor who had quit the business years earlier. The affidavit specified payments made to a top Chicago deejay. Claiming that he had actually seen the cancelled checks, Miller expressed opposition to a congressional investigation of payola.

"This is a job for policing by station management," he averred. "The main trouble with congressional investigations is that a few get named but the whole group gets hurt."

Advised of Miller's statement and Lind's exposé, another Chicago deejay reportedly said: "Well, there goes my Christmas."

By the following week, music business was like an erupting volcano, with the country's newspapers and radio and TV indulging in sensational headlines. A third governmental agency had now joined the payola hunt. On November 19 the New York District Attorney's office served subpoenas on a string of record labels, demanding their books. It was concerned with possible violations of a statute forbidding commercial bribery, a matter that also interested the Federal Trade Commission.

But a possible underlying motive was revealed by the counsel for the House Subcommittee who stated: "Suppose John Smith owns a record company and then buys a broadcast station. Suppose he dumps its personnel and its good music format to push his own label generally only rock and roll. . . . Now, that's not in the public interest . . ."

"The payola hearings would never have taken place," Carl Belz of Brandeis University has written, "if rock had been esthetically pleasing to the popular music audience. . . . The impetus behind the hearings was undeniably related to an assumption that rock was 'bad' music, that it encouraged juvenile deliquency and that it could only have been forced on the public by illegal business activities . . ."

Writing in *The Nation,* Paul Ackerman stated: "Payola may be ethically deplorable, but it is unlikely that it has ever changed, or ever could change the course of popular American music."

As sleuths for the House Subcommittee fanned out into six

cities seeking evidence of payoffs, also of performer kickbacks and *sub rosa* deals for product plugs, several "canaries" began singing. A Philadelphia record distributor admitted in a filmed interview that he had to sell ten thousand copies of any record to cover "gifts" of cash, household articles, and baby items to local deejays. The name of Dick Clark's producer, Tony Mammarella, figured in his narrative of the success of "Get a Job," a record cut by a local deejay and sold to a New York label. Wildcat Music, of which Mammarella was part owner, was listed as the publisher. Mammarella admitted also that he was Anthony September, a cowriter of Charlie Gracie's '57 hit, "Butterfly." Claiming that he had used the pseudonym at the request of the two actual writers, he acknowledged that he had received $7,000 in royalties on the song.

From Cincinnati, the president of King Records—one of eleven companies whose books were subpoenaed by New York District Attorney Frank Hogan—announced that at one time, he had a monthly payola nut of $2,000. "Payola is plain blackmail," said Syd Nathan, "and a dirty rotten mess that has gotten worse and worse."

From Hollywood, the president of Dot Records announced the availability of his books, even though no officer of the label was located in New York to accept a subpoena. Randy Wood stated that the label never contributed to the payola evil. But publishers whose songs were recorded by Dot claimed that they were expected to grant an allotment of seventy thousand royalty-free records for promotion purposes. That represented $1,400 a side from which songwriters and publishers derived no royalties.

Predictably, one of the first casualties of the hullabaloo was the man credited with coining the phrase rock 'n' roll. On November 21 Alan Freed was dismissed by WABC when he refused "on principle" to sign a statement that he had never received funds or gifts to plug records. His fans learned that he was going off the air while he was spinning "Shimmy Shimmy Ko-Ko-Bop" by Little Anthony and the Imperials. Sobbing, he interrupted the record to announce his "resignation." Fred Robbins took over his slot. Two days later, ostensibly "by mutual consent," WNEW-TV replaced him on his "Big Beat" video dance show with singer–disk jockey Richard Hayes. At his final telecast, tears were visible on the faces of many of the youngsters and one girl was heard to cry, "Now they've taken away our father."

In Detroit deejay Tom Clay was fired by Station WJBK when he admitted accepting about $6,000 in a year and a half from small record companies. Another WJBK broadcaster, Jack Le

Goff, was pink-slipped after he quoted an editorial defending payola "as a part of American business." Within a thirty-six-hour period, still another deejay, Don McLeod, took a walk.

In Boston three top jockeys—Stan Richards, Bill Marlowe, and Mike Eliot—were separated from their turntables at Station WILD in what was described as a move "to de-emphasize the role of the deejays and to emphasize the role of the Station from now on." Two other deejays, Joe Smith and Ken Malden, originally scheduled to leave as a consequence of the station's new policy, decided to remain. Emphasizing that payola was not at all involved, Smith stated that the contracts of all five were up and the station wanted to re-sign them for less money. He remained by accepting the cut.

In Philadelphia Joe Niagara, a key disk jockey, moved his previously announced resignation up from December 19 to November 23. Payola was not necessarily involved, it was said, though the updating came after conferences with Station WIBG's managing director.

As more and more stations, apprehensive about their licenses, circulated affidavits among their personnel—"I have never taken payola . . ."—controversy developed within broadcasting circles as to the meaning of "payola." Did it mean *cash* or *conflict of interests?*

The general managers of WNEW and WINS in New York City both felt that it was not payola "unless it affects the music." It was okay for WNEW deejay Lonny Star to own several publishing firms and for WINS jockey Murray Kaufman to be involved in publishing and recording. As for William B. Williams at WNEW, its general manager said: "I don't care if Frank Sinatra gives him a Cadillac because he would be playing Sinatra records regardless—thus such a gift wouldn't affect the music."

Westinghouse Broadcasting took an opposite view: "We do not condone disk-jockey ownership of record companies, distributing companies, publishing companies or talent. That is because of the actual or potential conflict of interest between ownership and the creative selection of programing."

There was no question of what it was when it came to Joe Finan and Wes Hopkins of Westinghouse Station KYW in Cleveland. In an inspection of the books of the RCA Victor distributor in the area, the FCC uncovered a flock of checks made out to the two deejays. Although they contended that they were paid to act as consultants in selecting potential record hits, the distributor's advertising director denied this and pointed out that checks varying from $25 to $100 each bore the title of a different disk.

Before they were paid by check over a fifteen-month period, the duo had received their emoluments in cash. The ad director stated that the cash was given by field representatives in KYW's third-floor men's room, which was affectionately known as "the payola booth." Finan's combined annual radio-TV salary was reported at more than $45,000—$30,000 for radio, $12,000 for TV, plus $300 per record hop.

A Westinghouse executive urged the investigators and public to recognize that "There must be one who tempts as well as one who accepts. No matter how intense the competition among record companies, distributors, talent managers and others, it cannot justify practices aimed at compromising broadcasting talent . . ."

Despite his disappearance from the air and TV tube, Alan Freed continued to be the focus of considerable attention. In a December 3 story in the New York *Post* the head of Jubilee/Josie Records and of Cosnat Distributors claimed that he had given Freed an $11,000 loan in 1956. Jerry Blaine stated that Freed had made payments of principal and interest during '56 but that he had returned the interest and turned the loan over to Roulette Records.

At the same time, a steady stream of record artists was seen flowing in and out of the New York District Attorney's office. Bobby Darin, Eileen Rodgers, Les Paul, and Mary Ford were all queried about appearance on the "Alan Freed Show" on WNEW-TV, how they were paid and whether they kickbacked the payment.

Urged by President Eisenhower to clean up "this whole mess," the FTC served formal charges on three record companies and six record distributors. RCA Victor, London Records, and Bernard Lowe Enterprises of Philadelphia were each accused of paying deejays to plug records, "thereby deceiving the public and causing a chain of artifical boosts in sales and chart ratings," which in turn worked unfairly to suppress the disks of competitors. Five of the distributors were located in Philadelphia and the sixth was in Cleveland. All were advised that they could defend themselves at a public hearing on February 8, 1960.

The FCC did not make charges. Of fifty-three hundred radio-TV licensees, it requested a detailed accounting, under oath, of all programing for which payment of any kind had been made but not acknowledged since November 1, 1958. Licensees were given until January 4, 1960, to supply the information as well as complete details on how tabs were kept on payola among employees.

Implicit in the request was the threat of revocation of license.

That this was not an idle possibility became clear when the plight of Station WGMA came to light. The station was owned by Dan Enright and Jack Barry, packagers of TV quiz shows under fire for fraud. In a letter to Enright, dated November 30, the FCC indicated that the station would have to answer charges that testimony before the Harris Committee on Legislative Oversight "raises serious questions concerning the character qualifications of Mr. Enright . . . and whether he is qualified to own and operate a broadcasting facility." Stations could not help concluding that just as Enright was culpable for malpractices of employees on the NBC-TV quiz shows, so they would be held accountable for fraudulent practices even if they were ignorant of them.

Reacting to the FCC inquiry, NBC required all of its deejays, performers, and executives to fill out a notarized questionnaire covering every aspect of direct or indirect conflict of interest and payment of any kind for plugging a record, person, firm, corporation, product, or service.

CBS radio issued a directive to its owned-and-operated stations requiring deejays to submit to station managers the titles of all records to be programed twenty-four hours before airtime. Air mentions of movies, cafés, or events had to be cleared in advance on pain of instant dismissal.

The most extreme probe of payola was put into practice by Station KDAY of Santa Monica, California, which literally utilized a lie detector and forced its personnel to take the test with KTLA-TV telecasting the proceedings.

"I detect symptoms of fear, frenzy and flight," commented the secretary-treasurer of the Disk Jockey Association, " on the part of several station managers." The voice of Bill Gavin was one of the few raised against the developing witch-hunt atmosphere. "They are hurriedly making protestations of purity by large-scale firings and inquisitions of their program staffs," he added. "Is their purpose to convince Washington investigators that they are just now aware of how record promotion pressures have for years been infiltrating and undermining their programs.

"Is it their belief that they can cure the evil by publicly sacrificing some of their name disk jockeys? Are they also willing to announce their discontinuance of gifts, rebates, and 'deals' to time buyers?"

While the investigators of the Harris Committee continued to dig, the country's newspapers kept the panic raging. Many innocent people found themselves mentioned, but had no personal involvement in the payola game. In payola headlines were such strange and contrasting figures as Bob Hope, gospel singer Clara

Ward, disk jockey Bill Randle, and inevitably, Alan Freed.

Hope was in a hassle with NBC because of a skit in which he played a deejay on Station KLIP and Ernie Kovacs appeared as an investigating senator. NBC objected to the mention of a product, which the comic defended as necessary to the skit.

Clara Ward made the headlines because of an appearance on the "Today" show a year earlier. The NBC network had a red face, as it was forced to admit that the gospel group had not received its full fee. But it contended that it was common practice to recapture part of the fee for promo purposes.

Alan Freed's name figured in headlines in the New York *Post* because of his dealings with Roulette Records. Freed was summoned to the office of the New York State Attorney General and quizzed about his dealings with Morris Levy, head of Roulette, and about two mortgages held by the record company with a face value of $21,000 and an unpaid balance of $16,293.

In Cleveland, police were summoned by attorneys of Station WERE. Disk jockey Bill Randle reported receiving blackmail threats by phone and through the mails for over a month. The blackmailer threatened to involve him in the payola scandal unless he paid a substantial sum of money.

With Christmas just around the corner, *Billboard* offered a chart of what a disk jockey might expect in '59 compared with '58:

1958	1959
Cashmere suit	Pair of gloves
Leather jacket	Wool muffler
Color TV set	Japanesee transistor radio
Stetson hat	Beret
Case of whiskey	Bottle of scotch
Cadillac	Vespa
Cash	Nothing

In Philadelphia five record distributors were sweating out charges leveled against them by the FTC; one admitted that the business of promoting a new record had undergone a drastic change. "All you do," he said, with obvious pain, "is leave it at the station. Since you are not paying anymore, you can't say, 'I want you to lay on this or that!' You just leave it." And apparently after you left it, the full music staff of the station decided in committee which records would be added to the playlist. Temporarily at least, disk hyping had stopped, as disk jockeys were not available even for a social lunch or dinner. The so-called "lootless era" had begun.

Another effect of all the investigations and publicity was a developing tendency by radio stations to play non–rock 'n' roll disks. This was explained in two ways: 1) while their programs were being scrutinized, disk jockeys were curving material that had evoked the wrath of pressure groups, and 2) stations were sensitive to the tendency of the nation's press to link payola with rock 'n' roll, even though the entire history of song plugging rejected the linkage. (In an editorial warning the probers and press against taking seriously allegations by embittered has-beens, *Billboard* said flatly: "The cancer of payola cannot be pinned on rock and roll.")

Out of Philadelphia came the news that an early sale was expected of three publishing companies owned by Dick Clark. It was known that the emcee of "American Bandstand" had been given the alternative by ABC-TV of giving up the show or divesting himself of conflict-of-interest ownerships. Producer Tony Mammarella had turned in his resignation. But Clark was selling Sea Lark Music, a BMI affiliate whose catalog included "At the Hop" and "Party Time," January Music, another BMI affiliate whose hits included "Sixteen Candles," and Arch Music, an ASCAP affiliate.

According to the New York *Post*, Clark was also the owner of Mallard Pressing Corporation of Philadelphia—but an executive of the firm claimed that Clark had sold his interest. To whom? The exec did not think this was "a proper matter for inquiry."

Tie-ups between Clark and Bernard Lowe, head of Cameo/Parkway Records, were detailed by the *Post*. Lowe was a vice-president of Clark's Mallard Pressing plant. Clark owned a one-third interest in Swan Records of Philadelphia, distributed by Lowe. Three of the tunes in Clark's Sea Lark Music were split copyrights with Mayland Music of which Lowe was one of the heads.

When public hearings were finally held in Washington in April 1960, Clark was the central figure. By then he had divested himself of all ownerships involving a conflict of interest. Though Rep. Peter F. Mack of Illinois called him, "Top dog in the payola field," he swore that his hands were never dirtied by play-for-pay. "I have never agreed to play a record," he stated, "in return for payment in cash or any other consideration."

What came out in the proceedings, however, was that he owned sixty songs as a publisher, most of which had come to him without any payment on his part. "Sixteen Candles" was cited as an instance of a song that he had played only four times in ten weeks. But after his January Music became part owner, he programed it twenty-seven times in less than thirteen weeks.

A songwriter named Orville Lunsford told of how his song, "American Boy" was going nowhere until he gave Mallard Pressing Corporation an order for fifty thousand records. "Almost immediately," Lunsford told the Subcommittee, "I heard my song played every other day on Clark's show." As the hearings continued, [it became clear that] Clark's music-business interests included six publishing companies, three record labels, a record pressing plant, a record distributing concern, and a firm that managed singers.

But Clark was a self-possessed and unyielding witness. Trading blows, occasionally even humorous, with committee members, he stubbornly insisted that his investments were not uncommon, improper, or illegal. He exhibited a kind of cleverness, poise, and canny cool that at the end of his testimony, led Rep. Oren Harris, the subcommittee chairman to commend him as a fine young man: "You're not the inventor of the system or even its architect. You're a product of it."

While he came out of the mess smelling like roses, though just a bit tarnished, and went on to a still-active career as "American Bandstand's" emcee, a television packager and film producer, not to mention actor, Alan Freed's path from the time of his ouster by WABC and WNEW was a depressing downcurve. Although he landed a daytime show on Station KDAY in Los Angeles, he and six others were arrested on May 20, 1960, on charges of commercial bribery. He was indicted for receiving $30,650 from six record companies whose disks he had plugged. Most tradesters felt that it was a small percentage of what Clark derived from the sale of all of his music business interest. In 1962 by which time he was spinning records at Station WQAM in Miami, Freed pleaded quilty to part of the charges and received a $300 fine and a suspended six-months sentence.

But his troubles were not over. In 1964 he was indicted for evading $47,920 in income taxes between 1957 and 1959, based on revenues which ostensibly came to him via the payola route. Less than a year later and about eleven years after he was crowned king of rock 'n' roll, he was dead of uremia. He was just forty-three years old.

More than one music business observer has suggested that the difference between Clark and Freed was the difference between

"American Bandstand's" annual advertising income of over $10 million as against Freed's $250,000. There was also the matter of Freed's image, which had kept him off network TV—he favored black artists out of respect for the basic contribution of blacks to the birth of rock 'n' roll. That he, to, was not the inventor or architect, but a product of the system, seems obvious. But resenting, as he did, the big record companies, he did not, perhaps could not, learn how to work within the system.

In a sense, he was the victim of the same prejudices and pressures that made rock 'n' roll so bitterly controversial in the 1950s. His rise and rapid fall were symptomatic of the vigor and vitality of the Big Beat, also of the tensions, confusions, and volatility of a new generation. It was a matter of their sound and the older generation's fury.

On one of his "Open End" shows, David Susskind read the lyrics of a song by Phil Spector. No music. Just the words. Susskind was trying to ridicule rock 'n' roll, and the words of "A Fine, Fine Boy" were repetitious. As he read on, Spector began drumming on the table, accenting the afterbeat with the palm of his hand.

"What you're missing is the beat," he said, as the monotony of the words began to dissolve in the pattern of the dance rhythm.

"That's why I go for that rock 'n' roll music," Chuck Berry wrote and sang. "It's got a back beat you can't lose . . ."

What a difference a decade made . . .

DISCOGRAPHY

This list of albums is oriented around the original single recordings that made up the sounds of the 1950s. Albums are arranged alphabetically by artists, chapter by chapter. The seventeen albums that precede the chapter listings are anthologies of singles by different artists. This list is arranged alphabetically by record companies and is keyed for easy reference. Digits preceding a record label indicate a more-than-one-platter set. An artist's name appears in italics and when there is no other title on the album.

ANTHOLOGIES

A 1. *History of Rhythm & Blues, The Roots 1947–52.* Atlantic SD 8161.

A 2. *History of Rhythm & Blues, The Golden Years 1953–55.* Atlantic SD 8162.

A 3. *History of Rhythm & Blues, Rock & Roll 1956–57.* Atlantic SD 8163.

A 4. *History of Rhythm & Blues, The Big Beat 1958–60.* Atlantic SD 8164.

A 5. *Country Hits of the '50s.* Capitol ST 885.

A 6. *Anthology of Rhythm and Blues,* Vol. 1. Columbia CS 9802.

A 7. *18 King Size Rhythm and Blues Hits.* Columbia CS 9467.

A 8. *The 50's Greatest Hits.* 2 Columbia G 30592.

A 9. *Rock 'N' Roll Survival.* Decca DL 75181.

A 10. *Collector's Records of the 50's and 60's.* Laurie SLP 2051.

A 11. *Solid Gold Rock 'N' Roll,* Vols. 1 and 2. Mercury SR 61371/72.

A 12. *Your Old Favorites.* Old Town OT LP 101.

A 13. *Oldies But Goodies.* Vol. 1–10. Original Sound OSR LPS 8850-60.

A 14. *Golden Goodies.* Vol. 1–19. Roulette R 25219.

A 15. *20 Original Winners.* Vol. 1. Roulette R 25249.
A 16. *This Is How It All Began.* Specialty SPS 2117.
A 17. *Rock Lives.* Sunset SUS 5281.
A 18. *The Cruisin' Series.* Increase Records.
A 19. Shanana. *The Golden Age of Rock 'n' Roll.* 2 Kama Sutra
  KSBS 2073.
A 20. *Grease.* A New 50's Rock 'n' Roll Musical. MGM 1 SE-34
  Original Cast.

1. SUMMER OF 1955

Elvis Presley. RCA LSP 1254.
Elvis. RCA LSP 1382.

2. IT'S LATER THAN YOU THINK

Call Me Madam. Decca 9022.
Kiss Me Kate. Original Cast. Columbia OL 4140.
South Pacific. Original Cast. Columbia OL 4180.
Songs by Frankie Laine. Mercury 20069.
Floyd Tillman's Greatest. RCA Victor LPM 1686.

3. MUZAK AND MISTER IN-BETWEEN

Nat "King" Cole. *Best.* Capitol SKAO 2944.
This Is Perry Como. 2 RCA VPS 6026e.
Billy Eckstine. *Golden Hits.* Mercury 60796.
Johnny Mathis. *All-Time Greatest Hits.* 2 Columbia KG 31345.
The Essential Frank Sinatra. 3 Columbia S 35842.
The Frank Sinatra Deluxe Set. 6 Capitol STFL 2814.
Frank Sinatra: A Man and His Music. 2 Reprise 1016.

4. THE BEARD

Rosemary Clooney. See A 8.
Mitch Miller. *Mitch's Greatest Hits.* Columbia CS 8638.
Mitch Miller. *Sing Along with Mitch.* Columbia CS 8004.
Guy Mitchell. *Guy's Greatest Hits.* Columbia CL 1226. Also
  see A 8.

5. THE EXCITERS

Ames Brothers. *The Ames Brothers Concert.* Coral 57031.
Gene Autry. *Country Music Hall of Fame.* Columbia CS 1035E.
Harry Belafonte. *Calypso.* RCA Victor LSP 1248.
Tony Bennett. *Tony's Greatest Hits.* Columbia CL 1229. Also
  see A 8.

Teresa Brewer. *Music, Music, Music.* Coral 57027.

Percy Faith. *All-Time Greatest Hits.* 2 Columbia KG 31588. See also A 8.

Four Aces. *Sentimental Souvenirs.* Decca 8227.

Georgia Gibbs. *Song Favorites of Georgia Gibbs.* Mercury 20114.

Joni James. *Award Winning Album.* MGM 3346. *Sings Songs of Hank Williams.* MGM S 3739.

Eartha Kitt. *That Bad Eartha.* Victor LPM 1183.

Julius La Rosa. Cadence 1007.

Mario Lanza. *Greatest Hits.* 3 RCA VCS 6192 E.

Guy Lombardo and His Royal Canadians. *Greatest Hits.* Decca 74812.

Tony Martin. *I Get Ideas.* Camden 412.

Mills Brothers. *Old Golden Favorites.* Decca 74084. *Vol. 2.* Decca 75174 E.

Patti Page. *Golden Hits.* Mercury 60495.

Les Paul and Mary Ford. *The Hit Makers.* Capitol T 416. *Paul & Ford.* Pickwick S 3122.

Edith Piaf. *Deluxe Set.* 3 Capitol DTCL 2953.

Jo Stafford. *Jo's Greatest Hits.* Columbia CL 1228.

The Weavers. *The Best of The Weavers.* 2 Decca DXSB 7173.

Hank Williams. *24 Greatest Hits.* 2 MGM 54755.

6. THE BEATS AND THE BELTERS

Eddie Fisher. *This Is Eddie Fisher.* 2 RCA Victor VPM 6069.

Frankie Laine. *Greatest Hits.* Columbia CS 8636. See also A 8.

Johnnie Ray. *Greatest Hits.* Columbia 1227. See also A 8.

9. "SH-BOOM"

The Chords. See A 2.

The Crew Cuts. *Rock 'n Roll Bash.* Mercury 20144. See A 11, Vol. 2.

10. BLUES WITH A BEAT

Louis Jordan. *Let the Good Times Roll.* Decca 8551.

11. THE BACK OF THE CHARTS

Johnny Ace. *Memorial Album.* Duke DLP 71.

Earl Bostic. *The Best of Bostic.* King 500. See A 7.

Ruth Brown. *Rock & Roll.* Atlantic 8004. See A 1, A 2.

Chester Burnett a.k.a. Howlin' Wolf. 2 Chess CH 60016.

The Clovers. *Their Greatest Recordings: The Early Years.* Atco SD 33-374. See A 1, A 2, A 3.

Fats Domino. *Sings Million Record Hits.* Imperial 12103.

The Drifters. *Their Greatest Recordings: The Early Years.* Atco SD 33-375. See A 2, A 3, A 4.

The Five Royales. See A 6, A 7.

Lowell Fulson. *Early Recordings.* Arhoolie R 2003.

Ivory Joe Hunter. *I Get That Lonesome Feeling.* MGM 3488.

B. B. King. *Blues in My Heart.* Crown 5309.

Joe Liggins and his Honeydrippers. See A 16.

Little Esther and Johnny Otis. See A 13, Vol. 9.

Clyde McPhatter. See A 2, A 3, A 4.

Percy Mayfield. See A 16.

Memphis Slim. *Messin' Around with the Blues.* King S 1082.

Roy Milton and his Solid Senders. See A 16.

The Orioles. See A 1.

Lloyd Price. *Mr. Personality.* ABC S 297.

"Big Mama" Thornton. *She's Back.* Backbeat BLP 68.

Billy Ward and the Dominoes. See A 6, A 7.

Chuck Willis. *His Greatest Recordings.* Atco SD 33-373.

12. ROCK 'N' ROLL'S SUPERPROMOTER

Alan Freed and his Orchestra. Coral 57063, 57115.

13. CONFRONTATION

Hank Ballard and the Midnighters. See A 6, A 7.

Roy Hamilton. Epic BN 26009.

Joe Turner. *His Greatest Recordings.* Atco SD 33-376.

Muddy Waters. *The Best of Muddy Waters.* Chess 1427.

Otis Williams and the Charms. See A 6, A 7.

14. BLACK ORIGINALS AND WHITE COVERS

LaVern Baker. *Her Greatest Recordings.* Atco SD 33-372.

Pat Boone. *Ain't That A Shame.* Dot DLP 25573. *Pat's Greatest Hits.* Dot S 25071.

Ray Charles. *Rock and Roll.* Atlantic 8006. See A 2, A 4.

Bo Diddley. *16 All Time Greatest Hits.* Checker 2980. *Boss Man.* Checker S 3007.

The El Dorados. See A 14, Vol. 11.

Little Walter. *The Best of Little Walter.* Checker S 3004.

Little Willie John. See A 6, A 7.

The Robins. See A 3.

15. "ROCK AROUND THE CLOCK"

Chuck Berry. *Chuck Berry's Golden Decade.* 2 Chess LPS 1514 D.
Bill Haley. *Rock Around the Clock.* Decca 29214.
The Platters. *Golden Goodies.* Mercury MG 20511. *Encore of Golden Hits.* Mercury S 60243.

16. THE GOD OF R 'N' R ARRIVES

Elvis Presley. *Elvis Golden Records.* RCA LSP 1707. *50,000,000 Fans Can't Be Wrong, Elvis' Gold Records,* Vol. 2. RCA LSP 2075.

18. TEEN-AGE ERUPTION

James Brown. *Please, Please, Please.* King 909. See A 7.
The Cadillacs. See A 14, Vol. 3, 5. See A 15.
Johnny Cash. *Original Golden Hits.* 2 Sun 100 E. *Living Legend.* 2 Sun 118 E.
The Coasters. *Their Greatest Recordings, Early Years.* Atco SD 33-371.
Bill Doggett. *Honky Tonk.* King 531. See A 6, A 7.
George Hamilton IV. *On Campus.* ABC Paramount 220.
Little Richard. *Here's Little Richard.* Specialty 2100. *Well, Alright!* Specialty S 2136 E.
Frankie Lymon and the Teenagers. See A 14, Vol. 1, 2.
Carl Perkins. *Original Golden Hits.* Sun 111E, 112. *Blue Suede Shoes.* Sun 112 E.
Gene Vincent. *Greatest.* Capitol DKAO 380.

19. THE AMERICAN BANDSTAND

Sonny James. *Best.* Capitol ST 2615. *Young Love.* Camden S 2140.
Dick Clark. *20 Years of Rock 'n' Roll.* Buddah BDS 51332.

20. THE AUDACIOUS AMATEURS—AND THE COUNTRY ROCKERS

The Bobbettes. See A 14, Vol. 3.
Jimmy Bowen. See A 14, Vol. 9.
Duane Eddy. *Have Twangy Guitar.* Jamie S 3000. *16 Greatest Hits.* Jamie S 3026.
Everly Brothers. *Greatest Hits.* Epic BGP 350 E. *Wake Up Little Susie.* Harmony 11304.
Bobby Helms. *Fraulein.* Harmony 11209. *My Special Angel.* Vocalion 73874 E.
Buddy Holly. *Best.* 2 Coral 7CX 8. *Story.* Coral 757279. See A 9.

Bill Justis. *Raunchy*. Sun 109 E.
Buddy Knox. See A 14, Vol. 9.
Jerry Lee Lewis. *Original Golden Hits*, Vol. 1, 2, 3. Sun 102 E,
103 E, 128 E.
Sal Mineo. *Sal*. Epic LN 3405.
The Rays. See A 14, Vol. 16.
Tommy Sands. *Steady Date*. Capitol T 848. *Sing Boy Sing* (sound-
track). Capitol T 929.
Shirley and Lee. See A 13.
The Tune Weavers. See A 13, Vol. 10.
Link Wray. Polydor 244064.

21. WE'RE SO YOUNG—AND THEY'RE SO OLD

Paul Anka. ABC S 371.
Eddie Cochran. *Summertime Blues*. Sun 5153.
Eddie Cochran. 2 United Artists UAS 9959.
Sam Cooke. 2 *Sides*. Specialty S 2119 E. *Hits of 50's*. RCA LSP
2236.
Del Vikings. See A 11, Vol. 1, 2. See A 13, Vol. 3.
The Diamonds. See A 11, Vol. 1, 2.
Ricky Nelson. *Million Sellers*. Imperial S 12232.
Mickey and Sylvia. *New Sounds*. Vik LX 1102.
Della Reese. *Best*. Jubilee S 5002. *Classic Della*. RCA LSP 2419.
Jimmie Rodgers. *Yours Truly*. Roulette 42006. See A 14, Vol. 8, 9.
Larry Williams. See A 14, Vol. 14.

23. GOING STEADY

Frankie Avalon. Chancellor 5001. See A 13, Vol. 10.
The Champs. *Go Champs, Go!* Challenge 601.
The Chordettes. Cadence 3001. *Listen*. Columbia CL 956.
Danny and the Juniors. *Million or More*. ABC S 216.
Four Preps. Capitol T 994.
Connie Francis. *Rock 'n' Roll Million Sellers*. MGM S 3794.
Bobby Freeman. *Get in the Swim*. Josie 4007.
Laurie London. Capitol T 10169.
The Silhouettes. See A 14, Vol. 7.

24. HULA HOOPS, CHIPMUNKS, AND THE KINGSTON TRIO

The Big Bopper. See A 11, Vol. 1.
The Chipmunks, David Seville. *Original Golden Greats*, Vol. 4.
Liberty S 7574.
Cozy Cole. Savoy 14010.

Bobby Darin. *This Is Darin.* Atco S 115.
Bobby Day. See A 13, Vol. 5, 9.
Dion and the Belmonts. See A 10. Also A 13, Vol. 6. A 14, Vol. 7.
Tommy Edwards. MGM GAS 123 E. See A 13, Vol. 7.
The Elegants. See A 13, Vol. 5.
The Kingston Trio. Capitol D 7996. *Tom Dooley/Scarlet Ribbons.* 2 Capitol STBB 513.
Little Anthony and the Imperials. See A 13, Vol. 3. Also A 14, Vol. 10.
Domenico Modugno. *Nel Blu Dipinto di Blu (Volare).* Decca 8808.
The Olympics. See A 13, Vol. 10.
The Playmates. See A 14, Vol. 7.
Perez Prado. *Hits.* Victor LSP 2104.
Harry Simeone Chorale. *Climb Every Mountain.* 20th Fox 4169.
Conway Twitty. *Hits.* MGM S 3849.

25. WHAT A DIFFERENCE A DECADE MAKES

Brook Benton. *Golden Hits.* Mercury 60607.
The Browns. RCA LSP 2260.
Ray Charles. *The Greatest.* Atlantic 8054 E.
The Drifters. *Golden Hits.* Atlantic S 8153.
Johnny Horton. *Makes History.* Columbia C 58269.
Brenda Lee, *10 Golden Years.* Decca 74757.
Bobby Rydell. *Biggest Hits,* Vol. 1, 2. Cameo 1009, 1028.
Neil Sedaka. *Sings His Greatest Hits.* RCA Victor LSP 2627.
Nina Simone. Philips 600148.
Ritchie Valens. See A 13, Vol. 7.
Sarah Vaughan. *Golden Hits.* Mercury 60645. *Golden Goodies.* Mercury MG 20511.
Dinah Washington. *What A Diff'rence.* Mercury 60158.
Jackie Wilson. *Greatest Hits.* Brunswick BL 754185.

SELECTED BIBLIOGRAPHY

Belz, Carl. *The Story of Rock*. Oxford University Press, 1969.

Gillett, Charlie. *The Sound of the City*. The Rise of Rock and Roll. Outerbridge and Dienstfrey, 1970.

Goldberg, Joe. *Jazz Masters of the 50's*. The Macmillan Company, 1965.

Gruen, John. *The Party's Over Now*. Reminiscences of the Fifties— New York's Artists, Writers, Muscians, and Their Friends. The Viking Press, Inc., 1972.

Guralnick, Peter. *Feel Like Going Home*. Portraits in Blues and Rock 'n' Roll. Outerbridge and Dienstfrey, 1971.

Laing, Dave. *Buddy Holly*. The Macmillan Company, 1971.

Malone, Bill C. *Country Music, U.S.A.* University of Texas Press, 1968.

Millar, Bill. *The Drifters*. The Rise and Fall of the Black Vocal Group. The Macmillian Company, 1971.

Passman, Arnold. *The Deejays*. The Macmillan Company, 1971.

Rohde, H. Kandy, ed. *The Gold of Rock & Roll 1955–1967*. Edited with special annotations. Arbor House, 1970.

Shapiro, Nat, ed. *Popular Music*. An Annotated Index of American Popular Songs. Vol. 1, 1950–1959. Adrian Press, 1964.

Shaw, Arnold. *The Rock Revolution*. What's Happening in Today's Music. Crowell-Collier Press, 1969.

Shaw, Arnold. *The World of Soul*. Black America's Contribution to the Pop Music Scene. Cowles Book Company, 1970.

INDEX

ABC-Paramount Records, 156, 195, 196, 218, 219
Abramson, Herb, 78, 83, 92, 144
Academy Awards, 8, 22, 23, 25, 33, 36, 37, 38, 123, 127, 208, 219, 232
Accents, the, 70
Ace, Johnny, 93–94, 116, 122, 187, 227, 239
Ackerman, Paul, 218–19, 272, 273
Acuff, Roy, 55
Aladdin Records, 82, 84, 103, 135, 168, 209, 222
Alberts, Al, 36, 41, 242
"All the Way," 23, 208, 219, 235
Allen, Fred, 17
Allen, Rex, 43
Allen, Steve, 151, 170, 241, 271
"American Bandstand," 63, 143, 175–81, 183, 220, 225, 239–40, 241, 247, 279, 281
Ames Bros., 16, 34, 42, 59, 209, 251
Anderson, Leroy, 17, 39
Anka, Paul, 187, 194–97, 200, 228, 234, 257, 266
Annette, 196
Anthony, Ray, 40, 42, 262
"Anytime," 39, 50, 51, 53
Apollo Records, 82, 84, 102, 103
Apollo Theatre, 88, 89, 103, 119, 226
Aristocrat Records, 117
Arlen, Harold, 250
Armen, Kay, 30
Armstrong, Louis, 47, 96, 246, 254
Arnold, Eddy, 2, 6, 10, 212, 253
ASCAP, 91, 92, 115, 157, 158, 211, 212, 222, 229, 236, 243, 279
"At the Hop," 208, 218, 251, 279
Atco Records, 157, 233, 234
Atlantic Records, 74, 78, 82, 84, 86, 91, 92, 94, 102, 116, 118, 128, 129, 135, 144, 164, 206, 218
Auric, Georges, 43
Autry, Gene, 35, 37, 157, 212
Avalon, Frankie, 143, 177–78, 183, 220, 252, 255, 256, 266

Baby Cortez, 242
Bacharach, Burt, 32, 242–43, 259
Bagdassarian, Ross, 30, 226, 248
Bailey, Pearl, 156

Baker, LaVern, 3, 79, 85, 125, 126, 129, 205, 233, 256, 261
"Ballad of Davy Crockett," 123
Ballard, Hank, 117, 118
"Barry Gray Show," 212
Bartholomew, Dave, 95, 250
Basie, Count, 83, 86, 91, 99, 101, 110, 202
Bass, Ralph, 103
"Battle of New Orleans, The," 252–53
Baxter, Les, 33, 114, 173
Beach Party, 221
Beatles, the, 95, 96, 130, 145, 150, 165, 187, 189, 196, 197, 223, 226, 239, 245, 249
Bee, Molly, 164
Belafonte, Harry, 43, 171, 172, 200
Belting, 45–60
Belvin, Jesse, 124
"Be My Love," 37
Bennett, Boyd, & his Rockets, 125, 128, 165
Bennett, Tony, 4, 21, 29, 30, 37, 59, 64, 114, 237
Benton, Brook, 250, 260
Berle, Milton, 149, 151
Berlin, Irving, 20, 51, 157, 220
Berry, Chuck, 81, 82, 100, 108, 122, 132, 138, 144–47, 153, 163, 164, 165, 178–79, 182, 187, 194, 200, 208, 229, 230, 236, 239, 281
"Big Bad John," 254
Big Bands, 18, 22, 62, 71, 87, 156
Big Bopper, 246, 255
Big Maceo, 84
Big Maybelle, 157, 229
Bihari, Jules, Sol, and Joe, 98, 99
Billy and Lillie, 178, 219
Biondi, Dick, 154, 263
Birdland, 35
Black, Bill, 123
Black & White Records, 83
Blackwell, Bumps, 200
Blackwell, Otis, 147, 189, 221
Bleyer, Archie, 41, 114, 188, 216, 217, 218
Blackboard Jungle, The, 109, 122, 136, 138
Block, Martin, 61, 62, 176, 220, 248
"Blue Suede Shoes," 164, 205
Blues, 46, 116, 117, 135, 138, 233
"Blue Tango," 17, 35
BMI. See Broadcast Music, Inc.

Bo Diddley, 122, 126, 130–31, 132–34, 186, 238
Bob and Ray, 63
Bob B. Sox, 249
Bobbettes, the, 183
Boogie woogie, 87, 93, 139, 191, 243
Boone, Pat, 12, 89, 116, 126–27, 129, 152, 161, 162, 164, 173, 182, 193, 197, 200, 220, 251, 262, 266
Bop, 119
Bostic, Earl, 81, 93
Boswell, Connee, 121
Bowen, Jimmy, 185–86
Boyd, Jimmy, 40
Bradshaw, Tiny, 81
Brand, Oscar, 29
Brando, Marlon, 134, 180
Braun, Bob, 248
Brecht, Bertolt, 254
Brenston, Jackie, 93, 137
Brewer, Teresa, 34, 44, 59, 121, 201
Brill Building, 15, 44, 216, 237
Britt, Elton, 11
Broadcast Music, Inc., 91, 92, 157, 158, 211, 212, 222, 228, 229, 279
Bronze Peacock, 103
Brooklyn Paramount Theatre, 109, 147, 242
Brown, Charles, 84, 95, 100, 103, 135
Brown, James, 163
Brown, Nappy, 4
Brown, Roy, 81, 106, 162
Brown, Ruth, 78, 81, 82, 85, 86, 91, 116, 123, 157
Brown, Ted, & the Redhead, 63
Browns, the, 252
Brubeck, Dave, 142
Brunswick Records, 186, 233
Bryant, Boudleaux and Felice, 188, 250
Bullet Records, 98, 99
Burke, Sonny, 123
Burton, Robert J., 228, 229
Busch, Lou, 35
Bye Bye Birdie, 238, 246, 256
"Bye Bye Love," 188, 199
Byrnes, Ed, 183, 262

Cadence Records, 41, 184, 188, 216, 217, 218, 223
Cadets, the, 167
Cadillacs, the, 167, 227, 257
Call Me Madam, 17
Calloway, Cab, 47, 246
Calypso, 99, 171–72, 205
Cameo-Parkway Records, 178, 184, 279
Cannon, Feddy, 178, 257
Cantor, Eddie, 51, 81

Capitol Lounge, 56
Capitol Records, 22, 23, 27, 35, 39, 44, 49, 56, 119, 122, 166, 195, 224, 227, 245
Cardinals, the, 118
Carlton, Joe, 27, 50, 125, 214
Carmichael, Hoagy, 47, 48
Carnegie Hall, 155
Carr, Cathy, 128
Carr, Leroy, 84
Carroll, David, & his Orchestra, 124
Carson, Jenny Lou, 120
Carson, Mindy, 29, 164
Cash, Johnny, 79, 165–66, 190, 193, 208, 231, 245
Cash Box magazine, 57
Cavanaugh, Dave, 56
Celler House Anti-Trust Commission, 157, 211, 224
Chacksfield, Frank, 42
Champs, the, 223
Chan, Charlie, 207
Chancellor Records, 178, 183, 184, 186, 220, 256
Chaplin, Charles, 42
Charles, Ray, 163, 191, 230, 233, 260–61
Charles, Ray ("Your Hit Parade"), 68–69, 71
Charms, the, 118, 119, 126, 127, 128
Chase, Lincoln, 115
Checker, Chubby, 117
Checker Records, 91, 131, 222
Cheers, the, 134
"Cherry Pink and Apple Blossom White," 123
Chess, Leonard, 179
Chess Records, 79, 82, 87, 93, 95, 108, 117, 133, 138, 145, 222
Chessler, Deborah, 89
Chipmunks, the, 30, 248–49, 251
"Chitlin' circuit," 96, 103, 130
Chordettes, the, 31, 217, 218
Chords, the, 74, 75, 76, 77, 119
Clanton, Jimmy, 239
Clark, Dick, 63, 111, 142, 176–81, 183, 184, 220, 221, 222, 223, 225, 227, 228, 239–40, 241, 242, 247, 256, 257, 265–66, 271, 272, 274, 279, 280
Clayton, Bob, 63
Cleftones, the, 167
Clement, Jack, 188, 191
Clooney, Rosemary, 4, 29, 30, 36, 39, 59, 91, 114, 121, 172
Clovers, the, 78, 79, 81, 92, 106, 116, 227
Coasters, the, 167, 206–208, 234, 241, 261, 266
Cochran, Eddie, 166, 198–99

Cole, Cozy, 246
Cole, Nat "King," 1, 21, 24–25, 33, 44, 48, 80, 82, 84, 90, 96, 103, 114, 119, 129, 143, 146, 185, 200, 201, 209, 212, 227, 251
Collins, Al "Jazzbo," 63
Collins, Dorothy, 69, 70, 71, 266
Columbia Records, 22, 25, 27, 28, 29, 38, 56, 92, 115, 124, 141, 158, 164, 206, 221, 222, 229, 248
Commodore Record Shop, 248
Como, Perry, 2, 12, 16, 19–21, 25, 43, 44, 59, 68, 73, 74, 80, 87, 113, 114, 123, 124, 128, 165, 171, 172, 182, 209, 219, 221, 227, 251
Cooke, Sam, 101, 130, 200–230, 248, 259
Cooley, Spade, 142
Copa, the, 21, 25, 45, 52, 194, 255
Copas, Cowboy, 4, 17
Coral Records, 38, 120, 121, 124, 128, 131, 170, 201, 220
Corey, Jill, 70
Cornel, Don, 21, 39, 59
Coronets, the, 108
Costa, Don, 195
Country & Western, 8, 9, 10, 14, 17, 30, 40, 43, 44, 114, 122, 126, 136, 137, 140, 142, 152, 165, 166, 184, 188, 229, 230, 253, 254
Cousin Lee, 139
Cover syndrome, 124–26
Craft, Morty, 73–74
Craig, Francis, 243–44
Crests, the, 258
Crew Cuts, the, 4, 64, 76, 114, 119, 120, 124, 131
Crewe, Bob, 184, 257
Crickets, the, 186, 255
Crosby, Bing, 4, 16, 17, 26, 34, 59, 67, 96, 127, 157, 158, 182, 202, 212
Crosby, John, 151, 256
Crows, the, 77, 118
Crudup, Arthur "Big Boy," 44, 79
"Cry," 52, 56, 58, 93
Crystal Caverns, 85
Crystals, the, 249
Curtis, King, 207

Dale, Alan, 21, 109
Damone, Vic, 21, 29, 50, 209
Dances: Bunny Hop, 40; calypso, 99, 171–72, 175, 205; cha-cha-cha, 175, 243; chalypso, 175; Chicken, 134; Circle, 179; Dish Rag, 134; Fish, 179; Hucklebuck, 90; Lindy Hop, 117, 155; Madison,

179; Mambo, 99, 123, 232; rumba, 123; Slop, 134, 179; Stroll, 179, 205
Daniels, Billy, 59, 259
Danny & the Juniors, 178, 208, 215, 219
Darin, Bobby, 178, 187, 194, 233–34, 239, 252, 254
David, Hal, 243, 259
Davis, Eddie "Lockjaw," 88
Daxis, Maxwell, 99, 101
Davis, Miles, 58, 119
Davis, Sammy, Jr., 194, 213
Day, Bobby, 244
Day, Doris, 29, 33, 85, 114, 173, 237, 251
de Mille, Agnes, 179–80
Dean, James, 112, 170–71, 180, 187
Dean, Jimmy, 254
Del Vikings, 209
Denny, Jim, 2–3
Desmond, Johnny, 8, 21, 42, 70, 124, 243, 266
Diamonds, the, 168, 179, 200, 205, 208
Ding Dongs, the, 233
Dion & the Belmonts, 241–42, 255
Dixieland Jazz, 48, 58, 87, 139
Dixon, Willie, 131
Dr. Jive, 155, 176
Doggett, Bill, 173
Domino, Antoine "Fats," 35, 71, 87, 90, 95, 96, 100, 136, 143, 153, 157, 162, 164, 173, 192–93, 194, 197, 200, 203, 233, 250
Dominoes, the, 78, 102, 106, 116
Don't Knock the Rock, 109, 138
Dorsey, Jimmy, 158, 209
Dorsey, Tommy, 11, 99, 233, 242
Dot Records, 126, 128, 152, 104, 100, 100, 184, 209, 241, 244
Down Beat magazine, 62, 63
Dragnet, 42
Draper, Rusty, 171, 213
Dreyfus, Max, 143
Drifters, the, 78, 93, 102, 115, 116, 157, 261–62
Driftwood, Jimmy, 253
Dubs, the, 238
Duke, Vernon, 32
Duke Records, 93
Duning, George, 173
Dupree, "Champion" Jack, 108
Dylan, Bob, 145, 182, 189

"Earth Angel," 118, 124
Easy Listening, 26, 173
Eckstine, Billy, 21, 25, 33, 119, 146, 202
"Ed Sullivan Show," 31, 151, 155, 165, 241

"Eddie Cantor Show," 17
Eddy, Duane, 193, 250, 262
Edwards, Sherman, 50, 125, 199, 259
Edwards, Tom, 159, 264
Edwards, Tommy, 243
Eisenhower, Dwight, 19, 26, 59, 112, 149, 175, 276
El Dorados, 122, 127, 131
Elegants, the, 237, 240
Ellington, Duke, 99
Ember Records, 131, 167, 219
End Records, 106, 118, 168, 238
Enright, Dan, 277
Ertegun, Ahmet, 74, 78, 83–86, 92, 116, 118, 206, 234
Essex Records, 38, 44, 93, 132, 137, 140
Everly Brothers, 187–88, 200, 227, 229, 250, 257
"Every Day I Have the Blues," 91, 95, 99, 101

Fabian, 143, 177, 183, 256, 262, 266
Fain, Sammy, 232
Faith, Percy, 17, 37, 40, 43, 212
Falcons, the, 118, 257
Federal Communications Commission, 275, 276
Federal Records, 93, 117, 132, 135
Feller, Sid, 195
Fender Bass, 193
Fiestas, the, 257
Fifty-second Street, 24, 35, 65
Fillmore West, 101
Finan, Joe, 275, 276
Finch, Dee, 65
Fisher, Eddie, 15, 21, 22, 39, 42, 51–52, 53, 59, 114, 125, 171, 172, 213, 214, 252, 266
Fitzgerald, Ella, 119, 131, 171, 173, 202, 234
Five Keys, 119, 122, 227
Five Royales, 102, 116
Flame Show Bar, 53, 201, 205
Flamingos, the, 118, 127
Fleetwoods, the, 252, 257–58
Flower Drum Song, 262
"Flying Saucer, The," 169
Foley, Red, 4, 34, 137, 141, 158, 191, 245
Folk song revival, 232
Fontane Sisters, 125, 128, 129, 168
Ford, Art, 231
Four Aces, 36, 41, 59, 114, 143, 144, 242
Four Fellows, 4, 131
Four Freshmen, 251
Four Lads, 29, 30, 56, 59, 114, 199, 236, 251
Four Preps, 226
Four Tunes, 116
Francis, Connie, 178, 220,

223, 234, 255, 257
Fratto, Russ, 108, 145
Freberg, Stan, 42, 77, 80
Freed, Alan, 35, 88, 103, 104–11, 116, 117, 120, 124, 127, 129, 130, 138, 141, 145, 154, 155–56, 172, 176, 180, 222, 228, 231, 236, 242, 248, 276, 280, 281
Freeman, Bobby, 231
Friendly Persuasion, 159
From Here to Eternity, 22, 197
Fulson, Lowell, 91, 96, 99

Gabler, Milt, 27, 141, 142, 213, 248
Gaillard, Slim, 48, 49
Gale, Sunny, 38, 39, 131
Gallagher, Eddie, 63, 65
Garner, Erroll, 85, 202
Gavin, Bill, 277
Gaylords, the, 114
Gee Records, 167, 168
Gene & Eunice, 124, 168
Gershwin, George and Ira, 260
Giant, 170
Gibbs, Georgia, 2, 3, 39, 59, 125, 126, 171, 214, 240–41
Gibson, Don, 166, 230
Gigi, 232
Gilkyson, Terry, 28, 209
Gillespie, Dizzy, 58
Girl Can't Help It, The, 100, 162
Gladiolas, the, 200
Glaser, Joe, 141
Glenn, Darrell, 43
Glory Records, 4, 129, 131, 171
Glover, Henry, 117, 163
Godfrey, Arthur, 41, 98, 265
Goldner, George, 168, 238
Gone Records, 168
Goodman, Benny, 61, 62, 87, 155, 159, 212, 246
"Goodnight Irene," 33, 65, 158
Gordy, Berry, 260
Gorme, Eydie, 131
Gospel music, 102, 162, 202, 226, 230, 258, 261
Gould, Jack, 151
Gracie, Charlie, 184, 208
Grady, Joe, 63
Grammy, 90
Grand Ole Opry, 1, 2, 140, 141, 165, 166, 188
Grant, Earl, 242
Grant, Gogi, 173
Grean, Charles, 27, 34, 240
Great Caruso, The, 36
"Great Pretender, The," 12, 144, 173
Green, Abel, 43, 269
Green, Al, 55, 205
Greenfield, Howard, 223, 256, 257
Grevatt, Ren, 70

Griffin Brothers, 127
Grossinger's Hotel, 51
Guthrie, Woody, 33
Gypsy, 262

Haig, 58
Haley, Bill, 12, 31, 44, 58, 71, 81, 82, 93, 100, 109, 112, 116, 117, 119, 120, 122, 123, 136–43, 160, 164, 173, 203, 208, 213
Hamblen, Stuart, 14, 114
Hamilton, George, IV, 166, 208, 235
Hamilton, Roy, 59, 119–20, 230
Hampton, Lionel, 83, 84, 173, 259
Happenings, the, 168
Hardin, Louis "Moondog," 107
Harlem charts, 35, 49, 87
Harmonicats, the, 62
Harris, Phil, 34
Harris, Thurston, 244
Harris, Wynonie "Blues," 81, 106
Harrison, Thurston, 209
Harrison, Wilbert, 261
Hart, Lorenz "Larry," 15
"Have Gun Will Travel," 175
Hawkins, "Screamin" Jay, 173
Hawthorne, Jim, 264
Hayes, Bill, 123
Hayes, Edgar, 48
Hayes, Richard, 28, 274
Hayman, Richard, 42
Haynes, Dick, 61, 224
Hazelwood, Lee, 193
"Heartbreak Hotel," 150, 173, 205, 228
Heath, Ted, 160
Helms, Bobby, 184
Henderson, Jocko, 176
"Hey There," 114
Heywood, Eddie, 173
Hibbler, Al, 59, 120
"High Hopes," 23
"High Noon," 38, 46
Hilliard, Jimmy, 27
Hilltoppers, the, 209, 227
Hit Parade, Your, 13, 36, 67–72, 77, 113, 175, 180, 220, 251, 266
Holiday, Billie, 15, 24, 48, 53, 54, 90, 202, 204, 266
Holly, Buddy, 81, 186–87, 199, 233, 234, 246, 255
Hollywood Flames, 244
Hollywood Ten, 17
Holmes, Leroy, 114
Homer and Jethro, 42, 55
"Honky Tonk," 173, 174, 205
Honor Roll of Hits, Billboard's, 3, 11, 28, 30, 34, 39, 44, 77, 134, 137, 145, 150, 157, 168, 184, 199, 200, 218, 220, 221, 224, 227, 234, 236, 237, 240, 243, 244, 248, 255, 259

Hooker, John Lee, 134
Hope, Bob, 43, 277–78
Horn, Bob, 63, 142, 176, 177, **225**
Horton, Johnny, 253
"Hound Dog," 103, 135, 151, 173, 205, 214, 235
Hound Dog Man, 183
House of Wax, 51
Houston Juvenile Delinquency and Crime Commission, 115, 117
Howard, Don, 38
Howard, Eddy, 39
Howard Theatre, 83
"How High the Moon," 37, 42, 58
Howlin' Wolf, 87, 94–95
Hubbard, Eddie, 62, 63
Hugo and Luigi, 75, 185, 198, 203, 231, 240
Hula Hoop craze, 240–41
Humes, Helen, 84
Hunt, Pee Wee, 49
Hunter, Ivory Joe, 54, 79, 91, 163–64
Hunter, Tab, 183, 184
Hyman, Dick, 173

"I Believe," 43, 46
Impalas, the, 257, 258
Imperial Records, 35, 82, 87, 129, 197, 241, 249
Impressions, the, 90
Ink Spots, 81, 92, 118, 173
Isley Brothers, 108, 261
"It's All in the Game," 70
Ives, Burl, 17, 209

Jackie Gleason's Stage Show, 156
Jacks, the, 168
Jackson, Bullmoose, 87
Jackson, Mahalia, 202, 204
Jackson, Stonewall, 253
Jacobs, Dick, 213
Jailhouse Rock, 215
Jamboree, 184, 186
James, Etta, 125, 126
James, Joni, 38, 40, 44
James, Sonny, 183, 208
Jarvis, Al, 49, 61, 62, 176
Jayhawks, the, 118
Jenkins, Gordon, 16, 33
Johnny and the Hurricanes, 258
"Johnny B. Goode," 230, 236
Johnson, Betty, 240
Johnson, Buddy, 81, 108
Jolson, Al, 46, 47, 52, 81, 190, 269
Jones, George, 246
Jones, Spike, 41
Jordan, Louis, 64, 81–82, 83, 84, 96, 100, 137, 139, 142, 173, 213
Josie Records, 167, 276
Joyce, Jolly, 109, 141
Jubilee Records, 43, 77, 82, 118, 170, 201, 203, 276
Juke Box Jury, 77, 128

Justis, Bill, 193, 208

Kallen, Kitty, 73, 74, 113, 114
Kapp, Dave, 27
Karas, Anton, 33
Kaye, Sammy, 17, 155, 212
Kelly, Grace, 38, 109
Kelly's Stable, 24
Kenton, Stan, 85, 142
Kern, Jerome, 143, 224, 261
Kerouac, Jack, 59
Kessler, Danny, 54, 56
Khrushchev, Nikita, 252
King, B. B., 81, 87, 91, 93, 95–102, 103, 143, 191
King, Pee Wee, 38, 42, 164
King and I, The, 262
King Creole, 233
King Records, 82, 91, 103, 106, 117, 118, 125, 128, 135, 163, 174, 222, 274
Kingston Trio, 244–45, 253, 262
Kiss Me Kate, 16
Kitt, Eartha, 42
KLAC, 61, 62, 222, 224
Klavan and Finch, 63
Knox, Buddy, 185–86, 200
"Kukla, Fran and Ollie," 17

Ladd, Alan, 13
Laine, Frankie, 17, 21, 28, 29, 38, 43. 45, 46–50, 59, 96, 243
Lake, Veronica, 170
Lanin, Lester, 220
Lanson, Snooky, 69, 70
Lanza, Mario, 21, 36, 37, 143
La Rosa, Julius, 41, 265
"Late Show," 40, 175
"Lawdy Miss Clawdy," 95, 205
Leadbelly, 33, 95
Lecuona, Ernesto, 1
Lee, Brenda, 257
Lee, Peggy, 130, 163, 234, 237, 251
Leiber and Stoller, 92, 103, 134–35, 147, 167, 182, 206–208, 214, 223, 234, 249, 261–62, 266
Lennon, John, 164, 182, 188, 189, 249
Leonetti, Tommy, 70, 271–72
Lerner and Lowe, 232
Les Compagnons de la Chanson, 255
Les Paul and Mary Ford, 37, 43, 276
"Let Me Go, Lover," 120
"Let the Good Times Roll," 168
Lewis, Jerry Lee, 110, 161, 188–93, 200, 214, 220, 231, 245
Lewis, Joe E., 194, 255
Lewis, Smiley, 12, 128
Lewis, Ted, 184
Liberty Records, 198, 213,

226, 244
Liggins, Jimmy, and his Drops of Joy, 90
Liggins, Joe, and his Honeydrippers, 89
Lindy's, 11, 28, 62, 169, 268
Lip-sync, 179, 236
Little Anthony and the Imperials, 178, 238, 274
"Little Drummer Boy, The," 250
Little Esther, 85, 90, 103, 106, 135, 238
Little Richard, 12, 59, 87, 96, 100, 101, 120, 126, 127, 138, 161–63, 165, 189, 193, 198, 200, 209–10, 233, 236, 259
"Little Things Mean a Lot," 73
Little Walter, 122, 131
Little Willie John, 122, 130, 163, 237
"Lollipop," 31, 216–18, 251
Lombardo, Guy, 17, 33, 62, 65, 157, 227
London, Julie, 42
London, Laurie, 224, 226
London Records, 65, 276
"Lonely Boy," 194, 195–96, 257
"Long Tall Sally," 126, 127, 152, 162
Lopez, Vincent, 269
Lor, Denise, 121
Lorenz, George "Hound Dog," 194, 235
Loudermilk, John, 166, 198
Louisiana Hayride, 10, 123, 165, 253
"Love Is a Many-Splendored Thing," 8, 123, 232
"Love Letters in the Sand," 200
Lowe, Bernie, 184, 276, 279
Lowe, Jim, 126, 164, 209
Lubinsky, Herman, 4
"Lucille," 96, 102
Lucy, Autherine, 149
Luke, Robin, 244
Lulu Belle and Scotty, 139
Lymon, Frankie, 110, 168, 194, 238
Lynn, Vera, 39

MacArthur, Douglas, 13
McCarthy, Joseph, 13, 17, 46, 113, 175
McDevitt, Clyde, Skiffle Group, 213
McDonald, Skeets, 44
McGhee, Stick, 85
McGuire Sisters, 59, 124, 220
Mack, Peter F., 180
"Mack the Knife," 252, 254
McKenzie, Ed, 63, 64, 263
McKenzie, Gisele, 69, 70
McLendon, Gordon, 66
McNeely, Big Jay, 88
McPhatter, Clyde, 78, 86, 93, 102, 250, 256, 260
McRae, Carmen, 204

McRae, Gordon, 17
McVea, Jack, 83
Maddox Brothers and Rose, 55
Magid, Lee, 203, 204, 205
Make Believe Ballroom, 49, 176
Mancini, Henry, 262
Mann, Kal, 184
Mantovani, 40, 64, 262
Marais, Josef, 29
Marcucci, Bob, 178, 183, 184
Marigolds, the, 128
Markham, Pigmeat, 83
Marks, Edward B., Music Corp., 1, 3, 4, 118, 125, 129, 131, 132, 217
Marshall, Jerry, 151
Marterie, Ralph, 44, 114, 137
Martin, Dean, 11, 21, 41, 114, 173, 194, 227, 236
Martin, Roberta 202
Martin, Tony, 33, 124
Martin, Vince, 171
Martino, Al, 39, 41
Mathis, Johnny, 25–26, 29, 199–200, 226, 232, 263
"Maverick," 175
Maxin, Arnold, 213
"Maybellene," 108, 126, 145
Mayfield, Percy, 90, 182
Me and Juliet, 43
Meditations, the, 202
Memphis Slim, 91, 99
Mercer, Johnny, 26, 39
Mercury Records, 8, 27, 28, 29, 38, 49, 75, 89, 118, 121, 124, 126, 128, 168, 170, 179, 249
Merman, Ethel, 17
Merrill, Bob, 28, 29
Mexican Hayride, 157
Meyerson, Harry, 27
MGM Records, 30, 33, 40, 63, 91, 102, 114, 116, 131, 155, 159, 164, 170, 213, 223, 230, 243
Mickey and Sylvia, 205
Midnighters, the, 116, 117, 118
Milburn, Amos, 84
Miller, Dave, 38, 137, 140, 141
Miller, Howard, 63, 273
Miller, Mitch, 8, 27–31, 40, 45, 54, 56, 57, 120, 121, 124, 141, 155, 158, 173, 199, 212, 213, 221, 222, 235, 262
Millinder, Lucky, 90, 108, 117, 127, 137
Mills Brothers, 39, 81, 92, 200
Milton, Roy, and his Solid Senders, 90
Mineo, Sal, 112, 178, 183
Mitchell, Guy, 21, 29, 59, 200, 243
Modern Records, 98, 135, 222
Modugno, Domenico, 236

"Moldy Fig," 58
"Mona Lisa," 25
Monroe, Marilyn, 100
Monroe, Vaughn, 17, 96
"Moon Dog Coronation Ball," 107, 116
"Moon Dog Rock 'n' Roll House Party, The," 35, 106
Mooney, Art, 18, 33, 63, 170
"Moonglow and the Theme from Picnic," 173
Moonglows, the, 120, 125
Moore, Scotty, 123
Morgan, Jane, 209
Mormon Tabernacle Choir, 254
Morris, Joe, 84, 86
Morse, Ella Mae, 39
Most Happy Fella, The, 168
Muddy Waters, 87, 94, 117, 133, 146
Mullican, Moon, 191
Murray the K, 233, 239, 275
Music City, 2
Music Man, The, 262
"Music, Music, Music," 34, 65
My Fair Lady, 262

Nader, Richard, 139, 143, 147
Nashville, 1, 2, 3, 4, 9, 34, 38, 186, 187, 223, 257
Nathan, Syd, 117, 118, 274
National Records, 17, 82, 118
Neal, Bob, 6, 9, 10, 122–23, 191
Nelson, Ricky, 197, 199, 200, 232, 239, 250, 256, 257, 262
Nervous Norvus, 169
Newborn, Phineas, 99
Newman, Jimmy, 127
Newsome, Gil, 63
Niagara, Joe, 275
Nichols, Red, 49
Nighthawk, Robert, 99
Norman, Gene, 61, 224
No. 1 Plugs, 69
Nutmegs, the, 122

O'Brien, Jack, 150
O'Day, Pat, 137
Okeh Records, 52, 54, 56, 141, 206
Olympics, the, 241
One-shot artists, 183–84
Orbison, Roy, 79, 193, 245
Oreo Rock, 163
Orioles, the, 43, 77, 89, 118
Otis, Clyde, 259
Otis, Johnny, 90, 135, 238
Over-dubbing, 37
"Ozark Jubilee," 245
"Ozzie and Harriet," 197

Paar, Jack, 175
Page, Patti, 4, 36, 38, 41,

42, 114, 119, 121, 173, 227, 251
Pal Joey, 33
Palace Theatre, 18
Paladin, 175
Palitz, Morty, 27
Paramount Theatre, 19, 45, 51, 109
Parker, Charlie "Bird," 35, 48, 58
Parker, Fess, 123
Parker, Col. Tom, 2, 4–6, 9–11, 41, 152
Pastor, Tony, 30
Patience and Prudence, 157
"Patricia," 232
Pauling, Lowman, 102, 103
Payola, 69, 111, 178, 180, 222, 244, 267, 268–81
Peacock Records, 83, 87, 162
Pearl, Minnie, 188
Peatman Sheet, 43, 53
Pelicans, the, 118
Penguins, the, 116, 118, 119, 124
Perkins, Carl, 164–65, 188–89, 245
"Person to Person," 225
"Personality," 100, 252, 258
"Peter Gunn," 262
Peterson, Ray, 117
Petty, Norman, 186
"Phil Silvers Show," 151
Phillips, Sam, 8, 9, 10, 79, 189, 191, 245
Piaf, Edith, 33, 255
Piano Red, 106
Platters, the, 12, 143–44, 157, 168, 170, 173, 194, 239, 242, 251
Playmates, the, 249–50
Plough chain, 221, 264
Pompelli, Rudy, 138
Poni-Tails, the, 237–38
Porgy & Bess, 260
Porter, Cole, 16, 157
Potter, Peter, 61, 77, 128, 222, 224
Prado, Perez, 123, 232
Presley, Elvis, 4, 7–11, 57, 64, 79, 81, 86, 103, 122, 131, 135, 136, 138, 145, 147, 150–53, 154, 157, 161, 164, 165, 166, 172, 173, 177, 180, 185, 186, 187, 189, 191, 196, 197, 198, 200, 203, 208, 209, 211, 214, 227, 232, 233, 234, 235, 239, 245, 251, 257, 266, 270
Preview Lounge, 141
Price, Lloyd, 95, 96, 100, 143, 205, 252, 258
Price, Ray, 188
Prima, Louis, 92, 250
Primitivism, 182
Proser, Monte, 21
Prysock, Red, 105
Purple Onion, 245
"Purple People Eater, The," 227, 230, 251

Quality Music Shop, 83
"Quiz Kids," 271

Race records, 87
Raeburn, Boyd, 85
Ram, Buck, 144
Rama Records, 77, 118, 168
Randle, Bill, 7–10, 56, 63–64, 105, 140, 170, 179, 248, 278
Randolph, Boots, 207
Ravens, the, 106, 118
Ray, Johnnie, 21, 29, 39, 45, 52–58, 59, 64, 93, 115, 116, 220
Rayburn, Gene, 65
Rayburn, Margie, 213
Rays, the, 178
RCA Victor, 9, 10, 22, 27, 34, 43, 50, 51, 79, 90, 92, 108, 115, 116, 121, 124, 125, 131, 141, 150, 151, 162, 170, 171, 191, 196, 201, 203, 213, 214, 215, 216, 221, 235, 240, 253, 261, 266, 268, 272, 276
Rebel Without a Cause, 112, 170, 180
Record hop, 172, 179, 239
Reed, Carol, 33
Reed, Jimmy, 134
Reese, Della, 201–5
René, Henri, 17, 42, 114
Reynolds, Debbie, 51, 200, 209
Rhodes, Todd, 106
Rhythm and Blues, 2, 3, 4, 14, 17, 31, 43, 44, 50, 60, 74, 75, 77, 78, 79, 80, 81, 84, 85, 86, 87, 90, 91, 92, 94, 95, 96, 99, 102, 103, 106, 111, 114, 115, 116, 118, 119, 120, 122, 123, 125, 126, 127, 128, 129, 130, 131, 135, 136, 137, 140, 152, 155, 157, 162, 167, 168, 173, 174, 180, 189, 195, 200, 206, 226, 244, 258, 259, 262
Rhythm Orchids, 185
Richman, Harry, 53, 269
Richmond, Howard S., 29, 65–66, 78
Riddle, Nelson, 22, 33
Righteous Brothers, 249
Ritter, Tex, 38
Robbins, Fred, 274
Robbins, Harold, 233
Robbins, Jack, 266, 270
Robbins, Marty, 142, 208, 253–54
"Robert Montgomery Presents," 69
Robey, Don, 87, 93, 103
Robins, the, 118, 157, 167, 206
Rockabilly, 59, 136, 138, 146
Rock Brothers, 125
Rock Around the Clock, 109
"Rock Around the Clock,"
44, 71, 122, 124, 136, 138, 141, 143, 145, 234
"Rock 'n' Roll Dance Party," 110
Rock 'n' Roll, 23, 29, 30, 60, 66, 71, 101, 105, 106, 111, 124, 135, 136, 137, 138, 155, 162, 172, 180–81, 182, 187, 197, 207–8, 212, 214, 222, 231, 234, 247, 258, 262, 265, 266, 267, 279, 281; origin of term, 106
Rock 'n' roll revival, 143, 168, 219
"Rock 'n' Roll Revival," 139, 143, 147
Rock, Rock, Rock, 109
Rodgers, Jimmie ("Singing Brakeman"), 190, 191, 192
Rodgers, Jimmie, 197–98, 200, 231, 235
Rodgers and Hammerstein, 16, 20, 43
Rodgers and Hart, 15, 33, 157
Rolling Stone, 30, 67, 95, 117, 130, 145, 147, 189
"Roll Over Beethoven," 146
Rolontz, Bob, 247, 268
Ronald and Ruby, 217–18
Ronettes, the, 249
Rose, Billy, 115, 157, 159
Rose, David, 17, 47
Ross, Beverly, 30–31, 216–17
Rosza, Miklos, 38
Roulette Records, 185, 198, 240, 241, 250, 276, 278
Rover Boys, the, 195
Roxy ending, 60
Roxy Theatre, 155
Royal Sons Quintet, 102
Royal Teens, 208
RPM Records, 95, 98
"Rudolph, the Red-Nosed Reindeer," 35
Rupe, Art, 95, 210
Rydell, Bobby, 256

Sachs, Manie, 22, 27
Saddlemen, the, 137
Saga songs, 253–54
St. Nicholas Arena, 108
Sands, Jodie, 184
Sands, Tommy, 184–85, 231
Santo and Johnny, 258
Saroyan, William, 30
Satins, the, 167
Savoy Records, 4, 82, 90, 118, 129, 135, 157
Schiffman, Frank, 89, 226
Schiffman, Jack, 119
Scott, Jack, 230
Scott, Raymond, 68, 69
Sears, "Daddy" Zenas, 94
"Secret Love," 114, 232
Sedaka, Neil, 223, 255–56, 257
Seeger, Pete, 245
Senate Commerce Subcommittee on Communications, 222
Sensations, the 157
Sepia records, 87
Sevareid, Eric, 155–56
708 Club, 133
"77 Sunset Strip," 183, 262
Seville, David, 226, 249
Seymour, Robin, 56, 140, 221, 263
"Shake, Rattle and Roll," 100, 112, 116, 119, 136, 137
Shaw, Arnold, 1–11, 14, 30–31, 32, 46, 50, 52, 58, 62, 73–77, 80, 83, 118, 120, 125, 126–27, 129, 131, 132, 140, 171, 178, 199, 216–18, 226, 243, 259
Shaw, Artie, 246
Shaw, Georgie, 120
"Sh-Boom," 73–77, 118, 119, 120, 125
Sherman, Bobby, 57
Shirelles, the, 103
Shirley and Lee, 168
Sholes, Steve, 10–11, 141, 150, 214, 216, 217
Shore, Dinah, 42, 65, 124, 208, 212
Shuffle, 87, 114, 188, 209, 243
Sigman, Carl, 65, 243
Silhouettes, the, 208
Silverman, Max, 83, 84, 85
Simeone, Harry, 250
Simone, Nina, 260
Sinatra, Frank, 2, 11, 16, 19, 20, 21, 22–24, 25, 42, 45, 49, 50, 51, 57, 59, 65, 67, 80, 87, 91, 96, 109, 114, 119, 124, 126, 142, 150, 158, 173, 177, 194, 197, 208, 212, 219, 228, 234, 235, 251, 255, 263, 275
Six Teens, the, 168
"$64,000 Question," 271
Skiffle, 213
Slim and Slam, 48
Smathers, George, 212, 228, 234
Smith, Hoey, and the Clowns, 209
Smith, Keely, 250
"Smoke Gets in Your Eyes," 93, 143–44, 157, 261
Snow, Hank, 6, 9, 10
Snyder, Bill, 33
"Song from Moulin Rouge," 28, 43
Songwriters Protective Association, 211, 222
Soul Stirrers, 200
South Pacific, 16, 37, 262
Sparkletones, the, 208
Specialty Records, 87, 95, 135, 162, 200, 210 222, 239
Spector, Phil, 249, 281

Stafford, Jo, 4, 29, 30, 38, 42, 73, 114
Starr, Kay, 39, 42, 59, 172, 201
Steiner, Max, 38
Steel drums, 172
Stevens, Connie, 262
Stevens, Dodie, 266
Stoloff, Morris, 173
Stone, Cliffie, 164
Stone, Jesse, 102
Stop the Music, 271
Stordahl, Axel, 22
Storm, Gale, 12, 128, 168
Storz, Todd, 66, 235, 264
"Stroll, The," 200, 208
Strouse, Charles, 238
Subcommittee on Legislative Oversight, 268, 270, 273, 277, 280
Sun Records, 7, 8, 10, 79, 95, 150, 188, 193, 214
Susskind, David, 281
Swallows, the, 118
Swan Records, 184, 257, 279
Syncopators, the, 17

Talking style, 254
"Tammy," 200, 209, 219
Tampa Red, 99
Tarnopol, Nat, 214
Tarriers, the, 132, 171
Taubman, Howard, 52
Taylor, Elizabeth, 51, 252
Taylor, Sam "the Man," 110, 165
Teddy Bears, 248–49
"Teen-Age Crush," 185
"Teen-ager in Love, A," 241
Teenagers, the, 168
Teen Queens, 128, 168
Telephone Box Squash, 252
Tennessee Ernie Ford, 17, 123, 184
"Tennessee Waltz," 4, 36
Tex-Mex sound, 185–87, 230
"Thing, The," 33–34, 65
"Third Man Theme, The," 33
Thomas, Rufus, 97
Thompson, Hank, 142
Thornton, Willie Mae "Big Mama," 44, 103, 135
"Three Coins in the Fountain," 114
Threepenny Opera, The, 252, 254
Tiomkin, Dmitri, 38, 159
Three Suns, 144, 269
Tillman, Floyd, 17
Tin Pan Alley, 3, 14, 15, 16, 25, 32, 33, 43, 46, 92, 113, 114, 123, 229, 243, 266–67
Tobias, Fred, 238
"Today Show," 270
Tom and Jerry (Simon & Garfunkel), 208
"Tom Dooley," 244–45, 247, 253

Toombs, Rudolph, 92
"Too Young," 25, 36, 185
Top Forty, 66, 72, 213, 220, 221, 222, 224, 227, 229, 235, 239, 250, 263–65
Torme, Mel, 50
Toscanini, Arturo, 175
Townsend, Ed, 230
"Transfusion," 169–70
Treniers, the, 141
Truman, Harry, 13, 21–22
Tubb, Ernest, 158
Tune Weavers, the, 183
Turbans, the, 167
Turner, Ike and Tina, 249
Turner, Joe, 78, 79, 87, 95, 100, 112, 116–17, 120, 136, 137, 142, 143, 229
"Tutti Frutti," 12, 127, 152, 162, 205
Twentieth Century Limited, 75
"Twenty-six Miles," 223
Twitty, Conway, 245–46

"Unchained Melody," 120, 123

Vale, Jerry, 21
Valens, Ritchie, 246, 255
Valente, Caterina, 1
Valli, June, 43
Van Doren, Charles Lincoln, 270–71, 272
Van Doren, Mamie, 196
Vanguard Rocket, 175
Variety, 43, 46, 109, 115, 195, 269, 270
Vaughan, Sarah, 119, 259
Vaughn, Billy, 124, 127, 223
"Vaya Con Dios," 43
"Venus," 178, 221, 252, 255, 256
Versailles, 33
Vincent, Gene, 166, 199, 233
"Volare," 70, 236–37, 243

WABC, 110, 220, 228, 274, 280
Wakeley, Jimmie, 17, 171
Walker, Aaron "T-Bone," 82, 87, 96
Wallace, Jerry, 241
Waller, Fats, 84
"Wanted," 73, 114
Ward & the Dominoes, Billy, 93, 195, 259
Ward, Clara, 277–78
Warnow, Mark, 68
Warren, Fran, 243
Washboard Sam, 84
Washington, Dinah, 85, 86, 87, 89, 96, 101, 204, 258–59
Wayne, John, 183
"The Wayward Wind," 173
WDIA, 96, 97, 98
Weavers, the, 33, 158
Webb, Jack, 42
Weber, Joan, 120, 121
Webster, Paul Francis, 232
Weems, Ted, 62

Weill, Kurt, 254
Wein, George, 229
Welch, Joseph N., 113
Weld, Tuesday, 196
Welk, Lawrence, 165, 212
Wells, Kitty, 184
WERE, 7, 159, 179, 264
Wexler, Jerry, 74, 75, 78–79, 206
WFIL, 51, 63, 142, 177, 178, 225
"What'd I Say," 130, 260–61
Whiting, Margaret, 17
Whitman, Walt, 33
Whiteman, Paul, 47, 63, 155, 269
The Wild One, 134, 180
Willet, Slim, 43
Williams, Andy, 184
Williams, Billy, 200
Williams, Hank, 4, 30, 40, 137, 139, 141, 166, 187, 190, 191, 192, 253
Williams, Joe, 91, 95, 99, 143
Williams, Larry, 205, 219
Williams, Mel, 132, 135
Williams, Otis, 118, 127, 128, 173
Williams, Paul, 90
Williams, Roger, 8, 244
Williams, Tony, 144
Williams, William B., 272, 275
Williamson, Sonny Boy, 95, 97, 99
Willis, Chuck, 78, 93, 205–6, 220, 227
Wills, Bob, and his Playboys, 142
Wills, Johnny Lee, and his Boys, 34
Wilson, Jackie, 59, 93, 101, 108, 214, 259–60
WINS, 100, 107, 108, 109, 110, 228, 275
Winterhalter, Hugo, 17, 50, 114, 173, 213
Wiswell, Andy, 27
"Witch Doctor," 226, 227, 230, 248, 251
WJW, 104, 106, 107, 116
WNEW, 61, 62, 63, 65, 111, 121, 151, 224, 272, 274, 275, 276, 280
Wood, Natalie, 112
Wood, Randy, 126–28
Wooley, Sheb, 230
Wray, Link, and his Ray Men, 193, 208
WSM, 2, 9, 10

"Yakety Yak," 207, 234, 261
Youmans, Vincent, 224
Young, Lester, 58, 119
Young, Victor, 33, 114, 209
"Young at Heart," 2, 22, 114, 119, 158
"You, You, You," 16, 42

Ziegfeld Theatre, 74

522-5372
My Boy!